ETHIOPIA AND
THE MIDDLE EAST

ETHIOPIA AND THE MIDDLE EAST

Haggai Erlich

LYNNE RIENNER PUBLISHERS

BOULDER
LONDON

To Omri

Published in the United States of America in 1994 by
Lynne Rienner Publishers, Inc.
1800 30th Street, Boulder, Colorado 80301

and in the United Kingdom by
Lynne Rienner Publishers, Inc.
3 Henrietta Street, Covent Garden, London WC2E 8LU

Library of Congress Cataloging-in-Publication Data
Erlich, Haggai.
Ethiopia and the Middle East / Haggai Erlich.
p.   cm.
Includes bibliographical references and index.
ISBN 1-55587-520-3 (alk. paper)
1. Middle East—Relations—Ethiopia.   2.   Ethiopia—Relations—
Middle East.   I. Title.
DS63.2.E7E75 1994
303.48263056—dc20
94-18824
CIP

British Cataloguing in Publication Data
A Cataloguing in Publication record for this book
is available from the British Library.

Printed and bound in the United States of America

The paper used in this publication meets the requirements
of the American National Standard for Permanence of
Paper for Printed Library Materials Z39.48-1984.

CONTENTS

Preface   vii

Part I
From Muhammad to Iyasu:
Political Islam and the Uniqueness of Ethiopia

1   Muhammad's Message: "Leave the Abyssinians Alone"   3
2   Relations up to the Sixteenth Century:
    Isolation, the Nile, and Muslim Sultanates   21
3   The Trauma of *Gragn* and the Diplomacy of Habesh   29
4   The Beginning of Modern Times:
    Muhammad 'Ali and Tewodros   41
5   Yohannes, Isma'il, and the Ethio-Egyptian Conflict   53
6   Yohannes and Menelik: Between Religious
    Confrontation and Diplomatic Dialogue   65
7   Iyasu, the Somali *Mawla*, and the Demise
    of the Ottoman Empire   83

Part II
Ethiopia and Arabism: From Arslan to Nasser

8   The Arabs, Mussolini, and the Abyssinian Dilemma   95
9   Pan-Arabism, Arslan, and Conquered Abyssinia   111
10   Nasser, Haile Selassie, and the Eritrea Problem   127
11   Egypt's View of Ethiopia During the Nasserite Period   141
12   The Arabs, Ethiopia, and the Arabism of Eritrea   151
13   Israel and the Fall of Haile Selassie   165
14   Conclusion: The Struggle for Diversity   179

Notes   191
Selected Bibliography   215
Index   223
About the Book and the Author   228

PREFACE

My research for *Ethiopia and the Middle East* began as something else. Five years ago I was given a generous grant by the United States Institute of Peace to work on "Autonomy as a Solution to the Eritrea Problem." In my research proposal I had sought to study the various approaches to the idea of autonomy by each of the concerned parties: the Ethiopian government, the liberation fronts, and Ethiopia's Middle Eastern neighbors. But as I was gathering the source materials for this study, two things happened. First, contemporary history, as it is wont to do, moved faster than my ability to digest the massive piles of documents, and in no time rendered irrelevant the very premise of my proposal.

Second, as I was studying the material, I was repeatedly struck by the contradiction between the importance of the Middle East to Ethiopian political strategy and how Ethiopians and Middle Easterners have historically ignored each other, despite the fact that they share so much history—ancient, medieval, modern, and contemporary.

Not that either the Ethiopians or their neighbors lack a sense of history. On the contrary: The two civilizations are enormously rich in legacies on which they draw constantly. The Ethiopians and Middle Easterners have historically mas and the Muslims and Arabs have had their own concepts of Ethiopia, stemming from their own historical experience. Yet there has hardly been an effort on either side to understand the other. There is too little curiosity and too much obscurity.

Thus, although *Ethiopia and the Middle East* is an attempt to reconstruct the main meeting points in the political and strategic relations between the two civilizations, it is also an effort to understand how each culture has viewed the other and to review the basic concepts behind their histories. Pursuing the reasons for this dichotomy between practical involvement and conceptual detachment I was sucked back to the history of early formative episodes. Islamic and, later, modern Arab concepts of Ethiopia were greatly influenced by the legacy of an early seventh-century story. It left a dual message about the very legitimacy of Ethiopia but quite a clear one about the need to keep a distance between Ethiopia and the Islamic Middle East. The Ethiopian view of the Middle East as a potential threat to be avoided—and ignored—stemmed from a sixteenth-century

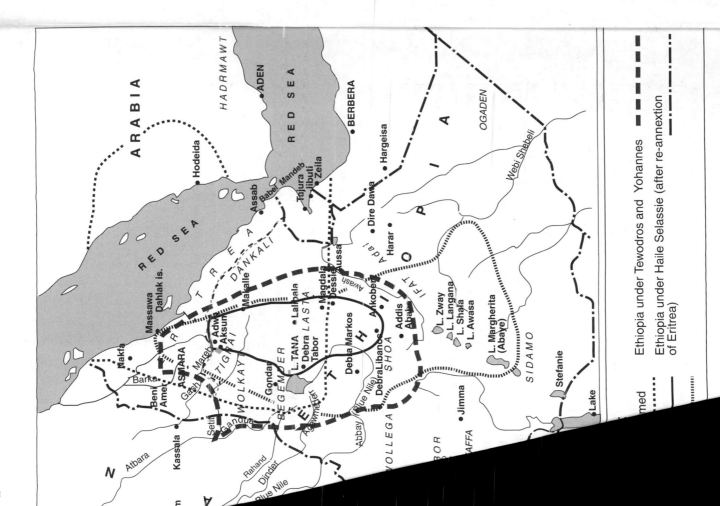

Ethiopia under Tewodros and Yohannes

Ethiopia under Haile Selassie (after re-annexion of Eritrea)

experience. The book begins with the earliest meetings, before the seventh century, surveys the interplay between politics and concepts, and ends with the contemporary era.

In using the term *Ethiopia*, I refer to the entity that has existed for some twenty centuries, held by the political institutions headed until 1974 by the royal dynasties. The fact that these institutions were identified with Ethiopian Christianity permits the use of the term *Christian Ethiopia*, connoting its homogeneity and continuity. I use this term for the sake of convenience and because I am dealing with foreign relations. Ethiopia itself is a diverse entity. This is a premise without which its history cannot be understood or, in my view, its future be assured.

Neither do I intend to tear Ethiopia from its African and Africanist context. An important aspect of Ethiopia has always been "black" and "African." Throughout history Ethiopia has been so recognized by members of all cultures, including Ethiopians themselves and by Middle Easterners. In the 1960s Ethiopia's African dimension began to attract the scholarly attention it has long deserved. The old guard of modern Ethiopianists (Trimingham, Cerulli, Conti Rossini, Ullendorff, to name but a few), who approached Ethiopia from Oriental studies, was gradually being replaced by Ethiopianists with backgrounds in emerging African studies. The new generation (trained mostly in the leading universities of the United States, the School of Oriental African Studies of London, and the University of Addis Ababa) applied the new methods of the social and political sciences, doing more scholarly justice to Ethiopia's ethnic, linguistic, and religious diversity. They were thus able to better analyze the role of that diversity in history and more profoundly relate to the issues of Ethiopia's modernization.

In this book I concentrate on Ethiopia's relations with the outside world. Throughout its history, the country has been closely integrated into the strategies of the Red Sea and of the Nile Basin, and through them, as well as through its culture, to the Oriental world. Relations with the Middle East have always been central to Ethiopia's major historical developments, and particularly so since the 1950s.

Ethiopia was born in ancient Aksum: the Middle East, both as term and as political reality, was born in the twentieth century. *Middle East* means a region of modern states and a political culture struggling with the legacies of Islam, of modern Arabism, of Egyptianism, Zionism, and other national affiliations. Prior to World War I and the fall of the Ottoman Empire, the region was known as the political *Land of Islam*, an essentially different concept from that of the Middle East.

Part I traces Ethiopia's political history and its relations with the rulers and dynasties of the Land of Islam from the days of the Prophet Muhammad to the collapse of the Ottoman Empire. Part II explores Ethiopia's new political identities and its relations with the modern Middle

East. The book's thirteen chapters follow the chronology of Ethiopian history.

This study is intended to be a contribution to the history of Ethiopian foreign relations. If it also serves to prepare for a future that is better tha[n] the past, I shall be doubly rewarded. The student of Middle Eastern histor[y] will also find much of interest here. From medieval Mecca to contempo[rary] Cairo, many issues involving the region's identity are discussed. By e[xam]ining how the region's politicians have dealt with their non-Islam[ic] non-Arab neighbor over the course of more than fourteen centuries[, I] attempted to shed light on the single most enduring issue of th[e Middle] East—the region's ability to deal with its own diversity.

The research for *Ethiopia and the Middle East* was made p[ossible by a] generous grant from the United States Institute of Peace. [...] advanced students at Tel Aviv University, notably Elda Ye[...] translated pieces of Turkish literature for me), Rahamim[...] Melzer, helped collect material. I tried to mention them[...] wrote the work during my 1992–1993 sabbatical lea[ve...] University and appointment as the Visiting Israeli Prof[essor...] University.

I am grateful to the founders and supporters of t[...] Chair, Professor Viliiam O'Brien, Professor Rob[...] Professor Marver Bernstein, for their patience and[...] wife, Martha, friends of Ethiopia and leading exp[...] developments, offered invaluable advice as we[ll...] Fawzi Tadros, the librarian of the Near East[...] Congress, a true gentleman and a professio[n...] tude for responding to my repeated naggi[ng...] loged or not. Hanan Aynor, Israeli amba[ssador...] and 1974 and the president of the Afri[...] gave me precious material. He remaine[d...] Hanan read my last chapter and sig[...] some twelve hours before dying of ca[...]

I take pleasure at thanking all[...] ways, I shall mention only a few: [...] script), Nehemia Levtzion, Israel [...] I thank also the keepers of the [...] well as Dagefe Walda-Tsadiq, [...] at Addis Ababa University. [...] and Jeanne Remington for [...] and to Lynne Rienner an[d...] The responsibility for m[i...] is, however, all mine. And I am grateful

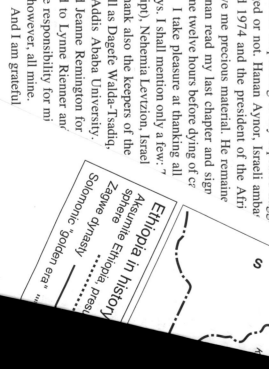

Ethiopia in history
Aksumite Ethiopia, pre[...] sphere
Zagwe dynasty
Solomonic "golden era" [...]

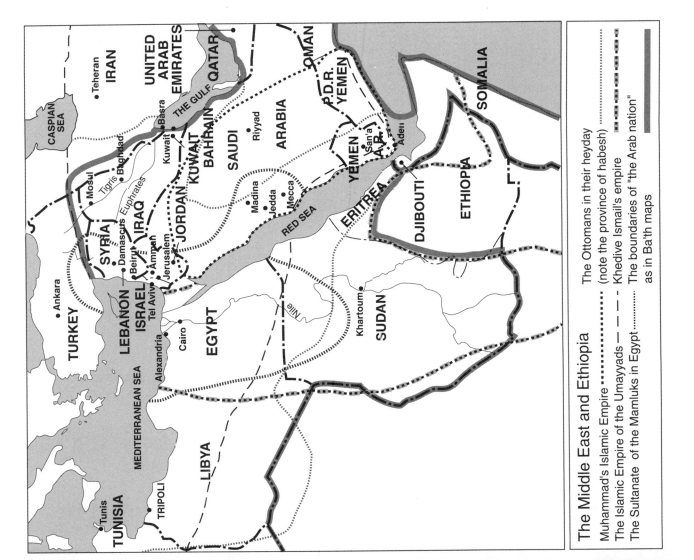

The Middle East and Ethiopia

Muhammad's Islamic Empire ·················· The Ottomans in their heyday ··············
(note the province of habesh) ··············
The Islamic Empire of the Umayyads — — — Khedive Ismail's empire — · — · —
The Sultanate of the Mamluks in Egypt ··········· The boundaries of "the Arab nation"
as in Ba'th maps

| I |

From Muhammad to Iyasu: Political Islam and the Uniqueness of Ethiopia

1

Muhammad's Message: "Leave the Abyssinians Alone"

AKSUMITE ETHIOPIA: AN ORIENTAL ENTITY

Ethiopia came into being as an extension of the Oriental world. Waves of immigrants from the southern parts of the Arab Peninsula imported their Semitic culture and languages, beginning in the seventh century B.C., settling on the African coast of the Red Sea and on the Ethiopian Plateau. Influenced by these immigrants, and as a result of their intermingling with local cultures and ethnic groups, the kingdom of Aksum, the first stage of today's Ethiopia, emerged in the first century A.D.[1]

Aksum developed an urban culture, an advanced peasantry, patriarchate, a legal system establishing the right of primogeniture, territorial organizations, and other institutions imported from the Semitic world. Aksumite culture was expressed in the Semitic language of Ge'ez, from which developed other Ethiopian Semitic languages, primarily the Tigrinya and Amharic. The culture was open and dynamic enough to assimilate existing local cultures and, at the same time, to connect further with the Oriental East. From there, from beyond the Red Sea, and from the direction of the Nile additional influences continued to flow. Judaic concepts and traditions were chief among these, producing far-reaching implications for the development of the country's spiritual and religious life as well as for Ethiopia's future relations with Jerusalem and with the people of Israel. Hellenic cultural influences were no less significant, for it was from the Hellenic Orient and through the Greek language that Christianity was introduced to Aksum.[2]

The adoption of Christianity by *Negus* (king) Ezana in the fourth century A.D. strengthened the bridge between Aksum and the Orient, or, to cite the phrase of the Ethiopian historian Sergew Hable Sellassie, the ties with the "civilized world." It was two brothers, Frumentius and Aedesius, from the town of Tyre who, saved from a shipwreck while en route to India, brought the precepts of the Christian religion to the Aksumite royal court. Aedesius ultimately returned to Syria to tell his story; Frumentius went to Alexandria, where he laid the groundwork for the connection between the

3

Egyptian Coptic Church and the future church of Ethiopia.[3] He then returned to Aksum to be the first Alexandria-appointed *abun* (bishop) over Ethiopia. In Ethiopian history Frumentius became known as *Abuna Abba Salama*. This Ethio-Egyptian Christian connection established in the fourth century A.D. was to survive until the 1960s, often important and problematic enough to contribute to the vicissitudes of political relations.

Ethiopian Christianity was further enhanced following another event in the Orient, the Council of Chalcedon, in A.D. 451. The so-called Nine Saints, monks from various places in the Roman Empire who resisted the doctrine laid down by the majority (that there were two natures, one divine, one human in Christ) found in Aksum shelter as well as a fertile field for spreading their Monophysite belief. They provided the young Ethiopian church with translated Ge'ez scriptures, and founded the first chain of monasteries.

Allied with the royal house and connected with the institutions and the spirit of Oriental churches, Ethiopian Christianity spread rapidly. It was not, however, merely a set of imported dogmas. Rather, it followed the path of other influences from the Semite Orient that had combined with and were assimilated in local cultures. Indeed, Ethiopian Christianity developed in such a way as to absorb components of other local spiritual beliefs and rituals. Assimilating aspects of Judaic traditions as well as local pagan customs, by the sixth century the Ethiopian church had become an all-embracing Ethiopian culture.

Aksum's Red Sea port, Adulis (today's Zula, south of Massawa), had begun to develop into a lively center of trade with the Arab Peninsula in the third century A.D. Although Aksum was a peasant culture, it nonetheless built a commercial fleet to sail the Red Sea. Moreover, its diplomatic and religious contacts with Constantinople drew Aksumite kings into the political and economic strategy of the East, which revolved around the Byzantine-Persian rivalry.[4] In 524 the intense Aksumite involvement in Arab Peninsula affairs culminated when the army of Emperor Kaleb (Ellesbaas to the Greeks), crossed the Red Sea and conquered Yemen, destroying the Jewish kingdom of Himyar and liberating the local Christians. The Aksumites ruled in Yemen and turned Ethiopia into a Red Sea empire for three generations before their eviction by the Persian army in about 590.

One of Kaleb's generals, Abraha, had built churches in the provincial capital of San'a. Equipped with armored elephants, he launched an expedition in 570 to Mecca to destroy the then-pagan shrine of the Ka'ba. It was only through the intervention of Providence, according to later Islamic tradition, that the holy place was saved. In that "year of the elephant," the Prophet Muhammad was born.

Indeed, by the sixth century Ethiopia had emerged as an Oriental state, deeply immersed in the affairs of the Eastern world and fully accepted as an equal if not a superior in the development of the strategy of the Red Sea. Arabs, Jews, and Greco-Romans of the period, to judge by their writings, revealed no racism in their dealings with the Ethiopians. Rather, for the Arabs of the peninsula the Ethiopians were deemed the representatives of an even higher civilization.[5] Words from the Ge'ez vocabulary penetrated the Arabic language as Ethiopians—traders, conquerors, and slaves—intermingled with Arabs in the urban centers of the Arab Peninsula.

Of particular significance was the high rate of intermarriage. Many prominent Arabs in pre-Islamic Yemen and the Hijaz were of mixed Ethiopian origin, such as the poet and warrior 'Antara bin Rabiba, whose mother was Ethiopian.[6] A lively Ethiopian community existed in Mecca, where the elite was especially known to favor Ethiopian women; centuries later foreigners observed a typical Meccan darker "golden" complexion.[7]

During the centuries immediately preceding the rise of Islam, Ethiopia emerged as a political entity of obvious Semitic cultural characteristics. It had a church that was dynamic enough to spread a literary civilization and to support a political order under a royal dynasty residing in a flourishing urban center. Aksum was an Ethiopian state linking the gradually assimilating local "African" ethnic and cultural groups, on the one hand, into the dynamism of the Oriental East, on the other. Although perhaps not yet up to the standard of most other capitals of the Orient, Aksum had proved its ability to face the challenge of participating in international relations and to benefit from its growing involvement in world affairs.

The emergence of Islam in the early seventh century was to have far-reaching consequences for Ethiopia. The great monotheistic revolution that was soon fundamentally to change the Oriental world started in nearby Mecca. The first chapter of Islamic history was closely connected to Aksum, and for Islam this was a vital episode. For Ethiopian history it was a moment that seemed to carry the promise of further cementing its ties with neighboring civilizations.

THE FIRST FORMATIVE CHAPTER: MUHAMMAD AND THE *NAJASHI*

Ethiopia played a role in the life of Prophet Muhammad. Indeed, Muhammad's own nurse was an Ethiopian woman named Baraka 'Umm Ayman. She looked after him from his birth, throughout his boyhood, and until his marriage to Hadija. It was said that "Muhammad loved her like a mother and confessed to that in public." After his death, his successors, the four Rashidun *caliphs*, continued to pay her visits following the Prophet's wish.[8] The many Ge'ez words in the Quran suggest that Muhammad himself acquired some of that language from the Ethiopians of Mecca. When Muhammad started recruiting followers, preaching his universal message, one of his earliest converts was an Ethiopian. In fact after his wife, Hadija, the first to answer his call was Abu Bakr (later the first *caliph*, 632–634), and then the Ethiopian, Bilal bin Rabah. Bilal had been the slave of a prominent Meccan who is said to have tortured Bilal so that he would deny Muhammad. When Abu Bakr heard about this he hurried to purchase Bilal from his master, brought him to his home, and set him free. Bilal ("the first fruit of Abyssinia") was to attain prominence by becoming the first *mu'ad-hdhin*, the caller for prayers in Islam. By tradition, this function was to stay in Ethiopian Muslims' hands ("The *khalifa* shall be of Quraysh, judicial authority shall be in the hands of the Auxiliaries, and the call for prayers with the Abyssinians"). By the same tradition and because Abu Bakr had rescued Bilal, it also became part of Islamic tradition that "who brings an Ethiopian man or an Ethiopian woman into his house, brings the blessings of God there."[9]

The first to host their neighbors, however, were the Ethiopians. They gave shelter in Aksum to the first group of Muhammad's followers, the *sahaba* (the term *sahaba* was coined later). The famous episode of the persecuted *sahaba* finding refuge in the Aksumite court, undoubtedly a true historical event, is mentioned in various Islamic chronicles written centuries later (by Ibn Yishaq, Ibn Hisham, al-Tabari, al-Nisa'i, Ibn Sa'ad, Ibn Kathir, al-Baladhuri, among others).[10] Although their recounting contains fictitious elements as well as legends, it is nevertheless pivotally important to my study and shall be summarized in the following paragraphs. This early encounter of Ethiopia with Islam was to become a formative event in shaping Islamic (and later, Arab) attitudes toward Ethiopia. The concepts created following that episode (although not necessarily stemming directly from it) were to influence the course of Ethio-Islamic relations as well as to influence the domestic history of Ethiopia to this very day.

In general, this early seventh century episode left a legacy of two contradictory messages for future generations of Muslims. The dominant of the two was a positive one in that it guided Muslims to be tolerant of the existence of Ethiopia. The other, a more latent message, would resurface at later historical junctures, when radical Muslims would reinterpret the same episode to mean that Ethiopia was illegitimate in the eyes of Islam.

In A.D. 615, five years after Muhammad had begun his preaching and when the Qurayshi Meccan nobility were intensifying their persecution of his followers, Muhammad urged them to emigrate to Aksum. He told his *sahaba* (early followers), what he thought of Aksum's civilization: "If you go to Abyssinia you will find a king under whom none are persecuted. It is a land of righteousness where God will give you relief from what you are suffering."[11]

A group of seventeen followers including Muhammad's son-in-law, who later became the *Caliph* (644–656) 'Uthman bin 'Affan, and the Prophet's daughter, Ruqayya (and her maid, the same Ethiopian who had nursed Muhammad, Baraka 'Umm Ayman)[12] fled secretly to Aksum.[13] They were well received by the Ethiopian king (most probably Adriaz, 610–630), whom some Arab chroniclers called Ella Saham, or, as he came to be better known in Islamic tradition the *Najashi* (Ethiopic: ruler) Ashama. (Read *As-hama*. In Ibn Ishaq he is referred to as "*al-najashi al-Asham bin Abjar*".[14] In some texts he is referred to as Asmaha.)[15] Three months later, having heard a false rumor that the Qurayshi Meccan leadership accepted Islam, the refugees returned to Mecca only to discover to their horror that persecution had instead intensified.

A much larger group of the now growing *sahaba* was then organized by the Prophet to flee and find shelter in Aksum.[16] It consisted of at least 132[17] newly converted Muslims—a substantial portion, at that time, of the core of Muhammad's followers. They were headed by Ja'far bin Abu Talib, Muhammad's cousin and the brother of the future *Caliph* Ali. Other prominent immigrants were 'Abdallah bin Jahsh and his brother 'Ubaydallah, the latter married to 'Umm Habiba, a daughter of one of the Quraysh leaders, Abu Sufian.

The group reached Aksum in 616. In Aksum, they were warmly welcomed and in response they composed songs of glory for the *najashi*: "Thou art noble and generous. . . . No refugee is unhappy with thee."[18]

Soon, however, the Qurayshis sent for them. A Meccan emissary led by 'Amru bin al-'As (who was himself of Ethiopian descent) came to Aksum, distributed gifts among the clergy and the nobility, and then approached the king about surrendering the Muslims. "Some foolish fellows from our people," they told the *negus*, "have forsaken our religion and not accepted yours, but have brought in an invented religion which neither we nor you know anything about. . . . Surrender them to us and do not speak to them."

It was a moment of importance in the early history of Islam. Had the king of Ethiopia chosen to surrender the group to Quraysh, as he was said to be advised by his generals, the Prophet might well have suffered a disastrous defeat. *Najashi* Ashama, however, saved the day and Muhammad's followers. He ordered the Muslim refugees to meet with his bishops, and, in the presence of the Qurayshi emissaries, he questioned the *sahaba*.

First, he asked them about abandoning the faith of their fathers, to which Ja'far bin Abu Talib answered by recounting their previous primitive, cruel, and merciless paganism. Then he went on to tell how Muhammad brought the light and progress of monotheism: "He ordered us to worship God and associate no other with him, to offer prayer, to give alms and fast. . . So we trusted in his word and followed the teaching he brought us from God. . . . Wherefore our countrymen turned against us and persecuted us to try to seduce us from our faith, that we might abandon the worship of God and return to the worship of idols."

After this speech on the oneness of God, the *najashi* asked Ja'far about

Jesus Christ. On that, Ja'far quoted the Quran (Sura 4:169): "Verily Christ Jesus, son of Mary, is the apostle of God and his word, which he conveyed into Mary and a spirit proceeding from him." When the *negus* asked him about Mary he recited Sura 19:16–34, which is copied from the Gospel of Luke: "And my spirit hath rejoiced in God, my Savior...."

By making Islam appear to be a form of Christianity, Ja'far bin Abu Talib managed to convince the king to grant the *sahaba* continued asylum. The *najashi* returned the gifts to the Qurayshis and sent them back to Mecca. ('Amru bin al-'As, perhaps influenced by this event,[19] would soon convert to Islam, thereafter becoming one of the most important generals, the occupier of Egypt in 640.)

When Muhammad made his hegira from Mecca to Madina (622) he sent for the *sahaba* in Aksum, but only sixteen returned with a ship generously provided by the *negus*. The rest remained for the next nine years, enjoying the hospitality of Aksum, marrying into local families, and furthering relations between Ethiopia and early Islam.[20] Some twenty of the *sahaba* died in Ethiopia; the rest, under Ja'far, returned to Mecca in 631.

At least one marriage of that era had far-reaching implications. One of the *sahaba* residing in Aksumite Ethiopia, the aforementioned 'Ubaydalla bin Jahsh, was said by later Islamic tradition to have joined Ethiopian Christianity (thus being the first Muslim to do so). Thereupon his wife, 'Umm Habiba, divorced him. (By another version he did not convert to Christianity but died.)[21] Upon hearing of the couple's separation, the Prophet sent to Ja'far to propose to her in his name. When she consented, the *najashi* betrothed 'Umm Habiba to the Prophet and sent her across the Red Sea with a wedding present of 400 dinars. This marriage would soon facilitate Muhammad's way to victory because the bride's father, the Qurayshi leader Abu Sufian, then joined his camp.

In the sixth year of the hegira (628) the story of Muhammad and the *najashi* reached its climax. The Prophet sent emissaries to eight rulers of the Oriental world: five local princes or viceroys and three kings and emperors: Chosroes of Persia, Heraclius of Byzantium, and Ashama, the *najashi* of Ethiopia. According to the Muslim historian al-Tabari, the emissary to Aksum, 'Amru bin 'Umayya al-Damari, carried the following message. It started with a Quranic verse inviting "the people of the book" to reconsider their allegiance to Jesus and to adopt Islam:

In the name of God, the merciful, the compassionate. Muhammad, the apostle of God, to *Najashi* Ashama, King of Abyssinia, greetings... I testify that Jesus, the son of Mary, is the spirit and Word of God, and that He sent them down to Mary, the blessed and the immaculate virgin, and she conceived. He created Jesus of his own spirit and made Him to live by His breath.... I summon thee to worship the one God... Accept my mission, follow me, and become one of my disciples. For I am the Apostle of God.... Set aside the pride of thy sovereignty....

According to another source, Muhammad's letter ended with a threat: "and if you refuse you would be responsible for the guilt of your Christian people."[22]

According to medieval Islamic sources, the Ethiopian king did convert to Islam. When he received this letter, the king was said to have placed it on his head, stepped down from his throne and, seating himself on the ground, uttered the *shahada*, the prayer of testimony of recognizing Muhammad and accepting Islam.[23] According to this version the *najashi* sent the following reply: "In the name of God. . . . To Muhammad the Apostle of God. . . . There is no God but Allah, who has brought me to Islam. . . . What thou said about Jesus is the right belief. . . . I testify that thou art the Apostle of God, and I have sworn this in the presence of Ja'far, and have acknowledged Islam before him. . . ."[24]

When Muhammad later learned of Ashama's death, it was said that he mourned over him as for a departed Muslim and prayed for the repose of his soul. Islamic tradition was, indeed, to argue (contrary to modern Western[25] and Ethiopian historians) that the *najashi* did convert to Islam and that he refrained from proclaiming his conversion publicly, having to leave his generals and fanatic bishops in ignorance out of fear that it would cause riots.[26] This story carried the latent negative message of a Christian people resisting Islam. But the overt message of the *sahaba* story, as it was accepted generally, was one of gratitude to Ethiopia for helping Islam. It was embodied in the *hadith* (prophetic saying or tradition), attributed to Muhammad: "Leave the Abyssinians alone, so long as they do not take the offensive." This *hadith* ("*utruku al-habasha ma tarakukum*") became over time a long-enduring legacy of detrimental influence on Muslims' attitudes to Ethiopia.

The following three sections of this chapter summarize the reasons for the ninth century *hadith* of "leave the Abyssinians alone," and discuss its legal implications in declaring this orthodox Islamic attitude toward an accepted though ignored Ethiopia.

The final section of the chapter presents the opposite idea, that of Ethiopia's political illegitimacy, inspired and legitimized by the same *sahaba-najashi* story, but held by what may be labeled as "radical Islam."

MECCA, ETHIOPIANS, AND ETHIOPIA

Following the return of the *sahaba* in 630, Muhammad ordered his admiral 'Alkama bin Mujazziz to destroy the Ethiopian trading post in the port of Shua'yba, thus bringing to an abrupt end the ancient Meccan-Aksumite commercial relations. After the death of the Prophet (632), a competition arose over the Red Sea trade between the new Islamic state and Ethiopia, for we know that the same admiral was sent by *Caliph* 'Ummar in 640 to raid Aksum's port, Adulis. He sailed with four ships and two hundred men but was routed.[27]

However, the image of Ethiopians and of Ethiopia in Islamic eyes remained positive. In Mecca in this early phase of Islamic history many newly converted Muslim Ethiopians played significant roles. Sadiq al-'Azm, the author of *Rihlat al-Habasha* (1908), gathered from the Islamic medieval literature some relevant data and included it in an appendix to his book. He summarized the stories of twenty-one Ethiopians among the *sahaba*, Muhammad's close followers, noting that there were many more. All the stories are full of praise and reflect no racial discrimination. Bilal bin Rabah, noted above, is perhaps the most famous. He was not only the first *mu'adhdhin* but also became a *jihadi* warrior. Following the army of Caliph 'Umar (whose grandmother had also been an Ethiopian), Bilal " al-Habashi" died later in Damascus, where his grave remained a sacred shrine.

Like Bilal, many other of the Ethiopians in the *sahaba* had been slaves who were liberated and Islamized by the Prophet himself. Some other members of the *sahaba* were Ethiopians who had converted under the influence of the *sahaba* in Aksum. Seventy-two of them are said to have gone to Mecca in 631 with the returning *sahaba*. They were led by Dhu Mahjar al-Habashi, a nephew of *Najashi* Ashama, who is reported to have been close to the Prophet. Another member of the same group was Dhu Mahdam al-Habashi. He was known for the poems (*qasidas*) he read to Muhammad, in which he narrated the history of the Ethiopians as the descendants of the Arab tribe of Bani Hud, who had emigrated from Arabia. Abrahah bin Sabbah al-Habashi was a grandson of "Abrahah the owner of the elephant" who had threatened Mecca in 570, "the year of the elephant."

Some of Muhammad's close associates and important figures in Mecca during the times of the four *caliphs* were sons of Ethiopian women. One such member of the *sahaba* was Asama bin Zayd, the great Arabian poet and a grandson of the famous pre-Islamic poet Imru al-Qays. He was the son of Baraka 'Umm Ayman, Muhammad's nurse and life-long friend. 'Umm Ayman herself was mentioned by Sadiq al-'Azm as one of the Ethiopian *sahabiyyat*, the female followers of the Prophet. His list contains the names of four more such women. Of those Ethiopians who adopted Islam after the death of Muhammad it is notable that the *Faqih* 'Ata' ibn Rabah became the *mufti* of Mecca at the time of the 'Umayyad *Caliph* Sulayman ibn 'Abd al-Malik. It was said that the same *caliph*, passing through Mecca, came to study under the Ethiopian *mufti*, who died in 735 at the age of ninety.[28]

By the time the center of Islam moved from Arabia to Damascus, with the establishment of the 'Umayyad dynasty in 661, the period of Ethiopia's importance in Islamic history had ended. The 'Umayyads continued what the successors of the Prophet had begun: the expansion of the Islamic

Empire away from the Red Sea. Islam extended into "Middle Eastern" Asia, to Egypt, to North Africa, and into Europe. It did not attempt, however, at least not until the arrival of the Ottomans in the sixteenth century, crossing into Ethiopia with armed forces.

Throughout the seventh century, the Aksumite navy was still among the strongest in the Red Sea. In 702, the Ethiopians even attempted to invade the Hijaz, occupying the port of Jidda and causing a panic in Mecca. *Caliph* Sulayman ibn ʼAbd al-Malik hurried from Damascus to expel the invaders. He then went on in the same year to occupy the islands of Dahlak, opposite Adulis, and appointed an *amir* over that strategic position.[29] Under such a blockade, Adulis, Aksum's port, began to deteriorate.

An Ethiopian presence in the Red Sea was revived occasionally later, in the eighth century and in the late ninth and early tenth centuries (but these were discrete episodes). The image of Ethiopia in Islamic eyes as a respected nation remained at least until the middle of the eighth century. It is clear from a painting that survived in the ruins of Qusayr ʼAmra (in today's Jordan), that the ʼUmayyads regarded "the *Negus* of Ethiopia" as one of the six members of "the family of kings," the major rulers of the world, worthy of being their own predecessors. The *negus* is depicted in this painting as equal to the last Visigothic king of Spain, the *shah* of Sassanian Persia, the Byzantine Emperor, the Emperor of China, and a Turkish or Indian ruler.[30] But while the Umayyads and their Abbasid successors (after 750, in Baghdad) remained much concerned with their Spanish, Byzantine, or Persian fronts, they never actually dared to challenge the mountainous Ethiopian citadel—they simply neglected the Red Sea, ruined Aksum's seafaring, and condemned Ethiopia to isolation. For them, Dahlak would serve as a prison island, not as a point of departure for the African coast.

RACE, SLAVERY, ISLAM, AND THE "HABSH"

What was the historical significance and the cultural legacy of the Islamic tradition to "leave the Abyssinians alone"? Many of the pertinent facts concerning this tradition remain unknown. Did the *najashi*, in fact, adopt Islam, as contended by the Muslims and denied by the Christian Ethiopians? Did the Prophet really utter this sentence and, if so, was it in response to the conversion of the Ethiopian king as well as in gratitude for the shelter Ethiopia gave to the *sahaba?* Or was this *hadith*—first published in the ninth century[31]—fabricated at a later stage to justify the fact that Islam was unable to launch a combined sea-and-land operation against the mountainous citadel of Ethiopia, and was, in any event, more attracted elsewhere?

Whatever the case, much of ensuing Islamic-Ethiopian relations, as we shall see, would be affected by the spirit of that *hadith*. However, as history unfolded, Muhammad's utterance acquired an additional meaning. It came to reflect not only a benevolent, charitable exemption from *jihadi* conquest, but also the deeming of Ethiopia as marginal, irrelevant, and isolated.

Generally speaking, the rulers of "Middle Eastern" Islam, from the end of the *sahaba* story, ignored Ethiopia. Their strategic interest in the Red Sea and the Horn of Africa was only slight. Prior to the emergence in the sixteenth century of the Ottomans, a strategic interest in Ethiopia was revived only by the Mamluk dynasty in Egypt (1250–1517). Also, medieval Arab geographers and travelers had little curiosity concerning anything beyond the immediate Red Sea coast. Ethiopia or Abyssinia, "the land of the *habasha*," is mentioned in the writings of such chroniclers and travelers as Ibn Hawqal, al-Mas'Udi (tenth century), Ibn Khaldun (fourteenth century), and some others, but it seems that only one of them, Ibn Batuta (1304–1369), had first-hand knowledge of the Horn of Africa. Another medieval Arab writer who provided some reliable information was al-Maqrizi, whose 1434–1435 small treatise (*Kitab al-ilmam*) described the spread of Islamic emirates in southern Ethiopia, to which we shall return later. The Christian kingdom, however, was barely mentioned.32

Although Ethiopia as a Christian entity was thus abandoned and ignored by medieval "Middle Eastern" Muslims, Ethiopians remained an intellectual subject of some importance—but, to be sure, not the Ethiopians of the Horn of Africa, only *habasha* (black natives of the Horn of Africa, who joined Islam and lived under its sway).

In his book *Race and Slavery in the Middle East*, Bernard Lewis analyzes the medieval Islamic Arab literature and prophetic traditions (*hadith*) that referred to Ethiopians, their color, and their role in Islam. In general, the literature cited by Lewis conveyed a positive view of Muslim Ethiopians and reflects Islam's supraethnic concepts: "I was sent to the red33 and the black," said the Prophet in one relevant *hadith*. Another *hadith* referring to the meaninglessness of ethnicity and the centrality of religious authority in Islam quoted the Prophet: "Obey whoever is put in authority over you, even if he be a crop-nosed Ethiopian slave."34

Books written by medieval Islamic writers in defense of black Muslims were chiefly concerned with *al-habasha* (the Ethiopians). Ethiopians, because of their role in early Islam, could better serve the cause of supraethnicity and the primacy of spiritual universalism over race and color. There are a few such books, Lewis found, which survived in only a few copies, and none of them has yet been printed. One of the earliest, written by Jamal al-Din Abu Faraj ibn al-Jawzi (d. A.D. 1208), is entitled *The Lightening of the Darkness on the Merits of the Blacks and the Ethiopians*. In explaining the purpose of his book al-Jawzi wrote, "I have seen a number of outstanding [Muslim] Ethiopians whose hearts were breaking because of their color. So I let them know that respect is based on the performance of good deeds, and not on beautiful forms. I therefore composed for them this book, which deals with a good number of Ethiopians and blacks."[35]

Other books studied by Lewis include the work of the Egyptian historian Jalal al-Din al-Suyuti (d.1505), *The Raising of the Status of the Ethiopians*, and the sixteenth-century book entitled *The Colored Brocade on the Good Qualities of Ethiopians.*

All of these books, according to Lewis, dismissed color and emphasized Islamic piety as the only valid criterion for distinction. In seeking to convey their message of universal supraethnicism, these medieval writers went back to the aforementioned formative Ethio-Islamic episode, that of the *sahaba*, and discussed the many Ethiopians among the slaves and the freedmen in the *sahaba*. They also discussed the *najashi*'s vital help to the Prophet's followers and repeated the *hadith* concerning Christian Ethiopia: "Leave the Abyssinians alone. . . ."

As for Islam itself, Lewis argues, the very need on the part of Islamic thinkers to refer to the subject of color and preach ethnic equality among Muslims suggests that racism among the peoples espousing the tenets of Islam was a problem. In fact, these same writers sometimes resorted, subconsciously perhaps, to racist insinuations. One tradition, for example, attributes to Muhammad the saying concerning the Ethiopian: "When he is hungry he steals, when he is sated he fornicates." In another *hadith*, Muhammad is said to have promised the Ethiopians that if they proved to be pious Muslims on Earth, they would become white in heaven.[36]

Lewis's analysis confirms that in the initial stage, the period of Muhammad and the four *rashidun caliphs*, color and race were not issues. Ethiopia and Ethiopians, as we have seen, were not looked down upon by contemporary Hijazi or Yemeni Arabs. If anything, they accepted Ethiopians as equals and respected Ethiopia as a civilized neighbor.

It was only later, in the eighth century, when the 'Umayyads tended to emphasize their "Arab" leadership in Islam, and during the period when Ethiopia—indeed, the whole of the Horn of Africa—was abandoned and ignored by Islam, that racist attitudes surfaced. With the creation of a vast multiethnic Islamic empire, ethnically diversified, Arab Muslims, contends Lewis, began to view blacks as inferiors. At that time they also started distinguishing between the *habasha* (the dark natives of the Horn of Africa) and the even darker natives of the inner continent (whom they now called Zanj or Sudan). In daily life, Lewis writes, the *habasha* were regarded by "Middle Eastern" Muslims as above the other blacks. (*Habsh* in Arabic means a mixture, and in popular usage it connoted a mixed ethnic origin, partly black, partly brown.) The literature cited by Lewis, produced by Islamic purists, was intended to protect black Muslims and to protect the purity of Islam itself from existing racist tendencies. However, it also served to maintain throughout the centuries the notion of Ethiopia itself as a Christian kingdom. Although Ethiopia was practically ignored, it was also seen as a legitimate entity.

Lewis's discussion of slavery in Islam sheds additional light on our subject. Because Islam forbade enslaving fellow Muslims but did not abolish the institution of slavery itself, it created the need to import slaves (*mamluks*) from beyond its boundaries. Thus, a religion and an empire that spread the universal concept of racial equality nonetheless engaged at the same time in slave trade as an intercontinental business. Inescapably, this trade enhanced racist attitudes. Islamic racism was further increased by the fact that slaves imported from "the land of the *habasha*"—the Ethiopian Horn of Africa (enslaved pagan Oromos, Gurages, Sidama, or the considerably fewer enslaved Christians)[37]—were preferred to and higher priced than Zanj slaves. The same was true of the *habashi* eunuchs.[38]

Islamic slavery, it must be emphasized, was neither the cruel institution of the industrial West, nor were racist attitudes of medieval times similar to the modern "scientific" ones. Rather, slaves in Islam were often integrated into society through marriage, even achieving political positions, including even political and military leadership, through official appointments. Many of the aforementioned Ethiopian members of the *sahaba* were slaves in such positions. Other Ethiopian slaves or eunuchs were later to obtain social or political prominence.

It is thus apparent that Islamic rulers and traders viewed the non-Muslim populations on their peripheries as appropriate sources of manpower. The Abbasid *caliphs* brought their *mamluks* from the Turkish peoples of the Caucasus, and the Ottomans imported their "slaves of the *sultan*," the backbone of Ottoman administration and army, from the Caucasus and the Balkans. It was most convenient for these rulers of Islam, in the Prophet's phrase, "to leave" those territories and refrain from converting their inhabitants en masse to Islam. It was equally convenient to "leave" the Horn of Africa as a major source of domestic slavery, and to refrain from a costly conquest of Ethiopia.

"LEAVE THE HABASHA ALONE" AND "DAR AL-HIYAD"

The cultural message of the famous *hadith* as interpreted in daily life in medieval Islam was mixed. On the one hand, it carried the legacy of gratitude and respect (the heritage of the Meccan period), but on the other it also reflected some racist attitudes (surfacing during the 'Umayyads). Whatever was the original practical reason for "leaving" the *habasha*, a desire to have a comfortable distance from a strong and mysterious neighbor, or the interest in keeping the whole Horn as a slavery reservoir, the operational mes-

Ethiopia as long as Ethiopia committed no aggression against Islam. It was a unique case.

Islam was, and remains, a comprehensive religion, a total world order aimed at including and organizing all mankind within its sole and only legitimate empire. By its very nature, it is in a constant state of rivalry with the rest of the world. Ethiopia, as a political entity (the *najashi*, adopting Islam or not) nevertheless remained Christian.

Islam at the apex of its military expansionist power refrained from trying to challenge the mountain citadel of Ethiopia. It is doubtful that the early Islamic empires could muster the combined naval and ground forces necessary to the task. It failed, as well, to attract the Ethiopians through its cultural message. What Islam offered so appealingly to other peoples—combining monotheism with a comprehensive harmonious set of legal answers to problems of earthly existence—Ethiopians already possessed in their own form of Christianity.[39] For a variety of reasons, both cultural and strategic, Ethiopia was to retain its uniqueness and not to be absorbed into "the world of Islam." Islam, however, and against its own grain, in principle accepted Ethiopia. It was to be the only such case.

By Islamic law the world is divided into *dar al-Islam*, namely, the house or the land of Islam, and *dar al-harb*, the land of war, the territories of the infidels, where *jihad* must be conducted. Medieval Islamic jurists occasionally accepted interim stages (*dar al-'Ahd, dar al-Sulh*, namely, territories enjoying a temporary agreement with Islam). However, as analyzed by Majid Khadduri in his *War and Peace in the Law of Islam*,[40] in early Islam there were, apart from Ethiopia, only three other cases of exemption by tradition from *jihad* without such an agreement. These were Nubia, the island of Cyprus, and the land of the Turks, each exempted for practical reasons. The Turks, it was said in a *hadith*, because of their toughness and difficult physical terrain of their country should be the last people the Muslims should attack. The arrangement was thus temporary; and indeed the Turks, although not by means of a holy *jihad*, would join Islam and even become, in their time, its very leaders.

According to one version of the Abyssinian *hadith*, as analyzed by Van Donzel, the Turks and the Ethiopians were combined into one case (*"da'U al-habasha ma wadda'Ukum wa-'truku al-turk ma tarakukum"*). This case may suggest that "leave the Abyssinians alone" (*"utruku al-habasha ma tarakukum"*) might well have implied only an interim arrangement.[41] However, while the other peoples and lands in question had long been conquered by or absorbed into Islam, the Islamic neutrality toward Ethiopia was said to be a matter of gratitude and did, indeed, remain in force.

Khadduri discusses in a full chapter the legal meaning of neutrality in Islamic jurisprudence. It referred to a status granted by the leaders of Islam, not a self-declared position by non-Muslims. His conclusion is that the only case of such a "land of neutrality" (*dar al-hiyad*) was Ethiopia. Writing in

1955 and referring to the crucial tale of the *sahaba* Khadduri concludes: "Perhaps with the exception of Ethiopia, no land or people has ever been declared immune from the *jihad* in the authoritative sources of Islamic law. . . . In the case of neutrality, the law is still valid regarding Ethiopia."[42]

The special status granted to Ethiopia by medieval Islam was a positive one for Ethiopia. Although reflecting some racist attitudes (beginning in the eighth century) and perhaps convenient in permitting slave trade of *habashis*, it was in essence a declaration of Ethiopian legitimacy as a sovereign, albeit non-Islamic state. Individual Ethiopians making a pilgrimage to Jerusalem were often treated like *dhimis*, non-Muslim subjects of the Islamic state, rather than as foreign infidels.[43] It may be argued that this recognition stemmed primarily from Ethiopia's geographical inaccessibility and military impregnability and was couched in terms of gratitude (or even patronizing charity). But whatever the reason, Ethiopia's right to exist was unique in Islam, and the legacy of gratitude to Ethiopia remains. Moreover, in the eyes of many fundamentalist (as distinguished from radical) Muslims in today's Middle East, Ethiopia, because of the formative episode of the *sahaba* and their hegira, not only deserves the right to exist, but also serves as the ultimate historical model for righteousness and justice. For example, *Shaikh* Nimr al-Darwish, head of the Islamic Movement (an offspring of the all-regional fundamentalist "Muslim Brethren"), in Israel in the early 1990s, made the Ethiopian case a pillar of his political platform. The *shaikh* argues that in countries where Muslims are the majority, an Islamic government should be constituted. But in countries (like Israel), in which Muslims are a minority, they are allowed to recognize and even to cooperate with the existing governments, provided these governments do not interfere with their rights as Muslims. The theological-historical legitimacy to such recognition stems, according to *Shaikh* Nimr al-Darwish, from the story of Muhammad and the *najashi*. "If the Israeli government," he wrote, "would render justice to Muslims the way the *najashi* and Christian Ethiopia did with the *sahaba*, I am full ready to follow in the line of Ja'far bin Abu Talib, who, as instructed by the Prophet himself, lived respectfully under the Ethiopian government and the *najashi* 'under whom none are persecuted.'"[44]

"ISLAM AL-NAJASHI" AND
THE LEGACY FOR THE RADICALS

Islam was and is *din wa-dawla*, both religion and state. Its spiritual message was often compromised by the dictates of political reality. However, in pursuing the aims of radical "pure" Islam, free from such compromises, leaders such as the sixteenth-century *Imam* Ahmad bin Ibrahim *Gragn*, or the late nineteenth-century *mahdi*, the Sudanese Muhammad Ahmad, did declare *jihad* against Ethiopia. We shall return to these cases and their implications for Ethiopian history, but at this point we must turn our attention to the theoretical legitimacy of such an anti-Ethiopian holy-war approach.

Radical Islam is oriented fully to the past: For its followers, Muhammad's period is the ultimate source of guidance and legitimacy and a model of conduct. This fact is true of the radicals of today who in referring to Ethiopia return inevitably to the *najashi* story. The radicals' interpretation of the *najashi* story reflects the opposite of the *"utruku"* concept, namely, the concept of Ethiopia as the historical enemy, which has also existed, usually latently, throughout the centuries.

What is the message of the *najashi* story for radical Islamic literature? Some of the books published in Cairo in the late 1980s make it clear that in radical Islamic literature, Ethiopia has been, and remains, the country of the infidels, of fanatic crusaders, who denied Muhammad and hated Islam.

One such book is *The Immigration to Ethiopia and the Arguments over the Issue of al-Najashi's Islam*, published in 1987.[45] The author, an al-Azhar professor, Muhammad 'Abd al-Fattah 'Aliyyan, fails in 120 pages of details even to mention the *"utruku" hadith*—in fact, he hardly mentions anything that even suggests that Ethiopia contributed to the Prophet's effort to survive. The book makes two points relevant to our concerns: The first is that the king of Ethiopia, being a just individual, did see the light of Islam and convert.[46] That conversion was recorded by the great early Islamic writers (Ibn Ishaq, Ibn Sa'ad, and al-Tabari, among others).[47] To dispute these learned sources, the author maintains, is an anti-Islamic act, and much of his book is devoted to accusations against Muslim historians who dared to doubt (especially against the author of a London School of Oriental and African Studies 1960 M.A. thesis, "Muhammad's Diplomacy," the Sudanese 'Awad al-Sharif Qasim).[48]

'Aliyyan's second point is that Ethiopia did not follow the *najashi* in conversion but rather forced him to conceal his devotion to Islam.[49] The Ethiopian people led by the priests derided Ashama for his harboring of the *sahaba*. After his death, his son destroyed the Prophet's letter to him. There is no mention in 'Aliyyan's book that Muhammad was grateful to the *habasha* in general. Ethiopia, says the author, was not occupied by Islam for concrete military reasons, not because of the Prophet's gratitude.[50]

For the Islamic radicals the premise of the whole *sahaba-najashi* episode lies not in Ethiopia saving the *sahaba* but in the conversion of the *najashi* to Islam. The idea of Muhammad and his successors was to expand the Land of Islam by first convincing the political rulers to convert. What mattered was that the kings themselves would recognize the Prophet, and this was the essence of Muhammad's letter of 628 to the *najashi*. If the ruler did declare his allegiance to the Prophet, then the country fell within the boundaries of the Land of Islam and actual conversion of the inhabitants could follow later. By opposing a Muslim *najashi*, Christian Ethiopia betrayed Islam. It follows that only the return of a *najashi* to Islam can redeem the country. Prior to such redemption the very existence of a Christian Ethiopia is an offense against the legacy of the Prophet.

Another such book, published in 1985, reflecting the radical Islamic attitude toward Ethiopia, is *The Political Relations between the Muslims of Zayla' and the Christians of Abyssinia in the Middle Ages*.[51] It is mainly devoted to later events but does include a chapter on the *najashi*. The author, a Cairo University professor,' Abd al-Halim Muhammad Rajab, writes that Ethiopia is one of the main historical enemies of Islam, and a loyal, but by no means junior, partner to Europe in an on-going Christian crusade.[52] In dealing with the *najashi* episode, Rajab makes the following points:

First, the Ethiopians, even before the time of Muhammad, were crusaders who wanted to destroy the Ka'ba and Christianize the whole Arab Peninsula.

Second, a *najashi* by the name of Ashama did convert to Islam, but he was not the emperor of Ethiopia, only a provincial ruler, a *bahr negash* (a position and title that were, in fact, established much later). This provincial functionary (*negasi* in Ge'ez, indeed, means a ruler, although not necessarily an emperor) adopted Islam out of fear (for a reason that had to do with his personal background). But again, he had to conceal the adoption out of fear of his own people, the Christian enemies of Islam (pp. 31–38).

Third, Muhammad himself understood that Ethiopia was an enemy and that the *najashi* who converted was not a significant ruler. Indeed, Muhammad warned the Muslims from Ethiopia, saying: "The lean-legged from the Ethiopians, they will destroy the Ka'ba." (The *hadith* is quoted from al-Bukhari.) It was a warning regarding Ethiopia, Rajab emphasizes, that the Prophet also said: "Leave the Abyssinians alone" (pp. 31–38). The Dahlak Islands, he adds, were occupied to prevent the Ethiopians from invading and destroying Mecca and the Ka'ba. Rajab concludes: "Indeed the Ethiopians revealed their enmity to Islam from the very beginning. It was mostly out of their fear from Islam, for the new religion proved so powerful in uniting the Arabs on the other shore of the Red Sea. They were hostile from the very start . . . and the *najashi* affair made no difference, for when he died it ended in any case, and their fanatic priests took over in fighting Islam" (p. 37).

These two different legacies from the formative episode were to shape Middle Eastern attitudes toward Ethiopia. They were not of equal importance. The concept of Ethiopia's illegitimacy (I shall call it "*Islam al-najashi*") was a distant second in motivating Islamic politics. In the thirteen centuries between Muhammad and Mussolini it surfaced rarely, but it was in the background ready to be called forth. It was transmitted, we shall see much later, into modern pan-Arabism during the 1935–1936 "Abyssinian Crisis."

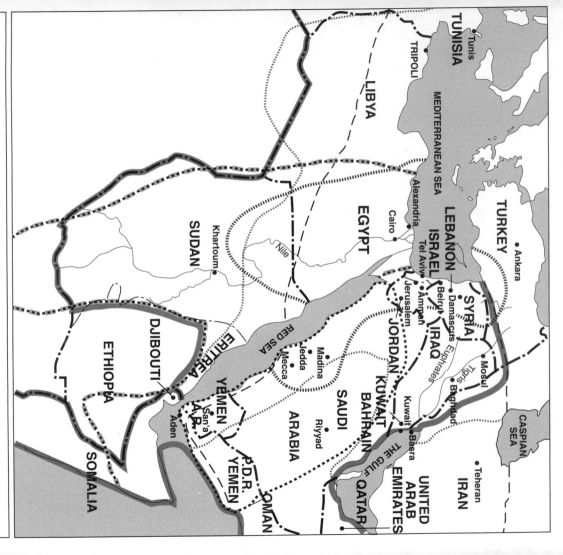

The Middle East and Ethiopia

Muhammad's Islamic Empire
The Islamic Empire of the Umayyads
Khedive Ismail's empire
The Sultanate of the Mamluks in Egypt

The Ottomans in their heyday
(note the province of habesh)
The boundaries of "the Arab nation"
as in Bath maps

xi

"Utruku al-habasha" or "Leave the Ethiopians as long as they do not take the offensive" was the major principle guiding the Middle Eastern Muslims. (I shall call it the *"utruku* legacy.") It meant that Ethiopia enjoyed a special, symbolic status and had the right to exist, but only as a marginal, irrelevant entity, isolated, and ignored. The Ethiopian case, though rarely in the center of events, became "one of Islamic history's most delicate questions."[53] This was because the argument stemming from the ambivalence over the *sahaba-najashi* story revolved in fact around the principal issue of accepting or denying the legitimacy of a non-Islamic entity, and turned often into a discussion among the believers over the very significance of Islam itself.

2

Relations up to the Sixteenth Century: Isolation, the Nile, and Muslim Sultanates

Islam was to remain until the twentieth century the major political identity of today's Middle East. From the very beginning, we have seen, it declared Ethiopia neutral to its goals and purposes and therefore irrelevant. This principle, couched as it was in terms of piety, would remain virtually unchallenged until the creation of the modern Middle East out of the Ottoman Empire following World War I.

Throughout these centuries Islam, as a Middle Eastern culture and state, isolated Ethiopia from its notion of the civilized world. It deprived Ethiopia of most of the Oriental connections that had been essential to its creation. Islam's empires inherited all the Oriental political entities with which Aksum had been in contact, and then left Ethiopia to its own.

Until the sixteenth century there were two exceptions to this story of benevolent indifference. First, Egypt, although it was an Islamic province, always stood out as a country interested in Ethiopian affairs. Second, Islam, as a culture rather than a political entity, penetrated the Ethiopian sphere of the Horn of Africa. This phenomenon of local Islam became an integral part of Ethiopian history, often linking it, at least potentially, with the strategy of the Middle East.

ETHIOPIA IN ISOLATION

Following the occupation of the Dahlak Islands in 702 Islam began strangling Aksum as a maritime entity. Cut off from its link to the Red Sea, Aksumite Ethiopia began to decline. Ethiopian Christianity was left with only an indirect contact with the Coptic center of Alexandria, and lost much of the momentum—political, commercial, and spiritual—that had marked the century prior to the emergence of Islam. What followed was the gradual decline of a landlocked Aksum, and the inescapable movement of the realm's center to the south, with important implications for its ethnic and cultural development.

The process that led to the final fall of Aksum is in itself outside the scope of this study. Aksum, as has been described by Sergew Hable Sellassie, Taddese Tamrat, and others,[1] had disappeared by the tenth century. It fell victim to the Islamic policy of condemning Ethiopia to isolation by neutralizing it as *dar al-hiyad*, Islam, because of its beliefs, was unable to accept Ethiopia as an active neighbor and a partner in commercial and cultural relations. Deprived of the stimulus of international relations, Middle Eastern Islam meted out to Ethiopia the greatest punishment, that of indifference. Occasionally, as we shall see, Muslim rulers deviated, for concrete strategic interests, from the principle of "leaving the Abyssinians alone." However, the initial exemption of Ethiopia from *jihad* left the country to survive by depending on its own strength. Ethiopia managed to do this quite successfully,[2] mainly by feeding on its own cultural and regional diversity and by maintaining political continuity. But the price of isolation was high.

The strength that made Ethiopia's continuity possible was aided by the Oriental connections that survived the Islamic blockade. The main one was with the Coptic Church of Egypt. The head of the Ethiopian Church, the *abun*, remained until 1951, as we shall see, an Egyptian bishop appointed by the Alexandrian patriarch. His presence in the royal Ethiopian court and his contribution to the maintaining of the Church of Ethiopia as a branch of Oriental Christianity was no doubt essential for the continuity of the country's religious as well as political institutions.

For example, the Coptic influence can be seen in the revival of Ethiopia under the Zagwe dynasty (from 1133) and then, even more forcefully, under the Solomonic dynasty (from 1270). The country's renewed judiciary code, the *Fetha Negast*, the implementation of which was consistent with the process of that revival, was imported from Egypt. It was compiled by an Egyptian Copt, al-As'ad bin 'Asal, and consisted of two parts. The religious part was based on the Coptic code, and the penal code was based on the Islamic *shafi'i* school, especially on *Kitab al-tanbih* by Abu Yishaq al-Shirazi.[3]

The revival of the institution of the emperorship owed much of its legitimacy to the ethos of the *Kebra Negast*, "The Glory of the Kings," which was also an importation from the Arab East. According to this officially adopted legend, translated into Ge'ez from an Arabic translation of a Coptic version, the founder of Ethiopia's ruling dynasty, Menelik I, was the son of King Solomon and the Queen of Sheba. Menelik removed the Ark of the Covenant from Solomon's Temple in Jerusalem and brought it to Aksum, which became Zion, the dwelling place of the Lord.[4] By the fifteenth century, the sanctuary of every Ethiopian Church edifice had come to be regarded as a copy of the Holy of Holies in Solomon's Temple.[5] The

Solomonic myth providing the main political ethos of Ethiopia thus owes its existence to the cultural link to the Orient in general, and to Jerusalem in particular.

EGYPT AND THE NILE-COPTIC CONNECTION

While the Middle Eastern Islamic empires under the 'Umayyads in Damascus (661–750) and the Abbasids in Baghdad (from 750 to 1517 officially) turned their backs on Ethiopia, Islamic Egypt continued to maintain relations. The issue of obtaining an *abun* from Alexandria made it imperative for the Ethiopian emperors to communicate with Egypt's rulers.[6] Upon the death of the *abun* they sent emissaries and presents to placate Egypt's Islamic rulers, who were not always tolerant of their own Copts. Egypt's rulers were, however, most concerned about the Nile, the lifeline of their country. More than two-thirds of the Nile waters reaching Egypt come from Ethiopia (and more than four-fifths of the summer flood waters, which irrigate Egypt) by way of the Blue Nile (the *Abbay* in Ethiopic), its tributaries, and the Atbara.[7] The notion of Ethiopia's potential control of Egypt's very existence has worried Egyptians from time immemorial.

The first written record of such a concern dates from the days of the Fatimid dynasty (909–1171). Around 1090, with the Nile waters at a low ebb, the Fatimid ruler al-Mustansir bil-Allah sent an appeasement mission headed by the Coptic patriarch to the Zagwe court. Ethiopian tradition has it that the greatest Zagwe king, Lalibela (1133–1173) had discussed the idea of diverting the Nile but refrained from so doing because other Muslims, in Ethiopia's east, would benefit from it, and also because the Egyptians had agreed to pay an annual tribute. As a demonstration of good will, the ruler of Egypt and the Islamic victor of the crusades, Salah al-Din of the Ayyubi dynasty (1171–1250) restored the Ethiopian community in Jerusalem in 1187, which had existed from the beginning of Ethiopian Christianity.[8] (The Jerusalem connection, as we shall see, would become a political issue only in the nineteenth century.)

The rule of the Mamluk dynasties in Cairo (1250–1517) coincided with Ethiopia's "Golden Age" under the early Solomonids, 1270–1529.[9] The Mamluks turned Egypt into the center of Middle Eastern Islam. Although the caliphate remained in the hands of the 'Abbasid dynasty, the latter's capital of Baghdad had long been politically ineffective, and it was destroyed by the Mongols in 1258. The Mamluks hosted the *caliph* in Cairo and built up their capital as an Islamic theological center. But vis-à-vis Ethiopia, however, they had to deviate from the Islamic legacy: they could hardly afford "leaving the Abyssinians alone."

The major concerns of the Mamluks were Middle Eastern: expanding their territory and facing repeated Mongol raids. They were also interested in Red Sea commerce and were heavily involved in the affairs of Yemen, Aden, and the Hijaz.[10] But like other rulers of Egypt, they, too, were worried about the Nile. The contemporaneous emergence of a powerful Ethiopia under the Solomonic dynasty put the issue on their agenda. Between the Mamluks and Ethiopia's emperors there developed a hostile series of exchanges: The Mamluks delayed sending *abuns* to Ethiopia, mistreated their own Egyptian Copts, and punished the Ethiopian community in Jerusalem, and the Ethiopians threatened to block the Nile. The correspondence between Ethiopia's Yekuno-Amlak (1268–1285) and *Sultan* Baibars I (1260–1277), and between Emperor 'Amda-Zion (1314–1344) and *Sultan* al-Nasir Muhammad (1309–1340) expresses these positions. In 1381 Emperor Dawit (1380–1414) sent an army that reached Aswan before appeasement had been effectuated by the Coptic patriarch. Emperor Yishaq (1413–1430) sent letters to European monarchs offering an alliance against Egypt. Zar'a-Ya'qob, Ethiopia's greatest emperor of the time (1434–1468), tried at first to be cooperative and sent a constructive message in 1437 to *Sultan* Barsbay (1422–1437). When, three years later, Zar'a-Ya'qob learned from the Coptic patriarch that *Sultan* al-Zahir Jaqmaq (1438–1453) had ruined an important church in Egypt, he again sent a message, this time threatening to block the Nile unless the church was restored. *Sultan* Jaqmaq responded in 1443 with kind words and presents but refused to rebuild the church. Zar'a-Ya'qob replied, warning the Mamluk to cease persecution.[11] He kept the Egyptian envoys as hostages for two years.[12]

These diplomatic exchanges bespeak the Mamluks' relations with Ethiopia.[13] Although Egypt was Islamic in its culture it was always forced to deal with the territorial importance of the Nile River. This concern arose again in the early nineteenth century with the reemergence of Egypt as a state, simultaneously with the revival of Egypt's special interest in Ethiopia.

Mamluk Egypt, as distinct from the rest of Islam in the medieval era, expressed some modest intellectual curiosity in Ethiopia. A book by Ibn Fadl-Allah al-'Ummari, *Masalik al-absar fi mamalik al-amsar* (written between 1342 and 1349) and al-Maqrizi's *Book of the True Knowledge of the History of the Muslim Kings in Abyssinia* (written in 1435–1436) are two important sources for this period. They were both concerned with the Muslims of the Horn, and in discussing the Muslims they also refer to the Christian kingdom. However, by expressing any curiosity about Ethiopia at all, they were the exceptions.

Mamluk Egypt's relations with Ethiopia contributed to Ethiopia's Golden Age. Emperor Saifa Ar'ad (1344–1371) used Egyptian experts, in both his political administration and his armed forces. Emperor Yishaq (1414–1429) was even more fortunate to host a group of Mamluks who had fled from their rivals in Egypt. The group, led by al-Tabingha, was said to help the emperor reorganize his army, introduce to Ethiopia the use of naphtha, and to build an arsenal that produced swords, spears, and other weapons. Among the refugees from Egypt there was also the Copt administrator Fakhr al-Dawla, who helped Yishaq reform his financial system.[14]

The demise of Egypt as a separate political entity following the fall of the Mamluks in 1517 deprived Ethiopia of the constructive challenge of an active relationship with an Oriental neighbor. The Ottomans, after a brief but important period of active interest (which we shall discuss), returned in the late sixteenth century to the policy of ignoring Ethiopia, with all concomitant implications for its premodern history.

THE CHALLENGE OF LOCAL ISLAMIC SULTANATES

Islam in the Horn of Africa and in the Middle East forms two distinct sets of political cultures and histories. In the East, Islam managed from its earliest days to fulfill itself as a dominant political philosophy. In the Horn, in facing Ethiopia, Islam was less politically cohesive and, indeed, less powerful.

From Muhammad to the abolition in the Middle East of the caliphate in 1924, Islam represented religion and state inseparably. The Islamic state and empire were not always unified under effective dynasties, but they were always the only legitimate order in the eyes of Middle Eastern Muslims. Also, Islam as an Oriental empire, from the failure of *Caliph* 'Ummar to take Adulis until the advent of the Ottomans, virtually never even attempted to cross the Red Sea. ('Ummar is said by tradition to have sworn never to fight again in the sea.)[15] It not only "left alone" Ethiopia, it also "left alone" the Muslims of the Ethiopian Horn of Africa.

Failing to assert itself in the Horn as an extension of its Oriental political order, Islam crossed the Red Sea with traders[16] and holy men, rather than with armies. Even so, the movement was far from a failure. Indeed, ever since Islam spread in the Horn of Africa in the eighth century it has competed up to the present time with Ethiopian Christianity over the cultural and political order in Ethiopia and the adjacent areas.

Following the occupation of the Dahlak Islands in 702 Islam continued to spread during the eighth century down the Red Sea coast to Zeila and beyond. Zeila became a trading post that helped to diffuse the new faith to the southern parts of modern Ethiopia. In Zeila, Massawa, and other coastal towns Arab immigrants settled, and the Arabic language was adopted by other indigenous groups. These Islamic communities maintained contact with the spiritual centers of Middle Eastern Islam, like the great *madrasa* of al-Azhar in Cairo, the holy cities of Mecca and Madina, and even Damascus. They also coordinated the annual pilgrimage to Mecca, the *hajj*, an institution central for the spreading of Islamic influence. In al-Azhar of Cairo there was established a special *riwaq* (literally, a hall; an institution devoted to the support of students of the *madrasa*) called *Riwaq al-jabar-*

tiyya in which several notable Islamic scholars emerged from these towns over the centuries (the most famous being the early nineteenth-century Egyptian historian 'Abd al-Rahman 'Abd al-Jabarti).[17] This connection between the elite of the coastal towns of the Horn and al-Azhar in Cairo would last, as we shall see later, to become relevant to the emergence of today's Eritrean nationalist movement. But the peoples of the interior who came under the Islamic influence from the coast did not adopt Arabic: Arabic was usually spread where migrating tribes from Arabia served as a cultural and military backbone for the Islamic Middle Eastern empire. In the Horn of Africa and the hinterland of southern Ethiopia this was never the case (I shall underline the significance of this fact in discussing twentieth-century history). The indigenous peoples, be they Sidama peoples or Afar (like the Somalis in the coast), preserved their languages and their ethnic identity. Their adoption of Islam was shallow. For example, they barely developed the Islamic educational system based on quranic schools, nor did they, with the notable exception of the town of Harar, develop urban centers, so essential for the spread of a universal message such as that of Islam. But Islam in the hinterland proved useful in converting the traditional political organization of the Sidama into political principalities under continuous dynasties.

From the eighth century to the sixteenth there existed at least fourteen such Islamic political entities on the territory spreading inland from the coast into southern and southwestern Ethiopia.

The history of these principalities was reconstructed by scholars such as E. Cerulli, S. Trimingham, Taddesse Tamrat, Zahir Riyad, J. Cuoq, and more recently by U. Braukamper, and 'Abd al-Halim Muhammad Rajab.[18] The detailed story is outside our scope. Generally, the most important principalities were Shoa (from 897 to the end of the thirteenth century), Ifat (1285–1415), and Adal (1415–1577). The Islam they adopted failed to unite them, and they fought each other almost constantly. Islam was more of a success as a political identity when they faced Ethiopia, for as the Christian kingdom moved southward, and particularly after the rise of the Solomonic dynasty, the collision was inevitable.

From the point of view of Ethiopian history the two and one-half centuries of conflict with these Islamic principalities was of great importance. Ethiopia was invariably the victor and the conqueror of the enemy territories. The conflict provided a continuing challenge that turned Ethiopia's kings into "kings of kings" and emperors. The conquests gave Ethiopia some access to Red Sea commerce[19] (an access that had been lost since the fall of Aksum in the tenth century). The Ethiopian Church was revitalized because of the stimulus of a religious confrontation and because of the opportunities to spread the word and extend its chain of monasteries into new lands.

Victories and expansion to the south thus contributed to the restitution of a central imperial authority, combined with the spiritual and political strength of a revitalized church. In terms of cultural and political creativity, this was, indeed, the Golden Age of Ethiopian history. The extent of the revival was such that Ethiopia was able to return to the north and attempt to regain its place as a maritime power once again. Emperor Zar'a-Ya'qob (1434–1468), reoccupied Massawa (after it had been temporarily taken by 'Amda-Zion [1314–1344]) and made the Muslim *Amir* Dahlak his tributary. The entire region of the present province of Tigre, combined with the present Christian Tigrean-populated regions in Eritrea (the districts of Hamasien, Serai, and Akelle Guzai), were known as Ethiopia's Bahr Midir (the land of the sea), headed by a provincial ruler (*bahr negash*, literally a "ruler of the sea").[20]

Enjoying stability and their military superiority over their local Islamic neighbors, Ethiopians of this Golden Age developed their own concept of Islam as reflected in the emperors' chronicles. Islamic leaders were described as the ultimate embodiment of evil. In the chronicle of 'Amda-Zion, his rival Sabr al-Din, the *sultan* of Ifat, is described as: "This rebel son of a viper, seed of a snake, son of a barbarian, from the origins of Satan" and "enemy of righteousness who opposes the religion of Christ." On the Muslims in general this chronicle says: "All Muslims are liars" and "hyenas and dogs, sons of vipers and seeds of evil ones. . . ."[21] Christian Ethiopian confidence in facing Islam was also demonstrated at the time in the contacts with Egypt's Mamluks, as was described above.

What was the role of Middle Eastern Islam in this long chapter? In their struggle with Christian Ethiopia the Muslim rulers of the southern principalities sought their own salvation from the Muslim rulers of the Middle East. Within their limits they sought to establish contacts. Members of the Walashma' dynasty, which ruled in the principality of Damot and later in Ifat, were said to be descendants of 'Aqil ibn Abu Talib, the brother of *Caliph* 'Ali and of Ja'far ibn Abu Talib, the leader of the *sahaba* in Aksum. (According to other tradition they claimed to be descendants of 'Ali's son, Hasan.) The Makhzumi dynasty ruling in Shoa were said to be descendants of a Meccan tribe (from which had come Khalid ibn al-Walid, the Muslim conqueror of Syria).[22]

Islamic holy men, some arriving from Yemen or Arabia, others emerging from among the indigenous peoples, arose mainly in times of war with Ethiopia and attempted to unite local Islam and connect it with the rulers of the Middle East. Two such cases in point were *Shaikh* Muhammad 'Abdallah, who appeared in 1298–1299, and *Qadi* Salih, who appeared during the last days of Sabr al-Din, both in Ifat.[23] Of the Adalites, worth mentioning is *Sultan* Badlay's mission of 1452 to Cairo begging help in facing Zar'a-Ya'qob. He was not answered and was destroyed by the Ethiopian.

Until the end of the fifteenth century, with few exceptions, the rulers of the Islamic Middle East ignored their fellow Muslims in the Horn. Their own political order was in a state of crisis. The Abbasid caliphate had long been a political fiction and its capital of Baghdad as well as other centers like Damascus were, during this period, subject to Mongol raids. These two centers of Islamic power were not interested in contact with Ethiopia. The Mamluks, as we have seen, were not desirous of a relationship with Ethiopia after having a conflict with it, and the rising Ottomans were still busy conquering Constantinople and waging *jihad* in Europe. The Ottomans of this period, until their occupation of Egypt in 1517, knew nothing of Muslims fighting Ethiopians beyond the Red Sea. In the Arabic literature of the period as well as in later publications, (as distinct from literature of today's radical Islam)[24] the Muslims of the Horn principalities were often referred to as the "Muslims of *al-habasha*."[25] As *"habasha,"* they were hardly worthy of interest. Indeed, leaders of Islam in Ethiopia from Badlay to the present who hope for politicizing Islam in the Horn at the expense of Ethiopian integrity, yearn for the Middle East to come forward to help them. Such help has never arrived on time. At least not yet.

Not that Middle Eastern Muslims were always so indifferent. When it suited their purposes they put tradition aside and did intervene in Ethiopian affairs. But occupying Ethiopia in the name of Islam was not a goal for the Middle Easterners, and their occasional interventions were never seriously coordinated with the efforts of local Muslims.

3

THE TRAUMA OF GRAGN
AND THE DIPLOMACY OF HABESH

The events unfolding throughout the second and third quarters of the sixteenth century present a story of intense Islamic anti-Ethiopian effort. First, local Islam united in the south and launched a devastating *jihad* on Ethiopia. Then, the Ottomans entered the scene and occupied the northern coast of the country. But, though effective enough to be the major trauma in Ethiopian history, the Islamic assault lacked strategic coordination between the local and the Middle Eastern Muslim centers of power.

AHMAD GRAGN, ETHIOPIA, AND THE MIDDLE EAST

The first decades of the sixteenth century were marked by a revival of Islam as a politically unifying factor in the Middle East. The revival was diverted into external *jihadi* efforts. The Ottomans fought in Europe, the Persian Saffawids in the Caucasus, and the Mamluks against the Portuguese, who had penetrated the Red Sea as they worked to solidify their control over their newly discovered sea route to India.

A contemporaneous awakening of Islamic zeal in Arabia motivated holy men and *ashraf* (that is, members of leading Arab families who were descendants of the Prophet's family and tribe) to migrate from the southern Arab Peninsula. Their destination was the other shore of the Red Sea, and from 1490 to 1540, as described by B. G. Martin[1] and 'Abd al-Halim Rajab,[2] many such individuals from Yemen, Hijaz, and especially from Hadrmawt reached Zeila and traveled inland to Harar and into the various Islamic emirates. (Martin mentions members of such Hadrami families as Ba 'Alawi al-Husayni and al-Shatiri.) Their influence was most significant in Harar, the only major urban center in the hinterland, which in the thirteenth century had been reorganized as an Islamic center of learning by a pioneer of Sufism in the region, *Shaikh* Abadir of the Qadiriyya order.

In Harar, the now revitalized religious spirit served as a background for a revolution. The Walasma' *sultans* were ignored by the newcomers from Arabia and soon disappeared altogether. Political power shifted into the hands of military-religious leaders allied with the holy men. One of these, *Amir Mahfuz* of Zeila, restored a new spirit of anti-Ethiopian *jihad*. He was in touch with the *amir* of Mecca, the *Sharif* Barakat II (1495–1522), who had managed to control the Hijaz and spread the word of Islamic militancy beyond the Red Sea. *Amir* Mahfuz proclaimed himself an *imam*, hoisted Islamic holy-war flags, and erected velvet holy-war tents from Arabia in his camp. He even scored some victories over the Ethiopians before he was killed by Emperor Lebna Dengel in 1516. It was his son-in-law, Ahmad ibn Ibrahim, nicknamed *Gragn* (the left-handed) who managed (from 1525) to unite around Harar and under the banners of *jihad* all of Islam of southern Ethiopia.

The contemporary Yemeni (from Jizan) chronicler of Ahmad *Gragn*, Shihab al-Din Ahmad bin 'Abd al-Qadir, better known as 'Arab Faqih, emphasizes repeatedly in his *Futuh al-habasha* (History of the conquest of Ethiopia) that *jihad* is central to, indeed, the essence of Islam.[3] He also stresses the direct daily contact between the *imam* and the Arab *'ulama* (learned holy men), and in one passage reveals the way these holy men legitimized the anti-Ethiopian *jihad*. Two of them recount the story of a vision experienced by Yunis al-'Arabi:

As I was sleeping one night, I suddenly saw the Prophet, peace and prayer be upon him. "Ummar bin al-Khattab was standing to his right, Abu Bakr to his left, and 'Ali bin Abi Talib in front of him. And in front of 'Ali there stood *Imam* Ahmad ibn Ibrahim. And I asked him [the Prophet]: Oh Messenger of God, who is this man in front of 'Ali? And he, peace and prayer upon him, said: This is the man by whom God will bring peace and Islam [*yuslimu*] to the land of the *Habasha*.[4]

Ahmad *Gragn*'s was an Islamic revolution in full.[5] He assumed the title of *Imam*, which appears to indicate a Zaydi-Yemeni influence. He succeeded in combining religious zeal with military leadership and attracted many Muslims of the region: the Sidama of the interior and the Afar as well as the Somalis. The latter had converted in previous centuries, and Ahmad himself could have been a Somali, an Afar, or even an Arab—in the revolution he led, his exact origins were meaningless, for with the new Islamic unity, ethnicity and language were rendered marginal. The later controversy over *Gragn*'s origin[6] is insignificant. In his time and place he was nothing but the *imam* of Islam. He was, of course, also *al-Ghazi*, the conqueror.

Gragn's conquest of Ethiopia needs no retelling. The Ethiopian kingdom had been weakening as Islam united, seeking its destruction and its replacement. Muslim nomads were hungry for the richer upland pastures,[7] and their new movement led by the holy men and commanded by the *imam* turned into a successful *jihad*. The Islamic army conquered Shoa in 1529, Amhara in 1531, and Tigre in 1535. Emperor Lebna Dengel, some of his family captured and sent to Yemen, fled from one mountain top to another and died in 1540, as the whole country was virtually conquered. Thus, for the local Muslims the *futuh* of Ethiopia was accomplished: a conquest that opened the country for full integration into the Land of Islam.

Ethiopia's conquest by Ahmad *Gragn* was surely the single most important chapter in Ethiopia's long history. It was a far more traumatic experience than even Mussolini's conquest of Ethiopia in 1936–1941.[8] By Ethiopian records nine out of every ten Christians were forced to convert to Islam. The destruction of cultural assets and national pride was immense.[9] "The very texture of Ethiopian civilization was being torn into a thousand pieces in the course of this era of pillage."[10]

The implications in terms of Ethiopians' concept of Islam were far reaching. If the *sahaba* story was the formative episode for the Middle Easterners as they viewed Ethiopia, *Gragn* was the central experience for the Ethiopians. From that sixteenth century event until today the idea that Islam, once politically revitalized, could well unite to destroy their national existence, has been an integral and central part of Ethiopian consciousness. A sixteenth-century Ethiopian chronicler and poet prayed: "May God exalted take vengeance on the house of Mujahid [that is, he who wages the *jihad*] for a thousand generations." A few modern Ethiopian scholars and historians still call this chapter "Ethiopia's holocaust."[11]

Ethiopian fear of Islamic unity focuses on the idea that local Islam always contains the potential of being supported by, indeed, even allied with, the mighty Middle East. This fear, as we shall see, would turn into a central factor in Ethiopian history. During the *Gragn*'s conquests, however, such an Islamic unity did not exist.

In general, *Gragn*'s was an effort by a united local Islamic front with the backing of the Arab Peninsula only. This backing was certainly important. According to Martin, the *sharif* of Mecca, a major authority in Islam, was involved in sending holy men and arms.[12] *Gragn* possessed at least one cannon, some two hundred firearms, and a similar number of trained warriors from beyond the Red Sea. It was enough to destroy Ethiopia.

The cannon and firearms that *Gragn* used were newly introduced to the area. They had been brought to Arabia by the Ottomans, the emerging great power of Islam. By the time *Gragn* was launching his *jihad* in Ethiopia, the Ottomans were already the masters of the Middle East. After two centuries of successful holy wars in Europe, during which they had perfected their art of cannon warfare and use of firearms, the Ottomans turned to occupy and reunite the "land of Islam." They were in the process of creating the strongest Islamic empire, and one of the largest in history. It brought them into direct contact with Ethiopia.

In 1517 *Sultan* Selim the Terrible captured Egypt and established a navy in the Red Sea. His successor, Suliman the Magnificent (1520–1566), the greatest of the Ottomans, annexed the whole of North Africa (with the exception of Morocco, which prevented the Ottomans from entering the ocean). He also returned to the Red Sea seeking to defeat his great rivals, the Portuguese. His navy clashed with the Portuguese, who had penetrated the Red Sea in 1502, and engaged in decisive sea battles on at least five occasions between 1520 and 1555. In 1538, when *Gragn* was solidifying his control over Ethiopia, the Ottomans appeared to be on the threshold of a strategic victory. They sent their Red Sea navy to India under the command of the governor of Egypt, Suliman *Pasha*. En route, Suliman captured Yemen and Aden. In India the local Muslims betrayed Suliman, and he was defeated by the Portuguese. The latter retaliated by launching a daring campaign into the Red Sea, which proved to be unsuccessful.

The mighty Ottomans, in a sea war, paid little attention to Ahmad *Gragn* and his Ethiopian *jihad*. When in 1538 *Imam* Ahmad appealed to the new Ottoman *pasha* in Zabid, Yemen, for military aid to effectuate the Islamization of Ethiopia, he asked for three thousand men. *Gragn* promised in return his allegiance to the Ottomans once he fully stabilized his new Islamic entity in the Horn.[13] But the Ottoman commander in Yemen was too busy fighting against the Zaydis in San'a to care greatly what happened in Ethiopia.[14] He gave *Gragn* nine hundred trained warriors—Arabs, Albanians, and Turks—as well as ten cannons. Although an impressive force, it was nothing compared with what the Ottomans might have dispatched had they identified with the cause of *jihad* in Ethiopia.[15]

The Ottoman failure to help *Gragn* to a final victory of Islam stands in contrast to the fact that the Portuguese expeditionary force to the Red Sea did land in Massawa to rescue Christian Ethiopia. Headed by Christopher da Gama, four hundred highly trained Portuguese soldiers helped Emperor Galadewos to recoup his strength. Da Gama himself was captured and executed in August 1542, and *Gragn*, overconfident, sent the Ottoman contingent together with da Gama's head to the *pasha* in Yemen. Dispensing with Ottoman help proved premature. A few months later, on 21 February 1543, in the battle of Zantara, *Gragn* himself was killed. The entire local Islamic enterprise, losing its leader and lacking Ottoman support and interest, collapsed. The remnants of the Islamic armies of *Gragn* returned to Harar. *Gragn*'s successor, Nur al-Din, assumed the title of *Amir* of the Believers and built walls around the city. In 1559 he even dared to venture out of his defenses, attacking Ethiopia's Emperor Galadewos and killing him in battle.

By that time, the Ottomans had already become interested in Ethiopian affairs and in 1557 landed in Massawa. They were concerned with their own strategic goals and did not attend to Nur al-Din and Harar. However, they did save the town for Islam. Their landing in Massawa attracted Ethiopia to the north, and it was the Oromos, the new invaders from the south, not Christian Ethiopians, who captured Harar. In 1577 the political center of the Adals moved to the remote oasis of Awsa, in the land of the

Afar, and Harar remained under a local dynasty, a small center of Islam in the midst of Oromo territory.

As Harar declined, the memory of Ahmad *Gragn's jihad* faded. It meant little to the Muslims of the Ottoman Middle East. But to the Muslims in the Horn of Africa, *Gragn* became their greatest historical hero. In Middle Eastern medieval literature, by contrast, he is hardly mentioned. The manuscript of *Futuh al-habasha* (The conquest of Ethiopia) written by 'Arab Faqih was never completed, and it was little known. A summary was published for Middle Eastern Muslims and Arabs in 1933 by Shakib Arslan[16] (on whom I shall elaborate later). In 1904 a high-ranking Ottoman official visiting Ethiopia, Sadiq al-'Azm, the author of *Rihlat al-habasha*, was knowledgeable enough to lecture to his Ethiopian hosts on the history of Islam and Ethiopia. He knew only little about *Gragn*, about whom he was curious.[17] The Turkish historian C. Orhonlu, who worked extensively in Istanbul's archives on the history of the Ottomans and Ethiopia, found there only brief mention of *Gragn*.[18] Radical Muslims today lament the fact that no significant contact existed between Middle Eastern Islam and Ahmad *Gragn's jihad*,[19] for the Ottomans were hardly interested in a holy war against Ethiopia.

THE OTTOMANS AND THE HABESH *EYALETI*

The Ottomans soon became interested in occupying a part of Ethiopia. In 1555, after another frustrating clash with the Portuguese navy, it became clear to the Ottomans that they were not going to dominate the sea route to India. They decided instead that they wanted to control at least the Middle East trade route to the Far East and sought to solidify their position in the Red Sea. For this purpose, they established *Habesh Eyaleti* as their province of Ethiopia.

A second reason for this decision was that the Ottomans, following the European discovery of America, were now desperate to discover new sources of gold and silver. In 1551 they had occupied Tunisia for that purpose and now they sought access to Ethiopia's minerals.

Habesh was the Ottoman term referring to all the territory lying to the south of Egypt, east to the Nile and down to the land of the Zanj.[20] The Ethiopian project was therefore more of an Egyptian-Ottoman enterprise than a matter of international political strategy planned by Istanbul. In 1555 Suliman *Pasha*, the governor of Egypt, entrusted the conquest of Habesh to one of his generals, Ozdemir *Pasha* (previously an aide to the governor of Zabid in Yemen with whom *Gragn* had been in contact, and later the conqueror of San'a in 1547). Ozdemir's first move was to march in 1555 from Egypt down the Nile and capture the sultanate of the Funj. He then had to return to Egypt and in the same year landed in Suakin (which had been in

Ottoman hands since 1517). In 1557 he proceeded to Massawa leading three thousand soldiers, established his headquarters there, and ascended the escarpment to Debaroa, the capital of Bahr Midir, Ethiopia's coastal province.[21] Debaroa was taken easily because the *Bahr Negash* Yishaq was at that time accompanying Emperor Galadewos in his campaign against Harar. Ozdemir *Pasha* erected a tower and built a wall around Debaroa, in the midst of which he also constructed a mosque. He then proclaimed the establishment of a new Ottoman province, the *eyalet* of Habesh. The proclamation, officially made on 5 July 1557, was significant. *Eyalet* was the term used for the basic Ottoman provincial unit and was applied to entities such as Egypt, Damascus, or the Hijaz. The entire empire, stretching from near Vienna to the borders of Morocco, was divided at the time into only twenty-five such units. The establishment of Habesh as an *eyalet*, itself divided into five *sanjaqs*—Suakin, Massawa, Arkiko, Zeila, and Jidda on the opposite shore, complete with a supreme *qadi* (residing in Suakin)—was a clear indication of an intention to control the country permanently. However, soon afterward (in 1559), Ozdemir died of sunstroke, and *Bahr Negash* Yishaq returned and forced the Ottoman garrison from Debaroa.[22] An Ottoman conquest of Ethiopia, or of some hinterland for Massawa on the Ethiopian Plateau, was never to materialize.

From the available information it is not clear whether the whole idea of Habesh was really adopted at the time by Istanbul. It seems far more likely, judging by the fact that the resources allocated for the enterprise came from Egypt and that Ozdemir as well as all governors who were later to engage in enterprises directed against Ethiopia were from Egypt,[23] that the enterprise was a local initiative of the *pasha* of Egypt rather than a full-scale imperial effort. Two years after the death of Ozdemir, his son, 'Uthman, was sent from Egypt to replace him. His first act was to contact the *bahr negash* and make a treaty with him.

During the next thirty years, from 1559 to 1588, the Ottoman effort was not to occupy Ethiopia but to return from Massawa to Debaroa. It appears that they concluded (as would the Italians centuries later) that they should control some of the highlands in order to secure their hold on the coast. It is hardly conceivable that they desired or planned anything more than that.

If the Ottomans had desired to occupy all of Ethiopia they would have had to muster a huge army. In the 1550s they were, at least in terms of ground forces, the strongest military power on earth. But it is apparent that they confined themselves to a Red Sea province having the necessary hinterland. In any event their Habesh enterprise was by no means a matter of an anti-Christian *jihad*. They were not aiming at the Islamization of the country. Indeed, in the large territories the Ottomans had captured in eastern Europe, where they would remain for some four centuries, the Ottomans refrained (for practical reasons mentioned in Chapter 1) from

Islamizing Greeks, Serbians, Bulgarians, Rumanians, and others. In Habesh they were not seeking the spread of Islam but rather promoting their own political interests.

Once the Ottomans presented themselves in Ethiopia as participants in a strategic game rather than as religious warriors, they were free to play politics. Their trump card was *Bahr Negash* Yishaq.[24] By the time Ozdemir invaded in 1557, *Bahr Negash* Yishaq had long since acquired his reputation as an Ethiopian patriot. His northern province was the only one *Gragn* had not managed to destroy. And it was through this territory and Yishaq's personal mediation that the Portuguese came and helped in reuniting the land against *Gragn.* Although Yishaq's father and brother had adopted Islam to enter the service of *Gragn,* Yishaq remained a loyal and most efficient supporter of Emperor Galadewos. In return he was allowed to exercise an autonomous government over Bahr Midir, the land of the proud Tigrinya speakers (*Tigrai Tigrinya*), the core territory of Aksumite Ethiopia.

When 'Uthman *Pasha* contacted Yishaq in 1561 the *bahr negash* of the Tigreans was in revolt against the new emperor of Ethiopia, Minas (1559–1563). The latter (who as a child had been taken hostage by *Gragn* and kept in Yemen) deviated from the internal politics of pragmatic and flexible decentralism pursued by many successful Ethiopian emperors. He tried to force a rapid centralization of the government, with the same disastrous consequences experienced later by Ethiopian rulers. It led directly to revolts by various regional leaders resorting to *shiffnnet*, an Ethiopian sociopolitical institution of semilegalized defiance of established authority. We shall return to discuss this central phenomenon and its modern development in the context of Ethiopia's twentieth-century relations with the Middle East.

Like many such rebels, Yishaq found it natural to cooperate with outsiders against such an emperor. This cooperation was acceptable under the Ethiopian cultural code, provided that the outsiders were playing a political game and not threatening Ethiopia's Christian identity.

Yishaq allied himself with 'Uthman *Pasha,* and they united their armies to defeat Minas in 1562 in Tigre. Minas fled to Shoa, where he died the following year. His successor, Emperor Sertsa Dengel (1563–1597) appeased the *bahr negash* and restored Tigrean autonomy. Yishaq broke relations with 'Uthman (he was now supported locally by the Portuguese), and for a brief time the Ottomans stopped meddling in Ethiopian affairs. They had their hands full in nearby Yemen, where, upon the death of the great *Sultan* Suliman in 1566, the Zaydi tribesmen and their *imam* had started a revolt.

Suliman's successor, Selim II (1566–1574), did his best to restore the Ottoman position in the Red Sea. He sent his emissary and architect, Sinan *Pasha,* to quell the Yemenites (he scored a success in 1570), and in January

1568, ordered his *pasha* to Egypt to start working on the construction of a canal at the isthmus of Suez. *Sultan* Selim wanted to send his Mediterranean fleet to the Red Sea and then finally defeat the Portuguese in India. But in 1571, the Ottoman Mediterranean fleet was destroyed at Lepanto by a coalition of European navies, and the entire project was put aside. It led to yet another attempt at solidifying the Ottoman hinterland of Massawa.

Radwan *Pasha* was sent from Egypt with new forces, and he captured Debaroa in 1572. Two years later he was evicted from the highlands by Yishaq. In June 1577 Ahmad *Pasha* was appointed over Habesh. He came with substantial forces and eight cannons and, like 'Uthman *Pasha* sixteen years earlier, offered an alliance to the *bahr negash*. The latter, now an aging man of undiminished ambition, was at the time in disgrace with the emperor, who was considering abolishing his title and reorganizing the north. In the ensuing clash (the so-called "Turkish-Ethiopian War")[25] Yishaq and Ahmad *Pasha* were twice defeated by the imperial army that Sertsa Dengel was able to amass. They were both killed at Addi Quro on 17 December 1578.

Entering Debaroa, the emperor destroyed the town and abolished the Bahr Midir arrangement that had united the Tigrinya speakers since the days of Zar'a-Ya'qob. He also assembled the remnants of the local garrison and built around them the first Ethiopian army unit equipped with firearms. Its commander held the title of *Turk Basha*—"the Turkish Pasha"—which would connote the king's commander of such units until the beginning of modernization.

An Ottoman force of seven thousand men had to rush from Yemen to ensure the safety of Massawa. In 1588 the Ottomans managed for a short time to reoccupy the site of Debaroa. But then they gave up. They confined themselves to Massawa where they would nominally stay and maintain Habesh as a *sanjaq* subordinate to Jidda until the nineteenth century. But in the seventeenth century they lost all hope of competing on the sea route to India, especially after the British and the Dutch had replaced the Portuguese in the Indian Ocean.[26]

It has been written that "the Turks made between 1576 and 1579 their most serious bid to conquer Ethiopia."[27] It has also been observed that for the Ottomans, Debaroa was the "Poitiers of Ethiopia,"[28] referring to the town in southern France where the Islamic armies of the 'Umayyads invading from Spain were stopped in 732 from advancing into the heart of Europe. The analogy is valid only if the Ottomans were truly seeking the occupation of all of Ethiopia. Orhonlu provided no evidence that this was the goal of the Ottomans. It appears, rather, that the Habesh enterprise, an Ottoman Egyptian provincial project, was aimed at Massawa and its hinterland; it was never an effort to destroy Ethiopia as a Christian nation.

How the Habesh developments, from the invasion of Ozdemir in 1577 to the Ahmad *Pasha* War (the 1578 defeat as it was referred to by the Ottomans of the time),[29] were conceived in Istanbul we do not know. We have, however, interesting evidence of what may have been a theoretical discussion of Ethiopia in the Ottoman court that took place just after the last failure in 1588 to return to Debaroa. *Sultan* Murad III (1574–1595) ordered the preparation of a Turkish translation of an Arabic biography of Prophet Muhammad (by al-Waqidi). The Turkish version was handed to the *sultan* in 1594–1595 complete with illustrations, which provided the only way to add some contemporary interpretation to the earlier text. Two of the drawings are of interest to us.[30] One of them accompanies the story of Muhammad sending the *sahaba* to *al-habasha*, the land of justice, and to the court of Aksum. The drawing depicts the *najashi* seated with four members of the *sahaba* as they exchanged greetings. The other drawing is of "Bilal al-habashi" and the *sahaba* with Bilal (black like the *najashi*, but not as dark as *Zanj* Africans in other drawings), much distinguished as a leader of Islam.

In the sixteenth century the power of the Ottomans was such that even the partial effort they made in Habesh may be deemed an Islamic Middle Eastern threat to Ethiopia. But such a threat was not to be revived before the nineteenth century. The Ottomans did stay in Massawa, but their history in their *sanjaq* of Habesh is of marginal significance. Gradually, with the loss of any hope to use Massawa as a station en route to India, the Ottomans lost interest in the region. They stayed there for local commercial considerations as well as for regulating the Red Sea pilgrimage to Mecca. Their province of Egypt, the base and reason for Red Sea policies, began slipping from Ottoman grip, and, torn by its own internal rivalries, briefly lost its strategic role. In addition, new Islamic movements, such as the ones which in early sixteenth-century Arabia had influenced events in the Ethiopian Horn, were not to reappear in this manner until the early nineteenth century.

In the first half of the seventeenth century the Ottomans in Massawa still played an active role in Ethiopian affairs. They were, for example, involved in the efforts by the Catholic Jesuit missionaries to convert Emperor Susenius (1608–1632) and reform Ethiopian Christianity. When the inevitable tension culminated with Emperor Fasiladas's expulsion of the Catholics in 1632, the Ottomans in Massawa helped Ethiopia briefly counter European Christianity. In 1647 Fasiladas and the *pasha* in Massawa agreed that the latter would kill any missionary attempting to enter Ethiopia.[31] The Ottomans were interested in preventing the strengthening of Ethio-European relations as well as the reform and change they might bring to the country. The significance of the episode from our perspective was the extent of Ottoman readiness to legitimize Ethiopia's existence as a *dar al-hiyad*, a concept that did not identify with Christian infidelity.

The Ottomans, in decline as an effective all–Middle Eastern government, in time lost interest in Massawa itself. The town, deprived of its hinterland, remained dependent on Ethiopia for water and other basic necessities. These were usually obtained in return for not damaging Ethiopian trade and passage. Such a petty game was not important enough to justify a permanent Ottoman functionary on the spot. Ottoman authority was therefore delegated to a "replacer," a *na'ib*, a title given to a local Beja family from the nearby town of Arkiko. The *na'ib* of Arkiko, with nothing but a poor Ottoman military unit at his disposal, took care of local matters in the name of the Ottoman Islamic Middle East until the Italian occupation of Massawa in 1885.[32]

Thus, by "leaving the Abyssinians alone," the Ottoman Empire ceased to have any direct influence on internal Ethiopian matters. Significantly, there was no important connection between this Islamic Middle Eastern empire and the process of Islamic conversion by the Oromos during the seventeenth and eighteenth centuries. It was a major phenomenon in Ethiopian history to which I shall soon refer.

The real significance of the Ottoman presence in Massawa lay in its implications. The Ottomans guarded the gateway of Ethiopia, controlled the Red Sea, and thus "left" Ethiopia alone. Their presence was efficient enough to continue Ethiopia's isolation from Europe.

The Ethiopian emperors after Susenius (1608–1632), it is widely accepted, were for their part ready to close themselves off by withdrawing into political isolation in the town of Gondar. They resisted change, fearing the conservative clerics and nobility. But it was even more convenient for yet another reason. The isolation of the coast by an indifferent neighbor meant the continuing marginalization, in the Ethiopian context, of the Tigrean northerners.

The Middle Easterners were ready to see Ethiopia left alone. Indeed, when Emperor Fasiladas (1632–1667) attempted to reach out to build contacts with the Middle East, his efforts were rebuffed. According to Van Donzel's analysis,[33] Fasiladas sought contact with Istanbul and even sent letters to the *shah* of Persia and the *mogul* in India. These attempts yielded nothing of substance.

More significant was Fasiladas's effort to build an alliance with the Zaydi *imams* of Yemen. The latter had been successful in 1635 in ousting the Ottomans from San'a; Fasiladas, much impressed, offered them an alliance. He wanted not only arms but also an alternative outlet to the Ottoman-occupied Massawa by way of Beylul and its connection to the Yemeni port of Mukha.[34] In 1642, Fasiladas initiated a correspondence with *Imam* al-Mu'ayyad bi-Allah, who would only respond if he believed that the Ethiopian was considering conversion to Islam. Fasiladas finally sent a mission to Gondar (1647–1649), headed by the *qadi*, Hasan bin Ahmad al-Haymi. When al-Haymi learned that Fasiladas sought only friendship, he returned to Yemen. But Fasiladas did not give up and thereafter sent presents to the *imam*, now al-Muayyad's successor, al-Mutawwakil 'Ala-Allah, whose response was categorically negative. In 1651–1652 he wrote to Fasiladas saying the only gift he wished was the Ethiopian's conversion. Citing the *najashi* episode in the life of the Prophet, he wrote: "We have forefathers [who acted] like that: Our ancestor, the Messenger of God . . . and you have forefathers [who acted] like that: the *najashi*."

Then, quoting lengthy passages from Muhammad's letter to *Najashi* Ashama, and reproducing the alleged response in which the *najashi* recognized the Prophet and professed to have adopted Islam, the *imam* continued: "Since the matter stands like that, it is our duty to call you to that which called our forefather, and it is your duty to agree to that which [was] agreed [to by] your forefather, if God permits. These are, from ourselves and yourself, the presents and the greatest gifts."[35]

The *imam* chose to give weight to that aspect of the *najashi* legacy that implied that a Christian Ethiopia was not a legitimate entity unless it accepted Islam. But the Zaydis never sought influence beyond their mountainous Yemen, and the *imam*'s response to Fasiladas was, in fact, a dismissal of Fasiladas's desire for cooperation.

Ethiopia, according to the analysis of Abir,[36] drifted into its "Era of the Princes" (1769–1855), a long period of renewed isolation, political anarchy, and lack of cultural or economic creativity because the Red Sea was ignored by the Ottomans who, as we saw, isolated Ethiopia and deprived it of the challenge of international relations.[37]

Viewed from the Middle Eastern Ottoman perspective, the sixteenth-century Islamic encounter with Ethiopia was a story of noncooperation. There was no significant contact, in terms of a coordinated effort, between the local Islamic enterprise under *Gragn*, and the powerful Ottoman empire. *Gragn*'s was a *jihadi* movement inspired by Islamic awakening in the Arab Peninsula. The Ottomans neither paid attention to him nor did they supply him substantially. When the Ottomans finally became interested in Habesh, it was not in the name of *jihad*, and *Gragn* and his movement had been long dead. And the Ottomans never made a concerted, unified effort. The *eyalet* of Habesh had been initiated in Egypt and in the context of Red Sea affairs. It was not consistently coordinated with Istanbul, which remained more interested in the maritime struggle over the route to India than in the affairs of Ethiopia.

However, from the Ethiopian perspective the picture and legacy of the sixteenth century may be viewed differently. The Ethiopians distinguished, both contemporaneously and later, between *Gragn*, the *jihadi* destroyer of their country, and Ozdemir, the invader who became an ally of the *bahr negash*.[38] But the trauma of the sixteenth century was engraved in the Ethiopian consciousness as the threat of Islamic political unity. It left a very clear legacy: the idea that local Islam could well eventually reunite, and with the backing of the Islamic Middle East could again threaten to annihilate Ethiopia's state and culture.

But, the seventeenth and eighteenth centuries witnessed no such effort. The Middle East, under Ottoman decline, had little interest in the Horn affairs, and the local Muslims had no more Ahmad *Gragns* or political unity.

4

THE BEGINNING OF MODERN TIMES:
MUHAMMED 'ALI AND TEWODROS

MUSLIMS AND ISLAM IN
ETHIOPIA IN LATE MEDIEVAL TIMES

Although the history of Islam in Ethiopia during the periods of Ottoman disengagement is outside our scope, we must nonetheless turn briefly to developments before the nineteenth century because they will become important before our story is over. The periods after the demise of *Gragn* were marked by the penetration of Islam into the core of Ethiopia. The conquest opened the country to new waves of immigration from the south, and the remnants of the Muslim invaders—those who preferred to stay—were not expelled. It has been estimated that by the early seventeenth century no less than one-third of Ethiopia's population were Jabarti Muslims.[1]

The Jabartis were originally Muslims who had emigrated from the territories of the Emirate of Ifat, which had also borne the name of Jabarta, namely, "the burning country."[2] They settled in the highlands of Ethiopia, mainly integrating into the local communities, occasionally forming their own communities. Mixing with the indigenous population and spreading their beliefs, they adopted Ethiopian languages, mainly Amharic. (An older but rather small Muslim community had lived in Tigre and spoke Tigrinya. Its origins date to the eighth century, when Dahlak Island was an important Islamic cultural center. It is still known today as Jabarti.) The Jabartis settled predominantly in urban centers and thrived on commerce, which required frequent travel to Islamic territories. Commerce happened to be a profession despised by the Christians. Over time, all Muslims of Ethiopian origin and speakers of Ethiopian Semitic languages came to be called Jabarti.

By the seventeenth century the term *Jabarti* had changed to connote religious affiliation in a cultural and a social sense. It lost the political meaning from the days of the conflict with Adal. In fact, Ethiopian Islam, since the demise of *Gragn*, had become largely depoliticized. The Jabartis, being ethnic Ethiopians and following an Islam that was not based on an institutionalized quranic educational system, never stood for the political fulfillment of the Islamic identity. Instead, they formed an integral part of an increasingly diversified Ethiopian society.

The record of Christian-Muslim relations during this period is multifaceted.[3] Some contemporary observers reported discrimination against the Muslims, but others were impressed by the cultural similarities, indeed, the harmony between the communities. Naturally there were vicissitudes, as would be expected. For example, in 1647 Emperor Fasiladas allied himself with the Ottomans against European Catholic meddling in Ethiopia; at the time he was, as we have seen, seeking to establish ties with the Zaydi *imam* of Yemen. The *imam*'s envoy to Gondar (1648), al-Haymi al-Hasan, was impressed by the thriving Muslim community in the Ethiopian capital.[4]

Fasiladas's successor, Emperor Yohannes I (1668–1682), was alarmed by the extent of the spread of Islam. He convened his nobles and clergy and declared Islamic segregation, forcing Muslims in Gondar and throughout the realm to move to separate neighborhoods. Muslims were now also barred from owning land and from holding high offices, their leaders being reduced to the position of *nagadra*, a functionary in charge of commerce and markets.

Through both contemporaneous literature and popular expressions, we see an era marked by cultural tension, if not of outright enmity. In daily life Muslims were looked down upon by Christians, who called them *eslam* or *naggade* (trader) with a contemptuous connotation. Christians wore a blue neck cord, the *matab*, to distinguish themselves from the Muslims or pagans, who in some respects were regarded as equally impure. Christians would not eat from the same table as Muslims. Making love to a Muslim woman was considered a sin. "The sky has no pillars," according to a saying that succinctly reflects the attitude of the Christians, and "Muslims have no land." Another saying ridiculed the male Muslim as measuring his wealth by women instead of by land, as did the Christians. When a Christian met a Muslim he saluted him with his left hand (instead of the right one) to show his disrespect. When two Christians quarreled, they were said to have "become like Christian and Muslim."

Muslims, in their turn, developed similar attitudes. They looked down on Christians as semipagans. Christian ceremonies of the *tabot* (the sacred "ark" carried during festivals in procession around the church) were regarded by Muslims as tantamount to pagan worship. "Instead of cleansing himself in the river, the Christian goes to a priest," according to a Muslim saying.[5] We shall return to this theme suggesting uncleanliness in our subsequent discussion of modern Middle Eastern attitudes.

But beyond these tensions, the general picture was one of functional coexistence if not of partial assimilation between Muslims and Ethiopian Christians. The apolitical Muslims even played a constructive role in Ethiopian economy and society. Their economic contributions as traders and artisans were obvious. Socially, and even politically, they became integrated into the general Ethiopian social fabric. Because the Jabartis claimed no ethnic differentiation and used Ethiopian languages, they contributed to the diversity of Ethiopian culture, rather than polarizing it. Those who aspired to national leadership had to convert to Christianity, but in lower regional or state positions and in daily social and economic life, they could participate as Muslims. Taken as a whole, the general record of Islam within premodern Ethiopian society was one of flexibility and openness.[6] It certainly compares favorably in terms of religious tolerance with the Ottomans and with most contemporaneous European empires.

John Markakis found a remarkable symbol for what he calls intimacy and enmity between the Christian and Muslim communities in Ethiopian history. He writes:

There is no more poignant illustration of the intimacy and enmity which characterize the relationship between Christian and Muslim communities in Ethiopian history than the legend of the Aksumite emperor who befriended the disciples of the Prophet. Ethiopian Muslim tradition venerates his memory under the name of Ahmad Negash. According to this tradition, Ahmad Negash travelled to Mecca and espoused Islam. Upon his return to Ethiopia, he was killed by Christians, and his death is attributed to the treachery of his Christian wife, Maryam. At the top of the hill in the village of Nagash, near the town of Wukro in the province of Tigre, a mosque houses the tomb of Ahmad Negash. It is a place of worship for Muslims in northern Ethiopia and the site of annual pilgrimage. At the foot of the same hill is a Christian church dedicated to Maryam, who is referred to by the Muslims as "Maryam the traitor." Although the two places of worship lie close to each other, neither is visible from the other—a fact which is regarded as symbolic of the historic relationship between Muslim and Christian in northern Ethiopia.[7]

Another element that added to the increasing Ethiopian diversity during this period were the Oromos (formerly known as the Galla).[8] We have already seen that the Oromos invaded the Sidama territories of the southern Islamic emirates, which had been exhausted following the demise of *Gragn*. There they settled, mixing with the Sidama, and were influenced by their political tradition. In the late sixteenth century some of the Oromo groups—the Wallo, the Raya, and the Yadju—went on to penetrate into the very heart of the Ethiopian Christian highlands. There they settled, and, unlike the Jabartis, they retained their ethnic identity and language.[9] During the course of the eighteenth century, they adopted Islam, further emphasizing their distinction.

The settling of the Oromos in the very core of Ethiopia was a major cause of the ensuing period of political disintegration ("the Era of the Princes"). The Ethiopian political culture was, however, sufficiently flexible to absorb these highland Oromos into the Ethiopian system. All that was required was that their leaders superficially adopt Christianity. Relying on the military power of their Oromo Muslim followers, Oromo chiefs could thus aspire to fuller political participation. A dynastic family of the Muslim Yadju Oromos (whose ancestor, 'Ummar Shaikh, was said to have emigrated from Arabia, arriving with *Gragn*'s army) dominated the late eighteenth century. Their *Ras* Ali I (d. 1788), *Ras* Gugsa (d. 1825), and *Ras* Ali II (from 1831) were in their time the most powerful individuals in the country. They were accepted by an Ethiopia in decline. But then, in the early nineteenth century, the Middle East re-entered Ethiopian political history.

THE MIDDLE EAST AND RENEWED SPREAD OF ISLAM

The nineteenth century was a period in which some of the features of the sixteenth century returned to rekindle the Ethiopian–local Islamic–Middle Eastern triangular story. Local Islam would again be revitalized in Ethiopia and its immediate periphery because of a religious reawakening across the Red Sea in Arabia. And, again, political and military revival in the Middle East would combine with the reinvigorated local Islam to threaten Christian Ethiopia's existence. In the second half of the century the danger as viewed by Christian Ethiopia's existence. This combination was the threat of a reunited and repoliticized Islam, actual or imagined, was at least as important in shaping the history of Ethiopia as the new, simultaneous challenge of Western imperialism.

At the beginning of the nineteenth century, a revival of Islam in Arabia was triggered by the Wahhabi-Saudi movement and dynasty in Riyad. Spreading fundamentalism into the Hijaz, it encouraged the revival of Sufism (mystical, popular Islam). *Tariqas* (religious orders) spread through the preaching of holy men, especially in Mecca. Of special importance was the work in Mecca of *Sayyid* Ahmad ibn Idris al-Fasi (1760–1837). Originally from Morocco, he sent his disciples to spread *Sufi* Islam in Africa.[10]

One of the most prominent of al-Fasi's disciples was Muhammad ibn 'Ali al-Sanusi (1787–1859), who established a chain of *Sufi tariqas* as well as a movement that was to constitute the backbone of the modern Islamic identity of Libya. Another student of al-Fasi, *Shaikh* Muhammad 'Uthman al-Mirghani (1793–1853), worked in northern Sudan and areas in today's western Eritrea beginning in 1817. It was due to his activities and to the *Sufi* movement he established, the Mirghaniyya (also called the Khatmiyya), that local tribes (some of whom had practiced Christianity) converted to Islam. The most important of these were the Bani 'Amir clans, which were the strongest in eastern Eritrea and were to play a major role in the later emergence of the Eritrean nationalist movement.

The son of Muhammad 'Uthman al-Mirghani, Hasan al-Mirghani (who died in 1869), established the headquarters of the Mirghaniyya in the town of Kassala and entered, as we shall see, into the service of Egypt.[11] Other "holy families" preached Islam at the same period in the area of what would become Eritrea. One of these was the Ad-Shaikh family, claiming Qurayshi origin and led at the time by *Shaikh* al-Amin ibn Hamad.[12]

During this period, Islam was also being revived in the south, in the areas of the defunct medieval Islamic emirates. The Oromos, who had swept over these territories in the late sixteenth century and who had inherited the political institutions from the Sidama, had established five such entities in southeastern Ethiopia. These were Jimma, Gera, Guma, Limmu-Enraya, and Gomma. At the end of the first half of the nineteenth century their leaders came under the influence of Islamic preachers from Ethiopia itself and from Yemen and the Hijaz. As a result, they adopted Islam. Islam helped to sanction the new *sultans* and kings, especially as the inhabitants followed their leaders by converting to Islam, as well.[13] The spread of Islam was also on the rise because of the growing demand in Arabia for Habasha slaves. In 1857 when slavery was abolished in the Ottoman Empire the Arab Peninsula was exempted from the decree of abolition, and the Habasha—mostly Oromo, Gurage, Walamo, and Kaffa—remained the best merchandise.[14] Since Islam forbids the enslaving of Muslims it was widely believed that conversion was the best preventive measure.

The most prosperous of these kingdoms was Jimma. The kingdom was established in about 1830 by Sanna Abba Jifar who, having united many of his Oromo followers, adopted Islam and encouraged its spread. He managed to convert the merchants and centralize his administration. When he died in 1855 Jimma Abba Jifar, as he came to be known, bequeathed to his successor a thriving sultanate. In southeastern Ethiopia the revival of Islam culminated in the reconstitution of Harar as the main center of Islamic diffusion.[15] The town again attracted *'ulama* (learned holy men) from Arabia and gradually began to spread Islam among the Arusi,[16] the Borana, and the Leqa.

The growth of Islam in Ethiopia during the first half of the nineteenth century was a far greater threat to the Christian character of Ethiopia than it had been during the similar period prior to Ahmad *Gragn*'s destruction. This situation was so for at least four reasons.

First, in the nineteenth century, Muslims held power in the very heart of Ethiopia—among the Oromos of the highlands, in Wallo and Bagemdir. (By Ethiopian oral tradition *Ras* 'Ali II was said to have contemplated renewing the cult of *Gragn* by organizing ceremonies at *Gragn*'s presumed burial place.)[17]

Second, Islam was spreading now through learned men and *Sufi* leaders, who were now establishing quranic education in mosques and had their centers in towns like Harar, Kassala, Massawa, and even in Gondar.[18]

Third, Islam was now on the rise because of the Muslims' monopoly of trade. Trade as well as *'ulama* were also helping to increase the communi-cation among these various centers of Islam.[19]

And fourth, Ethiopia itself, as a state based on the institution of the emperorship, was now in a clear decline. The emperors, by now political nonentities, resided in Gondar under the direct control of *Rās 'Ali* and his Muslim Oromos. The various provincial Christian centers, in contrast to the Muslims, were drifting into regional isolation. And, as occurred in the six-teenth century, the Middle East now witnessed a revival of its political energy, a revival now centered on Egypt rather than Istanbul. In the nine-teenth century, the attention of Cairo was inevitably drawn to the Red Sea and the Nile.

MUHAMMAD 'ALI AND ETHIOPIA

The Ottoman *pasha* of Egypt, Muhammad 'Ali (1805–1849), was the first and perhaps most effective modernizer of Egypt.[20] By the late 1820s he had introduced Western military methods and had created in his province the largest and the best armed forces in the Ottoman Empire, stronger even than the army of his official master, the Ottoman *sultan*. Imitating Western ways, Muhammad 'Ali also introduced reforms in the Egyptian economy (by introducing the cultivation of cotton) and its soci-ety. In order to build a new, modern armed force, he had to move away from old Ottoman traditions and recruit into his army the Arabic-speaking peasants of Egypt. He thus initiated the process of creating a modern Egyptian society and state, a process still going on in our own day, and one, as we shall see, with implications for Ethiopian history.

In his early years Muhammad 'Ali still had to answer to Istanbul. In 1813, Istanbul ordered his forces, which were still traditional, premodern, and modest, to Arabia to quell the Wahhabiyya. Five years later the *pasha's* attention was again focused on the Red Sea when the *sultan* gave his son Ibrahim the *eyalet* of Jidda including the *sanjaq* of Habesh. A small Egyptian garrison was then stationed in Massawa,[21] but the entire enter-prise was of little importance. With the goal of building larger forces, Muhammad 'Ali sent his forces to the Sudan. He also sought gold and min-erals, which were presumed to be available in eastern Sudan, but even stronger was his desire for black slaves to serve as the backbone of his Egyptian army. In 1820–1821, he occupied Sudan and established the capi-tal of Khartoum in 1830.

The occupation of Sudan and of Massawa also caused increased Islamic involvement on the Ethiopian periphery. We have already seen that the work of *Shaikh* Muhammad 'Uthman al-Mirghani among the Bani 'Amir had been carried out under the auspices of the Egyptian administra-tion in Sudan. In 1840, in order to control the region and the Bani 'Amir more successfully, the Egyptians established the town of Kassala as the capital of their new district of Taka and the headquarters of the Mirghaniyya. At the same time an increased number of Muslim youngsters began attending school in *riwaq al-Jabartiyya*, the corridor of the Cairo *madrasa* of al-Azhar designated from medieval times as the center of Muslim Habasha students from Massawa or Zeila. The *na'ib* of Arkiko also became involved as many Eritrean tribes joined Islam. All of these simultaneous movements caused the imperialist newcomers to the Red Sea region, the British and the French, to suspect that Muhammad 'Ali intended to occupy Ethiopia, a notion that remained alive for more than two decades. Europeans warned the *pasha* not to threaten Christian Ethiopia, and Muhammad 'Ali repeatedly declared that he never planned to do so.

At this time, new tensions were arising on the Sudanese-Ethiopian border stemming from differences in the understanding of the concept of a border. The Egyptians had adopted the Western concept of a demarcated line, which they were now pushing inland, claiming territories not inhabited by Habashis. The Ethiopians, by contrast, conceived of a border as the limit of their raiding and taxing abilities. The tension that inevitably arose occasionally took the form of serious clashes, including the harboring of Sudanese rebels by Ethiopian chiefs from Tigre or Bagemdir, and of Egyptian punitive expeditions.[22]

What rendered the situation more dramatic was the correspondence between *Ras 'Ali* in Gondar and the Egyptians. The *ras*, only superficially a Christian and the leader of the militarily powerful Oromo Muslims dominating the heart of Ethiopia, was reported by many contemporary sources to have invited Egyptian interference in Ethiopia. He is also said to have urged Muhammad 'Ali to refrain from dispatching a new *abun* from Alexandria to Ethiopia, a post that was essential to the Christian spiritual life in Ethiopia. No new *abun* was sent for an entire decade (from 1831 to 1841). The documentary evidence provided by Rubenson of this correspondence clearly indicates that *Ras 'Ali* conceived of himself (or at least that he wanted Muhammad 'Ali to think of him) as a Muslim *sultan of al-Habasha*, who yearned to solidify this position and rid himself of the rival Christian regional warlords with the help of Muhammad 'Ali.[23] However, as had occurred in earlier centuries, the Middle East Muslims were not forthcoming with their assistance.[24] "In spite of the disorder in Ethiopia, and the tension between Christians and Muslims in some parts, the Ethio-Egyptian problem was basically a question of border conflict . . . not one of interference in the internal affairs of the country."[25]

Muhammad 'Ali's chief, and perhaps only, interest was to inherit the all–Middle Eastern power of the Ottoman Empire, which he both defied and challenged. By 1824, he understood the futility of building a *janissary*-like traditional Ottoman army of Sudanese slaves. Instead, he began conscripting his own peasants en masse. With his newly formed, Western-style army and navy, he began in 1824 to involve himself in the internal affairs of the Ottoman Empire. First, he diverted his new army to help *Sultan* Mahmud II in facing the Greek nationalists' uprising (1824–1827), and then to undermine Mahmud's power. For this purpose he sent his son Ibrahim to invade Syria (1831–1832), to advance into Anatolia, and ultimately, in 1833, to defeat the Ottoman imperial forces. Halted only by the European ultimatum, the *pasha's* army remained in Syria for the next six years.

Like previous Islamic rulers, Muhammad 'Ali's theater of operation was the Middle Eastern lands of Islam. He wanted to placate the Europeans in order to win their approval of the strategic change he sought for the Middle East. He wanted to move the region's center from the shores of the Dardanelles to Cairo. He knew the British, fearing that the Dardanelles would fall into Russian hands, would be unlikely to agree. Nonetheless, he took a risk, and, in 1840 (after once again defeating *Sultan* Mahmud's army), lost all he had won when the British army forced him to retreat from Syria.

At the height of his power Muhammad 'Ali was never interested in Ethiopia, and in any case he would not risk a rupture with Christian Europe over Ethiopia. When he lost power he recognized Ethiopia as a Christian entity. In 1841 he finally relented, and permitted an *abun* to depart for Ethiopia from Alexandria.[26] This *abun, Abuna* Salama, was to become a pivotal figure in the unfolding saga of Christian Ethiopian revival. In the same year the Egyptians evacuated Massawa. They returned for a two-year stay in 1846–1848, but by then the aging *pasha* was too senile to initiate any further activity.

Muhammad 'Ali's importance to Ethiopian history was great. He revived Egypt, turning it from an Ottoman *eyalet* into a state that has become a leader and the center of Middle Eastern affairs ever since. Egypt, now an independent actor, pursued Red Sea and Nile policies that the Ottomans or earlier Middle Eastern dynasties had long neglected. From Muhammad 'Ali's conquest of Sudan in 1820, Ethiopia remained significant to Egypt.

By increasing Egyptian international standing, Muhammad 'Ali gave Ethiopia the long-needed challenge in its external relations. He provided both an incentive and the model. The first was the traumatic fear he incited in Ethiopia of Islamic local and Middle Eastern unity. The second was Muhammad 'Ali's centralized government, which would later serve Ethiopia's first modernizing emperor, Tewodros II, as a model.

TEWODROS II AND THE LEGACY OF MUHAMMAD 'ALI

Emperor Tewodros II (1855–1868) and Muhammad 'Ali are often compared as the initiators of modern eras in their respective countries.[27] By the time Tewodros assumed power in Ethiopia, Muhammad 'Ali had been dead for six years. Even so, the general programs created by Emperor Tewodros II were based on the assumption that he would rebuild Ethiopia fighting a formidable, threatening Muslim power. Muhammad 'Ali, as we have seen, never lived up to this Ethiopian image of him. His immediate successors, the contemporaries of Tewodros, were not ready to provide any such challenge. Indeed, they even sought his friendship.

Tewodros was born *Lij* Kassa Hailu, a local contender to overseeing in Quara, west of Lake Tana, a territory that had been in dispute with the Egyptian Sudanese authorities. The monastery he joined in his childhood was pillaged on one occasion by invading Egyptians, and this event was interpreted by later scholars as inculcating in him a lifelong anti-Muslim sentiment. Recently discovered documents, however, shatter this assumption. They reveal that in 1847 *Lij* Kassa, by now controlling much of the territory in question and on his way to assuming power at the center of Ethiopia, was not a fanatical enemy of Islam. At that time, still eager for domestic leadership, he corresponded with the Egyptians offering friendship. In his letters he even pretended to be close to Islamic culture if not a Muslim himself.[28] It is clear that he studied Arabic, a language he used, as did many other Christian Ethiopian leaders of that time, as the main means of communication with the outside world.[29]

But when Kassa came to power he adopted an anti-Islamic stance as an ideology. Upon coronation he took the name of Tewodros, who had been, according to an early Solomonic legend, a messianic king and savior of Ethiopia who would unite the country and would destroy Islam on his way to redeem Jerusalem.[30] The new Tewodros was, however, not a messianic visionary but, rather, a daring reformer[31] and a revolutionary. His general concepts and strategy were best reflected in a letter he sent to Queen Victoria in October 1862: "My fathers, the Emperors, having forgotten the Creator, He handed their kingdom to the Gallas [i.e., the Oromos] and the Turks. But God created me, lifted me out of the dust, and restored the Empire to my rule. He endowed me with power, and enabled me to stand in the place of my fathers. By this power I drove away the Gallas. As for the Turks, I have told them to leave the land of my ancestors. They refuse. I am going now to wrestle with them."[32]

The letter summarizes some of his own personal history. Tewodros was "lifted out of the dust" as a son of a remote district chief and a woman of humble origin. He made his way up as a *shifta* (usually a political rebel resorting to banditry). He "drove away the Gallas" by destroying the power of *Ras* 'Ali II (1853) and later by moving his capital to Maqdala, in the center of Oromo territory. Having defeated the provincial warlords of Tigre and of Shoa, he began to amass an all-Ethiopian army, judiciary system, and administration. His attempts at effective centralization, carried out by a Christian king and around a capital town located in the previously dominated Oromo territory, proved successful in at least one respect. He managed to neutralize the political power of the Oromos. The Oromos remained Muslims and a strong military power in the heart of Ethiopia but would henceforward be unable to return to their independent political role.

Until 1862, Tewodros was happy to concentrate his attention on his efforts to centralize Ethiopia. He fought the Oromos, the various contenders to power, and *shiftas* all over the country. He also struggled with the Church, which he wanted to subsume into his centralized state, but which, under *Abuna* Salama, was not ready to submit. But now Tewodros reached the stage of needing foreign aid, specifically, European technology and experts to solidify his government and begin serious economic development. Europe was, however, not interested and instead sent missionaries as well as some agents who were of little use. Earlier (in 1856) Great Britain had been ready to make some gesture. Its powerful ambassador to Istanbul, Lord Stratford de Redcliffe, approached the *sultan* about letting Ethiopia have the port of Massawa. *Sultan* 'Abd al-Majid (1839–1861) refused to give up the Habesh *Eyaleti*, and the British, even though they had just rescued the Ottomans in the Crimean War (1853–1856), let the matter rest.[33]

Having defeated a major rebellion in Tigre, Tewodros now had access to the coast. To modernize his country he sought British or French technicians and experts. He badly desired a port and European attention, and—as he saw it—he needed Middle Eastern Islam to serve as a common enemy. But he found none, nor was Egypt ready to help. On the contrary, Muhammad 'Ali's son, 'Abbas *Pasha* (1854–1863), shortly after the coronation of Tewodros, had sent the Coptic Patriarch Qerilos IV to the Ethiopian court. It was the first time in history an Alexandrian patriarch had paid a personal visit to Ethiopia, and the message he brought to Tewodros in December 1856 from the ruler of Egypt was one of appeasement and peace. The emperor was reported to be upset at seeing a Christian in the service of Muslims, and as false (or fabricated) rumors spread that 'Abbas *Pasha* had gone to the Sudan to prepare an attack on Ethiopia, Tewodros arrested the patriarch. Qerilos was allowed to return to Egypt only in November 1857, but in spite of this provocation the Sudanese-Ethiopian borderland remained quiet.

In 1859 'Abbas *Pasha* authorized the beginning of excavating the Suez Canal and gradually became interested in reviving the Egyptian government's claims to the Red Sea region and the Sudan. In 1862, tensions along the Sudanese border nearly brought about an Egyptian invasion of Ethiopia. Also, the French-British rivalry in the Red Sea had aroused the suspicion of the Ottomans. Indeed the new *sultan*, 'Abd al-'Aziz (1861–1876), was in no mood to suffer another humiliation. He had just been compelled by the Great Powers to agree to political autonomy for the Christians in Lebanon. In the Red Sea he ordered the raising of Ottoman flags along the coast of

Habesh and into the hinterland. Tewodros responded, as he mentioned in his letter to Queen Victoria, by issuing an ultimatum for "the Turks."

But 'Abd al-'Aziz, as had 'Abbas *Pasha*, refused to play the role of *Gragn*. He ordered the sending of the *na'ib* of Arkiko, Muhammad 'Abd al-Rahim, to Tewodros's court. In March 1863 the envoy came bearing gifts and a message of peace, but he was arrested. A month later he was permitted to return.[34]

Tewodros's idea of attracting European interest in his modernization effort through common enmity with Islam was a failure.[35] Perhaps he was overly frustrated by European indifference, for it appears that he was aware that the Ottomans and the Egyptians did not seek Ethiopia's conquest. He also knew that the British were the protectors of Ottoman survival and that the French were behind the modernization of Egypt. The fact that he nevertheless pursued that line may have been a symptom of the depth of the *Gragn* syndrome in Ethiopian Christian culture.

It was also a symptom of his own mental crisis. By 1860 he believed his country to be on the brink of modernization, but the lack of European support threatened a return to parochialism. At this point, he became merciless in dealing with his opponents, losing all sense of proportion. He alienated the country and its culture as he seemed bent on self-destruction. One example of his irrationality was his ordering in 1864 of mass Christianization of the Jabarti Muslims. (He began by burning a mosque in Gondar.) Tewodros's actions demonstrated that he was despairing of his entire efforts on behalf of his country. He was, however, in no position to carry out any policy, for he soon became involved in a dramatic struggle against the British, which ultimately led to his suicide in Maqdala in April 1868.

Both Tewodros and Muhammad 'Ali ended their lives in deep frustration. Muhammad 'Ali's dream of controlling the Ottoman Islamic empire was shattered because the West would not allow the fall of Istanbul. Tewodros failed because the West paid no attention to his efforts at modernizing his country. It is ironic that Tewodros's image in later Ethiopian historiography was overshadowed by his battle with the British, for Tewodros was not anti-European but rather a Westernizer. He dreamt of rebuilding a centralized Ethiopia around Western technology and even certain Western concepts. The British under Robert Napier, "Lord of Maqdala," fought him not in order to conquer Ethiopia but rather to disengage from it. (Indeed, the British had their own version of "leave the Abyssinians alone.")

Tewodros's failure to solidify the measures he introduced into the army, bureaucracy, land ownership, and state-church relations, prevented him from truly reviving the Ethiopian state. But he nonetheless succeeded in strengthening the all-Ethiopian awareness and identity to the point that it was better equipped than before to cope with the challenges that lay ahead.

Muhammad 'Ali failed to revitalize the identity he was struggling to fulfill. He was not an Egyptian. He was a Turkish-speaking Ottoman who only by accident found himself in Cairo at exactly the moment in history when the West began interfering in the affairs of the Ottoman East. In his effort to exploit the situation and create in Egypt modern Western military capabilities "he may have identified Egypt with himself," but to distinguish him from Tewodros, "he never identified himself with Egypt."36 Muhammad 'Ali's success was the by-product of his Islamic-Ottoman enterprise: He turned the Ottoman province of Egypt into a true state. He did succeed where Tewodros failed, in building around modern concepts the statehood and economy of Egypt. He thus paved the way for a Westernization process that was to create in the emerging identity of Egypt a tension between the heritage of Islam and the new concepts borrowed from the West. It is important to appreciate the difference between an Ethiopia of a revived traditional identity and an Egypt undergoing a quick-paced Westernization because this difference remained significant to their ensuing conflict.

5

YOHANNES, ISMA'IL, AND
THE ETHIO-EGYPTIAN CONFLICT

THE IMPATIENT EUROPEANIZER
AND THE CONSERVATIVE EMPEROR

By far the most important period in the modern history of Ethio-Egyptian relations was the decade of the mid-1870s to the mid-1880s; much has been written about the open conflict and the Ethio-Egyptian War.[1] *Khedive* Isma'il, Egypt's ruler between 1863 and 1879, departed from his grandfather Muhammad 'Ali's Ottoman Middle Eastern strategy and turned his attention to Africa. In 1865 he obtained Massawa from the *sultan* and initiated effective administrative reforms in the Sudan. After the opening of the Suez Canal in 1869, his forces occupied the African Red Sea coast and continued down the Somali coast of the Indian Ocean. An Egyptian province named Equatoria was then established in the African hinterland.

In 1875 the Egyptians occupied the Islamic center of Harar and simultaneously worked to strengthen the land route between the port of Massawa and the Sudan. They wanted to control the territory of today's Eritrea—this in spite of the fact that the nearby Ethiopian province of Tigre had just become the center of Ethiopia.

As we remember from the days of *Bahr Negash* Yishaq, Tigre had always been connected with the Tigrean-populated highlands of Eritrea, the Mareb Melash ("Beyond the River Mareb," in the Ethiopian terminology of the time). In 1872 the Tigrean *Dajazmach* Kassa Mircha was crowned Emperor Yohannes IV (1872–1889) and for the first time since the Aksumites shifted the country's political center back to the Red Sea sphere.[2]

The inevitable conflict between Egypt's new ruler, Isma'il, and the Ethiopian emperor, Yohannes, involved military clashes and diplomatic struggles that the Ethiopian side won. The Egyptian army suffered defeats (1875–1876), which contributed to the demise of Isma'il (1879). Egypt continued to deteriorate, both economically and socially, until it was occupied in 1882 by Great Britain.

The Ethio-Egyptian conflict of the decade under discussion exempli-

53

fied the major opposing trends in each society. The military aspect of the conflict was particularly important: The army of Yohannes defeated the Egyptian invading forces, doing so twice on Eritrean soil—in Gundet (November 1875) and Gura (March 1876). But these victories were effective only in preventing the Egyptians from advancing any farther than the territories they had occupied in Eritrea. The Ethiopian army was unable to loosen the Egyptian hold on Massawa, Keren, and other regions lying between the Red Sea and the Egyptian positions in the Sudan. Furthermore, as in the days of Muhammad 'Ali, the Egyptians erected a chain of forts in Eritrea, which the Ethiopians were unable to storm. A long war of attrition ensued (1876–1884), during which the Egyptians responded to Ethiopian raids into their territory by supporting, as *shiftas*, local Ethiopian adversaries to Yohannes and to his deputy in Eritrea, *Ras* Alula. Under circumstances such as these, a military solution was impossible.[3]

Neither was the conflict resolved through diplomacy. A historian would hardly deem Yohannes IV to be adept in the art of international diplomacy. Before coming to power he had been quite successful with the British mission against Tewodros. But after the British left him, as they had done with his predecessor, Yohannes despaired of the Westerners. He went on to alienate the French, and, more fatefully, shied away from negotiations with the Italians, when they appeared in Massawa beginning in 1885. His greatest diplomatic failure was in dealing with the Islamic fundamentalist Mahdist state that emerged in the Sudan in 1884 following a successful rebellion against the Egyptian government. As we shall see, instead of trying to avoid confrontation with the Mahdiyya, Yohannes undertook to fight them, with fatal consequences. He did so in the only treaty he did sign, the so-called Hewett Treaty of June 1884 with the British and the now British-controlled Egyptians.[4]

The Egyptian ruler, *Khedive* Isma'il, was a far more successful diplomat. Educated in Europe and fluent in both French and Italian, he personally befriended many Western heads of state, most notably Napoleon III. It was because of Isma'il's flexible diplomacy that he was able to secure Egyptian autonomy from the Ottomans. He even achieved some modest success with Ethiopia and managed at least until 1877, when it still mattered, to drive a wedge between Yohannes and his major vassal, *Negus* Menelik of the southern province of Shoa.[5]

What determined the outcome of the Ethio-Egyptian conflict of the late nineteenth century were matters beyond local warfare and diplomacy. In that period Ethiopia, facing both Egyptian aggression and pressure from the West while still recuperating from the devastation caused by Tewodros's attempt at radical centralization, revived many of its ancient political and cultural institutions. By contrast, at the same time Egypt was undergoing virtually the opposite process and was breaking away from its old traditions and experiencing quick-paced Westernization. These processes in Egypt were also marked by a social stratification that caused increasing polarization of the country. There was, as well, a growing involvement and interference by foreign individuals and countries in areas of Egyptian life such as its economy, its bureaucratic administration, and its army. In this regard, *Khedive* Isma'il has been accurately depicted as an "impatient Europeanizer,"[6] while Yohannes, in his confrontation with Westernization, gained the reputation of a rejectionist. Yohannes's policy emphasizing Ethiopia's traditional values culminated in October 1882 when he managed to bring about a unification, albeit an unstable one, of Ethiopia. In that month *Negus* Menelik of Shoa swore allegiance to Yohannes, thus temporarily uniting the houses of Shoa and Tigre. Just a few weeks earlier Egypt fell to the invading British army and lost its independence. Thus the demise of a rapidly Westernizing society, Egypt, and the tenacity of a traditionalist one, Ethiopia, determined the outcome of the conflict between them.

The differing characteristics and goals of the Europeanizer Isma'il and the traditionalist Yohannes had historic roots. The Ethiopian rose to power under the impact of Tewodros's failure and realized full well that Ethiopian society would continue to resist changes that were forced upon it from above. Isma'il, however, only continued the program of his predecessor, Muhammad 'Ali, and thus further deepened Egypt's Westernization. One of Isma'il's innovations was the diversion of Egypt's strategic orientation from the Muslim Ottoman Middle East to Africa. This diversion was carried out in accordance both with European interests and in line with changes within Egypt. Thus Isma'il, while pursuing old Egyptian expansionist goals in the Red Sea and the Nile Basin, actually paved the way for Western imperialism in Africa.[7]

Major differences are apparent in how these neighbors and rivals faced the challenge of Western penetration. Isma'il continued to encourage the proliferation of Western resources and concepts in order to effect Egypt's break with its past. Yohannes, by contrast, let Ethiopian development run its natural course. Isma'il followed an African strategy compatible with the interests of European powers, and during his rule the construction of the Suez Canal, turning Egypt into a bridge between Europe and the Afro-Oriental world, was accomplished. Yohannes, on the other hand, abandoned whatever all-regional role Tewodros cherished for Ethiopia, and he even attempted to avoid contact with European envoys to his country. He also made little effort to develop Ethiopia's infrastructure or urbanization. While under Isma'il, Cairo was replanned and largely rebuilt in imitation of Paris, and both this modernized capital and Alexandria flourished as cosmopolitan European-style cities with up-to-date municipal services, Yohannes abandoned Tewodros's plan of a central capital for all of

Ethiopia, and became, instead, a roving emperor, with campsites at Adwa, Dabra-Tabor, and Maqale. Insignificant changes were made at these royal campsites.

Of great significance was the difference in the two leaders' approach to their countries' economies. Isma'il greatly expanded Muhammad 'Ali's policy of converting to large-scale agriculture of cotton, mainly for export. Yohannes made no attempt to modernize or even to expand Ethiopia's traditional agriculture or to introduce any other economic innovations. Indeed, he even fought against the cultivation of tobacco, a crop of great economic potential that European missionaries in Eritrea and elsewhere had sought to introduce. Yohannes justified his tobacco policy in religious anti-Islamic terms, an issue to which we shall return. Yohannes expended considerable effort to revive Ethiopia's ancient alliance between Church and state. It was only in connection with the affairs of the Coptic Church that he was interested in relations with Egypt. (Yet it was not until 1881, two years after Isma'il's demise, that Yohannes finally received from Egypt the four Coptic bishops he needed for the restoration of the Ethiopian Church.) Isma'il, although unmistakably a Muslim (and certainly not a modern Egyptian nationalist) was nevertheless a child of European culture and acted accordingly. He put an end to the financial independence of Islamic institutions and of the *'ulama* by putting the whole *waqf* system (endowment of property) under state control. Much of the *waqf* income was then directed to the expansion of modern, semisecular education, and state examinations were imposed even on the Islamic university al-Azhar. In 1868 Isma'il inaugurated the French-oriented School of Law from which later emerged the future leaders of Egypt's liberal nationalism. Yohannes, by contrast, introduced no changes or new ideas in secular education. In fact, the opening of the first modern primary school in Ethiopia did not take place until the later years of his successor, Menelik II (1889–1913). In 1908, the year Cairo celebrated the inauguration of the Egyptian University, Menelik opened the Ecole Imperiale Menelik II. Even then the school was staffed largely by a group of Egyptian schoolteachers and headed by an Egyptian Copt, Hanna Salib Bey.[8]

In the fields of military affairs and imperial administration, Isma'il was again true to his reputation of being "the impatient Europeanizer" and Yohannes to his rejectionist reputation. Isma'il hired dozens of high-ranking officers, not only from Europe but also unemployed veterans of the U.S. Civil War, to train, advise, and command the Egyptian army. Other foreign personnel were employed to run the Egyptian Empire's administration in the Sudan, Eritrea, and Equatoria. It was under such personalities as Charles Gordon, Samuel Baker, Werner Munzinger, William Loring, William Dye, Soren Arendrup, and Eduard Schnitzer, to mention only a few, that Isma'il's African enterprise was built up, and was therefore in spirit and style fundamentally alien to Egypt's traditions. Yohannes—

unlike either Isma'il or his own predecessor, Tewodros—had little interest in foreign experts. He avoided them even after his early military success with the help of a British sergeant, J. C. Kirkham, whom General Robert Napier had left behind in 1868 after the campaign against Tewodros, along with a gift of firearms and a few pieces of light artillery. Kirkham's military guidance helped Yohannes to power, but when Yohannes became disillusioned with the British government's policy of ignoring Ethiopia, he ceased seeking such assistance. By the time the battles of Gundet and Gura took place, Yohannes's army was again purely Ethiopian in both its command and military strategy.

SOCIETIES AND LEADERSHIP
BETWEEN TRADITION AND CHANGE

Our perception of the personalities of Isma'il and Yohannes during this period is important because of the broad effects their divergent policies had on the social structure of both countries in the ensuing years. Isma'il was the autocrat who imposed his grandiose plans on the Egyptian populace; Yohannes was a flexible compromiser who realized how deeply embedded were the regional loyalties of Ethiopians, who recognized the rulers of Shoa and Gojjam as *neguses* (kings). In Egypt under Isma'il, socioeconomic polarization broadened the division between rich and poor. The country's agrarian elite, mostly of Ottoman-Circassian and non-Arab origin, and a newer element of recent arrivals from Europe and the Levant, was enriched and strengthened, while the landless peasants and unskilled urban laborers were reduced to ever-increasing poverty. The class stratification created during this period in Egypt was to endure for several generations. (We shall see the problem in Ethiopian history again during the Abyssinian Crisis of 1935–1936.) In Yohannes's Ethiopia no such radical reordering of the country's society, economy, or agriculture took place. Its agriculture remained diverse and small scale. None of its families, at least not in the territories under Yohannes's direct control, accumulated sufficiently significant wealth to lead to the creation of an economy-based aristocracy. Foreign influence and assistance were discouraged. Surprisingly, despite this economic stagnation, Yohannes's reign was outstanding for a great increase in sociopolitical mobility in Ethiopia, which was the basis of its strength. It provided Ethiopia with the best possible leadership in all ranks and at all levels of society. This situation could not happen in Egypt where the old and newly formed upper classes as well as the large number of foreigners pouring into Egypt monopolized the country's highest social, administrative, and economic positions.

To illustrate this point and to elaborate on its implications, let us return briefly to the battle of Gura, March 1876. Two young men were to emerge from that confrontation as leaders of central importance in their respective societies, the Ethiopian *Ras* Alula and the Egyptian *Amir alai* Ahmad 'Urabi:9 Both Alula and 'Urabi were born into simple peasant families but, by virtue of ambition, talent, and natural leadership qualities, they both emerged as figures of some military standing. However, although the internal mechanism of Ethiopia's sociopolitics allowed for Alula's talents and leadership to be accepted, 'Urabi's abilities to contribute and to lead were stymied. Unable to penetrate Egypt's rigidly delineated upper stratum of society and achieve a position of real leadership, his activities ultimately contributed to Egypt's loss of independence.

Alula, the son of peasants from Tambien, in Tigre, had received a traditional education as an *ashkar*, a trainee rendering services to a great chief, *Ras* Ar'aya Dimsu. He was lucky enough to be transferred to serve in the house of *Dajazmach* Kassa Mircha of Tambien who, in the late 1860s, made his way up the country's flexible sociopolitical ladder to emerge, in 1872, as Emperor Yohannes. Alula, excelling in administration, became the *balamwal*, the royal favorite, of the new emperor. On the eve of the battle of Gura, he was, at the age of twenty-nine, a trusted military counsellor with the rank of *shalaqa*, a commander of a thousand.

Ahmad 'Urabi, only seven years older than Alula and of similar military rank, that of *amir alai* (colonel), was stationed not far from the battlefield of Gura. Born near Zagazig in the Nile delta, 'Urabi's future changed when Sa'id *Pasha*, Isma'il's predecessor, decided to prepare a new cadre of military officers. In order to contain the power of the entrenched Turco-Circassian officers he had inherited from 'Abbas *Pasha*, Sa'id recruited promising young men from among the Egyptian peasantry. In 1862 'Urabi graduated from the military academy, received his commission, and rose quickly through the ranks. In the early 1870s, however, the climate changed again when Isma'il, as he was about to embark on his African venture, and in keeping with his dismissive attitude toward anything authentically Egyptian, lost faith in the officers of local Arab-Egyptian origin. He reinstated the former Turco-Circassian establishment as well as his European and U.S. mercenaries. By the time of Gura many of the Arab-Egyptian officers had left the army and 'Urabi had become an embittered *amir alai*, with no combat units under his command. In fact, throughout 1875-1877, he served as a commissariat officer along the communication lines between Massawa and the hinterland. From this vantage point he could observe the lack of motivation and the endless rivalries and jealousies that characterized the Turco-Circassian officers and the mercenaries and that led to the Egyptian defeat.

Shalaqa Alula won the battle and achieved personal renown at Gura. He initiated the tactical maneuvers that lured the safely entrenched Egyptians out into the open, where the Ethiopians overwhelmed them. After this brilliant victory he was promoted by Yohannes. Much to the anger of Tigre's nobility he was appointed governor of the territories of today's Eritrea and was given the title of *ras*. He was also given the title of *turk basha*, which meant—as we remember from the days of Sertsa Dengel's victory over the Ottomans in Debaroa in 1578—the commander of the elite royal units. From that point on, for the next two decades until the final victory over the Italians at Adwa, in March 1896, *Ras* Alula commanded many Ethiopian forces in successful battles against foreign invaders. He also contributed to the strengthening of Ethiopia's unity, especially in 1894 when he brought about the reconciliation between Shoa and Tigre under the supremacy of Emperor Menelik II.

Alula's career exemplifies Ethiopia's flexible sociopolitics. Throughout its history, and particularly in periods of crisis and trial, a fresh and robust leadership often emerged in that country. Natural leaders among the ever-competing leading families, as well as frequently persons of humble origins such as Alula, could make their way to positions of leadership through merit. Preeminent status was not guaranteed for the less talented sons of leading figures. It was this kind of flexible competition for power, combined with a sociopolitical mobility that gave Ethiopia its greatest strategic asset: a continually self-renewing leadership at all levels of the political and military command structure. This aspect of Ethiopia's political culture, at once competitive and hierarchical, would later be adapted to the changing realities of the twentieth century. Emperor Yohannes, in facing his challenges, promoted and encouraged this dimension of Ethiopia's political culture.

Amir alai Ahmad 'Urabi tasted defeat in Gura but, as noted above, the Ethio-Egyptian conflict was not determined militarily; 'Urabi's true role in Egyptian history was in the political sphere. For 'Urabi the war in Ethiopia exposed all the deficiencies of Isma'il's hasty Westernization. In his memoirs 'Urabi described the story of Isma'il's demise in a chapter entitled "The Abyssinian Campaign."[10] He admired the Ethiopian management of the war and despised the Turco-Circassian commanders of the Egyptian army because of their corruption and lack of motivation. Moreover, he blamed the Western mercenaries (particularly the American William Loring) for betraying the movements of their army to the Ethiopian enemy. He underlined, time and again, the distinction between these foreign, non-Egyptian elements and "the Egyptians," the poor peasant soldiers who died and the poor Egyptians at home who paid for the calamity. The only high-ranking combat officer of Egyptian-Arab origin who participated in the campaign, according to 'Urabi's memoirs, was *Amir alai* Muhammad Jabar. Although he fought bravely and wisely, because of the non-Egyptians no one could save the day.

When 'Urabi returned to Egypt his frustration increased as he witnessed the destruction of the social fabric of his country and the loss of its sovereignty due to economic dependency as well as despoliation by foreign-controlled interests. After Isma'il was deposed by the Great Powers (1879) 'Urabi's frustrations as a disenfranchised Egyptian-born officer, together with the humiliation he felt as an Egyptian patriot, combined to propel him to action. By January 1881 he had organized his fellow officers and became the leader of a protest movement whose slogan was "Egypt for the Egyptians." (He advocated fighting the European presence in the Red Sea.)[11] In 1882 this movement turned into an open revolt against both the local establishment (headed by *Khedive* Tawfiq, Isma'il's son) and foreign involvement in Egyptian affairs. This episode is considered as the first active manifestation of modern Egyptian nationalism. 'Urabi's movement was finally defeated by a British invasion on 13 September 1882. He was exiled by the British, who remained to occupy Egypt for the next seventy-four years.

The British thus ended Isma'il's dream of an African Empire. In facing the *mahdi* revolt in the Sudan and Egyptian eviction from that country, the British made the Egyptians sign the Hewett Treaty with Yohannes (June 1884), by which they evacuated the territories disputed with Ethiopia. In the same year the British forced the Egyptians to withdraw from Harar.

The end of imperial expansion combined with other major changes and heralded a new era for Egypt. As the century drew to a close, the British occupation gave rise to a nascent modern Egyptian nationalist movement. Spearheaded by young intellectuals who sought to introduce new political forms, these nationalists gave new interpretation to the Egyptian identity and to its image of the outside world. For them, and for the next forty years, Egypt included the Sudan, but Ethiopian affairs were left aside.

It may be that this new generation of nationalists in Egypt could not forgive the Ethiopians for the humiliation Egypt had suffered twenty years earlier in Gura. One source of evidence for this view are the military memoires of an Egyptian officer, Muhammad Rif'at, who had been taken prisoner in Gura. The image of the Ethiopians as reflected in his 1896 published book was of merciless, ferocious warriors, hardly a model of a respected civilization.[12]

The Egyptian public under the yoke of the British yearned for sources of political inspiration. In 1905, when the news of Japan's victory over Russia reached Egypt, the Japanese were quickly adopted as representatives of the Orient who had managed to defeat the imperialistic representatives of the West. Mustafa Kamil, a young Egyptian intellectual of that time, wrote a book, *The Rising Sun*, on Japan's victory as a symbol for Oriental nationalism. But Ethiopia, which had itself mounted a stunning victory against Italian imperialism in 1896 and, unlike Egypt, had managed to maintain its independence, was not to play any such role in Egyptian life. In fact, in 1905 a new book on Ethiopia was published in Cairo: Entitled *The Beautiful Pearls in the History of the Ethiopians,*[13] it had little to tell about contemporary affairs. Written by an al-Azhar religious scholar, the book is essentially a compilation of early Islamic sources on the *sahaba-najashi* story. Six al-Azhar scholars contributed introductory remarks, all emphasizing the lack of informative literature in Arabic on Ethiopia; the short chapters on Ethiopia's history and geography, though informative and occasionally useful, carry no message of significance for the modern reader. Ethiopia's struggle with Italian imperialism is discussed, but is limited to a mere mention of Ethiopia's 1896 victory.

Even the admission of Ethiopia to the League of Nations in 1923, the year Egypt was granted a constitution under the British, had little resonance in the land of the Nile. Indeed, throughout the first three decades of the twentieth century, Ethiopia, independent and mysterious, was not on the Egyptian agenda. Immersed in the struggle to fulfill the newly discovered Egyptian identity and facing British occupation, the Egyptians would occasionally host an Ethiopian prince on his way to Europe, but they showed little curiosity. For the Egyptians as well as for the Ethiopians the only significant connection during this period was the Coptic Church.

YOHANNES AND ISLAM

Isma'il attacked Ethiopia for strategic reasons. He used Islam whenever it suited him. In the new Egyptian province of Harar, for example, the Egyptian conquest (1875–1885) spread Islam among the neighboring Oromos and others. The two Egyptian governors in Harar made substantial efforts to increase the spread of Islam in order to tighten their political control. *'Ulama* were brought from al-Azhar and began teaching Arabic—the language of politicization of Islam in the Horn of Africa—among the various local populations, distributing Islamic holy books printed in Cairo. These activities were accompanied by the coerced Islamization of pagans, complete with attempts to force circumcision and the construction of mosques.[14] But this had little to do with Ethiopian-held territories or with Christianity. In Eritrea, where the main confrontation with Yohannes had occurred, such activities were restrained. The Egyptians employed European mercenaries there as well as Christian Ethiopian *shiftas*. Moreover, from 1882–1883 they also faced an increased level of radical Islam from nearby eastern Sudan that aimed at their own destruction. As a result, they cautiously supported Islamic propaganda from Massawa and Kassala. Isma'il's strategic goal was to destroy Yohannes as a champion of a northern-oriented Ethiopia, and he was eager to recognize Menelik of Shoa as emperor.

Yohannes, however, and the clergy around him, clearly identified Isma'il with what Ethiopians conceived as a centuries-old Islamic threat to their very existence. They regarded the Egyptians as "the tribe of the Ismaelites . . . wicked and apostate men."[15] The concept of a renewed *jihad* was part of Yohannes's own religious policy. Yohannes's main effort was a religious reunification of Ethiopia: His policy was marked by a strong anti-Islamic element that had far-reaching implications on Ethiopia's relationship with external Middle Eastern Islam. Yohannes's aim was to convert all the natives of Ethiopia to Christianity. Whether his motivation was religious fanaticism or measured political calculation is debatable.

One contemporary Ethiopian source, not entirely sympathetic to Yohannes, quoted him as saying: "I shall avenge the blood of Ethiopia. Gragn Islamized Ethiopia by force, fire and sword." Yohannes himself, on the other hand, wrote self-righteously to Queen Victoria claiming that the "Muslims . . . begged me saying: We have no book handed down from our forefathers; so baptize us and make us Christians. And I replied: All right, if you like, become Christians. And the Ethiopian Muslims became Christians out of their own volition. There is nothing I have done by fire."[16]

Yohannes's Christianization policy was clearly coercive.[17] It contained harsh measures such as forcing Ethiopian Christian circumcision, and the building of churches. Many of the Jabartis in towns such as Gondar or Aksum were forced to convert; others, by the thousands, fled to nearby Sudanese territory. The more powerful Oromos of Wallo and Yadju presented a major problem. In May and June of 1878, Yohannes convened the prominent figures of Ethiopia in a religious council at Wallo. Two of the major local chiefs of the Oromos were also summoned. According to an Ethiopian chronicler, Yohannes and Menelik told them: "we are your apostles. All this [Wallo and the central highland] used to be Christian land until *Gragn* ruined and misled it. Now let all, whether Muslim or Galla [pagan] believe in the name of Jesus Christ! Be baptized! If you wish to live in peace preserving your belongings, become Christians. . . . Thereby you will govern in this land and inherit in this world the one to come."[18]

One of these two Muslim Oromo chiefs, *Imam Muhammad 'Ali*, is notable in Ethiopian history: Converted by Yohannes, he was granted a title and renamed *Ras Mika'el* and played a central role in future developments.

Yet, in spite of Yohannes's efforts, the majority of the Oromos in highland Ethiopia as well as the Jabartis in the urban centers remained Muslims. According to one source, by 1880 some fifty thousand Jabartis and half a million Oromos had been baptized.[19] But the policy of coerced Christianization was not carried out along Ethiopia's borders. Yohannes's major vassal, Menelik of Shoa, was in the process of expanding his kingdom by annexing vast areas in the south populated by Muslims and pagans. In 1887 his efforts culminated with the conquest of Harar. Yet Menelik, as we shall see, did not carry out in the occupied territories the mass Christianization prescribed by Yohannes.

This disobedience was true, as well, of *Ras Alula in Eritrea*. Alula sought to combine his military position against the Egyptians with the establishment of prosperous commerce between Asmara and the coast. He cultivated good relations with local Muslim traders, convinced Yohannes to exempt his province from his campaign of Christianization, and even had himself photographed dressed as a Muslim.[20] He came to terms with the British, who were now behind the Egyptians, and persuaded Emperor Yohannes to sign the Hewett Treaty in June 1884.

By this treaty, Yohannes and Alula undertook to rescue the Egyptian garrisons besieged by the Mahdiyya in eastern Sudan in return for Egyptian-held portions of Eritrea. This trading of the Egyptian enemy, modern but weak, with the Mahdiyya, radically Islamic and fresh, exposed Yohannes's Ethiopia to the first *jihad* since Ahmad *Gragn*.

6

Yohannes and Menelik:
Between Religious Confrontation
and Diplomatic Dialogue

A series of dramatic events at the end of the nineteenth century in Ethiopia would shape much of its twentieth-century history. First, Ethiopia collided with Western imperialism and emerged victorious. The confrontation with the Italians in Massawa led not only to the loss of Eritrea (established as an Italian colony in January 1890) but also to the military victory in Adwa (March 1896), which stopped the invaders and brought international recognition to Ethiopia. Second, Ethiopia managed to expand in the south, annexing what is today nearly the entire country south of Addis Ababa.

Middle Eastern Islamic involvement in this period took the form of the radicalism of the Mahdiyya, on the one hand, and the all-regional Islamic diplomacy of the Ottoman *Sultan* 'Abd al-Hamid II (1876–1909) on the other. In facing these two challenges Ethiopia's emperors, Yohannes IV and his successor, Menelik II, adopted two different approaches.

YOHANNES AND THE MAHDIYYA:
THE LEGACY OF RADICAL ISLAM

In late 1884 a period of active conflict began between Ethiopia and the newly established entity in the Sudan, the Mahdist state. The Mahdiyya movement represented an explosion of Sudanese local anti-Egyptian rage. It stemmed from a variety of grievances—social, economic, religious—and was led by a *Sufi* leader, Muhammad Ahmad, who claimed to be a *mahdi*, namely, one guided by God. The *mahdi* created the formative chapter in the modern history of the Sudan. His messianic Islam, spearheaded by an anti-Egyptian *jihad*, helped to build a supratribal unity that thrived on military successes in driving the Egyptian Turks from Khartoum (January 1885). The *mahdi* then established an Islamic state modeled on the early seventh-century state of Muhammad in Mecca. When he died the following June, he was replaced by 'Abdallah al-Ta'ishi, who took the title of *khalifa*, or *caliph*. The new Sudanese state was intended to redeem the whole Islamic nation. The *mahdi* and his successor viewed Egypt, and the modernizing Middle East beyond it, as led by Turks—Westernizing infidels. Their prime aim was to launch a *jihad* against these infidels.[1]

The Mahdiyya was not interested in fighting Ethiopia, and, indeed, in the beginning adopted the "leave the Abyssinians alone" approach. Yet, as a movement of radical Islam, it was in a position to reinterpret the Prophet's dictum. When Yohannes provoked the Mahdiyya a new line was adopted in Khartoum; the ensuing conflict lasted until the death of Yohannes by Mahdist bullets in March 1889.

The military history of this conflict has been well recounted elsewhere.[2] In brief, there were two theaters of confrontation. One was in the area and district of the Sudanese town of al-Qallabat (in Arabic) or Metemma (the name given to a nearby border town by the Ethiopians). The other was around the town of Kassala and in western Eritrea.

Hostilities commenced following the signing of the Hewett Treaty when, in late 1884, Ethiopian forces, sometimes in cooperation with Egyptian officers, tried to rescue the besieged Egyptian garrisons in these two towns and two other posts. Most of these operations were successful: Ethiopian forces remained in the area around al-Qallabat, which was a commercial center and the strategic link between mainland Sudan and Ethiopia.

Until 1888 the Ethiopians were usually the victors. The Ethiopian ruler of Gojjam, *Negus* Takla-Haimanot (until his coronation as *negus* in 1882 he was *Ras* Adal, or "*Ras Adar*" in Mahdist literature), a leading contender in Ethiopian political competition, was encouraged by Yohannes to exert pressure on the Mahdists. In January 1887 he scored a major victory over his counterpart, the *Amir* Muhammad Wad Arbab.

In the second Ethiopian-Mahdist front, in western Eritrea, the Ethiopians had scored their main victory in September 1885 when *Ras* Alula crushingly defeated the army of *Amir* 'Uthman Digna in the battle of Kufit, located between Kassala and Keren.[3]

Much of the impetus for the escalation of Ethio-Mahdist hostility can be traced to center-periphery relations and to the personal rivalries and jealousies within both the Mahdiyya and Ethiopia. In addition, there was also the continuing issue of each group harboring the other's rebels. No less important a factor was the involvement and manipulation of the British, the Egyptians, and the newly arrived Italians. They were all interested in fomenting the Ethiopian-Mahdist conflict. Prior to the battle of Kufit, for example, the Egyptians sent the aging 'Uthman al-Mirghani to the Bani 'Amir clans in western Eritrea to organize them in support of Alula's anti-Mahdist campaign. At the same time British agents supplied Alula with arms to tempt him to march on 'Uthman Digna. However, both the Mahdiyya and Ethiopia had higher priorities than fighting each other. The

Mahdists sought the redemption of Islam. They wanted to engage in a *jihad* against Egypt and were thus on a collision course with Great Britain. The Ethiopians soon discovered that the Italians had replaced the Egyptians in coveting the Eritrean highlands and thus threatened Ethiopia's sovereignty. Some time after the *mahdi*'s occupation of Khartoum in January 1885, Yohannes sent him a letter. Its content is lost, but by the *mahdi*'s reply, which survives, it is clear that its message was straightforward and that the Ethiopian wanted to hear firsthand what the Mahdiyya's intentions were. The *mahdi* replied on 16 June 1885, only a few days before his death. He wrote to Yohannes that Islam had replaced all other religions including Christianity; that Islam deteriorated because of the infidel Turks; and that he, the *mahdi*, was sent by God to restore Islam. Then in a conciliatory tone, the *mahdi* praised Yohannes for trying to understand the "truth of the *mahdi*":

Know that we like your being a modest listener, and that I think well of you because you insisted on having a letter from me, so that we can explain to you what we are all about. This is an action of a reasonable and a justice-seeking person. So I write to you this letter as a response to your request and out of pleasure for your gifts, and in wishing you all the best and calling you to become a Muslim, be Muslim. . . .

The Lord gave you the honor to live in the prophetic period of my appearance as a *caliph* of our Prophet Muhammad. So be like your predecessor the *najashi*, God bless him, who, when the Lord gave him the honor to live in the time of our Prophet Muhammad, trusted and befriended him and sent him the *sahaba*. And the king of this world did not prevent him from doing justice, and he was given by the Prophet Muhammad all honor. And when he [the *najashi*], God bless him, died in his land, the Prophet prayed for him in Madina as a show of respect. And there were many *hadith* and wonderful stories on his high place with the Lord, because he followed our Prophet Muhammad and because of his lack of interest in this meaningless worldly kingdom. And I pray to the Lord who made you live in this blessed time that He will make you a successor to your predecessor by following me, and that He will lead you out of the darkness of the infidels to the light of the true belief.

The *mahdi* then ended his letter with a threat (similar to Muhammad's to the *najashi* as quoted by Ibn Kathir):[4] "but if you refuse . . . it will be your fault and the fault of your followers, for it is inevitable that you fall into our hands."[5]

Compared with similar letters of warning (*indharat*) the *mahdi* sent to other rulers, such as that to Tawfiq, Egypt's *khedive*, his letter to Yohannes was not particularly provocative. Ethiopia and the Mahdiyya were already at war initiated by the Ethiopian help to Egypt, a fact the *mahdi* refrained from even mentioning. Indeed, the letter contained both contradictory messages of ancient times. By mentioning the "Islam of the *najashi*" and calling on Yohannes to follow his example (as had been done by the *imam* of

Yemen in his letter to Fasiladas of 1647) or pay for his insubordination, the *mahdi* was expressing the idea that a Christian Ethiopia was illegitimate. However, by mentioning the positive *sahaba* story (which the *imam* had failed to do) the *mahdi* indicated that he was willing to leave Ethiopia alone. His message was far from overtly hostile: He was interested in disengaging from the conflict, not in escalating it. Several weeks later his successor, the *khalifa*, wrote to 'Uthman Diqna, who was contemplating an attack on *Ras* Alula in Eritrea, instructing him to "leave the Abyssinians alone" and return to fight the Egyptians and the British.[6] (The letter came too late, after 'Uthman had been defeated in Kufit.) However in pursuing his policy, Yohannes provoked the Mahdiyya, who, instead of following the *utruku* tradition turned to launch a *jihad* legitimized by Yohannes's refusal to follow the "Islam of the *najashi*."

Three and a half years later, in late December 1888, Yohannes sent to the *khalifa* an appeasing letter. In that letter Yohannes stressed the futility of the conflict between Ethiopia and the Mahdist state, in the face of a common enemy, Western imperialism. Yohannes described his wars with the Egyptian Turks and the threat of the *Ifranj*, the Europeans. "If they destroy Ethiopia," he argued, "they will surely storm the *ansar* [the Mahdists], and if they destroy the *ansar* they will storm Ethiopia." He therefore suggested a unified effort against the Europeans until victory is achieved, and then, in peace, "traders from our country will trade in yours, and your traders will come to Gondar for the welfare and prosperity of our two peoples."[7]

But this message was sent only in late 1888, after both sides had been for more than three years at each other's throat. In mid-1885, Yohannes, after having coerced Ethiopian Christianization of Jabartis and Oromos, was still in a militant, anti-Islamic mood. He despised the *darbush*, the dervishes, as the Mahdists came to be called by the Ethiopians, and his priests referred to them as "unclean pagans . . . [who] spoke great blasphemies against God . . . thought vanity and spoke it; they spoke lawlessness in the highest. They lifted up their mouths to heaven, and their tongues went to and fro on the earth, and their hearts passed the bounds of pride."[8] His written reply to the *mahdi* was handed to *Amir* Wad Arbab in September 1885. Its contents were highly provocative. He mocked the invitation to join Islam and derided as well the personality and pretensions of the *mahdi*. He concluded his letter by calling the *mahdi* (and *Amir* Wad Arbab) to convert to Christianity, the only true religion.[9]

It was at this stage, in late 1885 or in early 1886, that a discussion of Ethiopia took place in the new Mahdist capital of 'Umm Durman. Yohannes's response arrived with the news of Alula's destruction of 'Uthman Diqna in Eritrea, as Ethiopian forces of *Negus* Tekla Haimanot controlled the Muslim-inhabited territory around al-Qallabat. The following passage is from the contemporary Mahdist official chronicler, Isma'il 'Abd al-Qadir al-Kurdufani, whose book *The Embroidery Embellished with the Good News of the Death of Yohannes the King of the Ethiopians*[10] was published three months after the death of Yohannes in the battle of Mettema-Qallabat. This passage is from the first chapter, and details a discussion in the *khalifa*'s headquarters on the two old legacies of the *habasha*—a discussion that ended with a decision to declare *jihad* against Ethiopia:

Know that this nation, I mean the Ethiopian nation, are of the ancient nations, most famous among the kingdoms in bravery, their numbers and strength. And how much bravery [they show] in wars, their men storming like rivers of iron, confronting death as if it would not matter, and listening only to the talk of their swords. . . .

They were reputed for that among the nations for generations until God brought the light of our master [the Prophet] Muhammad bin 'Abdallah. . . . And when God instructed his Prophet about the duty of *jihad*, this was at a time when the infidels were still many even in the Arab Peninsula . . . and the Prophet instructed his nation and showed them what was first and what was most important. Therefore [he told them] to leave the Ethiopians alone and occupy in fighting the others in that time, and he said: "leave the Ethiopians alone as long as they leave you alone." It means that it is permitted to us to leave off fighting the Ethiopians at [a given] time and fight the others. The message of the *hadith* is that it permits us to leave them alone and fight the others. So if leaving them alone is optional, fighting them is optional too. And all this is on condition that they stay in their borders as they were in the early period [of Islam].

Later the kings of our time and especially the kings of the Turks, because of their weak belief . . . and their negligence of Islamic commands, and their abandoning of the *jihad* . . . enabled the infidels [the Ethiopians] to enter in the land of Islam and take control over portions of it, and build churches with bells.[11] And there was no one from the kings of Islam to defend Islam and the Muslims. [The reference is probably to towns in Eritrea like Keren handed over by the Egyptians to Alula.] And for this reason the Ethiopians managed to invade al-Qallabat and other places and they put agents of their king who force the Muslims to pay *jizya* [i.e., personal tax payable by non-Muslims only].

When Yuhanna [Yohannes] established himself on the Ethiopian throne he became arrogant . . . and he invaded Islamic territory and sent his army to capture from the Turks towns in the Red Sea coast [Eritrea] and place over them [men] from among the infamous people of his country, like *Ras* Alula and others. . . . And thus Yuhanna conquered from the land of Islam and he is the most hateful of the Ethiopians towards Islam. Someone who knew him told me that if he saw a Muslim in the morning it would depress him so that he would immediately take the cross which he worships, and put it over his face. . . . And when God sent the *mahdi* . . . he wrote to Yuhanna calling him to join God, but he answered in an ugly way and sent his armies to fight [the Mahdiyya].

And from this it is clear to any one who has the fire of God in him that the fighting of the Ethiopians today is not only a legal option, but a very emphasized duty for the Islamic nation. This is because they went out of their borders and they did not leave the people of Islam alone. So it is permitted for us to fight them in accordance with the saying of the

Prophet "leave the Ethiopians alone as long as they leave you alone." It shows clearly that the meaning of that is to leave them alone as long as they leave you alone, and if they do not, as happened with Yuhanna and his aggression towards the land of Islam, so do not leave them alone, oh you the people of Islam, but fight them. This is what every Muslim should identify with, and God is the guide and on Him only we rely.[12]

January 1887 witnessed the peak of Ethiopian power under Yohannes IV. *Negus* Takla-Haimanot defeated the Mahdists; *Negus* Menelik conquered the town of Harar; and *Ras* Alula ambushed and destroyed an Italian battalion in Dogali, near Massawa. But while the conquest of Harar strengthened Menelik, the victory at Dogali brought down upon Yohannes the wrath of Italy. An Italian army landed in April 1887 in Massawa, aiming to capture the Eritrean highlands and punish Yohannes and Alula. Tekla-Haimanot's (*Ras* Adal) victory over Wad Arbab also inspired the *khalifa* to build up an army for war against Ethiopia. Later, in the same January (1887) the *khalifa* wrote to Yohannes informing him of the new holy war: "We were watching you in accordance with the saying of the Lord of the Apostles, 'Leave the Abyssinians alone, while they leave you alone.' So we did not allow the army of the Muslims to raid your land until from your side serious aggression repeatedly took place against the weak Muslims who are near your country, with slaughter, the taking of captives, plunder and damage, while the apostates from their faith as Muslims take refuge with you."[13]

As the Mahdist buildup against Ethiopia was being overseen throughout 1887 by *Amir* Hamdan Abu 'Anja, the *khalifa* strengthened his resolve to depart from the policy of "leaving the Abyssinians alone." In early January 1888 he published a "prophetic vision" he had in which "the Prophet said to me, 'You are permitted to raid the Abyssinians in their land.' So . . . we commanded Hamdan Abu 'Anja to raid them. . . . He raided them in the midst of their land and was victorious. . . . Then the Prophet gave the battle cry against the Abyssinians repeatedly and we gave the battle cry with him."[14]

Three days after the publication in 'Umm Durman of this "prophetic vision," Abu 'Anja launched a deep penetration raid and captured Gondar. Before retreating, his army massacred those local Christians who were slow to flee and set fire to the churches of the Ethiopian capital (by tradition, forty-four in number). In Yohannes's camp facing the Italians in Eritrea, as reported in later Ethiopian historiography, the fire in Gondar was perceived as if heralding the return of Ahmad *Gragn*. The clergy of Gondar wrote to Yohannes: "O Lord, the pagans have invaded thy preserve, thy sacred shrine they have profaned, Gondar have they laid in ruins."[15]

Thus began a disastrous year for Yohannes. Unable to continue to face the Italians, he now pulled back from Eritrea to deal with the revolting Menelik and Tekla-Haimanot. At the end of the year, under pressure from all quarters, he wrote his conciliatory letter to the *khalifa*, the one of December 1888 mentioned above. It was, of course, too late.[16] Hamdan Abu 'Anja responded in early January 1889 with provocative mockery: "As for your request for peace while you remain infidel . . . it is a sign of your stupidity and ignorance. . . . If you want peace say it from the bottom of your heart that you testify that 'there is no God but Allah and that Muhammad is his Prophet.' For if not, we shall kill you, destroy your homes, and make your children orphans. . . ."[17]

In spite of the rhetoric the Mahdists were in no position to destroy Yohannes. They could at best raid Ethiopia when the imperial army was occupied elsewhere. Their own major effort was concentrated on their Egyptian front, and Hamdan Abu 'Anja himself died of an illness later that month (January 1889). But this religious-cultural conflict was heading toward a disaster. Yohannes, facing two threats, the Italians to the north and Menelik in Shoa, decided to move against the Mahdists (now under *Amir al-Zaki Tamal*). It was a decision (taken against the advice of his generals) that can be explained only in psychological terms and against the background of Yohannes's concept of Islam as the ultimate enemy. He was quoted saying: "Their religion says as follows: say 'No' to God, and 'Yes' to the demon which is Muhammad. . . . The Muslims want to massacre the Christians and burn the churches in Gondar.[18] Many dogs have surrounded me and a gathering of evil people holds me. . . . Here we are ready to fight against these Arabians, the doers of atrocities."[19]

On 9 March 1889, a decisive battle took place in Mettema-Qallabat. The Ethiopian army was winning the day when Yohannes was killed. The Ethiopian forces dispersed as victory turned into defeat. Yohannes's body was captured and his severed head sent to the celebrations in 'Umm Durman.

The strategic implications of the confrontation in Mettema-Qallabat were far reaching. When Yohannes decided to concentrate on fighting the *darbush* he ordered *Ras* Alula from Asmara to join him. It was a decision tantamount to giving up Eritrea,[20] and, indeed, the Italians, the real winners of the Ethio-Mahdist battle, advanced to capture the province without firing a single shot. They established their colony officially on 1 January 1890. Four years later they captured Kassala, thus heralding the end of the Mahdist state. With the fall of Yohannes there fell also Tigre as the political center of Ethiopia. Power shifted to the south where Menelik of Shoa was now in a position to become the next emperor. His policy toward the Mahdiyya was conciliatory, in keeping with his general cultural and political approach and—as we shall see—in accordance with the new strategic circumstances.

In the context of Middle Eastern history the Mahdiyya was one of the movements of Islamic revivalism that appeared at the end of the nineteenth century as a reaction to the Westernization process. One dimension of this revival was led by the Ottoman *Sultan* 'Abd al-Hamid II (1876–1909), whose Ethiopian connection (and his acceptance of Ethiopia's legitimacy) we shall soon discuss. Another dimension was the revival of Islamic values, in a modernized form, among members of the new intelligentsia located mainly in Egypt. The leading figures in the late nineteenth century, notably Jamal al-Din al-Afghani and Muhammad 'Abduh paid little attention to Ethiopia, but their disciples (headed by *Shaikh* Rashid Rida) will be relevant to our concerns. They also accepted Ethiopia's legitimacy, as we shall mention later in discussing the stormy 1930s. A third dimension of Islamic late nineteenth-century revival took the shape of supratribal unity movements in the periphery of the Ottoman world. These movements included the Wahhabiyya of the Saudis in Arabia, the Sanusiyya in Libya, and the Somali "Mad Mawla" movement. Each of these movements, although carrying the fundamental universal message of Islam, compromised at some point with the Western-imported phenomenon of the international boundary. The Mahdiyya, as a state, was either too strong or too short-lived, or both, to make this compromise with recognized boundaries. Throughout its existence it was the most radical anti-Western and politically successful Islamic movement. In its militant fundamentalist raison d'être the Mahdist state experienced little compromise. What little spirit of compromise it had was for Ethiopia. The *mahdi* and his successors, as we saw, wavered between the two basic Islamic approaches, that of *uruku al-habasha*, which accepted Ethiopia, and that of *Islam al-najashi*, which implied its illegitimacy. They decided for the latter and pursued *jihad* because Ethiopia under Yohannes was first provocative and later exposed as weak.

Indeed, the Mahdist *jihad* carried a message for the future: that in discussing the history between Ethiopia and Islam the radical Muslims (as had been done by *Gragn* and the seventeenth-century Zaydi *imam*) should declare Ethiopia illegitimate. It was a message that resurfaced during the Abyssinian Crisis of the 1930s and served other radical visionaries of an all-Middle Eastern cultural and political homogeneity.

MENELIK II AND 'ABD AL-HAMID II

The fall of Yohannes, and with him the short-lived Tigrean hegemony, heralded a change in Ethiopia's relations with the Islamic Middle East. With power shifting to the southern-oriented Shoa, Menelik's Ethiopia compromised with the Italians by acquiescing in the loss of Eritrea. The Italians, the British, and the French took over the defunct empire of Isma'il along the entire African coast of the Red Sea. During the mid-1880s they occupied the Somali and Eritrean coast and their hinterland, thus creating a buffer between Ethiopia and the Middle East.

The British, by occupying Egypt beginning in 1882, neutralized that pivotal Middle Eastern country for the next three generations (until the aftermath of World War II) as an independent factor in a regional strategy. The Mahdist state remained in existence for some time, but its attention was consumed in dealing with Egypt: first, offensively as a prime *jihadi* objective, and then, defensively in an effort to stem the Anglo-Egyptian invasion. Emperor Menelik (1889–1913)[21] did his best to avoid confrontation with the Mahdists. He was not interested in the border disputes of the north nor was he involved in the spirit of the anti-Islamic crusade. Menelik led Ethiopia in a period that saw the political defeat of Muslims in Egypt, Sudan, and Somalia. He himself occupied Harar (1887), the historic and symbolic capital of political Islam in the Horn. His confident policy toward Islam and Muslims was hardly influenced by the "Ahmad *Gragn* trauma."

Menelik was ready from the start to implement the relations Yohannes had offered the *khalifa* too late, in December 1888. Mahdist-Ethiopian relations from 1889 remained good, marked by mutual restraint, sometimes even rising to the level of cooperation. They remained constant until the fall of the Mahdiyya state into British (and Egyptian) hands in 1898.[22]

Menelik's period represented Ethiopia's introduction into the twentieth century. It witnessed two major phenomena, each constituting a watershed in Ethiopian modern history, and both marked by a military victory. The first involved Ethiopia's taking on the challenge of Western imperialism, a successful process that lasted a decade and culminated with the victory in Adwa, in March 1896, over the Italian army. The second phenomenon was the simultaneous Ethiopian occupation of the vast territories in the south, the annexation of which more than doubled Ethiopia's size. Both these demonstrations of Ethiopia's military strength must be seen against the background of the country's process of modernization.

We have mentioned briefly the sociopolitical aspect of the process, emphasizing the flexibility of the country's social mobility. Another important element of Ethiopia's process of modernization was its absorption of modern firearms.

In the pre-modern Islamic Ottoman Middle East warfare was exclusively the preserve of the Turkish-speaking elite. Absorption of firearms in quantities, and the need to build modern armies by resorting to massive mobilization of the peasantry, necessitated revolutionary changes such as those we saw in the case of Muhammad 'Ali (or later with Ahmad 'Urabi). In Ethiopia, the mass mobilization of the peasantry had traditionally been an integral part of the military structure. As long as the arms imported during the second half of the nineteenth century were guns or rifles, Ethiopian society could absorb them in unlimited quantities.

In the second half of the nineteenth century, the period that had begun with Ozdemir *Pasha* of Islam on the coast preventing the importation of firearms came to an end. Firearms began pouring into the country and were no longer a limited matter of small units led by a *turk basha*. Under

Menelik the combination of the traditional military mobilization system (with battle-tested, constantly renewed leadership at all levels), with modern, mainly individual, weaponry, proved enough to defeat Western forces. It also proved enough to resume Ethiopian expansion in the south.

Menelik's conquests in the south returned Ethiopia to areas that had been Ethiopian during the early Solomonic Golden Age and beyond. The occupation was a landmark in the history of local Ethiopian Muslims. But although lasting for two decades, the period went virtually ignored by fellow Middle Eastern Muslims. They were too busy in their own growing struggle with the challenge of the West to take notice. In fact, even the 1887 occupation by Menelik of Harar, the old capital of Islam, the town the Egyptians had renewed as a base for spreading quranic studies only a few years earlier,[23] received barely a headline in the Cairene press.

Even less Middle Eastern attention, if any, was paid to the demise of other Islamic sultanates of the Oromos and the Sidama. Menelik, equipped with unmatched superiority in firepower, accomplished the process in three stages: first, when still a vassal of Yohannes, he captured the country of the Tuluma Oromo, Jimma and Leka in the southwest, and Harar in the east. Second, before the Adwa victory he annexed to Ethiopia the vast territories of the Arusi, Sidama, and Bale. And third, after Adwa, more powerful than ever, Menelik expanded the empire to Ethiopia's current borders, destroying the kingdoms of Kaffa, Gimira, and Boran; annexing the Ogaden; and capturing Awsa of the Afars, which had been the last refuge (until the late seventeenth century) of *Gragn*'s successors.[24]

With the exception of Jimma, these southern entities were all officially abolished, their territories absorbed into Ethiopia's new provincial system. Christianity began to spread as the Ethiopian state religion, and churches were built for the colonizing newcomers as well as for members of the local elite, who opted for political cooperation and cultural integration.

Practitioners of Islam were not persecuted or oppressed. Islam was given cultural autonomy and the religion was permitted to be exercised, as both a judicial system and a social identity.[25] Under Menelik's confident flexibility, Ethiopia, no longer in conflict with external Islamic Sudan or Egypt,[26] returned to the religious tolerance of the pre-Yohannes and pre-Tewodros era. But Islam in the newly occupied territories lost its political message, whatever remained of it from the heyday of *Gragn*. Of all the sultanates only Jimma remained in existence because of Abba Jifar's surrender in 1883 without a fight. In return for his submission Abba Jifar was granted autonomy for Jimma, a promise that was kept until the eve of Mussolini's invasion in 1935.

As we shall see, the fact that the "Abyssinians" under Menelik did "take an offensive" against Islam would ultimately be put on the Middle Eastern agenda only during the Fascists' 1935 aggression. But at that time, no such hostility existed. To the contrary, the Ottoman *Sultan* 'Abd al-

Hamid II (1876–1909) was eager for a diplomatic channel to and a friendly dialogue with Menelik.

'Abd al-Hamid II, to be sure, was a restorer of political Islam in the Ottoman Empire. A short time after his accession to the sultanate, he abolished the 1876 constitution that was intended to integrate Ottoman politics around Western pluralism (including political equality for Christians). Instead, he revived the daily usage of his own title as "the *Caliph* of the Believers." Islamic ways were implemented in all parts of Ottoman life to the extent that contemporary Europeans and Ottoman nationalists depicted 'Abd al-Hamid as a theocratic reactionary. His renewed emphasis on the caliphate was also aimed at preserving Ottoman influence on Muslims in territories that had been lost to Russia in recent decades. But he cared very little about Islamic territories lost to Menelik's Ethiopia. The new Ethiopian-Ottoman dialogue revolved rather around the Ethiopian community in Jerusalem. We have already noted that a community of Ethiopian monks lived in Jerusalem from the earliest years of Ethiopian Christianity.[27] Their existence, combined with Ethiopian pilgrimages to Jerusalem, constituted a modest but a steady bridge into the cultural sphere of Oriental Christianity.

We have only sketchy references to the whereabouts of the Ethiopians in Jerusalem during the period before the thirteenth century (we have already mentioned their restoration by Salah al-Din al-Ayyubi), but there is no doubt that they coexisted and shared property with the other Monophysite local communities, the Syrians, the Armenians, and the Egyptian Copts.

The Ethiopian community in Jerusalem, and continuing pilgrimages from Ethiopia to the Holy Places, flourished during the period of the early Solomonic Golden Age. At that time Ethiopian emperors felt confident enough to look after Christianity in Jerusalem. When the Mamluk *sultan* Barsbay ended the Church of the Holy Sepulchre in 1422, Emperor Yishaq (1414–1429) retaliated by persecuting Ethiopian Muslims. But after the destruction of Ethiopia by Ahmad *Gragn* and the simultaneous Ottoman conquest of Jerusalem, the Ethiopian local community in Jerusalem declined. Although the Ethiopians themselves were deprived of a niche in Jerusalem's Church of Holy Sepulchre, at least as early as 1530, Ethiopian monks inhabited the roof of the St. Helena Chapel, which is a part of the church complex. They called it Dabra Sultan, better known by its Arabic name, Dayr al-Sultan (henceforward Deir al-Sultan), the monastery of the ruler. They believed it to have originally been Ethiopian property from the days it was given by King Solomon to the Queen of Sheba. From the sixteenth to the nineteenth century it remained the only site left to symbolize Ethiopia's Christian, biblical, and national link to Zion.

The place, small and shabby, gave shelter to the few monks who chose to remain in Jerusalem. During the Era of the Princes no aid was received from the motherland, and the Ethiopians lived on the charity of fellow Monophysite Armenians. They also coexisted with their fellow Egyptian Copts. The roof of the St. Helena Chapel forms a courtyard shared by the latter's Monastery of St. Antony, and next to it is a small edifice with an opening from which a passageway runs past the Chapel of the Four Martyrs and the Chapel of St. Michael. Control of the passageway, and thus of the two chapels, depends on who holds the keys to the padlocks of the gates at either end of it. For many generations possession of the keys alternated between the Copts and their fellow Monophysites, the Ethiopians, symbolizing the ownership of the two chapels and the passageway. In the middle of the nineteenth century this partnership soured into a dispute.

In 1838, when Jerusalem was under the government of Muhammad 'Ali's son Ibrahim, nearly the entire Ethiopian community perished in a plague.[28] The Armenians and the Copts obtained the governor's permission to burn the Ethiopians' belongings, which they hastened to do. The belongings included their library and its documents. When the Ethiopians returned several years later the Copts were ready to accept them as their guests, although not their partners. A complicated negotiation ensued, with British and Russian missionaries and lawyers pleading unsuccessfully with the restored Ottoman government on behalf of the Ethiopians.

Emperor Tewodros II had conceived of the redemption of Jerusalem as a symbolic Ethiopian nationalist goal. But his relations with Islam and with the British neutralized his ability to pursue this goal. Yohannes IV was more practical.[29] He sent money for the purchase of a plot of land outside the Old City in West Jerusalem for the purpose of building a new Ethiopian church. In 1884 he also sent an energetic priest, *Mamher* Walda-Sama'at Walda-Yohannes, to organize and lead the community and to oversee the construction that began the same year. The work was completed in 1893, and the Ethiopian church of Kidana Mihrat and the monastery of Dabra Gannat were inaugurated four years after the accession of Menelik II.

Menelik, unlike his predecessors, was in a position to build a constructive dialogue with an Islamic ruler. He reached out to 'Abd al-Hamid II, seeking mainly to solidify the Ethiopian position in Jerusalem.

As early as 1889, after the death of Yohannes but prior to his own coronation, Menelik sent emissaries to Istanbul. They carried a letter to the Ottoman *sultan-caliph* in which Menelik described the religious freedom he granted to the Muslims in his country. In return he asked for justice for the Ethiopians in Deir al-Sultan.[30] 'Abd al-Hamid was reluctant to intervene in the delicate legal case of Deir al-Sultan but the Ethiopians were given permission to purchase land and build elsewhere in Jerusalem.

The following year, *Ras* Makonnen, the conqueror and governor of Harar, passed through Istanbul with presents from Menelik and a renewed request to build in Jerusalem. Makonnen became a guiding spirit in what turned into a full-scale Ethiopian endeavor. He was overshadowed, however, by the energy of Menelik's wife, Empress Taitu.[31] In the next two decades more than a dozen buildings were built or purchased with Ottoman permission in West Jerusalem. Many were located near the new church in what came to be known as Ethiopia Street.

Menelik, nevertheless, did not give up his hope of restoring the heart of the Ethiopian presence in Jerusalem, the ownership of Deir al-Sultan. In 1902 he intensified his personal control over the community by organizing a conference there of Ethiopian clergymen, and by the appointment of his devotee *Mamher* Faqade, as a replacement for Walda-Sama'at. In June 1904 Menelik promised an envoy of 'Abd al-Hamid that he would permit the Muslim community of Addis Ababa to build a major mosque in that town, to be named after the *sultan*, al-Hamidiyya.

Following the visit of this Ottoman envoy, Menelik canceled the arrangement by which the Italian consul in Jerusalem had overseen local Ethiopian legal affairs and decided instead to deal directly with 'Abd al-Hamid. In May 1905 he sent a mission to 'Abd al-Hamid headed by *Dajazmach* Mashasha-Warq and *Ato* Hailu Mariam. In Istanbul they hired a Russian lawyer who looked into the Ottoman archives, as they collected more evidence in Jerusalem. On the basis of their findings an Ottoman court decided that one of the keys to the gates of Deir al-Sultan should be turned over to the Ethiopians, but because of a legal maneuver, this was not done. (Menelik, for his part, shelved his promise concerning the grand mosque in Addis Ababa, a fact that will become an issue much later in our account.)

In 1907, a ten-man Ethiopian delegation headed by *Dajazmach* Mashasha-Warq arrived in Istanbul. They obtained a court decree that an investigation be carried out in Jerusalem, but in March 1908 the governor of Jerusalem ruled against the Ethiopians. By that time Menelik had already been paralyzed by his illness and 'Abd al-Hamid was about to be deposed by a group of army officers, known as "Young Turks."

'Abd al-Hamid was the last Islamic Ottoman ruler of the Middle East. He was not, however, the fanatic religious reactionary often depicted by contemporary Westerners and local young nationalists. What concerns us is his attitude toward Ethiopia, which was both pragmatic and constructive. Ethiopia was not on his crowded agenda but, clearly, it was not totally ignored. Moreover, the Christian country was accepted by 'Abd al-Hamid as a legitimate neighbor, particularly after it proved a strong state in the aftermath of Adwa.

This attitude was apparent in 'Abd al-Hamid's authorization of the Ethiopian settling in Jerusalem. We also have implicit evidence in the form of an account produced by the envoy, Sadiq al-Mu'ayyad al-'Azm, that 'Abd al-Hamid had sent in 1904 to Menelik. The account was published in that year as a book in Turkish (under the title of *Habesh Siyahetnamehsi*) and translated into Arabic four years later. Entitled *Rihlat al-habasha* (*The

Ethiopian voyage), al-'Azm's written account became the most oft-cited standard work, a near classic on Ethiopia, in the twentieth-century Arab-Islamic Middle East.[32]

The author, a lieutenant general in the Ottoman army, gained diplomatic experience as an Ottoman representative in Bulgaria. In the 312 pages of his book the exact objective of the mission assigned to him by the *sultan* is not discussed. It appears that 'Abd al-Hamid's suspicion of Italian encroachment in Tripolitania drove him to explore the possibility of some anti-Italian cooperation with Menelik. (Sadiq al-'Azm was sent later by 'Abd al-Hamid to the Sanussis in Tripolitania.)[33] Moreover, as the Hijazi Railway was being constructed, Istanbul grew increasingly interested in Red Sea affairs. Sadiq al-'Azm carried a letter from 'Abd al-Hamid to Menelik which, we may infer from the narrative, mentioned also the issue of the Deir al-Sultan. Altogether, the general nature of the mission was to renew Ottoman intelligence of Ethiopia and pave the way for some eventual strategic cooperation. The sharp-eyed al-'Azm, traveling in Ethiopia between 11 March and 15 June 1904 (accompanied by two aides), provided a richly, multifaceted account.

Al-'Azm's descriptions of Islam in Menelik's Ethiopia show that his basic impression was one of an honorable existence under a benevolent Christian elite. The author entered Ethiopia by way of Djibouti and reached Harar on 11 March. His description of his meeting with the Islamic town (pp. 59–60) is enthusiastic. Nearly all of the thirty-five thousand Muslims (of forty thousand inhabitants) marched from the town to receive him as the *sultan*'s personal envoy. Headed by their *muftis*, *qadis*, and the *imams* of the numerous mosques they represented a flourishing town that thrived on both commerce and learning. In addition, some Ethiopian soldiers came to salute him. The only person who did not appear was *Amir* 'Abdallah, the last Islamic ruler (1884–1887). According to al-'Azm, Menelik had occupied Harar because of the arrogance of the *amir*. After the Egyptian evacuation of 1884, 'Abdallah had replaced the Ottoman-Egyptian flag with his own, and pretentiously proclaimed himself *Amir* of the Believers. He then challenged Menelik by inviting him to adopt Islam. Menelik, according to al-'Azm, tried to appease 'Abdallah and, failing that, he took the town. 'Abdallah confined himself to his residence out of shame, and the Ottoman envoy met only with his brother. Apart from a few hints elsewhere in the text this is the only mention of Menelik's recent occupation of vast Muslim-populated areas. There is no indication whatsoever of the various sultanates or other entities that, until their recent annexation to Ethiopia, had exercised political sovereignty under Islamic flags. In a later passage (p. 161) is a detailed description of his meeting with part of the ruling family of Jimma, the only kingdom surviving as an autonomous Islamic entity. Suliman, the brother of Muhammad bin Dawud Abba Jifar, came to see him in the outskirts of Addis Ababa. With his two sons, all speaking good

Arabic and dressed as distinguished Muslims, they asked him about Istanbul, Damascus, and Mecca and expressed the hope of making a pilgrimage to the holy city. They were overwhelmed with joy to see the emblem of the *sultan* (*tughra*) carved on al-'Azm's watch, and he promised to send them Islamic printed materials and a *fez* (headgear).

Wherever 'Abd al-Hamid's envoy went, Muslims were free to pray for the Ottoman *sultan*. Al-'Azm was especially moved when he attended a Friday prayer in Harar's main mosque with some two thousand local Muslims, who expressed great excitement when the *imam* mentioned the Ottoman *caliph* in his sermon. In Addis Ababa, however, there was neither a mosque nor an Islamic cemetery. As we have already seen, al-'Azm managed to obtain Menelik's promise to authorize the building of a major mosque to be named after 'Abd al-Hamid. The promise to build the mosque in Addis Ababa was made through al-'Azm to the local Muslim leadership, headed by 'Abdallah al-Sadiq (pp. 138–143, 201, 204). The latter was a prominent figure from Harar, where he had served under *Ras* Makonnen as *Ra'is al-Muslimin*, the chief of the Muslims, serving Menelik in important diplomatic missions to which we shall return later.

The picture given in *Rihlat al-habasha* of Christian Muslim relations is not a happy one. Al-'Azm discerned a cultural barrier between Muslims and Christians. A Christian would not touch the skin of an animal slaughtered by Muslims (pp. 160–161, 209). Neither Muslims nor Christians would eat from the same table. The Christians, he wrote, even their nobles, do not wash. One can easily "feel the difference" because the Muslims are required ritually to wash several times a day. The Christians "are too free in mixing with women," and as a result they suffer from diseases that Muslims have very rarely (p. 182).

Turning his analysis to the political dimension, al-'Azm's overwhelming impression was of the Ethiopian state's benevolent protection of Muslims and of Islam. He described how the Muslims of Gondar asked *Ras* Gugsa to act against one of them, a man named Zakarya, who became a false prophet (*zindiq*), whom they feared would turn into a new *mahdi* (pp. 167, 193). *Ras* Makonnen (a main figure in al-'Azm's book, a man who was just and noble) allowed the Muslims of Harar to celebrate in public, when news reached them of an Ottoman military success against the Greeks. He did so in spite of the local Harari Greeks' argument that it was an Islamic victory over Christians (p. 234). Another Christian community, the Armenians of Addis Ababa, had settled there after fleeing Istanbul following the 1894–1896 Ottoman anti-Armenian atrocities. According to al-'Azm, once in Addis Ababa they wanted to initiate anti-Ottoman propaganda activities, but Menelik prevented this by threatening them with expulsion (p. 168).

In addition to this portrait of Menelik's Ethiopia are the passages in *Rihlat al-habasha* concerning the history of Islamic-Ethiopian relations. It is apparent that al-'Azm made an effort not to emphasize conflicts or to blame them on Ethiopia. There is very little in the book about Ahmad *Gragn* apart from a brief mention (p. 186) and Tewodros II is mentioned (p. 151) without discussing his relations with Islam.

Two historical chapters of great relevance are presented, however. The first concerns Yohannes IV and Islam: In one passage referring to the conflict with Egypt, the author blames the war on Isma'il, and then proceeds to blame the British for diverting Yohannes to fight the Mahdiyya. Later, a full chapter is devoted to a discussion of Yohannes and the Mahdiyya (pp. 175–181). In al-'Azm's version the Mahdists are clearly the aggressors. He mentions how 'Uthman Diqna provoked Ras Alula (prior to Kufit), and how Abu 'Anja (in January 1888) massacred the priests of Gondar and committed atrocities there. What al-'Azm wrote was accurate, but only a partial view of history. Indeed, the Ottoman observer had nothing but harsh criticism of the Mahdiyya, and by comparison Yohannes fared much better in his analysis.

Al-'Azm went so far as to ignore basic facts and dates when he presented a kindly view of Yohannes's oppression of Islam in Ethiopia. According to al-'Azm's account Yohannes began his anti-Muslim campaign only after an Ethiopian Muslim named Muhammad Jibril went to serve the *mahdi*. Muhammad Jibril was returned to Ethiopia by the *mahdi* to convert the Christians to Islam: "When the *najashi* Yuhannis heard about it he became madly angry, and from that time he started oppressing the Muslims contrary to the policy of his predecessors, and maltreated them contrary to the spirit of religious freedom prevailing in his country. This spirit had been to the extent that even his own sister followed Islam with no restrictions and married one of the Muslim princes . . ." (pp. 176–177).

Al-'Azm writes that he saw people mutilated by Yohannes for clinging to Islam, and that many fled to the Sudan. But he then blames some of the refugees themselves for instigating many of the border problems that aggravated the conflict. Yohannes's generals and nobles, concluded al-'Azm, particularly Menelik, were against his anti-Islamic policy.

The second historical chapter in *Rihlat al-habasha* that is of significance to us is entitled, "The cordial relations between the Ethiopians and the Muslims in the early days of Islam" (pp. 193–197). It contains a detailed description of the Muhammad-*najashi* story, compiled from various sources, and clearly emphasizes the role of Aksumite Ethiopia in saving the Prophet's followers. It is obvious that al-'Azm made an intensive study of early Ethio-Islamic relations prior to undertaking his mission. His attitude to Ethiopia was clearly influenced by his knowledge of Muhammad's saying to the *sahaba*: "If you go to Abyssinia you will find a king under whom none are persecuted. It is a land of righteousness."

At the end of the book (pp. 315–323) al-'Azm annexed a long list under the rubric, "The famous Ethiopians," containing brief sketches and an extensive listing of Ethiopians who followed the Prophet in his early days, such as Bilal, "the first *mu'adhdhin*," Baraka 'Umm Ayman, and many of those we have already noted in discussing that first formative chapter of Aksum history. The climax of the mission was al-'Azm's meeting with Menelik himself, on 13 June 1904. He reveals little about the talks themselves, but perhaps the most illuminating point in the entire book is al-'Azm's telling Menelik in detail the story of Muhammad and the *najashi*:

He [Menelik] then asked me about the historical relations between Ethiopia and the Muslim world, and I started telling His Highness in general and in detail on the connection and the exchanging of presents between the Prophet and *Najashi* Ashama, and how the refugees found the best of shelters in Ethiopia, and how many of the followers of our master Muhammad were Ethiopians, the same as today there are Ethiopians in high position with our sultan ['Abd al-Hamid], and they are called *musahibun*. It all made the emperor very happy and he said he wanted the good relations to continue for ever, and that he loved his fellow Muslim Ethiopians like he loved the Amhara without distinction. (p. 230)

The book is filled with praise of Menelik as an enlightened king, a just ruler for Muslims and for Islam, and as a man who seeks knowledge and progress (p. 223).

Substantial parts of the book are devoted to the description of Ethiopia's military might. The Ethiopians' courage, tactical mobility, and resourcefulness impressed the Ottoman observer, and he described them, in combination with the Ethiopians' ability to mobilize hundreds of thousands of warriors in time of war (pp. 210–215).

This description provides the introduction to a detailed chapter (pp. 277–313) that concludes the book. In it, he describes Ethiopia's victory at Adwa. The chapter is clearly derived from Western sources and contains no new information on the diplomatic and military dimensions of the Ethio-Italian conflict. It is, however, of great value because it conveyed to generations of Arabic readers in the Middle East the notion that the Ethiopians, although in some respects a strange people "who do not wash," were not only legitimate neighbors but were also strong enough to succeed in what the Middle Easterners themselves were now failing: in maintaining independence.

Rihlat al-habasha became the standard work on Ethiopia for at least the period until the Abyssinian Crisis of 1935. Published in Cairo in 1908 it became the best source on Ethiopia for a new generation in Egypt and the Fertile Crescent. This was a generation that would experience the revival of Islam as well as the beginnings of modern nationalism, both Egyptian and Arab. The book was translated by two cousins of the author, Haqqi al-'Azm and his brother Rafiq. Both were pioneers of modern Arabism in its first form, namely, an emerging Arab identity and ideology compatible with the main messages of traditional (not radical) Islam. For when the Young

Turks toppled 'Abd al-Hamid in the name of Turkish identity, educated Arabic-speakers in the Middle East started discovering their own modern Arab identity. In 1913, Rafiq al-'Azm became the cofounder of the main prewar political party in Cairo advocating this line of Arabism and Islam. (Haqqi joined somewhat later.) It was called the Ottoman Party for Decentralization, and the other cofounder was one of the main advocates of Islamic spiritual (nonmilitant) revival in the Middle East between the world wars, *Shaikh* Rashid Rida. As we shall see, many members of this first generation of Islamic-Arab nationalists absorbed al-'Azm's image of Ethiopia.

7

IYASU, THE SOMALI *MAWLA*, AND
THE DEMISE OF THE OTTOMAN EMPIRE

The next chapter in the history of Ethiopian–Middle Eastern relations
was the Ottoman Turkish one. Under 'Abd al-Hamid the Ottoman
dialogue with Menelik did not turn into formal diplomatic relations.
Ottoman agents were sent to Ethiopia but a consulate was opened only in
April 1912, three years after the deposition of 'Abd al-Hamid by the Young
Turks.

From this movement of the Young Turks there would emerge in the
1920s the radically secular-nationalist leadership of Mustafa Kemal
Ataturk. But in the years leading up to World War I and the period of the
war itself, the movement was still a diverse one: a mixture of the Ottoman-
Islamic with the emerging new Turkish identity. Diverse too was the foreign policy of Istanbul. In Ethiopia the new Turkish leaders went on to
invest in local Islam. Their information on Ethiopia, as well as their image
of the country, stemmed clearly from al-'Azm's *The Ethiopian Voyage*,
which, as mentioned, was first published in Turkish in 1904.[1] The Ottoman
consulate was opened not in Addis Ababa but in Harar. The consul (from
March 1913), Mazhar Bey, had clearly adopted al-'Azm's concepts about
Ethiopia's close affiliation to the Oriental Middle East and about the poten-
tiality of Christian-Islamic alliance in Ethiopia in the service of Ottoman
strategy. Mazhar began his tenure by registering Ottoman subjects residing
in Ethiopia, and, even more important, began cultivating relations with the
local Islamic community.[2] Prominent among his local new associates in
Harar was Menelik's *Ra'is al-Muslimin* (chief of the Muslims) 'Abdallah
al-Sadiq (who, after meeting with Sadiq al-'Azm in 1904, had become a
member of Menelik's mission to Istanbul headed by *Dajazmach* Mashasha-
Warq). Harar was also an ideal location to establish contacts with the
Sayyid Muhammad bin 'Abdallah Hasan (the so-called "Mad *Mullah*" or
"the *mawla*") who, since 1899, had been leading an Islamic *jihad* against
the British in nearby Somaliland. Although modest in scope, this Ottoman
diplomatic overture to Ethiopia was soon to become part of a global storm.
For when World War I began, Istanbul, although under young nationalists,

reverted to Islam in its war effort against the British, French, and Russians.

By World War I, particularly after mid-1914, the internal situation in Ethiopia was ready for a new wave of influence. Menelik died in December 1913; he had been very ill and out of power beginning as early as 1907–1908. However, the political establishment he built was strong, and, unlike earlier cases in modern Ethiopian history, his power was not challenged by a new group of warlords headed by a chief of another region. Shoa and Addis Ababa remained the center of events, but the Shoan nobility was not homogenous. It was rather the product of Menelik's policy of integration. Composed mainly of Amhara elite, it also included many of Oromo origin and of others as well. When the struggle for power within this establishment began, some of Menelik's achievements at integration proved fleeting.

Ethiopian domestic events of this period have been presented and analyzed in detail by Harold Marcus, among others.[3] After the power of Empress Taitu was curtailed, *Lij* Iyasu, Menelik's grandson and only male descendant, was accepted by the Shoan nobility as the legitimate heir to the throne. However, he was not satisfied with being a mere figurehead for such a powerful group; his authority over its members was far from absolute. With Menelik still alive, Iyasu left Addis Ababa and traveled the country as a kind of roving emperor-to-be. He went about acquiring a network of loyalties throughout the provinces, especially in the newly annexed territories.

In so doing, the young Iyasu was laying the groundwork for the beginnings of a fundamental change in the country's political culture. Menelik had built his system on a Christian or newly Christianized center-oriented elite and tolerated Islam only as a cultural aspect of Ethiopian provincial life. Iyasu, in defying the Shoan elite, sought the repoliticization of Islam. It was not the only element of his strategy, but it was a main pillar of it. Iyasu was the son of *Ras* Mika'el, a prominent member of Menelik's establishment who had been the former *Imam* Muhammad 'Ali of Wallo, and who was converted to Christianity in 1878 by Yohannes and Menelik. By the time Menelik died, Iyasu had already cemented his new loyalties in the periphery by marrying, according to Islamic tradition, the daughters of various chiefs.

In early 1914, Iyasu did not insist on a coronation ceremony in Addis Ababa, a highly religious Christian event, but he made his father *negus* of Wallo and Tigre. *Negus* Mika'el, second to none of the Shoan warlords, went on to behave like a Christian, but the inscription on his new seal was more revealing. It was in both Ge'ez and Arabic. The Ge'ez words were the insignificant biblical quotation "The government shall be upon his shoulders" but the Arabic read: "Mika'el, the king of Wallo and Tigre, the son of

Imam 'Ali, the king of Wallo."[4] It is possible that he entertained the idea of reviving Islam politically, and through his son making it dominant in Ethiopia.

The story of Iyasu turned into one of the most controversial affairs in all Ethiopian history.[5] With the outbreak of the World War I, it acquired an international dimension. In the first week of November 1914 the Ottomans joined the German and Austrian side, and on 7 November 1914 the Ottoman Empire's chief *mufti,* the *Shaikh* al-Islam, issued a *fatwa* (an Islamic legal proclamation) declaring *jihad* on Britain, France, Russia, and on whoever sided with them.

The Ottomans' idea was to encourage Muslims under these empires to revolt: The main strategic object was India. In some cases the response was significant. The Sanussis of Libya invaded Egypt; the Zaydi *Imam* Yahia of Yemen did the same in threatening Aden; and *Sultan* 'Ali Dinar revolted in Dar Fur in western Sudan. More important were other consequences. In India the British were now ready to negotiate with modern Indian nationalists, and in the Middle East they encouraged the *amir* of Mecca, the *Sharif* Husayn bin 'Ali, to start the anti-Ottoman Arab revolt (to which we shall soon return).

However, beyond the *jihad* policy there lay an Ottoman-German grand scheme to reconstruct, after achieving victory, the whole Oriental East. German and Ottoman agents worked toward this goal in Iran, Afghanistan, the Caucasus, and elsewhere. During 1915 and the first half of 1916 the victory of the Ottoman side in the Oriental arena seemed likely. The Ottomans defeated the British at Gallipoli (in January 1916) and in Iraq (where some three British divisions surrendered in April 1916 in Kut-al-Amara). The Ottomans failed twice (January 1915 and April 1916) in their attempt to storm the Suez Canal from their staging area in Palestine. But their daring campaigns in Sinai were impressive, and their agents were in a position to promise that victory was near.

Ethiopia and the Horn of Africa were marginal to this Ottoman effort. The fact that a Somali *jihadi* movement (the Mad Mawla) was already in action[6] and that Ethiopia's emperor was potentially leaning toward Islam, was hardly important to Istanbul. The British, the French, and the Italians had long created a territorial buffer between the Ottomans and Ethiopia, and even in the heyday of Habesh *Eyaleti* it would have been too much to imagine a *najashi* of Ethiopia joining in an Islamic *jihad.* Yet the idea that Ethiopia might side with the Ottomans arose because of the activities of Mazhar Bey, the consul general in Harar, and because of his observations and dialogue with Iyasu.

Isolated as he was in Ethiopia, Mazhar was able to correspond with Istanbul only rarely through couriers infiltrating from Yemen. We are fortunate in having his correspondence with the Ottoman Foreign Ministry, and it is worth following some of it, as it recounts Iyasu's story.[7] It begins with Mazhar's report of 19 December 1914:

> The Ethiopian policy has not yet been established. It is possible to get the Ethiopians on our side if we manage some compromise with them. By using this situation we can have the profit in the Sudan and in Somalia. I sent the messengers to Somalia and the Sudan with the declarations [of *jihad* by the *Shaikh* al-Islam]. I even published the *fatwas*. . . . The *mawla* in Somalia has rebelled. I am trying to involve the other tribes. With all Muslims we are praying for the *sultan*.[8]

Mazhar's idea was that pushing Ethiopia with its known military ability into the war on the side of the Ottomans would prove fruitful. "We must follow the Ethiopian affairs closely," he wrote on 17 March 1915, "the importance of this is very obvious. There are so many important moments according to the phases of war, one should not lose the chance to sign an agreement."[9] In a previous letter of 13 February 1915 he mentioned the price:

> The Ethiopians want to have a harbor. If the British are thrown out of Ottoman Somalia, it might work to give Ethiopia part of the coast between Zeila and Bulkar and the territory between the coast and the eastern border of Harar. If an agreement is reached with the Ethiopians, this need can be covered from this place. The *mawla* is ready to conquer whatever the Sublime Port [The Ottoman government] orders, and his power is enough. He only applied for our help in ammunition for next year.[10]

To enhance his scheme and to be in closer contact with the German embassy, Mazhar moved to Addis Ababa in March 1915. He was now in constant touch with *Lij* Iyasu and helped to intensify the already existing connection between him and the *mawla*.

The idea of Ethiopian-Somali anti-British cooperation was not unthinkable. (Indeed, in the 1905–1908 period, the *mawla* and Menelik corresponded, and the *mawla* seemed ready to accept Somali autonomy—Jimma style—in the Ethiopian Ogaden in return for Menelik's help against the British.)[11] Istanbul was now in favor of such cooperation, although it never approved Somali autonomy under Ethiopia. In Istanbul, it was contemplated that after the war the *mawla* would have autonomy under the Ottomans. He was promised the title of *Shaikh al-mashayikh* and the military rank of *mushir* (field marshal) as well as power over all the territories he would liberate.[12]

Mazhar convinced Istanbul to recognize Ethiopia's future status as an independent state and did his best to convince *Lij* Iyasu that an Ottoman victory was forthcoming. His strategy was to lure Iyasu into the war by leading him to believe that upon victory he would have the Somalis under his sovereignty.

For his part, Iyasu reciprocated by showing the Ottoman his Islamic leanings. A letter Iyasu had sent to the *mawla* in May 1915 through Mazhar (accompanying some token military aid) opened with the Islamic *shahada* (the testimony that Muhammad was the Messenger of God). "*Lij* Iyasu is in favor of us with all his heart," wrote Mazhar on 3 June 1915. "He will give the imperial order [to enter the war] soon."

But Iyasu was in no position to declare war on Britain, France, and Italy. In any event the members of the Shoan establishment would not follow such a militarily suicidal and a pro-Islamic action. Iyasu's policy was to bide his time. It is apparent from Mazhar's reports that Iyasu was waiting for the Ottomans to invade Egypt and defeat the British. Meanwhile, he reassured Mazhar he would bring Ethiopia into the war. "The prince is firmly in favor of us," Mazhar reported to Istanbul on 23 June 1915, suggesting that two airplanes should be sent through Yemen as a present to Iyasu.

But the Ottoman government could hardly send written messages. As much as three months or more would pass before a response would arrive from Istanbul. In October 1915 Iyasu and *Negus* Mika'el told Mazhar they had made a decision to enter the war, and they gave him a medal of honor. A few days later Mazhar was told that "the *malik* [king in Arabic] Mika'el" was ill, and then he was even told the rumor that Mikael had died. "I am praying for the prince [Iyasu]," he concluded his dispatch, "who is entirely pro-Ottoman and pro-Islam."

Iyasu (and his father) were waiting not only for the Ottomans to win in Egypt but also for the *mawla* to beat the British in Somaliland and conquer the coast that Mazhar led them to believe would be theirs. If either of these was to materialize, they would be in a position to drag the country onto the Ottoman side, and, in what would be their greatest prize of the war, to eventually do away with the Shoan establishment.

But the war in the Middle East came to a deadlock and the *mawla*, without massive Ethiopian aid, was little more than a nuisance for the British. Mazhar's correspondence with the Ottoman Foreign Ministry was hopelessly delayed. His message of November 1915 was replied to by Istanbul only on 22 May 1916, six months later. It contained the decision of Enver *Pasha*, Istanbul's strong man:

> We are following with interest your relations with the *mawla* of Somalia. It is understood that he is ready for every action under Ottoman supremacy. A guarantee can be given that in case he conquers any place from the Italians or the British, that place will be given to him. The Ottomans and their allies are defeating their enemies and shall win. The enemy has been defeated in the Dardanelles, . . . in Iraq, . . . in the Caucasus, . . . the Sanussis won a victory on the borders of Egypt. . . .
>
> If Ethiopia takes action against our common enemy as we hope, you have the permission to say that whatever they capture from Britain, Italy

or *France* [emphasis mine], we will support the Ethiopians so that they will keep these territories even in peace time. [These territories] were captured [by the British, Italians, and the French] from the Ottomans in older times. We will support them [the Ethiopians] even in peace time to keep their conquests. This suits the Ottoman interest too.[13]

The Ottoman government's design for the Horn and that of Iyasu were incompatible. The Ottomans wanted the *mawla* to exercise autonomy of the Somalis within their empire, while Iyasu wanted such autonomy to be exercised under his new Ethiopia. From Enver's letter to Mazhar it is apparent that ultimately the Ottomans wanted to pressure Iyasu to capture "French territory," namely Djibouti. They wanted him to settle for Djibouti and the Eritrean highlands. Istanbul was far from convinced that suddenly Ethiopia would become a Muslim nation, worthy of controlling the entire Horn.

In May 1916 the Ottoman Foreign Ministry wrote to Mazhar that in order to encourage Ethiopia to enter the war he was authorized to promise the Ethiopians the return of the keys to the gates of Deir al-Sultan in Jerusalem. This was the most important spiritual goal of Christian Ethiopia, and, clearly, that was still how Ethiopia was viewed in Istanbul. (The Young Turks, for their part were wavering between religious and secular nationalist ideas and were ready, unlike their predecessor, 'Abd al-Hamid II, to use holy places as bargaining chips.) Mazhar, however, realized that such an Ottoman promise, once made public, would enhance Ethiopia's Christian nationalism and endanger Iyasu. In a letter of 4 September 1916 Mazhar responded briefly: "The decision about Jerusalem is all right. I would like to have the authority to use this decision according to the proper time and place."[14] Mazhar, in the short time left to him in Ethiopia, did not tell anyone about the Deir al-Sultan promise,[15] nor did he tell Iyasu that the Somalis were not to be under his emperorship.

Iyasu's strategy was his struggle with the Shoan establishment and his trump card, as agreed to on the spot with Mazhar, was the *mawla*. Only an Islamic buildup in the Ogaden and around Harar could make him powerful enough to face down his opponents at home. Indeed, since late 1914, Iyasu, encouraged by Mazhar, had been working on his Harar-Islamic-*mawla* connection. For that purpose he constantly sought to undermine the Harar government of *Dajazmach* Tafari, the son of *Ras* Makonnen, an equally ambitious contender for the throne, who, for his part, was ready to settle on the province.

A few days after hearing of the Ottoman entry into the war, Iyasu appointed 'Abdallah al-Sadiq, the *ra'is al-Muslimin* of Harar, deputy governor of the Ogaden. 'Abdallah, Menelik's (and Makonnen's) assistant in building Christian-Islamic social and economic coexistence, now became Iyasu's political channel to the Ogaden Muslims. He married one of his daughters to Iyasu and became Iyasu's tutor in Islamic customs and manners. In February 1915 Iyasu visited Harar and, accompanied by 'Abdallah, he prayed in a mosque for the first time. Then, between June 1915 and April 1916 Iyasu spent most of his time in eastern Ethiopia, in and out of Harar, Dire Dawa, Jijiga, constructing mosques and building contacts with the Muslims and with the *mawla*. He was reported to have married a daughter of the *mawla* and also sent him some military aid. His clear message for the local Muslims, and through them to the Somali clans beyond the border, was to unite under the *jihadi* banner of the *mawla*. The *mawla* and his *jihad,* Iyasu conveyed to the Somalis, had Ethiopia's backing. For his own part, mired as he was in his conflict with the Shoan establishment, Iyasu was in no position to drag Ethiopia into war against the Allies.

In early August 1916 Iyasu started to panic. Despite Mazhar's efforts and communications between Istanbul and Berlin, the Germans were reluctant to guarantee postwar independence to Ethiopia under Iyasu. Moreover, the Ottomans had begun losing their initial military momentum in the Middle East. In April 1916 they remained victorious in Iraq, but their Sinai campaign aimed at Egypt failed the same month. Earlier in March the Sanussis of Libya were driven back from Egyptian territory and, two months later, the *jihad* of *Sultan* 'Ali Dinar of Dar Fur was quelled by the British. In July 1916 the Ottomans' third attempt to cross Sinai met with a disaster.

Closer to the Red Sea and the Horn was yet another development of major significance: the outbreak of the Arab Revolt against the Ottoman Empire on 5 June 1916. The Arab Revolt had a double impact on Iyasu.

First, the Arab army of *Sharif* Husayn (the *amir* of Mecca), helped by British advisers, took control of Mecca (10 June) and went on in July and August to capture all of Hijaz (with the exception of Madina, which remained under siege until the end of the war). Thus, in August 1916 the total collapse of the Ottoman position in the Red Sea was in the offing (in both Arabia and Sinai), with clear implications for any possible Ottoman-inspired military enterprise in the Horn. (In fact, with the loss of Ottoman communications through Yemen, Mazhar could now correspond with Istanbul only through Europe, as the correspondence now became exposed to the Allies's counterintelligence.)

Second, the Arab army of the *sharif* was spreading anti-Ottoman propaganda. Instigated by the British and led by *Sharif* Husayn, the Arab Revolt was no less a traditional Islamic movement against the nationalist Young Turks than a modern Arab uprising. Husayn in his propaganda depicted the Young Turks as a band of secular infidels who had toppled 'Abd al-Hamid II and humiliated the caliphate. The British used the fact that the Islamic figure of the *amir* of Mecca was fighting the Ottomans to neutralize Istanbul's declaration of *jihad* against them. Again, their main concern was India, but they lost no time in spreading the word among the Somali rivals of the *mawla*.

Iyasu's time was running out. On 13 August 1916 Iyasu removed

Dajazmach Tafari from the government of Harar and appointed him over Kaffa. Tafari stayed in Addis Ababa as Iyasu himself left for Harar. Before he entered the town, Iyasu published a proclamation in leaflets distributed all over the Ogaden. He called the British "imperialist oppressors of Islam" who had humiliated the caliphate and promoted disunity. They had allied themselves with *Sharif* Husayn, Iyasu explained, and made him fight against the *sultan.* They, the British and *Sharif* Husayn of Mecca, destroyed the Holy Hijaz with their cannons and airplanes. The British had occupied India and Egypt and now they sought to oppress Islam in the Arab Peninsula and in Somalia. It was all, continued Iyasu, because they fear Islamic unity. William Gladstone, the British prime minister, cursed the Holy Quran in Parliament, and the British were about to steal the black holy stone from the Ka'ba in Mecca and put it in one of their museums. Iyasu concluded his proclamation by calling on all Muslims to unite in order to save the Ka'ba. The British, he promised the Somalis, because they had tried to destroy the holy Ka'ba and even the Prophet himself, were doomed. But the true Muslims should unite in action against the false Muslims and the infidels. As long as they were united, victory would be assured.[16]

On September 5, Iyasu entered Harar. During the next three weeks he acted feverishly, sparing no effort in seeking to prove to the locals that even though his name meant Prince Jesus he was a militant Muslim. He prayed in public, made speeches, published his own genealogy showing himself to be a descendant of Prophet Muhammad,[17] disbanded the local police and built a new one from Muslim recruits. On 21 September, he left for Dire Dawa where he inspected a parade of the new local Islamic forces and waved his new banner, an Ethiopian one with the Islamic *shahada* embroidered on it, complete with an Islamic red crescent.[18]

Iyasu's plan to instigate an all-Somali anti-British revolt, and to install himself as a future emperor of a new Islamic order in the Horn, was now an act of despair. He gathered the Muslim chiefs, telling them (what Mazhar probably still let him believe) that the Ottomans had promised him all the territory from Harar to Massawa. At the same time he asked them not to share this information with Christians so that the Shoans would not hear about it. But he was unable to create unity among the Somalis, and the British as well as the Italian Intelligence had no problem following his moves. In Addis Ababa the British, French, and Italian embassies did not have to work hard to persuade the Shoan establishment to depose Iyasu. This deposition was done on September 27. The *abun,* under pressure, excommunicated Menelik's heir and grandson on the basis of his conversion to Islam.

Menelik's daughter, Zawditu, was now proclaimed empress, with *Dajazmach* Tafari, promoted to *ras,* as her heir. In October *Ras* Tafari led the Shoan forces to defeat Iyasu's father, *Negus* Mika'el. *Ras* Tafari was crowned Emperor Haile Selassie in 1930. Iyasu himself survived to the mid-1930s, wasting his life between prisons and escapes, and resurfaced during his last days, in our Ethiopian–Middle Eastern story.

In the wider context of Ethiopian–Middle Eastern Islamic relations the 1915–1916 *Lij* Iyasu affair closed a circle that began centuries earlier in the story of Muhammad and the *najashi*. Through Mazhar Bey the Ottoman Middle East acted as if to adopt the *Islam al-najashi* version and abandoned the *utruku* approach, inviting an Islamic Ethiopia to rejoin the strategic and cultural sphere of the Islamic Orient. Iyasu, in the modern version of that old episode, was ready to pay the price: to convert to Islam, and, consequently, to gamble on the survival of Ethiopian culture and identity. "There are two paths to the future of this country," wrote Mazhar Bey to Istanbul, "either to leave her in her poverty or to spread our influence over her."[19]

His recommendation was not to "leave" Ethiopia any more, especially an Ethiopia under a Muslim *najashi*. One can imagine Harar as the capital of a Red Sea–oriented and Ottoman-affiliated state, with a tolerated Christian minority left.

After the war Ethiopia would enjoy continuity, safe for a time as a political system that was slowly paying the price of victory and conservatism. Islam in Ethiopia was again, as it had been under Menelik, reduced to an apolitical dimension of the country's cultural diversity.

A fundamental change had occurred in the Middle East. With the demise of the Ottoman Empire at the end of the war, there came to an end the last all-regional manifestation and embodiment of Islam as a political ideology. The Turks, the political and military leaders of Islam for four hundred years, now pursued secular nationalism. In March 1924 Ataturk abolished the caliphate. The Western occupiers of the Arab-inhabited areas in the Middle East demarcated international boundaries, splitting the Islamic nation and carving out new states and entities built upon Western political concepts: Syria, Lebanon, Transjordan, Iraq, and Palestine. Egypt was led now by a political class motivated primarily by a non-Islamic concept of Egyptian identity shared actively by fellow Copts. The Arab Peninsula, left independent, came under Saudi domination, based in Riyad, away from the Red Sea.

Indeed, in the 1920s and the first half of the 1930s the new Middle East sent no major messages to Ethiopia. Its inhabitants were busy struggling for independence and searching for their own identities. They were to find some of it in modern Arabism, through which, from the mid-1930s and in conjunction with the Abyssinian Crisis, the Ethiopian–Middle Eastern dialogue would be renewed and reinterpreted.

II

ETHIOPIA AND ARABISM: FROM ARSLAN TO NASSER

——

8

THE ARABS, MUSSOLINI, AND THE ABYSSINIAN DILEMMA

During the first third of the twentieth century Ethiopians showed little curiosity about the Middle East. After their Adwa victory in 1896, and especially in the aftermath of World War I, their country's independence seemed secure, and it seemed even more so after 1923, when the country was admitted to the League of Nations. The Middle East was now occupied by Europeans, and in itself presented no threat. Islam had lost its empire and presented no political challenge.

The only active Middle Eastern interest Ethiopians demonstrated in this period was in their Christian Middle Eastern connections, to Alexandria and to Jerusalem. The first Ethiopian newspaper, *Berhanena Selam,* appeared in the mid-1920s; in its pages, little was written on the Middle East. Of the twenty relevant articles published between 1926 and 1935 only three brought information on affairs in the region that were not related to Ethiopia or to its Christian interests. Four of the twenty were on Deir al-Sultan and the Ethiopian presence in Jerusalem. Nearly all the rest focused on Ethiopia's relations with the Copts in Egypt or on relations with the government of Egypt that had to do with Church affairs.[1]

Ethiopian attitudes to the modern Middle East are a subject of great importance for both an understanding of the past and for preparing for future events. So, too, are the post–World War I Middle Eastern attitudes to Ethiopia. The region has seen the emergence of new identities, Arab, Egyptian, and Zionist. How do Arab or pan-Arab nationalists view Ethiopia? What was transmitted in this respect to modern Arabism from Islam? Was it the *utruku* message of acceptance and tolerance or the *Islam al-najashi* message of illegitimacy? What are the approaches to Ethiopia stemming from the values of modern Egyptian nationalism? What were the legacies for modern Egyptian nationalism of the history we surveyed? What are the deeper considerations behind the policies of other Middle Eastern states, movements, and organizations? Are these monolithic? And do different Middle Eastern identities predetermine different basic concepts of their neighbor, Ethiopia?

In trying to answer these questions in the first third of the twentieth century a scholar would search in vain through Arabic literature and journalistic writings. During that time Middle Easterners, experiencing the traumatic humiliation of the conquered, ignored Ethiopia (which, during these years, was being adopted as a model of freedom by blacks in Africa and in the Americas) exercising some of the ancient attitudes. The pan-Arabists who led their countries during the 1950s and 1960s were interested in the Arabism of the Eritrean people, but they attached little legitimacy to—and therefore had little regard for—Ethiopia beyond the River Mareb. Dozens of Arabic books and innumerable journalistic pieces were produced in the 1960s and 1970s, when it was assumed that an Arab victory was about to be scored in an Arab Eritrea. This wave subsided with the demise of the Islamic wings of Eritrean nationalist movements. Arab public opinion in the last two decades has devoted only superficial attention to Ethiopia's revolutions and wars. As of the early 1990s, an Arab scholar in the Islamic Arab world[2] seeking to understand Ethiopia on its own terms has yet to appear.

The literature that reveals the undercurrents of the many modern Middle Eastern concepts of Ethiopia, and mainly of pan-Arabism, was produced during the Abyssinian Crisis of 1935–1936. This was a period during which political-strategic developments of great consequence took place, but also one that witnessed sociopolitical changes of a far-reaching character. In both Ethiopia and the major countries of the Middle East the sociopolitical establishments created at the turn of the century were on the verge of losing their power during these crucial years. In Ethiopia they were replaced (after 1941) by the autocratic rule of Haile Selassie, and in the Arab Middle Eastern countries by new social and ideological forces, which would pave the way for Gamal 'Abd al-Nasser and his generation. The ideas expressed in the events and writings of 1935–1936, and the struggle between them, are thus crucial to our understanding of the region today.

MIDDLE EASTERN BACKGROUNDS
AND MUSSOLINI'S PROPAGANDA

In the 1920s the Arabs of the Middle East had no political leader to admire. Sa'ad Zaghlul of Egypt came close to being a national hero for the younger generation of that country, but he was unable to accomplish anything heroic and died in 1927. Two other personalities, Ataturk (Mustafa Kemal) of Turkey and Muhammad Reza Shah of Iran, who were regarded in the Oriental Middle East as charismatic historical leaders, were non-Arabs, and, moreover, also ardent fighters against Islam. Both initiated Western-oriented reforms in their respective countries, which spread into the rest of the region the message of Islamic and Arab-Islamic weakness. The 1920s (and to a lesser extent the early 1930s) were indeed a period of Western-oriented modernization in the Middle East, of parliamentarian politics, and even of some attempts at liberalism. Having lost their political dimension, Islam's leaders in countries such as Egypt included thinkers who tried to modernize its concepts and make them compatible with contemporary Western values. It was also a period of nonviolent opposition to the British and French rulers of Egypt, Palestine, Syria, Lebanon, and Iraq. From the social perspective, it was a period of stability, verging sometimes on stagnation. Socially and economically, the land-owning urban elite of Arab societies enjoyed the nonviolent atmosphere, and they confined themselves to a parliamentarian, mildly nationalistic struggle against their occupiers.

This spirit of the 1920s was slowly eroding during the early 1930s. It was shattered in late 1935 and 1936, in the aftermath of the Abyssinian Crisis.

The Italo-Ethiopian conflict had a tremendous impact on the entire world, including the Middle East. The year 1935 was a time of tension during which the conquered peoples of the region began to redefine their attitudes toward Europe and European values. Italian, and later German, totalitarianism as a model of political organization began to compete with British and French parliamentarian democracies. Most of the established Arab leaders were still pinning their hopes on new flexible political generosity on the part of the British or the French, but others were praying for British and French humiliation in the face of Fascist inroads. Simultaneously, the political rank and file throughout the Middle East were busy during that year redefining their attitudes toward themselves: What are we? they asked. Are we Egyptians, Syrians, Iraqis, and so on, that is, members of communities defined by the newly Western-created and Western-modeled states? Or are we Muslims by our own political-cultural history and Arabs by our modern nationalism?

This ambivalence in their self-image led to two sets of closely connected questions: political-strategic and cultural-nationalist. Islamic pan-Arabism, as it emerged in the 1930s, meant a revolt against the parliamentarian methods and political restraint followed by the old generation of urban elites. This blend of politically revived Islam with the new sense of Arab identity provided a militant ideology against Western hegemony. It appealed to the young generation in Cairo, Jerusalem, Damascus, and Baghdad as well as to the representatives of newly emerging, nonprivileged social groups. The combination of Islam and Arabism was used by Mussolini who, seeking to generate and fan regional instability, presented himself as the champion of Islam and helped the propagators of pan-Arabism in various ways.[3]

Mussolini's propaganda dragged Ethiopia into the middle of these Middle East dilemmas. On the strategic level he challenged Britain and

France and appeared on the brink of humiliating them militarily on Ethiopian soil. On the cultural-ideological level *Il Duce* portrayed Ethiopia as a barbarous black Christian kingdom that had oppressed Islam and Muslims throughout its history. The message that he conveyed to his listeners in the Middle East was that by destroying Ethiopia, an illegitimate entity, Islamic and Arab prestige would be rebuilt. Arabs and Muslims should therefore support his anti-Ethiopian, anti-British, anti-French campaign.

British propaganda, and to a lesser extent that of the French, resorted to arguments contradicting Mussolini's. Mussolini, they maintained, was neither a pro-Arab nationalist nor a champion of Islam. He was, rather, a power-seeker who aspired to resurrect the Roman Empire in the East. His "civilizing mission" in Ethiopia was only a thin guise for racist aggression, which should fool no one in the Orient. The British and French hoped that in comparison to Mussolini's schemes, their own occupation regimes in the Middle East would be better appreciated, at least by the ruling elites of the Arab countries.

EGYPTIAN RESPONSE UNTIL THE BEGINNING OF HOSTILITIES: GESTURES OF SOLIDARITY

The Abyssinian Crisis was a pivotal issue in the Egypt of 1935. The country's relations with its British occupiers, the power struggle within the political establishment, the spirit and methods of participation in politics by the emerging new generation as well as by the representatives of the deprived classes—all these were directly affected by the drama between Ethiopia and Mussolini. After all, the Fascists' military enterprise was built up by passing through the Suez Canal, and the Italians were about to occupy the main sources of the Nile. This is not the place to discuss the details of the 1935–1936 domestic Egyptian story (part of which I have discussed elsewhere).[4] I shall only summarize here part of the action and focus my attention on the question of basic attitudes toward Ethiopia.

Generally speaking, the political establishment of Egypt was determined not to miss the opportunity to make progress on the road to independence. One wing of this establishment, consisting mainly of individuals and parties that had tired of the country's experiment with parliamentarianism, sought open hostilities with the British. They sought to benefit from the British weakness as exposed by Mussolini and effectuate political gains through violent riots. This wing believed the Fascist propaganda and was even instrumental in transmitting it to the public.

The other wing wanted to exploit the opportunity to promote the cause of independence by strengthening the autonomous parliamentarian life that Egypt had enjoyed since 1923. In 1930, the British (through the services of Prime Minister Sidqi) had suspended the constitution of 1923 in order to undermine the power of the popular Wafd Party, which had led the anti-British struggle. The Wafd, still the most powerful political organization in the country, wanted to show the British it was reasonable and moderate and a better partner for Great Britain than the rising tide of their antiparliamentarian rivals. Because the Wafd could not support the British directly it sent its message by showing sympathy for Ethiopia. Showing solidarity with Ethiopia demonstrated understanding for British interests as well as for law and order in international relations. Beneath the political calculation there was also a strand of secular liberalism motivating many of the intellectual elite. In addition, many of the young Coptic generation had joined the liberal wing of young Egyptian nationalism. In 1935 the second in command in the Wafd (and perhaps the moving power of the party) was the Copt William Makram 'Ubayd, who also supervised the party's youth organization. In this capacity he missed no opportunity to praise Ethiopia, "the nation in the Upper Nile, those who sacrifice their lives for their country, who had bought their existence with death,"[5] as a source of inspiration for the youth of Egypt. (Strengthening Egypt's relations with Ethiopia was to be a line pursued by future modern Copts. The Church itself abstained from action.)

No less significant was the position of the Islamic thinkers, mainly the modernists. Here the most important figure in 1935 was *Shaikh* Rashid Rida, the leader of the Salafiyya movement that had advocated rational and open reinterpretation of Islam most effectively in the liberal 1920s. (The movement had been established at the end of the 1890s.) In Rida's view, modernization was part of Islam, and Western values of liberalism and of diversity, unlike Western aggression and occupation, were not to be rejected. For Rida and his followers (soon to be challenged by a new generation of more militant Muslims), Mussolini was the embodiment of crude Western brutality, but Ethiopia was a victim and a neighbor. We have already noted that Rashid Rida was a close associate of the al-'Azm brothers, the translators and publishers, in 1908, of *Rihlat al-habasha*. It was this book that had conveyed to Arabic readers and to Islamic modernizers of that period the notion of "Ethiopia as the land of righteousness." Rida was the spiritual leader of the first Islamic association established in Egypt in the 1920s, the Young Men's Islamic Association (YMMA, *Jam'iyyat al-shubban al-muslimiyyin*). This association supported the pro-Ethiopian activities of Egyptians in 1935.

The Egyptian public, to be sure, could do little, and the political establishment was not willing to risk a confrontation with the Italian Fascists and their potential supporters at home. Ethiopian attempts to mobilize Egyptian diplomatic or other assistance yielded little. Some of the official missions sent by Haile Selassie (including one seeking contact in Egypt with the exiled remnants of the Sanusiyya movement, in an attempt to revive their anti-Italian revolt in Libya)[6] were virtually ignored. The government's policy was to remain uninvolved, and it was only a month after the beginning of active hostilities that Egypt joined the sanctions imposed on Mussolini by the League of Nations. Even that was done amid strong protest, by both the Wafd and its rivals.

Nevertheless, the degree of sympathy expressed at this stage in some of the press (we shall discuss it later), and the Egyptian public's gestures of identification with Ethiopia were all but unique.

The most important action was the establishment in Cairo in early 1935 of the General Committee for the Defense of Ethiopian Independence (*Lajna 'amma lildifa' 'an istiqlal al-habasha*). Its early formation began in January and the guiding spirit was the head of the Association of Islamic Youth, 'Abd al-Hamid Sa'id. Soon the committee came under the auspices of two princes of the royal family, *Amir* 'Ummar Tusun and the *Nabil* Isma'il Dawud. Other members were affiliated with the Wafd, and one other prominent was the Copt and ex-minister of war, Salib Sami.[7] The committee itself was torn by internal rivalries but it did effectively manage to spread its word. The historical record on this point is unclear, but the committee may have supported sending, early in February 1935, two al-Azhar teachers, *Shaikh* Mahmud al-Nashawi and *Shaikh* Yusuf 'Ali, to Ethiopia. The two Islamic scholars were welcomed in Addis Ababa by the Ethiopian government and were encouraged to establish a *madrasa,* an Islamic school.[8] They helped to rally local Islamic support behind the emperor.

The committee also supported a campaign in the press to prevent the hiring of Egyptian workers by Italian firms contracted to help with the military buildup, especially by constructing roads in Eritrea.[9] More significant and impressive was the initiative to enlist volunteers to fight in the Ethiopian army. By August 1935 it was reported that some eight thousand Egyptians had signed up. Later reports put the number at thirteen thousand.[10] Very few of those enlisted (who were not Ethiopians residing in Egypt) reached Ethiopia to experience battle. They were led by a colorful figure, an ex-Ottoman officer named Muhammad Tariq (called *al-Ifriqi*), to whom we shall return. The significance in any case was symbolic, reflecting wide popular identification at that stage with Ethiopia.

The most notable action initiated by the Committee for the Defense of Ethiopian Independence was the organization of medical aid. Though modest in scope it was nevertheless the most substantial official aid from the outside world for the Ethiopian defense effort. Two weeks after the Fascists' invasion, on 15 October 1935, *Nabil* Isma'il Dawud left for Ethiopia with three medical doctors. Meanwhile, an extensive effort to raise money and enlist doctors (in which the Syrian exile, doctor, and leader of the 1925 anti-French revolt, 'Abd al-Rahman Shahbandar, was involved) enabled the sending of another mission under the banner of the Red Crescent. It left for Ethiopia on 23 October 1935, and consisted of twelve physicians and sixty trained assistants. A third mission of the same size left at a later date.[11]

WHAT IS ETHIOPIA? FOUR BOOKS IN CAIRO

Throughout this period, from the beginning of the international Abyssinian Crisis and its first repercussions in the Middle East (in December 1934 and January 1935) to the beginning of the actual invasion by the Fascists (3 October 1935), a major debate raged throughout the Middle East.

The issue raised by the Abyssinian Crisis was the basic orientation of the Middle East. The public was fed by opinions and propaganda from all quarters, and the main stage for the competing currents was the daily press. The press was in daily touch with both the unfolding drama and with the public. It thus reflected changes in the attitudes toward Ethiopia as they were developing. It was in the daily Arabic press, in Egypt and the rest of the Middle East, that at the end of the crisis the image of Ethiopia was to be remolded.

However, in order to follow the essentials of the drama we should first focus our attention on four books of that period. In Cairo alone at least four books on Ethiopia appeared in 1935. They were published in October and November, just as the war erupted, and thus they reflected a full year of public controversies. More important, they were all published in order to acquaint the public in Egypt and in the neighboring Arab countries with Ethiopia in general, a subject they had long neglected. As such, they were devoted substantially to Ethiopian and Ethio-Islamic history.

Returning to Muhammad and the *najashi* as well as turning to later history was indeed the starting point of any discussion of Ethiopia. The four books may be viewed as two distinct pairs.

First, the pro-Ethiopians. In the introduction to *The Ethiopian Question from Ancient History to the Year 1935*,[12] the Egyptian lawyer, judge, and journalist 'Abdallah al-Husayn tells how he came to write this book. He had contributed throughout 1935 to a daily column, "The Abyssinian Question," in the Cairo newspaper, *al-Ahram*. Readers started turning to him for basic background information, and as their curiosity grew he realized that he himself knew next to nothing about Ethiopia. He had written a book on the history of Islamic Sudan, but, he admits, whenever Ethiopia appeared in the story he almost ignored it. He had to study from scratch.

The book he wrote is clearly a product of a liberal Egyptian nationalist. In the book he makes a point of emphasizing that the Ethiopian woman is free, drinks beer, divorces, and participates in wars when necessary.[13] Ethiopian society in general, he writes, with a few exceptions, is Semitic in culture and origin, similar in ethnicity to the Arabs of the Arab Peninsula. Much of Ethiopian culture came from the ancient Egyptians. Haile

Selassie, for example, used royal symbols with hieroglyphic script similar to the ones of the great pharaohs.

In the Egypt of the time this was a statement of particular significance, for Pharaohnism was the school of the liberal elite that believed in educating the public about the pre-Islamic past of Egypt. It was a pluralistic message that accepted the Copts into Egyptian identity, and it was Egyptianism that conveyed tolerance of, indeed, even sought regional solidarity with, neighboring non-Muslims.

Al-Husayn's interpretation of history is full of respect for Ethiopia. His recounting of the "Muhammad and the *najashi*" story is clear.[14] He quotes the *najashi*'s letter to Muhammad, in al-Tabari, and then adds that the Prophet, upon reading it, uttered the famous *utruku al-habasha ma tarakukum:* "And because of this order none of the rulers of Islam ever even contemplated occupying Ethiopia or exerting his influence over it. To the contrary, the states and principalities of Islam always were in peace and friendship with the Ethiopian Empire, until after the Middle Ages. Even now, some of the *'ulama* and the *mufti*s of Somalia published a decree forbidding the Muslims to fight Ethiopia."

Respect for and goodwill toward Ethiopia, however, were not enough to produce an accurate survey. The book, consisting of hastily compiled newspaper pieces, is full of factual mistakes. But the educational message was clear. Tewodros, al-Husayn writes, had a constructive dialogue with Sa'id *Pasha* and was convinced by peaceful means to evacuate areas he had taken from the Sudan (p. 28). Yohannes's conflict with Isma'il is reduced by al-Husayn to a brief mention, but his obtaining four bishops from Egypt in 1881 is emphasized (pp. 62–63). There is nothing negative on Christian-Muslim relations with Ethiopia, according to al-Husayn. Throughout, he emphasizes Ethiopia's affiliation to the Oriental world as well as its successful facing up to Western imperialism. A long chapter (pp. 151–170) devoted to the prospect of Italian use of poisonous gas in Ethiopia implies that it was the Fascists who were barbarians while Ethiopia is depicted as a respectful neighbor deserving full support.

The second member of the first pair, *Between the African Lion and the Italian Tiger,*[15] by Muhammad Lutfi Jum'a, appeared in the last weeks of 1935. Jum'a, a lawyer and a well-known intellectual, was one of the promoters of the cultural-national identity of Easternism, an idea developed at the time by secular-minded Egyptianists. The people of the Orient, they maintained, irrespective of their religious or ethnic differences, share a common culture and must unite in stemming Western aggression. For Jum'a (the author of *The Life of The East*)[16] Haile Selassie was thus a lion symbolizing the hopes of the East. The Italian tiger, he predicted, would be defeated. Oriental Ethiopia deserved sympathy and support and would reciprocate by helping fellow Orientals, Arabs, Egyptians, and others, in their common, secular, progressive struggle for the redemption of the entire Oriental world. He wrote:

Egypt and the rest of the East both Near and Far, and Arabism ('uruba) embracing its many peoples and states, are all concerned with Ethiopia, with its centrality in the world and its present crisis. If Europe is interested in the Abyssinian Crisis because of fear for the world order, or resistance to Italian aggression, with us it is different. We are interested in Ethiopia because it represents both the East and Africa at their very best and most lofty—in terms of beauty, form, quality and dignity. What is more honorable than maintaining freedom, generation after generation and era after era, and resisting foreign enemies whatever their might? And indeed the Ethiopians (like us) conceive freedom to be the most precious value in life.[17]

Jum'a's book, which is subtitled *A Social and Psychological Analytical Study on the Italo-Ethiopian Question,* is a historical survey. The first chapter is devoted to Ethiopia's early relations with Islam, particularly the Muhammad-*najashi* story. The emphasis is on Ethiopia's saving of the *sahaba* and on the "beautiful special relations" between the *najashi* and the Prophet. There is no mention of the possibility that the *najashi* converted to Islam. The reader is left with the impression that the Aksumite king remained a good Christian, together with his priests. At one point Jum'a notes that the priests, having received gifts from 'Amru bin al-'As, tried to persuade the *najashi* to send the *sahaba* back to Mecca, but then they accepted his decision to let them stay. The story of 'Ubaydallah bin Jahsh's conversion to Christianity, as told by Jum'a, was one of an open-minded person persuaded by his hosts, not a story of coercion: "The Ethiopians headed by the *najashi* and by the priests proved that they were a noble people, lofty in spirit and humanity, having mercy on anyone oppressed, be he of their religion or of other persuasion. They, the *najashi* and his people, proved that they were men of principles and justice, and that the Prophet was right in sending the *sahaba* to their country, the land of righteousness" (p. 18).

In later chapters the author chooses to gloss over Ahmad *Gragn* and other medieval conflicts, and focus instead on the relations of Egypt with Ethiopia's modern emperors. Here again the presentation is a positive one. "Tewodros's vision" of a unifying emperor is mentioned, but not in terms that show him as defeating Islam. To the contrary, when discussing Emperor Tewodros II (pp. 21–22, 76–77) Jum'a blames *Khedive* Isma'il for enabling the British army of Napier, the destroyer of the Ethiopian, to pass through Egypt. Tewodros, according to Jum'a, was a progressive modernizer who saw Egypt as a model. He failed to prevail over the British but he nonetheless united his people, "watering the tree of unity with his blood."

Yohannes IV in Jum'a's account was no less a hero, but a victim as well. There is no mention of his domestic religious policy or his coercive anti-Islamic measures. The conflict he waged with Egypt was the fault of European meddlers and spies, who had tempted Isma'il to invade Ethiopia. In describing Yohannes's victory at Gura, Jum'a praises the emperor for his bravery and criticizes the Egyptian army as commanded by foreigners who deprived the authentic Egyptian, Ahmad 'Urabi, of leadership (pp. 23–27). In a later chapter (pp. 77–78) on Yohannes, Jum'a blames the Ethiopian for being narrow-minded and thus unable to reach understanding with Egypt after Gura.

Menelik is Jum'a's hero. Although there is no word on his conquests, Menelik is praised for accomplishing the unity envisioned by Tewodros. His benevolence was such that "all his subjects, Christians and Muslims alike, loved him and admired his beauty" (pp. 79–80). The Egyptians, writes Jum'a, never forget that the Ethiopians never intervened in the flow of the Nile (p. 34). For the Muslims in Ethiopia, Egypt is the spiritual center, as is Alexandria for the Christians. Ethiopia is portrayed as a neighbor, an important part of the East. Its enemy was and still remains the West. The Italian conquest of Eritrea and the reducing of it to a colony, argues Jum'a, was "stabbing the heart of Ethiopia with a dagger" (p. 84). The Fascist Italians, he concludes, sought revenge for their defeat at Adwa, but Ethiopia, the Eastern, Christian-Muslim country, would prevail (p. 117).

The first member of the second pair is Yusuf Ahmad's *Islam in Ethiopia,* published in November 1935. This book finally took the place of *Rihlat al-habasha* as the standard volume on Ethiopia for the next generations of Arabic readers. Subtitled *Evidences and Authentic Documents on the Situation of Muslims in Ethiopia,*[18] it is a hate-filled condemnation of Ethiopia's culture and history. "Now that the Muslims all over the world have pity for Ethiopia I want to tell them the truth on her relations with Islam so that they exert pressure on Haile Selassie to depart in future from the way of his predecessors in that respect" (p. 3).

In the first chapter Ahmad writes:

> Some writers talk of the *sahaba* as a reason to support Ethiopia. We want to explain that if we have some sympathy to Ethiopia it is because Ethiopia is an Eastern country facing a Western one, not because of anything historical. As for the honor given to the *sahaba* it was by one man only, *Najashi* Ashama. Indeed he converted to Islam. But he had to conceal it from his people until he died. . . . As for the priests and the people, they gave the *sahaba* only troubles. They rebelled against the *najashi* because he was good to the Muslims. (pp. 4–5)

In late 1935 Yusuf Ahmad had no difficulty in focusing the attention of the Egyptian public on the *Islam al-najashi* version. Earlier, in March 1935, the great author and scholar Muhammad Husayn Haykal had published his most famous study *The Life of Muhammad.* The book highlighted the general return to traditional Islamic thinking typical of the 1930s in Egypt, and it turned instantly into the bestseller of the whole period (ten thousand copies were sold out by May 1935, and a new edition was published in November and sold out by mid-1936). In narrating the *sahaba-*

najashi story Haykal merely reemphasized the traditional version that the *najashi* did convert to Islam. He also added his own interpretation that the first group of the *sahaba* returned to Arabia (in 616) because the Ethiopians revolted against their Muslim king.[19] However, apart from thus raising the issue Haykal avoided passing any judgment on Ethiopia.

In presenting the background to his version of the story, Yusuf Ahmad discusses an inherent hatred the Ethiopians felt for Arabs from the beginning of history. The story of the *sahaba* represented for Yusuf Ahmad the culmination of that hatred. The Ethiopians forced 'Ubaydallah bin Jahsh to renounce Islam and convert to Christianity. The priests and the people, he writes, tortured the Muslim refugees, forced them to attend Christian churches, and ridiculed their arguments in favor of Islam. "The learned researcher will find it easy to prove, and after we show and prove our points by comparing what we know about the *sahaba* with the travellers' accounts of later Islamic visitors, you will see that what the *sahaba* met with in Ethiopia was only hatred. If it had not been for the *najashi* they all would have to become Christians, die, or be returned to Mecca so that Quraysh could do with them as they pleased."[20]

Ahmad concludes: "So what right do they have that we shall remember this story in their favor? They never respected them and only tortured them. If it had not been for the Muslim *najashi* they could not have lived in Ethiopia even one day!" (p. 20)

Failing even to mention the *"utruku"* hadith, Yusuf Ahmad assures his readers that it was only because the pioneers of Islam were so kind-hearted that "they left us with a positive story about the *najashi,* refraining from telling us about the terror and threats they suffered from the priests" (pp. 11–12).

The reason Ethiopia was never conquered by Islam, he asserts, was practical, and not because of gratitude. To the contrary, the entire history as Yusuf Ahmad tells it is permeated by the Ethiopians' hatred. He cites a story from al-Tabari, "which is another testimony to their [the Ethiopians'] bad nature and inherent inhospitality: When Marwan bin Muhammad, the last of the 'Umayyad *caliph*s, was killed [A.D. 750], his two sons fled to Ethiopia. But the Ethiopians killed one of them and forced the other to flee. And look at that savage people! How do they treat refugees who look for shelter in their country? They receive them with swords, killing and expelling them!" (pp. 28–29)

According to Yusuf Ahmad (pp. 34–39), in medieval times the Ethiopians fought the Islamic emirates because the Muslims were prosperous and they were jealous. Ahmad *Gragn*'s was a defensive war, which turned into an epic of Islamic bravery second only to the early Islamic conquests. Tewodros is dismissed as a fanatic crusader who burned the mosque of Gondar (p. 46). Yohannes, much to the delight of his savage followers, humiliated the Egyptian prisoners he captured in Gura. He then forced fifty thousand Muslims to become Christians, but God sent the *mahdi* to punish him for maltreating Muslims (pp. 47–49).

Menelik II fares no better in Ahmad's book. His conquests, culminating in his capture of Harar, sought the defeat of Islam and the Muslims. Menelik did away with flourishing Islamic entities and culture. Only in Jimma did he permit the Muslims to enjoy autonomy. In 1934, after the death of Abba Jifar, a jealous Haile Selassie put an end to that autonomy. "Thus ended the last Islamic principality in Ethiopia. . . . They were all destroyed not because of fear but because of fanaticism and hatred" (pp. 49–54).

The ending of Jimma's autonomy in 1934 was part of Haile Selassie's program of centralization that was to affect nearly every province of Ethiopia. But Yusuf Ahmad, and, as we shall see, many of the anti-Ethiopian, Fascist-inspired thinkers in the Middle East, equated Haile Selassie with Menelik and saw Yohannes as a destroyer of Islam. In an effort to mobilize the support of Ethiopia's Muslims, Emperor Haile Selassie made a number of gestures during 1935. These included proclamations emphasizing constitutional equality of religions as well as one promising to build a grand mosque in Addis Ababa (the mosque promised in 1904 to Sadiq al-'Azm). For Yusuf Ahmad it was a matter of mockery:

> Has anyone ever heard of such a way to keep a promise? Oh what a glorious gift from an Oriental country, ancient and deep rooted, to its Muslim citizens! A gift for Muslim citizens who lived there for thirteen centuries, for its neighbors and guests. Do they not know, the people of that country, that even in European capitals like London or Paris there are mosques? In any case thank you, Your Highness, I hope you do not soon forget your promise like your predecessor. . . . (p. 77)

Apart from the historical interpretations summarized above, Ahmad's book revolves around one theme: Ethiopia's savage ingratitude to its Muslims. In Yusuf Ahmad's view, the Muslims brought to Ethiopia their virtue, the richness of their commerce, and their connections with the outside world. They even defended Ethiopia. What they got in return was killing, religious coercion, extra taxation, the maltreating of their women, and social segregation (pp. 78–88, 98). The social segregation, Yusuf Ahmad remarks at one point, was the only action taken against the Ethiopian Muslims that turned out to be a blessing: "The Christian Ethiopian hatred for the Muslim brings the latter important benefit. The Ethiopians live in dirt and they have sexual habits which are hazardous to health" (p. 88) and on that he quotes al-'Azm's *Rihlat,* a passage I cited above.[21]

In contrast to Jum'a, who regarded the Italian occupation and colonialism in Eritrea as "a dagger in the heart of Ethiopia," Yusuf Ahmad viewed the Italians as having brought improvement to Eritrea. He compared Islam in Eritrea and in Somalia to the Ethiopian case and wrote that it fared much better under the Fascists (p. 91).

In conclusion, Yusuf Ahmad makes three statements: first, that the history of Ethiopia vis-à-vis Islam was a story of injustice. Second, that the majority of the Muslims in Ethiopia are not Ethiopians, that they differ essentially in language, race, and culture. (He implies that they are Arabs by stating that their main language is Arabic, "which they preserved since the time of their ancestors' arrival from Yemen and the Hijaz" [p. 61].) And third, that the majority of these Muslims live outside historic Ethiopia and they deserve full freedom (p. 104). In sum, Yusuf Ahmad believed the oppressed Muslims under backward Christian Ethiopia were entitled to both Islamic and Arab liberation. Yusuf Ahmad's writings, together with the writings of many of his contemporaries, marked a change from Islamic attitudes toward Ethiopia to modern, pan-Arab ones.

The author of the fourth book was a Lebanese Christian resident of Cairo, an advocate and a historian of modern Arab secular nationalism, the journalist and author Bulus Mas'ad. Entitled *Al-Habasha or Ethiopia in a Turning Point of Her History,*[22] his book was aimed at the young modern Arab rather than the Muslim reader. Islam in Ethiopia is one of his main topics, not in itself, but rather as a measure of how barbaric Ethiopia was. In describing Ethio-Islamic relations the Christian author returns inevitably to the Muhammad-*najashi* story (pp. 80–92) but he deftly avoids the issue of *Islam al-najashi*. *Najashi* Ashama, he writes, obtained a holy book from the Prophet and put it in an ivory box, and the Prophet said: "Let the Ethiopians prosper as long as they have this book." In referring to the Muslims in Ethiopia he echoes Yusuf Ahmad's condemnations of Tewodros, Yohannes, and Menelik, but attributes their behavior to a different motivation; he saw them as maltreating a minority group.

One of the book's themes is that Ethiopia has failed to uphold the standards of civilized modernity. Ethiopia, in Mas'ad's view, was a barbarous medieval entity; this was not unlike Mussolini's view.[23] The theme of savage Abyssinia is central and extensively elaborated throughout. Three pages (32–35) are devoted to descriptions of cruelty in the traditional Ethiopian punitive system, ten pages (60–70) to the argument that slavery is an organic part of Ethiopian culture and society. The various decrees abolishing it by Tewodros, Yohannes, Menelik, and Haile Selassie, argues Bulus Mas'ad, were of no avail.

Summarizing his attitude toward the Ethiopian domestic situation, Mas'ad writes:

> The Abyssinians are Semites in the general sense, but they are not the original inhabitants of the land. They are warlike people having no interest in anything but power and bravery. They raise their children to be

> obsessed by fighting to such an extent that they attribute no importance to
> anything else of what life can offer. They consider themselves the masters
> of the country, patronizing their fellow countrymen and neighbors, the
> Muslims and the pagans, and look down on them. (pp. 44–45)

Ethiopian savagery, according to Mas'ad, was manifested not only in
domestic affairs but also in fighting foreigners. He cites descriptions of
maltreating the Italian prisoners of the Adwa battle. Menelik, he says, quoting al-'Azm's *Rihlat,* was an enlightened man, but his attempts at introducing progress were defeated by his own people.

Much of Mas'ad's book (mainly pp. 96–128) is devoted to Ethio-
Egyptian relations, especially during the periods of Muhammad 'Ali and
Isma'il. He emphasizes that Egypt, as it was modernizing under these
enlightened leaders, was seeking to bring progress to Ethiopia. "It was a
period when Egypt renewed her youth and reached a golden era of modernity which astonished the whole world," he writes. The Egyptians, in
Mas'ad's view, came to Ethiopia to bring books and build houses. They
built Harar, including the castle where *Ras* Makonnen lived and Haile
Selassie was born. They brought the light of culture to that region. Mas'ad
observes that Yohannes in the north failed to see the advantage of Isma'il's
scheme to construct a railroad from Massawa to Khartoum. Thus the battle
of Gura was fought, which "ended with a truce, the first stipulation of
which was the freedom of commerce and trade between Ethiopia and
Egypt." Indeed, he asserts, "in spite of the conflict Egyptian occupation
enlivened solid and good Ethio-Egyptian relations."

Mas'ad implies that Egypt's role was to perform a "civilizing mission."
The reader needs little imagination to note the similarity to Mussolini's
enterprise. The British did all they could to undermine Egypt's mission,
expelling the Egyptians from Harar and from the Sudan. "It is well known,"
Mas'ad asserts, "that the Egyptians were forced out by the British not by
the Ethiopians. On the contrary, the Ethiopians remember that period with
favorable sentiments. It left them with good memories and served as the
basis for good relations" (p. 122). *Lij* Iyasu, writes Bulus Mas'ad, cooperated with the Ottomans and the Germans because he knew that Britain sought
to annex Ethiopia to its government of the Sudan.

On two issues Mas'ad expresses positive views toward Ethiopia. First,
he admires Haile Selassie, and spares no praise in depicting him as a modernizer, a man of diligence and insight, a great reformer and organizer, a
man of letters and humanistic approach, and a person who understood the
West (pp. 171–182). Second, he admires Ethiopia's military ability. The
Ethiopians had only a small modern standing army but they were able to
amass two million fighters when the need arose. Under a leader like Haile
Selassie, defending their country on their soil and with their patriotic zeal,
they were a formidable force (pp. 36–37).

It is apparent that when he wrote his book, finishing as the actual combat was in a very early stage, Mas'ad was uncertain of the outcome. He and many others in the Arab Middle East, as we shall see in the next chapter, admired Haile Selassie and what he represented as long as they thought Ethiopia could win the war.

When Bulus Mas'ad and Yusuf Ahmad were working on their manuscripts, the greater part of the Egyptian public was still sympathetic to Ethiopia. This was also true, as we shall see, in other Middle Eastern countries. Neither author had to worry about selling his book: the Italian legation in Cairo covered their expenses. Bulus Mas'ad (who rendered the legation various other services) also received source material and illustrations. The legation bought in advance 750 copies of his book out of the 2,000 published.[24] Yusuf Ahmad was subsidized even more handsomely. The Fascist propaganda machine covered the £E 75 for the proofreader and the printers and bought in advance half of the 4,000 copies printed. Both the authors and the Italians witnessed a wide distribution of their works in the entire Arab world. By Italian reports the first 1,000 copies of Yusuf Ahmad's book were sold or distributed in Egypt, Syria, Palestine, Lebanon, and Iraq in less than two weeks after publication.[25]

As the war progressed with sweeping Italian victories, *Islam in Ethiopia* by Yusuf Ahmad became immensely popular. The atmosphere in Egypt changed to such an extent that the Wafdist newspaper, *al-Balagh* (in Cairo) published chapters from the book in late 1935 and early 1936.[26] The Syrian paper, *al-Jazira,* published in Damascus,[27] and Cairo's *Ruz al-Yusuf* also reprinted parts of Ahmad's book. Very positive reviews were published in numerous newspapers, some of them of the highest reputation. In its January and February 1936 issues *al-Hilal,* the most respected Cairo monthly, published favorable reviews for both Ahmad Yusuf and Bulus Mas'ad. (As if to be on the safe side a no less favorable review of Jum'a's *The Ethiopian Lion* was published next to those.)[28]

Yusuf Ahmad quotes the anti-Ethiopian writings of the noted Islamic-Arab thinker and journalist, Shakib Arslan.[29] Arslan, the central figure of the next chapter, did his best to promote the book and the ideas of Yusuf Ahmad. In a review he published in the Egyptian newspaper *Kawkab al-Sharq,* on 23 February 1936, he praised Yusuf Ahmad for expressing the state of mind of the true courageous Muslim. Indeed, the ideas of Yusuf Ahmad and his book, which became a classic, would live through the era of pan-Arabism and would later be transmitted to the radical Muslims of today.[30]

PAN-ARABISM, ARSLAN,
AND CONQUERED ABYSSINIA

WHAT IS ETHIOPIA? AN ALL-REGIONAL PRESS DEBATE

Even more influential than books about Ethiopia were newspaper articles. Throughout 1935, thousands of articles dealing with the Abyssinian Crisis and with Ethiopia were published in the numerous dailies of Cairo, Alexandria, Jerusalem, Jaffa, Damascus, Aleppo, Beirut, and Baghdad.[1] Newspapers were the real political forums of the period. At that time, they were free to present extreme ideas and opinions and occasionally did so quite boldly. Enjoying full liberty of expression under British or French mandatory rule, politicians and thinkers often used newspaper columns as their popular outlet, their main connection to the emerging generation and to the wider masses. In the 1920s such articles could help them at the polls. In the mid-1930s, the discussion on Ethiopia, Mussolini, and on the British not only played a role in domestic political rivalries, it also became part of the preparations for future politics of a very different nature than heretofore.

The discussion of Ethiopia held in the Arabic press during this period was a unique show of curiosity and interest. No similar seminar by Arabs on that neighbor country has taken place since. The writers derived much of their information from European sources, but some also reread medieval Arabic literature or the new books discussed in the previous chapter. They were discovering their neighbor, a mysterious, ancient kingdom.

A variety of subjects were raised: Ethiopia's relations with Middle Eastern Islam from Muhammad to Lij Iyasu and the Ottomans; Ethiopia's treatment of local Muslims from Zar'a-Ya'qob's war against the Sultanate of Ifat to the conquests of Ahmad Gragn, and from Tewodros's and Yohannes's enforced Christianization of Muslims to Menelik's conquest of Harar and Haile Selassie's abolition of Jimma's autonomy in 1932–1934; and Ethiopian customs, culture, law, church, and Christianity. Much of the journalistic writings repeated the themes discussed more thoroughly in the current books already noted.

Of special interest, however, was the issue of slavery. It was a major theme of the Fascists and had also been emphasized by Bulus Mas'ad. Numerous anti-Ethiopian articles echoing or copying Italian and other European propaganda pieces condemned Ethiopia as practicing slavery.[2] They never mentioned the fact that it was Muslim Middle Easterners who had traded in *habashi* slaves for centuries and that Islam encouraged the existence of slavery in both principle and practice. Indeed, the anti-Ethiopian line was a blend of ideas typical of the period. It was based on the history of Islam but was now aimed at a generation motivated by the modern concepts of Arab nationalism.

Opinions in the press were polarized. At one end of the spectrum stood those who sought to exploit the international situation in order to force the British (in Egypt, Palestine, and Iraq) and the French (in Syria and Lebanon) into a more generous dialogue. These leaders and personalities were inclined to see Ethiopia in favorable terms. Many of these wrote of Ethiopia as an Oriental sister, Semitic by virtue of ethnicity and language, Eastern by virtue of its Coptic Church, and even Islamic by virtue of the religion of half of its population. Their concept of Ethiopia was generally in line with Jum'a's *African Lion:* a close neighbor that was able to maintain its independence, and, hence, a source of Oriental pride. They admired the country's ability to mobilize military power and face Europe with dignity. We have already seen the Wafdists, and the more liberal-parliamentarianist circles in Egypt that adopted that attitude. In journalism it was the leading newspaper of the country, *Al-Ahram,* that advocated the clearer pro-Ethiopian line. *Al-Ahram* sent a special correspondent to Ethiopia, who stayed in Addis Ababa until the Italian occupation (in May 1936) and sent many pro-Ethiopian dispatches to his newspaper, including interviews enabling the emperor to appeal directly to the Egyptian public.[3]

Similar articles appeared in other Arab countries, written by members of the political establishments that had emerged in the nonviolent parliamentarian 1920s. Among Palestinian Arabs, the pro-Ethiopian side was adopted by the moderately British-oriented wing, the so-called Nashashibis. Their attitude was clearly expressed by their Jaffa-based newspaper, *Filastin:* "The Muslims always remember Abyssinian favor with early Islam, the same as they remember the Fascists' recent atrocities against their fellow Muslims in Libya. The Arabs support Ethiopia because of Oriental solidarity and historical love."[4]

A "Friends of Ethiopia Association" was active in Jerusalem. According to *Filastin* of 31 October 1935, it held a symposium on Ethiopian history with a main lecture on the Ethiopian victory over the Italians at Adwa in 1896.

A number of politicians in Syria and their newspapers expressed sympathy for Ethiopia. A leading newspaper in that respect was *Al-Qabas* of Damascus (which, for example, published a favorable biographical piece on Haile Selassie on 13 February 1936). The most persistent pro-Ethiopian of the Syrians, however, was the exiled nationalist hero, doctor, and leader of the 1925 anti-French revolt, 'Abd al-Rahman Shahbandar. Based in Cairo (and pinning his hopes for Syrian liberation from France on the British) Shahbandar wrote:

> I shall not hesitate to sacrifice myself for Ethiopia in 1935 the same as I was not hesitant to do so for Syria in 1925. I do not hesitate to stand by Ethiopia and identify with her, for indeed the highest obligation for freedom and liberation commands us to do so. If we do not have the chance to fight for the freedom of our own country, at least we have to do so for others. And especially in the region neighboring us, with which we have so many historical and political ties. We are proud to see that we stand for freedom, and that our brothers in the Arab world pursue a noble line with regard to Ethiopia.[5]

As noted earlier, Shahbandar had been active in the sending of medical missions from Egypt to the Ethiopian army.

The Iraqi public and press was somewhat less involved than were the Egyptians, the Syrians, and Palestinian Arabs. Iraq was not a Mediterranean entity and her anti-British totalitarian spirit was oriented more toward Germany than toward Italy. It was mainly members of the non-Muslim minorities who raised the Ethiopian issue. The Christian Razuq Shammas, one of Iraq's leading journalists, was persistent in condemning the Fascists as barbarians and in declaring that "all the Oriental people regard Ethiopia as their sister who is brutalized and with whom they identify."[6] The Jewish Iraqi poet, Anwar Shawul, followed the same line in his Baghdad literary weekly, *Al-Hasid*. He composed a poem dedicated to an imaginary Ethiopian Joan of Arc leading four hundred Ethiopian girls in battle against the invaders:

> The feelings and hopes in my poem
> are dedicated to you, descendant of Menelik.
>
> They stem from Iraq, land of the light,
> land of the two rivers, Mesopotamia,
> which respects men and honor.
>
> Oh you Virgin of Ethiopia, you fight for justice
> when evil-doers try to extinguish freedom.
> They will not succeed as long as in one country
> there are still those who sacrifice their lives
> for their motherland.[7]

In addition to modern nationalists and politicians who cooperated with the British and French, there were Islamic thinkers of the older generation who identified with Ethiopia. We have already noted the most prominent among them, the Cairene *Shaikh* Muhammad Rashid Rida, the leader of the Salafiyya movement and the greatest promoter of Islamic modernism in that period. Rida, as noted, was the spiritual father of the Young Men's Muslim Association that was behind many of the activities of the Committee for the Defense of Ethiopian Independence. Rida was ready to exploit the opportunity in order to promote Islam in Ethiopia by sending books and *'ulama*. He had corresponded with King Ibn Sa'ud of Saudi Arabia, seeking to establish in Mecca a center to coordinate his plans. On the subject of politics he was quite clear: "As for the Italo-Ethiopian conflict, all people of the East and surely the Muslims have to side with Ethiopia. It is inconceivable that any of them will side with the imperialists. Even if the Muslims in Ethiopia were deprived of their rights it does not follow that Italian conquest is preferable. . . . We must avoid any support for the Italians and any humiliation for Ethiopia, or her smearing."[8]

The group in the Arab Middle East that stood ready to smear Ethiopia consisted generally of the elements that were frustrated by the liberal experiment of the 1920s. Parliamentarianism, after all, failed to address the region's deepening socioeconomic problems and had brought no national salvation. Indeed, the British and the French were not ready, at that time, to loosen their grasps and grant full political autonomy. With the growing economic, cultural, and international crisis many despaired of the hopelessness of the continuing dialogue between their parliamentarian leaders and the Western occupiers. New social forces, spearheaded by the educated youth, who yearned for immediate solutions and strong political leadership, were exerting growing pressure on the established politicians.

Mussolini's propaganda was falling on attentive ears. Islam was now politically reintroduced in a renewed, militant manner. Pan-Arabism presented itself in a new form, carrying the promise of unity and strength achieved through struggle. Mussolini appealed to them both, depicting his Ethiopian campaign as a war against the barbarian entity that had oppressed Islam as well as against the liberal imperialists who also had oppressed Arabism.

The man who played a central role in transmitting Mussolini's anti-Ethiopian propaganda into the rising anti-parliamentarian tide was the Lebanese Druze, *Amir* Shakib Arslan (1869–1946).[9] Based in Geneva, Arslan was one of the most important figures in Islamic-Arab history during the interwar period. A prolific author and journalist, he gained the epithet of the *mujahid* (the holy warrior) for being an ardent fighter for Islamic political revival and for the joining of Islamic unity with modern Arabism. He did not advocate a secular liberal Arab nationalism that had animated the nonviolent dialogue in each separate Arab country with the British and the French, but rather an all-regional spirit of revolt. The Islamic-Arab region for him included, as well, North Africa and the Horn.

Arslan had begun corresponding with Ethiopian Muslims in the late 1920s. In 1928 he wrote to *Ras* Tafari, the future Haile Selassie, calling upon him to improve their situation, but he received no reply.[10] However, his views of Ethiopia and of its relations with Islam before the Abyssinian Crisis were far from being totally negative. In 1933 he published a very long article, "The Muslims of Ethiopia." In forty-one pages of historical survey,[11] from the Prophet to *Lij* Iyasu, there is nothing to suggest the illegitimacy of Ethiopia or that Muslims suffered there. Tewodros and Yohannes are both mentioned briefly as acting against Islam, but the wording is very mild, and their actions are placed in a context of their fear of Egyptian aggression. The Ethiopia he presented in his 1933 article is a mixed Christian-Islamic entity in which, although it witnessed some religious tension over the centuries, its Muslims were not always in the most difficult situation. The majority of the piece is a long historical overview, with quotations from the description of the epic of Ahmad *Gragn,* 'Arab Faqih's *Futuh al-Habasha,* leaving the reader with the impression that Islam did have its share of victories and honor in Ethiopian history.

In 1930–1932, when the Fascists had brutally quelled the Sanusiyya movement in Libya, Arslan raised his voice against Mussolini, whom he otherwise admired. During that period, Arslan was particularly concerned with North African affairs: He supported the anti-French Moroccan, 'Abd al-Karim al-Khattabi (whom he considered the greatest warrior of the period for Islam and Arabism).[12] A generation later, 'Abd al-Karim al-Khattabi would go to Cairo to become a mentor to young Muslim students from Eritrea and to teach them the Arab North African experience with the politics of liberation fronts.

It was only in 1934 when Mussolini began appeasing Islam in Libya in preparation for his propaganda campaign in the eastern Mediterranean that Arslan changed his line and turned against Ethiopia. In October 1934 Arslan returned from a tour in Eritrea and published an article in his edited French-language journal, *La Nation Arabe* (published in Geneva), which was full of praise for Italian treatment of Islam in that colony. In January 1935 he published another article in the same journal warning Ethiopia that it should restore autonomy to Jimma and should grant autonomy to Harar or face destruction.[13] Around mid-February 1935 he was summoned to Mussolini's office. He presented *Il Duce* with three memoranda: on Palestine, Syria, and Libya. According to Arslan, the Italian leader promised him that he would support the Arabs and the Muslims and would do his best to prevent the British and the Zionists from evicting the Palestinian Arabs from their land. A few days later, on 20 February 1935, he wrote to his closest ally, the *grand mufti* of Jerusalem and the leader of Palestinian militancy, Hajj Amin al-Husayni:

I do not know if Ihsan al-Jabiri [Arslan's associate] told you about all that was agreed between me and the Italian government concerning what both of us had discussed together in Mecca, and what we had agreed upon in Jerusalem. Now I want to tell you that following the last meeting I had with Mussolini himself, my conscience is clean. I am sure Italy would treat us differently than the British and the French. If you send Jamal al-Husayni here I shall confide through him things I should not put in writing.

In any case, it was agreed to start at once a propaganda campaign in support of Italy. Mussolini said he was afraid of a world war, and that if we fail to start paving the ground right away, we shall not be able to exploit the opportunity. In my opinion we have to exploit the crisis between Italy and Abyssinia and begin emphasizing the Abyssinians' bad attitude towards Muslims. It is possible that the Italian Propaganda Ministry would provide our journals with relevant material. I gave them the addresses of *Al-Jami'a al-'Arabiyya* and *Al-Wahda*. . . . I wrote to Riyyad al-Sulh [a Lebanese Muslim and an associate of Arslan] that he would see to that matter in Syria, and asking him to meet with you so that you may give him the proper instructions.[14]

Soon afterwards, Arslan published the first of many articles on Ethiopia in Arabic for consumption in the Middle East. It appeared in *Al-Jami'a al-'Arabiyya* of 4 March 1935, one of the newspapers under the Palestinian *Grand Mufti*. In it, he wrote:

All those who would like to defend Ethiopia have first to read about its history and particularly regarding the Muslims living there and what they received from the Ethiopians. They will see that apart from the Muslims of Spain no other Muslim people has suffered over the centuries such atrocities as the Muslims of Ethiopia. We do not even talk about maltreatment in the early ages, of which we have historical records. We talk about events that took place in the not too distant past. It is enough to refer to what happened sixty to seventy years ago, in the time of Emperor Yohannes, and mention the number of means he used against the Muslims that were forced to become Christians.

The rest of the article was in the same spirit, claiming that six million Muslims were then living in Ethiopia, deprived of their rights, barred from access to governmental posts, and living in conditions worse than under European imperialism. Italy, he wrote, was the true friend of the Arabs and Islam. He was not justifying Ethiopia's occupation by Italy, but, he asked: "Are we so strong and secure as to forget our own needs and give our attention and aid to the land of the *najashi?* . . . We should not alienate such a power as Italy just for the beautiful eyes of a certain people who for years do nothing but oppress the Muslims who live on the same land."

In one of his articles published in *Al-Ayyam* of Damascus[15] Arslan attacked the entire generation of the 1920s in the Arab world, blaming them for their lack of solidarity. He enumerated instances in which Muslims and Arabs did or said nothing when fellow Muslim Arabs in other countries were attacked by imperialism. "And now, Palestine is about to fall to the Jews and I see no Muslims in the entire world do anything comparable to their interest and sympathy to Ethiopia. . . . Now Britain is about to declare war on Italy while she herself is in control of Egypt, Palestine, Iraq and Transjordan, countries which are far superior in culture to Ethiopia. . . . How many Islamic countries fell in British hands and nobody protested like now when it comes to Ethiopia. . . ."

Throughout 1935, Arslan wrote dozens of such articles, publishing them in Egypt, Palestine, Syria, and Lebanon. The major newspapers were forums for an Arab intrastate debate. Arslan began broadcasting in Arabic on the popular Italian Radio Bari. In September he organized a congress of orientalists, in Geneva, attended by some seventy scholars and politicians in which Italy was praised as the true ally of Islam and Arabism.[16]

The entire controversy concerning Ethiopia came to revolve around Arslan. Although widely praised, he was also attacked in many quarters. *Shaikh* Fahmi, for example, wrote in *Al-Jihad* of Aleppo: "The *amir* is wrong . . . all Muslims should support Ethiopia. . . . In preaching to the contrary, he ruins his lifetime contribution of twenty years' effort for Islam and Arabism. I regret to see us losing for that reason one of Islam's greatest leaders."[17] Salim Khayyata, a Lebanese author of a book on Ethiopia that was published in Beirut in 1936, mocked Arslan: "And if someone challenges the Arabs asking: But how can you explain that your spokesman on Ethiopia is a certain *amir* from Lebanon? You answer to him: There are in Lebanon ten thousand *amir*s of that type. If Mussolini represents Italy while he leads to its destruction, so is Shakib Arslan representing the Arabs as he trades in them."[18]

Arslan's articles reached Ethiopia where they made a significant impact. In the Amharic *Berhanena Selam* of 30 May 1935, the leader of the country's Muslim community, Muhammad Sadiq (a relative of Menelik's and Iyasu's *ra'is al-Muslimin*, 'Abdallah Sadiq) wrote:

> Some Arab journalists wrote about Ethiopia's need for help. But others, those who understand nothing about this country . . . say that Muslims are discriminated against. . . . Mussolini's men want to separate the Muslims and Ethiopia. My people, let us not fall into this trap. Let us prove that we are the same nation. Let us forget the old saying "Skies have no pillars, Muslims have no land." It is no longer the case that in Ethiopia people are selected for governmental posts by their religion. This is my message to anyone who wants to see Ethiopia free.

The most important figure to publicly dispute Arslan was his lifetime associate *Shaikh* Rashid Rida. Rida was against violence and he regretted Arslan's attack on Ethiopia. In an exchange of letters he admonished Arslan for supporting Mussolini and defaming Ethiopia.[19] Rida died in August 1935, but Arslan did not follow his advice. In January 1936 he published in *Al-Ayyam* of Damascus his last letter to Rida. He also quoted from Yusuf Ahmad's book, which had appeared two months earlier in November 1935 (and to which he had himself contributed).

> What do we remember about Ethiopia? That she ruined the seven flourishing Islamic emirates, the last one, Jimma, was ended by Haile Selassie only a year ago. The mass Christianization of 1880 by Yohannes. The destruction of mosques. If God had not punished Yohannes by sending the Muslims of the Sudan to finish him off, the whole Islamic community of Ethiopia would be Christian today. When did we ever see Ethiopia doing anything for Egypt, Syria, or Palestine? For ten years she has been a member of the League of Nations; has she done anything for us?[20]

The mentioning by Arslan of the Mahdiyya in the Ethiopian context as the messengers of God and doers of Islamic justice is significant. As remembered, the late nineteenth-century Sudanese militant Muslims wavered between the two basic approaches of Islam to Ethiopia. When Ethiopia was exposed as weak, they interpreted the historical past as justifying a *jihadi* approach. Ethiopia's weakness in facing the Fascists was soon to have a similar impact.

Arslan was not alone in his views. His ideas as well as those of Yusuf Ahmad were echoed in numerous articles. Newspapers such as *Al-Waqit* of Aleppo, *Al-Bilad* of Beirut, and *Al-Jami'a al-'Arabiyya* of Jerusalem were examples. The Palestinian-Islamic leader, *Hajj* Amin al-Husayni, helped Arslan, although he himself was careful not to be provoked into writing anti-British diatribes.[21] In Iraq, it was the journalist Yunis al-Bahri, through his newspaper, *Al-'Uqab,* who spread anti-Ethiopian propaganda, and in Damascus it was mainly the newspaper, *Al-Jazira.* The editor of *Al-Jazira,* Muhammad Zabiyan al-Kaylani, was particularly active in portraying Ethiopia as backward and anti-Islamic. He fully supported Arslan and, in the fullness of time, the two would together celebrate the fall of Haile Selassie.

HAILE SELASSIE'S IMAGE AND
THE OUTCOME OF THE DEBATE

The public discussion of the figure of Haile Selassie reflected the Ethiopian issue in its earlier stages, later development, and conclusion. His story can be divided roughly into two stages. The first one began in early 1935 and continued until approximately March 1936, when it became clear that Ethiopia was on the verge of defeat. Until then, Haile Selassie was widely regarded with respect. Some even considered him a hero. Throughout this period, only Shakib Arslan dared to criticize Haile Selassie as a person. In this he was persistent, referring to the emperor by his old name, *Ras* Tafari, and describing him as an illegitimate, arrogant, and unjust ruler. Tafari, argued Arslan, deserved no justice, for he himself, in addition to his other sins, had put an end to the last area of Islamic autonomy in Ethiopia, that of Abba Jifar's Jimma. Arab and Muslim solidarity should be solely with their own peoples and countries, he argued, and not with the vainglorious king of a primitive country.[22]

For the great majority of the writers, however, Haile Selassie was still a hero. In the daily *Al-Ayyam* of Damascus, for example, 'Abd al-Salam al-Jaza'iri attacked Arslan for confusing the public and attributing the anti-Muslim policy of Emperor Yohannes IV to Haile Selassie. "What the Abyssinians did sixty to seventy years ago, if they did it at all, is nothing in comparison to what the Italians did in Tripoli (Libya) six to seven years ago."[23] "Haile Selassie," wrote the Egyptian daily, *Al-Balagh,*[24] "is a progressive, enlightened ruler who works days and nights for his country." The Cairene newspaper *Akhir Sa'a* published "an open letter to his Imperial Majesty Haile Selassie, Emperor of Ethiopia and friend of the Egyptian people. . . . The Nile has united our two countries for thousands of years. Brutal imperialism tries to separate us. . . . We should have sent you half a million Egyptians to fight the Italian fascist aggressors. . . . May God help you blacken with shame the faces of the descendants of Nero, and whiten the faces of the people of Ethiopia."[25]

The *Al-Ahram* correspondent in Addis Ababa praised Haile Selassie's progressive policies, including his enlightened approach to Ethiopian Muslims,[26] and *The Egyptian Gazette*[27] spared no superlatives in describing the Ethiopian emperor as "the builder of modern Ethiopia, a successful reformer, a genius, a phenomenon, a leader and a brain far greater than any other Ethiopian of the time. . . ." The paper concluded: "If war is to occur, he will no doubt lead a united people, and fight for what the whole world recognizes as a just cause." In one other example, printed on 4 November 1935, a month after the commencement of hostilities, *Al-Ayyam* of Damascus still wrote with admiration: "Haile Selassie will win. In any case he will prefer to die rather than to surrender." Four days later *Al-Ayyam* published a fictitious letter by Haile Selassie, in which the emperor explained to the Syrian people how the Fascists distorted the truth about his country, aiming to subjugate their country. *Alif-Ba* of Damascus published "a letter by the Syrian youth to Haile Selassie" expressing sympathy and support for "Ethiopia, our Oriental neighbor."[28]

However, as the war continued and it became clear that the Italians were on the road to victory, such expressions of sympathy and identification with Ethiopia dwindled and then ceased altogether. In March 1936, with Ethiopia's defeat nearly a *fait accompli,* the Arab press portrayed Haile Selassie as a naive victim. Articles published in the Syrian and Lebanese press were still merciful, and compared him to the Hashemite King Husayn of the Hijaz and to his son, later to become King Faysal of

Iraq.[29] The Arab consensus was that both kings were deceived by the British during World War I and in its aftermath. Both went to war with a British promise, were deserted by perfidious Albion, and ended in exile. Haile Selassie, according to their analysis, was equally naive to drag his people into a hopeless war based on his own belief in the word of the British.

In May 1936, following Haile Selassie's flight from Ethiopia, he was viewed as a vanquished loser and a fainthearted traitor. *Al-Taqaddum* of Aleppo compared him to Emperor Tewodros and called him a coward.[30] *Al-Jazira* of Damascus wrote that he deserved his fate, for he had deposed *Lij* Iyasu, the legitimate Muslim successor of Menelik II.[31] *Al-Waqit* of Aleppo put the entire blame for the demise of Ethiopia on the shoulders of Haile Selassie, calling him the usurper, the tyrant, the oppressor of Islam.[32] *Al-Jazira* went so far as to blame the British for saving Haile Selassie's skin by enabling him to flee.[33]

In July 1936 many Middle Eastern Arab newspapers (for example, *Al-Waqit,* July 9; *Fattah al-'Arab,* July 19) repeated Italian propaganda to the effect that the ex-emperor was a mere thief, fleeing from his country with its stolen treasury. Only a few articles (for example, *Al-Qabas,* 18 May 1936) expressed disbelief in such allegations and still defended the Ethiopian emperor's honor.

After fleeing from Addis Ababa to Djibouti, the emperor sailed to Haifa and then went by train to Jerusalem. The British-controlled "Voice of Jerusalem" tried to turn his appearance into an anti-Fascist occasion. This move was to no avail: The Arab world was no longer interested. It was, in fact, becoming a new Middle East, and a different one from that of 1935. A violent anti-British, anti-French spirit was sweeping through the whole region. Anti-British riots had begun in Egypt on 13 November 1935. They were spearheaded by students and led to the emergence in January 1936 of youth organizations that imitated the Fascists. One of them, the Blue Shirts, was a branch of the Wafd Party, which had been the guardian of parliamentarianism. In December 1935 similar anti-French riots erupted in Damascus, and in April 1936 Arab-Palestinian revolt began.[34] Baghdad was also about to erupt, and disturbances began there later in the summer, leading to the first modern officers' coup, the Bakr Sidqi coup of October of that year.[35]

For all intents and purposes, 1936 witnessed the demise of the "liberal age" in the Arab Middle East. The Abyssinian Crisis was undoubtedly one of the main causes of that fundamental change in Arab politics. It coincided with momentous local developments in social, economic, and cultural spheres that had been long preparing for the upheaval that was triggered in the aftermath of the crisis. The fall of Ethiopia and the subsequent erosion of British and French prestige was another factor that defeated parliamentarianism and its methods; it thus contributed to the emergence of pan-Arabism and Islamic radicalism.

THE LAST WORD TO ARSLAN:
ARABISM AND ETHIOPIA'S ILLEGITIMACY

In these formative years of modern Arab and pan-Arab nationalism, Ethiopia was viewed by the Arab press as both an Oriental sister and as a mysterious, distant African country. An independent, valiant Ethiopia was a source of great pride to the Eastern self-image but Ethiopia as the oppressor of Islam was also viewed as a backward and unjust Christian monarchy.

For the new generation of Arabs who wavered nervously during 1935 and 1936 between these contradictory perspectives, the most important facts were that Ethiopia was suddenly exposed as weak and defeated and that the Italian occupiers practically abolished Ethiopia, and began preparing the ground for turning the Horn into an Islamic-Arab extension of the Middle East.

Haile Selassie had failed in his prewar attempt to mobilize help from the Arabs. He had thought of urging the Egyptians to block the Suez Canal, of encouraging the Sanussis' revolt against the Italians in Libya, and, more realistically, to persuade the Saudis and the Yemenites to refrain from selling camels and food to the Fascists.[36] But although nothing of substance came of his diplomatic missions, there were some signs of sympathy and help. We have already noted that the Egyptians sent medical missions. Thousands of volunteers registered in Egypt to help Ethiopia, but in the end it was only some one hundred and fifty Ethiopians residing in Egypt and Palestine who, with the help of the Egyptian Committee for the Defense of Ethiopia, traveled to the battlefields. Two former Ottoman officers of Arab origin also came to distinguish themselves in the fighting and to symbolize the solidarity with Ethiopia. One was General Wahib *Pasha,* a prominent officer in the Turkish army during World War I, who acted as General Nasibu's chief adviser in the Ogaden front.[37] The other was his old friend, the dark-skinned Sudanese, General Muhammad Tariq Bey, nicknamed *al-Ifriqi* (the African).

Al-Ifriqi gave several newspaper interviews[38] and wrote a book, *My Memories of the Italo-Ethiopian War, 1935–1936,* published in Damascus in 1937,[39] which reflect the transformation from the initial respect for Ethiopia to pity. In the early chapters of his book Tariq describes how he thought it was his duty to defend Ethiopia, the only African country able to retain independence, and how he traveled to Addis Ababa, the capital built by Menelik, the victor over the Italians and the "Bismarck of Ethiopia" (p. 16). He then met with Haile Selassie who, he wrote, was no less a man of skill and knowledge than any European leader. He quotes the emperor telling him: "I have confidence in the sympathy of the noble Arab nation toward Ethiopia, since between the Arabs and the Ethiopians there exists a historical bond of friendship from the very beginning, from the days of Muhammad. I believe and hope that the help the Arabs render us, and especially the Egyptians, will hoist the flag of civilization in the Near East" (pp. 14–15).

The Ethiopians, Tariq wrote, are truly brave, do not fear death, and can sustain all difficulties. But they cannot face warfare in the modern world. Their bravery is outdated. Their psychology is irrelevant. It is the era of technology and they have nothing of it (p. 112). And, he summarized his ultimate conclusion: "We have to understand that the only justice is power and power is the only justice" (pp. 4–5).

Ethiopia's defeat was analyzed in many articles as the ultimate proof of its backwardness and sins.[40] The policies of the Italian occupiers added to the Arab impression of Ethiopia as an entity of little legitimacy. The Italians all but abolished Ethiopia, divided the territory along religious and ethnic lines, and worked for the spread of Arabic, declaring it the official language of the Muslim-populated regions of eastern Ethiopia. (Earlier they had adopted the same policies in Eritrea.) The new Fascist rulers in Addis Ababa encouraged Islam in the whole Horn by building mosques, implementing the *shari'a* (Islamic law), and by subsidizing other Islamic institutions. They sought to repoliticize Islam and Arabize it in order to make their "Italian Oriental Africa" part of their Oriental Mediterranean dream. As summarized by Alberto Sbacchi, the Italian goals in Ethiopia were as follows:

> Italian interests in the Muslims of Ethiopia had international repercussions. Favorable treatment of the Muslims in East Africa made a good impression in the Middle East and in the Islamic countries in favor of Italy and it enhanced its claim to be the protector of the Arabic-speaking nations with a view to becoming the leader of the Muslim world. . . . Close relations with Arab states were maintained by means of cultural activities, health missions, official visits, trade, radio and newspaper propaganda. Besides the yearly pilgrimage of Ethiopian Muslims to Mecca, there were also special visits of Muslim chiefs to Egypt and Arabia to advertise the good treatment of Ethiopian Muslims by the Italians. . . . Mussolini was anxious to expand trade and commercial relations with the countries across the Red Sea. . . . Plans were made for a center of Islamic propaganda in Massawa, whose Arab elite had strong family, economic and cultural ties with the other side of the Red Sea. The political courting of the Arab countries paid its dividends during the Second World War. . . . While the Italian rule lasted, the Muslims dreamed of making Ethiopia Muslim and the Italians hoped to become a Muslim power.[41]

The fall of Ethiopia and the ensuing declarations of Italian Islamic policy in Italian Oriental Africa created a wave of enthusiasm in the Arabic

Middle Eastern press. The first thrill was caused by the rumor that the occupiers were about to install a son of *Lij* Iyasu on the Ethiopian throne. The name mentioned was of Menelik, a son of a former Arab wife of Iyasu, Fatima Abu Bakr, who lived in Djibouti. But the idea that a Muslim Menelik III—an Islamic *najashi,* after all—would rule in Addis Ababa was short lived.[42] The Italians did not seek to foster Ethiopian imperial continuity.

More substantial was the news about the declaration of Arabic as the official language, substituting Amharic in non-Christian areas, and that Harar was to be revived as an Islamic scholarly center. The appearance of Arabic newspapers in these regions, and most notably in Addis Ababa itself, the building of mosques, including the promise to build the long-awaited grand mosque of Addis Ababa, were all celebrated in dozens of articles, even in Egyptian newspapers that had been identified with the pluralism of the 1920s. *Al-Siyasa* of Cairo said on 9 September 1936: "The victory of Italy over Ethiopia is God's punishment of Ethiopia for maltreating Islam. God never fails to settle with the sinners and He sent the Italians to end centuries of crimes against Islam. The emperor fell like Iyasu had fallen. Those who oppressed Islam got what they deserved."

The *Al-Ahram* correspondent in Addis Ababa, who had been an enthusiastic supporter of Haile Selassie, turned into an admirer of Graziani, the new ruler. He sent to Cairo a long report praising the Fascists for restoring Islam and Arabism.[43] The liberated Muslims of Ethiopia, the press in Palestine and Syria reported, were interested in the struggle for the liberation of Palestine (the Arab revolt in Palestine, it will be remembered, had begun in April 1936). One of their missions was said to have been sent to Jerusalem to express solidarity "with their Arab brothers in Palestine."[44] The editor of the Damascene daily, *Al-Jazira,* was especially forceful in connecting the victory of Islam and Arabism in Ethiopia to the Palestinian issue:

> In Palestine the British expel Arabs to make room for the Jews. . . . In Ethiopia the Italians did the opposite. There, a government that had oppressed the Muslims was toppled. It was an uncivilized government of the kind that had deserved no existence in medieval primitive times, let alone in the twentieth century. The Ethiopians are a people which never knew enlightened government, yet they were spared the yoke of foreign rule, while the Arabs were conquered.[45]

The editor of *Al-Jazira,* Muhammad Tayasir Zabiyan al-Kaylani, wrote vividly of the new image of Ethiopia. In October 1937 he published a book in Damascus, *Muslim Ethiopia: My Experiences in the Lands of Islam.*[46] It is based on his tour of the new Horn of Africa under the Fascists. The text begins as a series of conversations with various Muslims who testified to the deprivation—economic, social, and cultural—they had suffered in the now defunct empire of Ethiopia. The second part of the book consists of descriptions of the situation under the Italians. It culminates in the author's visit to Harar, now no longer a Christian Ethiopian town but a lively and flourishing center of Islamic life and Arab studies. This new Arab-Islamic freedom in a Muslim Ethiopia was achieved because of the benevolence of Fascism and the Fascists. When the author describes the interview he had in Addis Ababa with Graziani (pp. 39–45), Zabiyan cannot conceal his admiration for the determined general. Neither does he hide his gratitude for the restoration of Islam, the building of mosques, the spread of Arabic, the implementation of *shari'a,* and the whole administrative reconstruction of the Horn. All these developments occurred under Graziani, who himself spoke Arabic from his days in Libya. Zabiyan extensively quotes Graziani, a man who systematically massacred the Sanussis and other Libyans, as presenting himself as the born friend of Islam and Arabism. Indeed, Zabiyan returned to Syria via Libya where he interviewed Mussolini himself. He quotes Mussolini: "We granted the Muslims of Ethiopia full religious freedom, we made Arabic the official language, built mosques all over, and replaced non-Muslim functionaries in the Muslim-inhabited regions with Muslims. For that we have received the gratitude of the Muslims" (p. 15).

Another theme in the book is the author's admiration for Shakib Arslan. For Zabiyan, he was the true hero of the Abyssinian war. To Zabiyan, Arslan was the man who, from the start, had foreseen where history was going—he was right about Ethiopia and about the Italians. There were times, writes Zabiyan, when Arslan stood alone against all those who were misled in thinking that in the name of humanity Ethiopia had to be supported. "We were then sorry to see that except for Arslan nobody stood up to tell the truth. . . . The Ethiopians destroyed six million Muslims by forced Christianization and enslavement . . . their government was much worse than imperialism and more awful than occupation . . ." (p. 12).

Arslan himself wrote the preface to Zabiyan's book. In October 1937 Arslan seemed to be in a position to celebrate his victory. He did it by combining the fall of Ethiopia with the hope for a triumph for Arabism. He said he had never supported the strong against the weak but had believed in persuading the Muslims and the Arabs that Britain and Ethiopia, not Italy, was their enemy:

> How can Britain blame Italy for her doings in Ethiopia when she is ten times more wrong? She kills the Arabs in Palestine in their homes in front of their women, and this is just because they are not ready to abandon their homes and leave them for the Jews. The Arab nation has been the owner of Palestine for fourteen centuries and the British want to wipe it out in order to establish an English-Jewish state. They have no right whatsoever to say anything about the Italians in Ethiopia.
>
> The blind Muslims who fell for British propaganda forgot what the Ethiopians had done to the Muslims in their country and in neighboring

countries. What indescribable atrocities, generation after generation, what enslavement, land confiscations, and forced Christianization! What primitive and hostile destruction inflicted on the seven Islamic emirates, what enslavement of Muslims who had been sovereign in their country! In the name of the Lord, it was strange to see Muslims still having pity on Ethiopia after all that. . . . Oh you Muslims who blame Italy for occupying Ethiopia, would you not remember Jimma, . . . Harar, . . . the tens of thousands of slaves, the majority of them Muslims, and that Tafari himself [Arslan refused to call him Haile Selassie] personally owned one thousand of them? Would you not remember Yohannes . . . ?

Two years ago the distinguished author Yusuf Ahmad wrote a book based on Arabic and European sources and documented all that. And now the distinguished author Tayasir Zabiyan al-Kaylani of Damascus went himself to Ethiopia and confirmed all we knew. You should all read it so that you will know the truth. (pp. 4–7)

Zabiyan's book vividly describes Arslan's final triumph in the 1935–1936 struggle over the proper image of Ethiopia. It also illustrates how Ethiopian concepts of radical Islam were transmitted to the emerging militant Arabists. Zabiyan declared that Islam was the only way to save humanity, but in Islam the Arabs formed a distinct nation. They were the pioneers of Islam in the Arab Peninsula (thus he called his newspaper *Al-Jazira* [the peninsula]) since they were destined to be its future leaders. Without mentioning him by name, he repeats the ideas of 'Abd al-Rahman al-Kawakibi, the pioneer proponent of Arab nationalism of the early twentieth century. Kawakibi's book, *'Umm al-Qura* (Mecca), considered the first expression of modern Arab identity, concerns a meeting of Muslims in Mecca. They complain about the weakness of Islam until one of them suggests that the Arabs should resume their initial leadership. Zabiyan tells a similar story (pp. 10–11). He had read about Ethiopia in Arslan's articles, but his active interest was aroused when he visited Mecca. There, in the holy city, just after the fall of Ethiopia, there was a gathering of Muslims from Ethiopia, Eritrea, and Somalia for the *hajj*. They told him at length about the plight of Ethiopia's Muslims. It was then and there that he decided to go to Ethiopia to see things for himself. Although he does not say so in so many words, the implication for Ethiopia's Muslims is the victory of Arabism. This was the essence of Arslan's message.

10

NASSER, HAILE SELASSIE, AND THE ERITREA PROBLEM

In May 1941 Haile Selassie, helped by the British, returned to his throne. He initiated an effective process of political centralization and, in 1943, he quelled the only serious challenge to his authority at home, the Woyane revolt in Tigre. He then proceeded to expel British advisers (accomplished in 1944) and to expand his empire. He managed to regain Somali-inhabited territories (the Ogaden, 1948, and the Haud, 1954) that Mussolini had annexed to Somalia but failed to incorporate Somalia in his envisioned Greater Ethiopia.[1]

Far more important, however, was his effort to reclaim Eritrea. The future of that colony, which the Italians had occupied in the late 1880s, became a very complex international issue. Finally, in December 1950 the United Nations decided to federate an autonomous Eritrea with Ethiopia under the sovereignty of the Imperial Crown.

The Middle Eastern Ethiopia agenda was reestablished in the 1950s. The countries of the Middle East regained their independence and began to pursue regional strategies. Their individual foreign policies became involved with Ethiopia and Eritrea. We have discussed Islamic concepts of Ethiopian history from Muhammad to Iyasu. There was, as mentioned, a tension between the orthodox approach toward Ethiopia's legitimacy and the rival version supporting *jihad,* but there was little argument on the question of Ethiopia's border. Islam was not concerned about drawing international boundaries and Ethiopia was abstractly and generally recognized as a non-Islamic entity lying south of Egypt and east of the Nile. (The Ottomans, for example, had no problem in identifying the Massawa coast and the hinterland, today's Eritrea, as their "Province of Habesh." Most Islamic writers discussed the Muslims in the whole area as the "Muslims of Abyssinia.")

However, in the modern Middle East, itself a region demarcated now by Western-conceived and Western-created international boundaries, this could no longer be the case. Furthermore, the modern concept of Arab nationalism, taking the place of universal Islam, necessitated a territorial definition and the drawing of national-political maps. We have seen that

Arabism burst into Middle Eastern politics in the mid-1930s. We saw the role of Ethiopian affairs in the important events of early pan-Arabist history. We also discussed the simultaneous early tentative conceptualization of the Muslims in Ethiopia and in Eritrea as Arabs.

In the aftermath of World War II, particularly from the mid-1950s to the late 1960s, pan-Arabism became the hegemonic all-regional ideology. What were the international boundaries of the revolutionary all-regional Arab nation? Was Eritrea a part of it? Was the rebellion there against Ethiopia's government a part of the all-Arab struggle for unity? Or was it a matter of strategic concern to the Middle East but not an issue of Arab identity? The discussion of the Arabism of Eritrea in these years was not as central as had been the discussion of Ethiopia in the days of Shakib Arslan and Rashid Rida—there were too many other more pressing issues on the region's agenda—but since the Middle East became directly relevant to Ethiopian affairs, the Arab concepts of the country's legitimacy were of greater importance.

Egypt remained, as it had been in the past, the main Middle Eastern country relevant to Ethiopia. It was to become, following its 1952 revolution and under the presidency of Gamal 'Abd al-Nasser, the center of pan-Arabism. The Egyptians-becoming-Arabs strove, especially beginning in the mid-1950s, to lead a struggle for the fulfillment of supra-Egyptian identities: Arab, and to some extent Islamic, as well as African. They saw Egypt as a pioneering leader of a great Afro-Asian revolution and they attempted to modernize the Nile economy and to look outward in their political and military efforts. They therefore focused much attention on Ethiopia, which was connected to Egypt through the Nile, to Arabism and Islam through Eritrea and through the issue of Ethiopia's Muslims, and to Africa by virtue of Ethiopia's special status in the emerging all-African politics.

PRE-NASSERITE EGYPT AND ERITREA

The first postwar Ethiopian-Egyptian encounter took place in the corridors of international diplomacy. Egypt, still a parliamentary monarchy in 1945, demanded Eritrea. The Egyptian political establishment was still motivated by the ideas of Egyptian nationalism as formed in the early 1920s. These included the slogan of Unity of the Nile Valley and the dream of building a Greater Egypt, including the Sudan. In the context of that strategy Egyptian diplomacy sought to realize *Khedive* Isma'il's dream of imperial expansion in claiming Massawa as the corridor from the Red Sea to the Sudan. As described by the Egyptian historian Muhammad Rajab Harraz of Cairo University,[2] the Egyptian diplomatic campaign lasted more than two years and was led by the Copt diplomat Wasif Ghali. In London, Paris, and then at the United Nations, the Egyptians collided with Ethiopian diplomats over the legacies of the Isma'il-Yohannes period. The Egyptians argued that the Italians had captured Massawa in 1885 from the Egyptian garrison and had promised at the time to preserve it under Egyptian sovereignty. Now that the Italians had left Massawa, they argued, the Arab-populated town should be restored to Egypt. The Ethiopians countered by referring to *Ras* Alula's government in Eritrea and to the June 1884 Hewett Treaty under which Egypt renounced Massawa. When bilateral contacts between the two missions failed, Egypt decided to claim all of Eritrea, and on 17 November 1947 submitted a memorandum to this effect. However, as it became clear that they stood no chance of regaining Eritrea, and since the Ethiopians countered by airing the issue of the Nile (in 1950, Haile Selassie declared that Ethiopia had the right to use its waters), the Egyptians abandoned their claim.[3] In December 1950, against the other Arab delegations, Egypt joined the majority at the United Nations in voting for Eritrean federation with Ethiopia.[4]

The shift in Egyptian policy was part of a major change developing gradually in the Egyptian self-image. Egyptianism, representing a set of political and social values, was now seen as failing to address the mounting postwar problems of Egypt. The British, who occupied Egypt until 1956, made it clear that they would not allow Egyptian-Sudanese reunification. Following the Nasserite revolution of 1952 Egyptian policy began to focus on the Middle East rather than on the African countries watered by the Nile.

In his book, *The Philosophy of the Revolution,* Nasser emphasized the Arab Circle as Egypt's main sphere of identity, taking primacy over the "circles" of Islam and of Africa. But while a serious effort would be made, until the demise and death of Nasser, in an attempt to unite the Arab Middle East, the African sphere was rendered secondary. Africa, even the Nile countries, were defined now as a sphere of influence rather than as a theater of the Arab unity struggle. Like Muhammad 'Ali in the 1830s, Nasser had to give up on the Sudan in order to focus on the more promising Fertile Crescent and Arab Peninsula. In 1953, he signed a treaty with the British concerning their 1956 evacuation of Egypt, in which he acknowledged Sudan as an entity separate from Egypt. Sudan was granted its independence in January 1956.

Did Nasser ever fully relinquish the hope of spreading Egyptian government along the length of the Nile? The answer cannot be given with certainty. An analysis of the scholarly literature produced in Egypt, including the writings and speeches of Nasser himself, make it appear that he sought, above all, stability along the Nile, and the welfare of Ethiopia, including Eritrea. I shall turn to that literature in the next section. It is clear that Egypt's order of strategic priorities was rearranged, but it is also clear that the possibility of future expansion into the Sudan and into Eritrea (as well as into Somalia) was never ruled out. Nasser was said to have never given up on the idea of unity among the Nile countries, including Ethiopia. In the second half of the 1950s, especially after the Suez War, he even toyed with the idea that Haile Selassie might be persuaded to form a Sudanese-Ethiopian-Egyptian alliance under Nasser's hegemony.[5] He was, however, to fail in both his diplomatic efforts to embrace Ethiopia and in seeking to eventually undermine it through Eritrea and Somalia.

THE BIRTH OF THE ERITREAN
LIBERATION FRONT IN CAIRO

Nasser used a variety of measures to spread his influence in Africa, but it was in the Nile and Horn countries that he concentrated his efforts. He was deeply involved in Sudanese affairs, a subject that in one respect is highly relevant to our concern with Ethiopia.

Sudanese politics in the volatile period leading up to the emergence of Ja'far al-Numayri in 1969 to a great extent revolved around the old Mahdiyya-Mirghaniyya rivalry. The Mahdist *Ansar* had, under the British, turned into the wing that supported Sudanese independence from Egypt, while the Mirghaniyya, from the days of Muhammad 'Ali and Isma'il under Egyptian auspices, was cultivated by the Egyptians. Nasser, while trying to reach a *modus vivendi* with the Khartoum government (in 1957 and finally in 1959 they reached an agreement on distribution of the Nile waters), continued playing the Mirghaniyya card. The Mirghaniyya were concentrated in and around the town of Kassala; a main pillar of theirs in northeastern Sudan was the Bani 'Amir tribes, 90 percent of which lived in Eritrea. These were the same Bani 'Amir who would come to constitute the main power behind the Eritrean Liberation Front (ELF), which was born in 1961. Thus, from a Nasserite Egyptian perspective, the struggle over Eritrea was detrimental to far more than just the future of the Red Sea province and Egyptian relations with Ethiopia. A future ELF-led independent Eritrea could also help Egypt to achieve an Arab-Egyptian unity with the Sudan, leading one day to the establishment of a Greater Egypt embracing the Nile countries.

The ELF was born in Cairo, in the bosom of Nasser and Arab nationalism.[6] As described by one of Nasser's chief aides for the African Circle affairs, Muhammad Muhammad Fa'iq,[7] Nasser decided in 1955 to encourage the organization of an Eritrean anti-Ethiopian community of exiles in Cairo. Nasser himself, because his priorities were not focused there, did not seek an open clash with Haile Selassie, but privately Nasser did see the Ethiopian emperor as an enemy. Haile Selassie was said to have helped the anti-Egyptian wing in the Sudan and to have had economic and other relations with Israel beginning in 1954. Moreover, he was undermining the autonomy of Eritrea and was depriving the Muslims of their rights. He made Amharic the official language of Eritrea in place of Tigrinya and Arabic. Arabic had been encouraged in Eritrea to some extent under the Italians as well as even more energetically under the British Military Administration (1941–1952). The British wanted to annex western Eritrea to the Sudan and did their best to emphasize the distinction between Christians and Muslims. They promoted Arabic by importing books and teachers from Egypt. Massawa flourished as a center of Arabic education, but the fundamental change was taking place in western Eritrea, among the Bani 'Amir, connected to Egypt traditionally through the Mirghaniyya. The Bani 'Amir were speakers of the Tigre language (as distinct from Tigrinya, the language of the Tigrean Christians) who had hardly used Arabic. Their younger generation, in revolt during the 1940s against the feudal elite of the tribe,[8] was attracted to an Arabic education.

When Eritrea was federated with Ethiopia many young Christians moved to Addis Ababa to pursue new careers. Young Muslims went instead to Sudan, and from there, traveled to Cairo. In 1955, Nasser decided to make their life easier in the capital's institutions of higher education, and primarily in al-Azhar. Al-Azhar, as noted above, had had its *Riwaq al-Jabartiyya* in the days of medieval Islamic Zeila and Massawa. It was swelling now with students from western Eritrea, their numbers during this period estimated at between 300 and 700.[9] (In 1962 it was estimated that the number of students from sub-Saharan Africa in al-Azhar was approximately one thousand.) They were given scholarships, jobs, other benefits, and access to a special club of their own. Like other students from Palestine, Algeria, Lebanon, Jordan, Iraq, and other countries in which the battle for Arab unity was soon to take place, they were exposed to the Cairene atmosphere of the time—that of rising revolutionary expectations.

Another decision made by Nasser in 1955 was to welcome Eritrean politicians who had had to flee into exile. The most prominent of them, the Christian proponent of Eritrean independence Wolde-Ab Walda-Mariam, had been in Cairo since 1953, having exerted some influence on the young Eritrean students there. Thanks to Nasser's decision, Wolde-Ab was allowed to broadcast daily to Eritrea and Ethiopia in Tigrinya. (There were also broadcasts in Arabic.) However, when, after the 1956 Suez War, Haile Selassie offered Nasser his diplomatic support, the broadcasts by Wolde-Ab were stopped.[10]

Nasser was in no rush to deal with Ethiopia and Eritrea. The Eritrean Muslim youngsters were not indoctrinated to conceive of themselves as Arabs. They were sent to al-Azhar (not to the secular Arab Cairo University) to advance their Islamic awareness, which was to be channeled politically into an African, not Arab, struggle. Nasser, according to the analysis of Muhammad Fa'iq, always accepted the principle of territorial integrity in Africa. But in his eyes Eritrea was a different case. As a former Italian colony it was recognized by the United Nations, and its people were entitled to postcolonial self-determination. Fa'iq wrote that Nasser believed Haile Selassie should have preserved Eritrea's identity by maintaining the spirit of its autonomy.

Not all Eritrean exiles turned to Cairo. Those who sought immediate action or who were dissatisfied with the prominence accorded the western Eritreans of the Bani 'Amir organized elsewhere. In 1958 five young students from eastern and northern Eritrea established an Eritrean Liberation Movement (ELM) in Port Sudan. They were joined by an Arabic teacher from Massawa (a Saho and native of Arkiko), 'Uthman Salih Sabbe, who would play a central role both in organizing the Eritrean movement in eastern Eritrea and in creating the myth that Eritrea was Arab.

When a new wave of Muslim Eritrean leaders of Bani 'Amir origin headed by Ibrahim Sultan and Idris Adam came to Cairo in 1959, the local Eritrean students were ripe for action. Some were being trained by the Egyptians in a special camp near Alexandria. They were excited by the Arab Algerian revolt against the French.

It was the atmosphere in Cairo even more than Nasser's policy toward the Eritreans that helped to create an Arab-oriented ELF. Indeed, the most influential non-Eritrean in the situation was not an Egyptian but the Moroccan exile 'Abd al-Karim al-Khattabi.[11] We have already referred to him as the leader of the anti-French Rif War in the Atlas Mountains in the 1920s. Living as an exile in Cairo since 1947, 'Abd al-Karim was active in spreading the ideas of Arab solidarity and of guerrilla tactics. 'Abd al-Karim, along with another hero of Moroccan Islamic nationalism and a fellow exile in Cairo, 'Alal al-Fasi, was a great favorite of students from various Muslim and Arab countries. But his special interest was the Eritreans. It may have been because of the similarities in the terrain of the Atlas Mountains and of Eritrea, and between the Moroccan royal house and the Ethiopian monarchy. He had been, as we have seen, a close friend of Shakib Arslan; the latter traveled to Morocco in the stormy year of 1935, and surely the two of them discussed Ethiopia and Haile Selassie.

In talking to the students in Cairo, 'Abd al-Karim preached action in the field. In addition to sharing with them his experience in waging tribal mountain warfare, he also lectured to them about the modern organization of the Algerian Front de Liberation Nationale (FLN). In fact, the Algerian liberation front, which had scored impressive successes and which was on the verge of defeating the French, was to become the source of inspiration and the model upon which the Eritrean Liberation Front was based. In Cairo, in July 1960, the ELF was established by Idris Adam, Ibrahim Sultan, and a group of students, prominent among them was Idris 'Uthman Qaladiyos (Galadewos). They established their base in Kassala (the headquarters of the Mirghaniyya) and began gaining momentum after the November 1962 annexation of Eritrea by Ethiopia. By 1965 they had established provincial commands (*wilayyas*) on the FLN model, a General Command, and a Supreme Council in Kassala, with Arabic as the language of their foreign relations and military affairs. Beginning in 1965, they were troubled by internal rivalries[12] as more elements joined the front from the Muslim coastal and northern Eritrea (the ELM had disappeared before achieving its goals), and from the new young Christians frustrated by the loss of political freedoms. The fact that the ELF was founded in Cairo was still reflected four years later in the August 1969 General Command of the ELF. Of thirty-eight members we have a list of thirty-one names, and we have specific background records given for thirteen of them. Of these, eight were al-Azhar graduates, two were trained by the Syrians in Aleppo, two were ex-servicemen in the Sudanese army, and one was trained in Iraq.[13]

THE ETHIOPIAN RESPONSE—
AVOIDANCE AND AFRICANIZATION

Throughout this period, Nasser showered Haile Selassie and Ethiopia with compliments. In 1955, the year he made Cairo the base for Muslim Eritrean separatists, Nasser also invited the emperor to Cairo in an attempt to persuade him to join in a show of unity. Although the emperor was inventing excuses to avoid such a meeting,[14] Nasser went on exerting pressure on Haile Selassie to visit Egypt, couching his repeated invitations in rhetorical flourishes on brotherhood, his admiration for the emperor, and Ethiopia's historical greatness.

Even though Nasser's major energies were directed to the Arab Middle East, he was viewed as their greatest threat by the Ethiopian political establishment.[15] Ethiopian functionaries were filled with fear as they watched Nasser undermine the monarchical regimes in Jordan, Iraq, Saudi Arabia, and Libya. In December 1956 the emperor sent an envoy (his ambassador to Sudan) to Nasser to explain why he would not visit Cairo. Returning to Khartoum, the envoy described his conversation with Nasser to the British ambassador:

> Nasser had then asked whether a military alliance between Egypt, the Sudan and Ethiopia would not be in their common interest. "We drink of the same water" he had said. My Ethiopian colleague had replied bluntly, to the following effect: You claim to be an Arab and to lead the Arab world but you interfere in the affairs of your Arab neighbors and have tried to cause trouble for the Governments of Iraq, Libya, Lebanon and Sudan. We Ethiopians are not Arabs. We are Africans and we are black. We do not belong to your world although like you we drink of the water of the Nile. Yet you have tried to interfere in our affairs also and make trouble for His Majesty. . . . Secondly, you have military objectives. We do not know exactly what they may be but we have no confidence in the strength of your armed forces, and we are strongly against the Communists who arm you. For these reasons your proposal is unacceptable and we are not prepared to discuss it even.[16]

A year later, in December 1957, this same envoy, Meles Andom, was appointed ambassador to Cairo.[17]

Nasser's view of royal houses as outdated and reactionary was echoed in Eritrean anti-Ethiopian propaganda. In 1958 when Nasserism was gaining strength in the Middle East the emperor appeared to have lost some of his confidence. He saw the winds of an Arab revolution sweeping the region, nearly toppling King Hussein of Jordan, removing the Iraqi royal family amid bloodshed,[18] and threatening to do away with Christian-dominated Lebanon. That year also witnessed the culmination of the Arab unity effort when Egypt and Syria united to form the United Arab Republic (UAR). Simultaneously, as the Eritrean movement in Cairo was beginning to take shape, the Egyptians opened another Islamic Arab bridgehead in the Horn. They worked to strengthen the Somalis, who would become independent in July 1960 in the idea of a Greater Somalia, in the name of which the Somalis started claiming the Ethiopian-controlled Ogaden, including the town and the rest of the province of Harar. In the first years after independence the Egyptians were very influential in Somalia.[19] As Haile Selassie told the visiting Israeli Agriculture Minister, General Moshe Dayan, in September 1960, "The Somalis would not have dreamt of such an idea without being incited by Nasser."[20]

The notion of a powerful united Middle East threatening to join forces with emerging Islam in the Horn reawakened the ancient Ahmad *Gragn* fear. Not only in Somalia and in Eritrea but even in the core of Ethiopia, Islam seemed to be responding to a call from a revitalized Middle East. Haile Selassie confided to a visiting Israeli diplomat in 1955: "The Arabs were always our enemies. Till lately they were weak and powerless. The Europeans, unfortunately, inflated their strength and will regret it. Meanwhile we Ethiopians have to be considerate of their power, especially as we have such a big Muslim minority in Ethiopia."[21]

"Colonel Nasser," he told a British journalist in early 1957, "is trying to stir up the large Muslim minority with the aim of dismembering this Christian kingdom."[22] In March 1957 Haile Selassie in Parliament blamed Egypt publicly for pursuing this strategy.[23]

Indeed, Haile Selassie's policy of Amharization and centralization, pursued forcefully after World War II, deprived many Muslims (as well as other groups) of important elements of their culture. Some of the Muslim elite were successfully integrated into the expanding state machinery and social establishment, but, as a prominent Ethiopian scholar and diplomat admitted, the government sought the cultural disconnection of the Muslim youth from the Arabic language and from the spirit radiating from the Middle East.[24] In the late 1950s many Muslims in Ethiopia demonstrated their admiration for Nasser and began expressing their resentment of their own government.[25] For example, in 1960 an underground Arabic book was published in Addis Ababa, entitled *The Wounded Islam in Ethiopia,* which blamed Haile Selassie for retaliating against the Muslims because they had supported Mussolini by depriving them of their basic rights. The book, not unlike the works of Arslan and Yusuf Ahmad, also estimated that Ethiopia's Muslims constituted 75 percent of the population, and claimed that therefore the country was Muslim.[26]

According to the contemporary analysis of a young Ethiopian diplomat, Yiftah Demitrios, the medieval "Ahmad *Gragn* syndrome" was increased by ignorance. Ethiopian politicians, even of the postwar generation, had not been trained to observe and study the new Middle East. Rather, they were accustomed to the Ethiopian-Christian affairs of Jerusalem, Cairo, and Alexandria. They now faced a Nasserite pan-Arab momentum and they seemed afraid even to learn about it.[27] We have mentioned Haile Selassie wishing to avoid Nasser, refusing to pay a visit to Cairo. Instead, the emperor sent his foreign minister, Aklilu Habte Wold, who had become the emperor's authority and closest adviser on Arab affairs.

Aklilu was the man who, more than anyone else, influenced Haile Selassie's Middle Eastern policy. It sought a low profile for Ethiopia and to placate the Arabs in hopes that the storm would soon disappear. One dimension of that policy in the 1950s was an attempt to avoid high-profile relations with Israel. The emperor said he was looking for non-Arab friends in the East. He saw Ethiopia as an island in an Arab sea and sought the friendship of Iran, Turkey, and India.[28] But these states were not interested in ties with Ethiopia. Israel was, but the Ethiopians were afraid of provoking the Arabs. Indeed, twelve days after the Egyptians, on 17 November 1947, claimed Eritrea, the Ethiopian delegation to the United Nations, seeking to avoid contact with the Zionist delegation, abstained from voting for the establishment of Israel.[29] When Nasser began to have prestige and influence, Ethiopia's Prime Minister Makonnen Endalkachew was not impressed. In 1955, in Bandung, he met with Nasser, by then having attained global prominence. He found the Egyptian leader "an unsophisticated theater actor and a shallow thinker rather than a statesman." He said he was glad that Israel was strong, because otherwise the Arabs would have been all over it.[30] But his foreign minister, Aklilu Habte-Wold, was taken in by Nasser. According to British sources, he traveled to see Nasser in Cairo, and returned as his admirer.[31] The emperor was more trustful of Aklilu and was careful not to alienate Nasser by responding to Israeli diplomatic overtures. In spite of the growing Israeli presence beginning in 1954, Ethiopia sent no diplomats to Israel. (In 1953, two persons were sent to the Israeli part of Jerusalem to look into a renewed effort to obtain the keys to the monastery of Deir al-Sultan, then in Jordanian Jerusalem.) In 1956 Israel finally managed to persuade the emperor to permit it to open a consulate in Addis Ababa, but, following Aklilu's advice, the emperor preferred relations to remain low key.

The Ethiopian policy of seeking to avoid contact with the Middle East became apparent in 1957 when the emperor canceled visits he had planned to Turkey, Jordan (the Deir al-Sultan issue), and Saudi Arabia (in response to King Sa'ud's friendly visit earlier that year, his warm approval of the state of Islam in Ethiopia, and the opening of diplomatic relations).[32] According to British sources the emperor canceled these visits to avoid irritating Nasser and in order not to be faced with the necessity of visiting him as well. When the following year, 1958, brought about the above-mentioned pan-Arab momentum, Haile Selassie began an active Ethiopian diplomatic campaign in Africa. The Israeli consul general analyzed the emperor's 1958 Crown Speech delivered on 12 November 1958 as follows:

> The speech was a declaration on foreign policy of historic importance. . . . Ethiopia is doing now its utmost to count itself among the African peoples which obtain independence, and break her isolation. . . . As remembered, Ethiopia was until lately hesitant to participate in African affairs and claimed she was for historical reasons a Middle Eastern and not an African country.[33] We have no doubt that Ethiopia would have continued in that line if not for the Nasserite threat. This threat increased to the extent that it forced Ethiopia to look for allies not only to her north but also to the south and her West. Relying on Africa will be the most natural result of the Arab and Islamic pressure.[34]

The Nasserite Middle Eastern challenge did contribute to the ensuing Africanization of Ethiopian diplomacy. It moved Haile Selassie to find comfort in African international relations, a field that provided prestige and glory as well as political assets to counter the Arab challenge to Ethiopia. Africa needed Ethiopia, already a source of inspiration for a generation of African nationalists. Africa admired Ethiopia's proud history,[35] it accepted Addis Ababa to be the headquarters for the Organization of African Unity (OAU), established in 1963, and it looked up to Haile Selassie, a man of global prestige and a symbol of the anti-imperialist stance, to be the continent's elder statesman. The emperor, encouraged mainly by Aklilu, was said to be happy to play that role rather than pay attention to the mounting problems at home. Many observers believed that he made the ultimate switch to engage in African affairs following the December 1960 abortive coup led by the commander of his body guard, General Mangistu Neway. The general and his associates were said to be inspired by Nasser's Free Officers' 1952 coup, and by the revolutionary antimonarchical spirit of Nasserism. (The coup was foiled partly because Israel passed information about the coup to the emperor, who was then touring Brazil.)[36] A semiofficial book on Ethiopia issued in Cairo in February 1961 devoted extensive paragraphs to the recent December 1960 coup. It made no mention of any direct Nasserite connection but it carried a clearly revolutionary message. Entitled *Abyssinia Between Feudalism and Modern Times,* it depicted Haile Selassie's Ethiopia as a medieval and backward system and urged

Ethiopian society to catch up with the world by moving immediately toward a fundamental revolution.[37]

The new African orientation and the new emphasis on Ethiopia's Africanism were not incompatible with Ethiopia's historical role. Not only did they provide Ethiopia with a welcome and deserved position of international leadership, but they also linked the country's foreign policy to many aspects of its multiethnic culture. However, from the perspective of our discussion of Ethiopia's Middle Eastern ties, the Africanization of the 1960s carried yet another message. African consensus had crystallized around the principle of the territorial integrity of the continent's nations. The Middle Eastern Nasserite momentum of Arab unity (and the war against Israel) ran counter to changing international boundaries and political entities.

As 1958 ended with some modicum of stability restored to the Middle East following U.S. and British intervention in Lebanon and Jordan, Haile Selassie's fear of Nasser subsided. He was finally ready to go to Cairo and visit Nasser in June 1959. Earlier he had been gratified to hear from Israeli diplomats that Prime Minister David Ben-Gurion looked forward to what he called Israel's "Periphery Strategy," meaning that Israel would outflank the Arab world by building an alliance with the non-Arabs: the Iranians, the Turks, and the Ethiopians. Though very interested in promoting Ben-Gurion's idea, the Ethiopian response was outwardly cautious. The emperor said he would tell Nasser he was ready to recognize Israel *de jure,* but he did not do so. He sent Nasser a signal by laying a foundation stone of a small hydroelectric plant in Bahr Dar on the Nile[38] and then, following the advice of Aklilu, left for Cairo.

The emperor's visit to the Egyptian capital highlighted the contradiction between the two leaders' rhetoric and the mutual suspicion in which each held the other. Haile Selassie was received with great warmth by Nasser and his people. Nasser made speeches that were full of praise and admiration for his guest. Nasser revealed that in 1940, as a young Egyptian officer stationed in Khartoum, he had the chance to meet with the emperor as he was preparing to reenter his country. Nasser said he had admired him ever since. In his speeches Nasser avoided any mention of, or even an indirect allusion to, Eritrea or to a Greater Somalia. Rather, he spoke as if quoting from Lutfi Jum'a's book on Oriental brotherhood. He did not fail to mention the *najashi*'s saving of the *sahaba,* delivering the message of his acceptance of Ethiopia as a legitimate neighbor—a subject to which we shall shortly return.[39]

Haile Selassie was less gracious. He showered praise on his host, but mentioned difficulties as well. The main outcome of his visit was to further distance Ethiopia from the Arab Middle East. He came to secure the independence of Ethiopia's Church from the Coptic Patriarchate of Alexandria.

During the Italian occupation, the Fascists had severed the ties between the two Churches and had appointed an Ethiopian as *abun*. The Egyptian Coptic Patriarchate, to the anger of some Ethiopians, did not recognize him. When Haile Selassie returned to Ethiopia, he restored the ties, but reached an agreement that the next *abun* would be of Ethiopian origin. Now, in 1959, he insisted on the Coptic Church recognizing the Ethiopian *Abuna* Basiliyos (who had been in office since early 1951) as a patriarch, equal in rank to *Abuna* Qerilus VI of Alexandria. The agreement, signed during the visit, made the Ethiopian Orthodox Church autocephalous. At the ceremony, Haile Selassie stated that the Ethiopian Church was a part of a reawakening Africa. (The final official agreement severing the Ethiopian Church from Egypt was signed in 1965.)[40]

1962–1967: CULMINATION AND RELIEF

Relations between Ethiopia and the UAR remained tense. Not long after promising Haile Selassie that Radio Cairo would refrain from broadcasting to the Somalis concerning Greater Somalia, the station resumed its propaganda. In November 1959 the Egyptians, preparing for the construction of the Aswan Dam, signed a new agreement with the Sudanese on the distribution of the Nile waters. They did so without notifying Ethiopia, in defiance of Haile Selassie's declaration of September 1957 that he would consider such disregard of Ethiopia to be a gross offense.[41] In 1960, Ethiopia and Israel drew closer,[42] and one Ethiopian minister, apparently guided by the emperor, floated an idea that Jordan, too, would be included in a Turkish, Iranian, Ethiopian, and Israeli front.[43] The interest in Jordan stemmed from the effort to obtain the keys to Deir al-Sultan, an issue which the Ethiopians had put on Jordan's agenda (with the advice of the Israeli Haim Vardi) in 1953. On 2 December 1960, a Jordanian committee ruled that the keys should be handed over to the Ethiopian monks, but soon afterwards, in early 1961, the Egyptians exerted pressure on King Hussein and the keys were returned to the Egyptian Copts.[44]

In 1961 Nasser suffered his first major setback on the pan-Arab front when Syria broke away from the UAR. Later, in October, Ethiopia recognized Israel, and the daily *Addis Zaman* (of 25 October 1961) openly mocked Nasser's efforts to undermine Israel. As the first Israeli ambassador was about to leave for Addis Ababa, the ELF began its armed struggle in Eritrea.

The next years were marked by dichotomy. On the one hand, Nasser became a more direct threat. In September 1962 his army landed in Yemen to launch a five-year war against the Yemeni Royalists and the Saudis who backed them. It would be a war over the future of the Arab Peninsula, its vast resources, and, ultimately, over the Arab Middle East and the Red Sea. The journal of Egypt's armed forces declared that Egypt was seeking to make the Red Sea an Arab sea.[45] Haile Selassie feared the implications of a Nasserite pan-Arab victory in Yemen. Such a victory would inevitably be linked to the drive of the newly independent Somalis (a united Somalia had gained its independence in July 1960) committed to restoring the Ogaden, as well as to the struggle of the Eritrean Muslims of the ELF. In fact, Nasser's landing in Yemen prompted Haile Selassie to annex Eritrea in November 1962.

On the other hand, Nasser was also involved in the African agenda. With his attention focused on the outcome of the Yemen War, Nasser paid relatively less attention to injecting anti-Western spirit in his African Circle.[46] When Haile Selassie inaugurated the Organization of African Unity in Addis Ababa in 1963, which created a consensus for each country's territorial integrity, Nasser was ready to participate. Moreover, he was eager to be part of the organization's leadership, even if it meant being second to Haile Selassie. The two leaders were now showing a mutual respect, which may even have been authentic. Haile Selassie asked Nasser to join him in leading the inaugural ceremonies, and Nasser hosted the next gathering in Cairo in 1964.

Despite outward appearances of cordiality with Nasser, the emperor and his advisers bided their time. Aklilu was ecstatic over the success of his diplomacy, but others were suspicious about the potential of a Nasserite Yemeni-Somali-Eritrean coalition.

In May 1963, an Ethiopian minister wrote later, when Nasser came to the opening of the OAU "hundreds of thousands of Ethiopian Muslims spontaneously travelled (many on foot) to the airport to welcome him, completely surprising the Ethiopian authorities, who had very little way of gauging people's sentiments. The thunderous cry of 'Nasser! Nasser!' still rings in the ears of many of the Ethiopian police and military."[47]

Meanwhile, also in 1963, Nasser ceased aiding the ELF[48] which, as we shall see, meant that the front had to move its Middle Eastern base to Syria. The anti-Arab wing in the Ethiopian political establishment was still not convinced that Nasser posed no threat. The head of the group that rivaled the one led by Aklilu, *Ras* Asrate Kassa, was appointed governor of Eritrea in 1964. In the field he found ample evidence that pan-Arabism was a major source of fueling the separatists.

To the majority of Ethiopia's elite the Nasserite pan-Arab active presence was undoubtedly traumatic. It combined the collective awareness of the two historic cases in which their country had been destroyed. The Nasserite potential threat was reminiscent of the Ahmad *Gragn* sixteenth-century disaster in aiming to unite and politicize Islam in the whole Horn of Africa and to recreate the Horn as an extension of a revitalized, monolithic Middle East. And it seemed to be aiming at doing so through Arabization of local Muslims, in both language and identity, and in a manner reminiscent of the Arabization campaign under Mussolini.

The general mood during this period among Ethiopia's political elite and the Christian public was revealed in June 1967. Bogged down in Yemen in May 1967 Nasser gambled on escalating the Egyptian tensions with Israel. He openly threatened Israel with destruction by a united Arab front—Egyptian, Syrian, Jordanian. As the Israeli ambassador wrote, following the Six Day War:

> From the moment the crisis began we suddenly had no need to persuade the Ethiopians, of whatever walk of life, of our case. More so, that the Israeli effort for survival is vital to Ethiopia. The identification with us on the part of the Christians—and there were some cases of sympathy expressed by Muslims—was nearly total, astonishing in depth and magnitude. Not only the members of the tiny intelligentsia but also the masses, workers, peasants, the poorest merchants in the "Mercato," they were all immersed in a wave of emotions. As tension built, and with it the repetitious threats by the Arabs to wipe Israel out, there was an intensively growing anxiety. It was manifested in a variety of ways. . . .
>
> Part of this can be explained by religious traditional feelings towards Israel, part by the recognition that the outcome of the Arab war against Israel would be detrimental to the future of Ethiopia. . . . The Emperor, the various advisers and Foreign Ministry functionaries, they all, on their own initiative, emphasized how much was the Israeli survival of vital importance to their own destiny. . . . Finally after the news of our victory penetrated to the public[49] there followed demonstrations of joy and an endless wave of congratulations, amazingly untypical of a society usually reluctant to show emotions. . . .[50]

The Six Day War had a major long-range effect on Ethiopia's relations with the Middle East. It dealt a fatal blow to active pan-Arabism. The region was not to see the triumph of Arabism as an ideology seeking a monolithic Arab entity. Moreover, the role of Egypt, both the leading state in the Middle East and the Middle Eastern state most important to Ethiopia, was to change course.

11

EGYPT'S VIEW OF ETHIOPIA
DURING THE NASSERITE PERIOD

During the 1960s and the 1970s, the ELF made an effort to depict Eritrea as an integral part of the Arab world. But, Nasser, despite the pan-Arab ideology he espoused, refrained from extending his rhetoric to include Eritrea. Surprisingly, the Egyptian scholarly literature and press as well as Nasser's own speeches were silent on the issue. We have seen that Radio Cairo permitted Wolde-Ab Wolde-Maryam to broadcast to Eritrea in the period prior to the Suez War. Significantly, these broadcasts were made in Tigrinya, not Arabic, and they emphasized Eritrea's uniqueness, not its Arabism. We have also seen that 'Uthman Salih Sabbe, the Eritrean champion of Eritrea's Arabism, was hardly a welcome guest in Cairo. Ethiopia was deemed in Egypt a close and dear sister, and the problem of Eritrea was nearly ignored.

MURAD KAMIL AND
THE PRE-NASSERITE CONCEPT OF ERITREA

This Egyptian silence on Eritrea is even more surprising given the fact that in the late 1940s, as we recall, pre-Nasserite Egypt had claimed Eritrea, arguing at the United Nations that the former Italian colony was an integral part of Egypt's historical legacy.

The idea of Eritrea being an Egyptian land was clearly expressed in a book published in Cairo in 1949, *In the Land of the Najashi,* by Murad Kamil.[1] A Copt and a noted historian, who had pursued Ethiopian studies in Germany (under E. Littmann), Murad Kamil was sent to Ethiopia in 1943 as the head of a group of Egyptian teachers. The group helped restructure Ethiopia's educational system as part of the Egyptian effort that had begun in 1908 to help Ethiopian education. The *najashi* of the book's title refers to the concept of a righteous benevolent king, a close ally, and a legitimate Oriental Christian neighbor. Ethiopia, according to Kamil, is an Oriental country of great culture, ancient tradition, and a rich literature. This has been expressed in its two major religions, Coptic Christianity and

141

Islam. Relations between the two religious communities, Murad Kamil asserted repeatedly (p. 91), are of tolerance, unlike in other Eastern countries. Ethiopia's hope of progress lies in promoting modern education in an ecumenical spirit, and Egypt must cooperate in this venture. More Muslim Ethiopians should be sent to *Riwaq al-Jabartiyya* in al-Azhar and more Copts should be sent to Ethiopia to build schools, particularly a secondary school in Addis, which is much needed as a vehicle for Egyptian influence. "The Ethiopians trust only us," he wrote, "for they know that the Egyptians carry no political ambitions when it comes to Ethiopia" (p. 91). They want and deserve their own patriarch, but they do not seek a severing of relations with Alexandria. (He quoted an Ethiopian song about the Armenians and the Syrians who have their patriarchs even though they have no kings, and that only the Ethiopians have no patriarch of their own.) In Kamil's view, Haile Selassie is an enlightened friend of Egypt. He told Kamil, "Egypt is our dearest sister. . . . She is the first to whom we turn in difficult times, and she never let us down" (p. 123).

The first part of the book is dedicated to Kamil's en route visit to Eritrea (which in 1943 was under the British Military Administration). He summarizes the history of Eritrea as if such an entity had existed from ancient times. There had been ties, he asserts, between Pharaohnic Egypt and Eritrea. Aksum, he says, was an Eritrean empire. It was the Egyptians who had occupied Eritrea in the sixteenth century (Ozdemir *Pasha* and the Habesh *Eyaleti,* we recall, were subjects of the Ottomans in Egypt), and Egypt lost Eritrea three hundred years later because of the Mahdiyya. But it remained connected to the Eritrean Church, and Muslim Eritreans continued to go to al-Azhar. Egypt, writes Kamil, should strengthen its educational and religious mission to Eritrea (he mentions as a good example the work of the Faruk Religious Institute, which was operating in Massawa).

Murad Kamil emphasizes the uniqueness of Eritrean culture, especially its oral poetry, citing two Eritrean poems that convey his political message. Both date from the period of *Ras* Alula's rivalry with the Egyptians over Eritrea (1876–1884). The poems deal with tribesmen who were wavering between the Ethiopian Alula in Asmara and the Egyptian garrison stationed in Keren. Alula is depicted as a predatory bird, but the Egyptians are portrayed as people of order and justice. The choice is clear, and the hero of one song calls his friend to join him in finding shelter in Egypt (pp. 40–45).

After Egypt decided to vote for the Eritrean federation with Ethiopia in December 1950, Kamil never referred in his later writings to the Egyptianness of Eritrea. In 1958, in Cairo, he published his annotated edition of *Sirat al-habasha* by the seventeenth-century Yemeni envoy to Fasiladas, Al-Haymi al-Hasan bin Ahmad.[2] In his annotations he did his best to emphasize al-Haymi's impressions of medieval Gondar as a town typical of Ethiopian tolerance toward Islam.

NASSERITE LITERATURE ON ETHIOPIA

After the Nasserite revolution in which Egypt began to spread its influence in the African Circle there was much written and spoken in Cairo about the similarities between the Arab revolution and the African one. At times, Nasser appeared to identify the two "circles" as if they were, in fact, but one anti-imperialist (anti-Zionist) revolution. He was, however, careful never to mention Eritrea in an Arab context. Even when the Ethiopian regime was criticized for being backward, as in *Abyssinia Between Feudalism and Modern Times* (Cairo, 1961), and where the recent history of Eritrea was discussed in detail, no mention of Eritrea's "Arabism" was made.[3] Moreover, in the Egyptian press, mention of Eritrea all but disappeared. From 1955 to 1959, for example, the years during which Nasser allowed the Eritrean students and the exiled Eritrean leaders to organize in Cairo, very little was published on Eritrea. In all the material published on Ethiopia in the influential daily *Al-Ahram* (edited by Nasser's closest adviser) throughout these years, there appeared only four brief items on Eritrea. On the other hand, Ethiopia was the subject of many favorable articles.[4] Nasser, in his annual speeches on Revolution Day, would invariably note that July 23 was also Haile Selassie's birthday and would make a point to bless him in his remarks.[5] All in all, Nasser avoided the "Arabism of Eritrea" because he had to accept Ethiopia in the African terms dictated by Haile Selassie. Ethiopia was the Nile and for the time being at least Nasser had no other option than accepting Ethiopia's territorial integrity and historical legitimacy.

The most prolific Egyptian scholar who wrote on Ethiopia during this period was Zahir Riyad. In 1934 he was sent from Cairo by the Egyptian ministry of education to teach history in the new secondary school opened by Haile Selassie. He stayed in Ethiopia until 1937, teaching history and learning Amharic. Then in 1943 he joined his fellow Copt, Murad Kamil, in returning to Ethiopia to continue the Egyptian effort to help building Ethiopia's modern education. He returned to Egypt in 1945 and in 1954 joined the African Section of the newly opened Institute of Coptic Studies. Riyad published his articles on Ethiopia mainly in the journal of Cairo University's faculty of humanities, which was widely read by the young Egyptian intelligentsia. He was very favorably disposed toward Ethiopia as a land of justice and as a good neighbor to Egypt. Of special interest is his twenty-one-page review of British scholar Spencer Trimingham's *Islam in Ethiopia,* published in late 1957.[6] Riyad was extremely critical of Trimingham. He tried to prove that Trimingham could read no Arabic or Ge'ez and that he had misunderstood much of the source material that he had derived from translations. By discrediting Trimingham, Riyad sought to demonstrate that the British scholar was wrong in describing Ethio-

Islamic relations as an endemic conflict. In Riyad's view, there were only twelve years of enmity—the Ahmad *Gragn* period. Other than that brief exception, it was mainly tolerance and mutual respect that characterized relations between the Ethiopian Christians and Muslims. Moreover, he criticized Trimingham for overemphasizing Ethio-Egyptian conflicts and for failing to view Egypt as the main outside source of inspiration for Ethiopia's Christian and Islamic cultures.

In 1958 Riyad published a study of Ethiopia's 1955 constitution, which granted Muslims and Christians equal rights under Ethiopian law. Then, in his 1961 article, "The Shifta in Ethiopia from Medieval Ages and Their Political and Social Significance,"[7] he analyzed the phenomenon of Ethiopia's political and social banditry. Drawing from European and Arabic sources, he described the constant tension between the established politicians and the *shifta,* the outlaw, the bandit, an institution of individual opposition that generated much energy to Ethiopia's political dynamism. He concluded by describing Haile Selassie's modernization of the 1940s and 1950s as ending *shiftnnet.* A particularly interesting point is that Riyad completely refrained from mentioning *shiftnnet* in Eritrea during that period. In the late 1940s the term was widely used by practically all observers to depict the terrorist activities of the Christian Eritreans working for reunification with Ethiopia. Much was published on the Ethiopian government's using *shifta*s against the proponents of Eritrean independence.[8] The Eritreans in Cairo, many of whom had been subjected to the violence of the Ethiopian-recruited *shifta*s, were spreading the word of their activities.

In 1964 Riyad published his book, *Islam in Ethiopia in the Middle Ages,* subtitled: "With Special Interest in Christian-Islamic Relations."[9] Relying on extensive reading of Islamic and European sources, Riyad undertook to shatter the picture of endemic Christian-Islamic enmity in Ethiopia, a picture that, he wrote, Trimingham had helped to engrave. Riyad devoted his first chapter (pp. 15–47) to the *sahaba-najashi* formative episode emphasizing time and again the Islamic tradition about Ethiopia as the "land of righteousness" and the amicable relations between the Prophet and the *najashi.* In analyzing the relations between Ethiopia and the southern emirates prior to *Gragn* (Chapter 2, pp. 49–94), Riyad argues forcefully that the conflict was essentially political, only occasionally couched in religious terminology. The same was true, he contends, of the nature of relations between Ethiopia's emperors and Egypt's Mamluk *sultans* (Chapter 3, pp. 95–152). Islamic-Christian religious and cultural enmity, writes Riyad, was aroused only during the twelve years of the Ahmad *Gragn* "revolution" (Riyad uses the modern-Arab term, *thawra*). In analyzing *Gragn*'s period (Chapter 5, pp. 195–259) Riyad's main point is that the religious hostility then revealed was mostly an import from the Ottomans on the one hand and the Portuguese on the other. The legacy of mutual suspicion and enmity was mainly due to foreign involvement and lack of historical understanding. In practice the record of Christian-Islamic relations in Ethiopia, he says, was good. It was the Fascist occupiers, he learned upon returning to Ethiopia in 1943, who spread among local Muslims the notion of *Gragn* as the redeemer of Islam, to foment problems. Ethiopians, both Christians and Muslims, as well as modern Arab Egyptians, should study the true history in order to promote mutual understanding.

In his 1966 book, *A History of Ethiopia,* Riyad repeats his very favorable version of the Muhammad-*najashi* story;[10] he devotes a chapter to the history of Eritrea but does not mention the rebellion (p. 213), and concludes by emphasizing the good contemporary relations between Egypt and Ethiopia as based on African fraternity (pp. 225–237).

Riyad's main ideas about modern Ethiopia and its relations with modern Egypt are summarized in his book, *Egypt and Africa.*[11] In it he discusses the relations between the two countries in modern times as essentially friendly, although occasionally marred by problems. Tewodros and Sa'id, he writes, came to terms after a misunderstanding; between Isma'il and Yohannes it was the Egyptian who provoked the conflict. However, the Church was particularly constructive in aiding political relations and very helpful in promoting Ethiopia's educational system. He notes that the Copt Hanna Salib served as Menelik's minister of education, and that all cultural and educational contacts until the death of *Abuna* Matewos in 1926 went through the Church. In 1927, diplomatic relations were established between the two countries and an Egyptian consulate was opened in Addis Ababa. Additional educational missions, organized by the Egyptian Ministry of Education, came to Ethiopia: one in 1928, another headed in 1943 by Murad Kamil (pp. 151–160, 165–174).

Riyad was an advocate of Ethio-Egyptian relations but he refrained from exaggerating the contemporary picture. He described relations under Nasser as tense and blamed Ethiopia because it recognized Israel. In 1964, he wrote, he visited Addis Ababa and was told by the head of a newly opened cultural center at the Egyptian embassy that the cultural attaché had instructions to respond generously to any Ethiopian request, but that the Ethiopians were suspicious and avoided him. Shortly afterwards the center was closed (pp. 241–245).

Riyad does not mention the Eritrean problem and also avoids discussing Eritrea's Arabism. The same was true of another book, *Lights on Ethiopia,* which appeared in Cairo, probably in 1957 or 1958. It was part of an official series entitled "We chose it for you" published by the Ministry of Indoctrination and personally endorsed by Nasser.[12] The last chapter of it carries the same message as Riyad's last chapter: It describes Ethiopia's overtures to the West, mainly to the United States and Israel, and suggests a sense of danger. The first chapter, by contrast, is positive in tone. It was written by Nasser himself, and under the title of "Ethiopia, a Sister State," it is extremely amicable toward Ethiopia. "Between us and Ethiopia there are eternal relations of love incomparable to anything else between two brothers," Nasser begins. He then summarizes Ethiopian history with European imperialism and claims that the Ethiopians resisted the imperialism of the Crusaders; then of the Portuguese; and in the nineteenth century, that of the British, the French, and the Italians. It was Western imperialism, he writes, that made the Ethiopians isolationists. (He mentions nothing of the role of Islam.) The last Italian aggression, that of Mussolini, was almost a blessing because it brought Ethiopia to the attention of Egypt and other friends. (Nasser himself was a young student participating in the anti-British November 1935 riots which, as noted, erupted in conjunction with the Abyssinian Crisis. Following the Abyssinian Crisis he decided to leave his university studies and join the military academy, then opened in Aswan.) Nasser hints at no conflict between Ethiopia and Islam. To the contrary, he presents the *najashi* story: "And we, first and foremost, together believe in one God and follow the same ideals. Our Muslims and the Muslims of Ethiopia remember in any of their thoughts that distant day in which the first emigrants, the *sahaba* of Muhammad bin 'Abdallah, found shelter with the *najashi* as they escaped from the infidels of Mecca. And that he took care of them, and gave them security and shared his land with them giving them all the best" (p. 6).

The legitimacy of Ethiopia is emphasized throughout the publication. That is not surprising because although it claimed to have been prepared by Amin Sakir, Sa'id al-'Ariyyan, and Mustafa Amin the publication, with the exception of the last chapter, and of Nasser's first chapter, is a shameless, occasionally condensed translation of A. H. M. Jones and Elizabeth Monroe's 1935 classic, *A History of Ethiopia*. It contains minor adaptations whenever the Ethio-Islamic conflict was too heavily emphasized by Jones and Monroe to serve Nasser's purposes.

The Nasserite message of brotherly acceptance of Ethiopia within the family of the Middle East is even more pronounced in another book to which Nasser contributed the identical introductory chapter he had prepared for *Lights on Ethiopia*. It was published in 1960 in Beirut by an admirer of Nasser and the owner of a publishing house, 'Abd al-Rahman Mahmud al-Huss. Entitled *Ethiopia in the Period of Haile Selassie*,[13] the book is a song of praise for the emperor. On the cover, just below the name of the emperor, is the quotation from Prophet Muhammad to the *sahaba*. "If you go to Abyssinia you will find a king under whom none is persecuted. It is a land of righteousness where God will give you relief from what you are suffering." Indeed, al-Huss writes that he went to see this phenomenon for himself and was received in Ethiopia with great respect. He was invited to broadcast over Radio Addis Ababa a message from the Arab people of Lebanon. The text of the message (pp. 16–19) was a combination of quotations from Nasser's welcome to Haile Selassie in Cairo, June 1959, with a detailed version of the *najashi* hosting the *sahaba*, sent by "the *Arab* [note, not the Muslim] Prophet Muhammad." The book claims that the Ethiopians are essentially Arabs who emigrated from Yemen, an Oriental nation that should be reunited with the East. It reports on the situation of Islam and Muslims in Ethiopia, on their flourishing educational system, and their history of good relations with the Christians. At one point (p. 108) he quotes al-'Azm's *Rihlat al-habasha* on *Ras* Makonnen and the equal treatment he gave to Harar's Muslims and Christians. Haile Selassie, he notes, inherited the same spirit of justice from his father. Another hero of al-Huss' was Aklilu Habte-Wold (whom he calls Ethiopia's expert on the Middle East), who had many friends in the Arab world (pp. 62–63).

The only mention of Eritrea in al-Huss' book is of the emperor's speeches there. He quotes in detail the speech the emperor gave in Asmara's main mosque in 1952 (just after the proclamation of the federation). The speech concerned religious equality and tolerance, to which al-Huss adds his own impressions of Ethiopia's pluralism. In the conclusion to the book al-Huss quoted in full an article that appeared in the Cairene weekly, *Al-Musawwar,* during Haile Selassie's visit in June 1959. It was entitled "The Lion of Judah Taught the World a Lesson," and summarized the emperor's pre–World War II dialogue with the League of Nations. First, he managed to have Ethiopia admitted to the international organization by successfully fighting slavery and bringing progress to his nation. Second, he addressed the league on 3 June 1936, swearing he would redeem Ethiopia, a task he ultimately accomplished.

BOUTROS-GHALI AND EGYPT'S STRATEGIC CONTINUITY

After the founding of the OAU and Nasser's joining Haile Selassie in its leadership, the pro-Ethiopian literature produced in Egypt became official. In 1965, the semiofficial Al-Ahram Institute founded a quarterly, *Al-Siyasa al-Duwaliyya* (International Affairs). The first editor was a Copt, Boutros Boutros-Ghali, an academician and diplomat of repute. (In his memoirs Boutros-Ghali describes how as a child he had dreaded hearing the news from the Italo-Abyssinian front, and how his family had volunteered to participate in the activities of the Committee for the Defense of Ethiopia;[14] Boutros-Ghali always remained interested in Ethiopia. At the time he undertook the editorship of *Al-Siyasa al-Duwaliyya,* he was also involved in archeological activities in Lalibela, which were sponsored by the United Nations Educational, Scientific, and Cultural Organisation [UNESCO].)

Under Boutros-Ghali *Al-Siyasa al-Duwaliyya* turned into the most serious forum of foreign policy analysis in Egypt, with a discernable emphasis on Africa. This emphasis was because Boutros-Ghali considered Africa as important to Egypt as the Arab Circle. Over the ensuing years, the quarterly became committed to enhancing the Egyptian understanding of Ethiopia.

Boutros-Ghali himself would, in 1977, become the most influential Egyptian formulating his country's Ethiopian policy, so we will return in the conclusion to his role under Sadat and Mubarak. However, under Nasser, the quarterly published writers such as Murad Kamil, Mirrit Boutros-Ghali, and others, who discussed Ethio-Egyptian history, Church relations, and the need to cooperate on the issue of the Nile.[15] The journal published no significant discussion of Eritrea during Nasser's time, and in later pieces it asserted that Nasser had never given any meaningful help to Eritrea's separatists. Instead, it emphasized that beginning in 1950 Egypt was consistent in demanding the implementation of the federation of Ethiopia and Eritrea in the spirit of the United Nation's autonomy plan.[16]

An article written by Boutros-Ghali immediately after the death of Nasser reemphasized the centrality of Africa for Egypt and described the bond between Nasser and Haile Selassie in promoting the OAU. Nasser, wrote Boutros-Ghali, had worked to create stability and, just before his death, had been working on a solution to the Ethio-Somali dispute and on bringing peace between Ethiopia and Sudan.[17]

Eleven years later, after the death of Sadat, Boutros-Ghali, writing again in *Al-Siyasa al-Duwaliyya,* returned to the subject of Nasser and concluded that when it came to Africa, indeed, when it came to the Nile, Egyptian policy had remained consistent in the pursuit of stability.[18]

The leaders of Egypt from the days of the Mamluks' dialogue with 'Amda-Zion and Zar'a-Ya'qob to Muhammad 'Ali, Isma'il, and Nasser, were concerned about the Blue Nile. They were always fearful of the Ethiopians interrupting the flow of the Nile, and dreamt of extending their control, or at least their influence, to the Ethiopian source of Egypt's life. For that reason, Ethiopia was always on their minds. In seeking to secure that vital interest they alternated between diplomatic friendliness toward Ethiopia and exerting pressure on Ethiopia, the latter through their leverage on the Church, their influence on local Islam, and through their control of the Red Sea. Nasser opted for both approaches.

His verbal messages were of friendliness toward Ethiopia. These messages were expressed in a variety of assurances, culminating with the *najashi-sahaba* message, that he accepted Ethiopia as a legitimate neighbor. In so doing he was first seeking an Egyptian-dominated Egypto-Sudanese-Ethiopian alliance, similar to his 1958 unification with Syria. When this approach yielded little in the way of a response from Haile Selassie (and as Ethiopia was gaining strategic strength) he then worked, more successfully, toward building relations with Ethiopia through the OAU.

Nasser was not viewed in this way in Addis Ababa. The Ethiopian establishment took note of Nasser's speeches but was far more impressed with the Eritrean separatists' efforts to establish an Arab Eritrea and with the Somalis' admiration for Nasser as they began working for a Greater

Somalia. When Nasser moved his base of Middle Eastern activity to nearby Yemen and continued to undermine the royal houses of Yemen, Saudi Arabia, Libya, and Jordan, seeking to fulfill his dream of pan-Arabism through revolutions and wars (rather than through the diplomacy of the 1950s), the Christians of imperial Ethiopia were reminded of Ahmad *Gragn*. The idea that the Middle East was about to unite and that local Islam in the Horn was fully prepared to join Nasser's victory was most vividly on the mind of many Ethiopians, and it made little difference in Addis Ababa if the terminology was modern Arab rather then traditional Islamic.

We can only speculate on how Nasser's Ethiopian strategy might have differed had he won in Yemen or had he defeated Israel in the 1967 war. As it turned out, Nasser died in 1970 with his dream of Arab unity still unrealized. The Ethiopian dimension of that unrealized dream was a combination of potentially the greatest threat to Ethiopia's existence since the days of *Gragn* and the Egyptian diplomatic recognition of Ethiopia as "the land of righteousness."

12

THE ARABS, ETHIOPIA,
AND THE ARABISM OF ERITREA

Nasser's death in September 1970 was received with relief in Ethiopia. Sadat seemed to be much less of a challenge to Ethiopia; his focus was Egypt's conflict with Israel. Sadat abandoned the ideas of pan-Arabism and put aside all dreams of regional grandeur. He established good relations with Sudan's new ruler, Ja'far al-Numayri, and helped him and Haile Selassie mend their differences. In February and July 1972 Ethiopian-Sudanese agreements were signed, under which Ethiopia agreed to refrain from interfering in southern Sudan in return for the Sudanese ceasing to aid the Eritrean separatists.[1] Sadat's reassuring relations with Haile Selassie and his abandoning of pan-Arab terminology (in November 1971 Sadat relinquished the name UAR and reverted to using Egypt) indicated to Haile Selassie that Aklilu's diplomacy of appeasing and waiting had finally proven successful. The fact that he had outlived Nasser was a significant factor in Haile Selassie's preferring of Aklilu to Asrate Kassa in the last three crucial years of his reign. Asrate, as we have seen, had been leading the pro-Israeli wing of the imperial establishment. We shall return to that rivalry in discussing the Middle Eastern angle in the story of Haile Selassie's demise in 1974.

As important as was the Egyptian role in Ethio-Arab relations there were other significant factors as well. Egypt continued to be concerned with issues of the Nile River and the African Circle; even at the height of Nasser's power, it still showed at least superficial respect for Ethiopia. Egypt now attached (perhaps only temporarily) less importance to Red Sea Eritrean affairs and to the ideology of Eritrean Arabism. Other Arab countries bordering on Ethiopia, such as the Sudan or Saudi Arabia, had also followed a similarly pragmatic approach in dealing with Ethiopia and the Eritrean separatists. But Arabs in more distant countries, primarily the Syrians, the Palestinians, and the Iraqis, had little to gain or to risk by meddling in the affairs of the Horn. They were more interested in the Red Sea within the context of the Arab-Israeli conflict, as a theater of operations for advancing anti-Israeli and anti-American strategies. They did not concern themselves with Ethiopia, but they *were* quite interested in the establishment of an Arab Eritrea. As such they were instrumental in shaping the history of the struggle over Eritrea in the years leading to the fall of Ethiopia's *ancien regime.*[2]

In 1963, when Nasser closed the ELF office in Cairo, the center of the Eritrean exile leadership moved to Damascus. It was once more the veteran Moroccan leader of the 1920s Rif War, 'Abd al-Karim al-Khattabi, who was said to have helped to establish in Cairo an earlier Eritrean-Syrian connection. According to the memoirs of 'Uthman Salih Sabbe's aide, 'Abd al-Karim had been trying since the late 1950s to mediate between the Eritreans and various Arab governments. Sabbe, perhaps because he was not particularly welcome in Cairo, did the majority of the mediation. In 1962, he made contact with the Syrian president, Nazim al-Qudsi, but scored a greater success by being introduced to Muhammad Amin al-Hafiz who, with the Ba'th Party, came to power in Damascus in March 1963. Soon thereafter, Sabbe brought to Damascus from Cairo some thirty of his students, mostly natives of eastern Eritrea and the Massawa area, headed by Muhammad Ramadan Nur.[3]

The accession to power of the Ba'th Party, just as Nasser had abandoned the Eritreans, was well timed. The Ba'th had been the party that had, since the very early 1950s, stood for pan-Arab nationalism and had undergirded this political identification with modern ideological philosophy. The founders of the Ba'th, notably Michel Aflaq and Salah al-Din al-Bittar, had no other "circles," or international strategic concerns, as had Nasser, to compete with Arabism. Their approach was based on secular interpretations of history. At any rate, in the 1952 Constitution of the Ba'th Party they defined the "Arab homeland" as "a national home for the Arabs. It consists of that area which extends beyond the Taurus Mountains . . . the Gulf of Basra, the Arabian Sea, the *Ethiopian mountains* [italics added] . . . the Atlantic Ocean and the Mediterranean Sea, and constitutes one single complete unit, and no part thereof may be alienated."[4]

The existing literature on the Ba'th provides no clue as to why the founders of the Ba'th Party made it a point to include Eritrea in their territorial definition of Arabism. (At the time of their drafting Eritrea was still not yet federated with Ethiopia.) They were most probably relying on the writings of Shakib Arslan, Yusuf Ahmad, and the many others who, as noted above, had transmitted this message during the Abyssinian Crisis to the younger generation, particularly in Syria and Palestine. Aflaq and Bittar were in their mid-twenties during the time of Mussolini's invasion of Ethiopia, studying in Damascus and Paris. They established their "al-Ba'th al-Arabi" group in Paris at around that period and their views on Ethiopia and on Islam in the Horn undoubtedly stemmed from their reading of the material discussed in my chapter on the Abyssinian Crisis.

In the 1960s the Ba'thist government translated the "Arabism of Eritrea" idea into politics. Ethiopia had recognized Israel; an Israeli embassy had opened in Addis Ababa in 1962; and Ethio-Israeli relations were gradually rising to the level of an alliance. Damascus declared the Eritrean revolt a part of the Arab struggle. Syrian maps of the Arab world, without exception, always included Eritrea. According to the weekly journal of the Syrian army: "The sons of Eritrea are of various Arab origins. . . . Eritrea formed from the year 80 after the Hijra [i.e., from the occupation of the islands of Dahlak in 702 A.D.] part of the Umayyad caliphate and later on of the Abbasid caliphate. . . . The revolt in Eritrea is a revolutionary tributary which flows into the main stream of the Arab revolution."[5]

In June 1963 the main office of the ELF, headed by Idris Adam, moved from Cairo to Damascus. The Guerrilla Academy near Aleppo opened its doors to Eritrean youngsters, but others came from Egypt and others still, directly through the Sudan. Their recruitment in the field and their transfer to Syria was supervised by Idris Qaladiyos and Idris Adam, and gradually the whole matter was taken over by the Bani 'Amir from western Eritrea. By 1968 it was estimated that some 300 ELF fighters had finished a year-long training course in Aleppo, further strengthening the dominance of the western *wilayyas* of the organization's General Command in Eritrea.[6] (The General Command, although officially still in control of all fighters in the field, was now identified with the western Eritreans, mainly of Bani 'Amir origin.) Sabbe, whose base was Massawa and its surrounding area, was experiencing difficulties in his overly ambitious effort to become the leader of the movement. Although he was the architect of the new Arab connection, his position as the secretary of the ELF's Foreign Mission meant that he had little influence in the field. In Syria he was allowed to broadcast from Radio Damascus and increase his public profile. He was successful in befriending the powerful Syrian head of intelligence and later the army's commander-in-chief, Ahmad al-Suwidani, but his rivals within the ELF, the leaders of the General Command in Eritrea, outweighed his influence in Syria by their ties with a rival wing in the Ba'th.[7]

In June 1965, these complications in Syria surfaced through a small political drama in the Sudan. In Syria, Sabbe had managed to organize two planeloads of arms and fly them, with some of his eastern Eritrean followers, to Khartoum. His goal was to smuggle them to the Massawa area where, the previous January, his local men had tried unsuccessfully to begin anti-Ethiopian activities. The Sudanese government was now a loose coalition, which in October 1964 had managed to topple the military government of General Ibrahim 'Abbud. The new regime, unlike its predecessor, was ready to challenge Haile Selassie but was not unanimous on Eritrea. The Mirghaniyya-Khatmiyya wing of the coalition (supporters of the Bani 'Amir and the ELF General Command) soon learned of Sabbe's move and leaked word to the Mahdiyya people, who, in turn, arrested Sabbe and notified the Ethiopian government. Sabbe was released following the intervention of the Syrian ambassador, but the Sudanese power struggle and the growing hostility among the Eritreans continued to feed on each other.[8]

In late 1965, having returned to Syria, Sabbe had his moment when the wing of the Ba'th establishment that supported him, headed by Amin al-Hafiz and the ideologue Michel 'Aflaq, managed to defeat their rivals, the so-called "military wing" of the party. Soon however, in February 1966, the military wing ousted their rivals, who fled to Iraq. The new rulers, notably General Sallah Jadid and General Hafiz al-Assad, favored the ELF General Command, and Sabbe's men now faced serious problems. The memoirs of Sabbe's aide, Abu al-Qasim Hamad, reported that it was only because of the personal intervention of Sallah Jadid that they were not expelled from Syria altogether.[9] Following the Six Day War, however, the military Ba'thist rulers of Damascus lost active interest in Eritrea. Under Assad, beginning in 1969–1970, they continued to train and equip their wing of the ELF, but the amount of aid was modest and had more impact on the internal affairs of the Eritrean separatists than on their guerrilla activities against the Ethiopian government.

We have already seen the impact of the Six Day War on Nasserism and on pan-Arabism. It dealt a nearly fatal blow to the idea of secular Arab all-regional unity. In a span of two to three years after the traumatic defeat, a period began of strengthening the various regimes in the Arab Middle Eastern world. With the notable exception of Lebanon (as hosting the Palestine Liberation Organization [PLO]) all the other states began to enjoy a considerable amount of internal stability. The states of the region continued to pay lip service to the idea of Arab unity, but the idea inspired little more than that. The 1970s witnessed little of the rapid political change of the previous two decades and far less of the propaganda warfare and violent subversion of the kind that had fed the ELF.

Moreover, the 1967 war had resulted in the closing of the Suez Canal, which, in turn, rendered the Red Sea strategically marginal. Syria was ready to invest modestly in the ELF through the Sudan, but it had nothing to gain from Sabbe and his eastern Eritrean groups.

It was at this point that Sabbe initiated a connection between the ELF and the PLO, an action that would have serious consequences for Ethiopia and Eritrea. It is clear that the PLO adopted the Ba'thist concept that the Eritreans were Arabs. As one PLO journalist wrote: "The Arabs have to understand that in Eritrea a revolution in an Arab country is in the making, a revolution that is inseparable from the Arab liberation movement or from the struggle to liberate Palestine or from the Arab revolution in any other Arab country. We are therefore obliged to support the struggle of this people and do so in words and deeds."[10]

The PLO, according to its radio station, was working to liberate "Arab Eritrea from Ethiopian occupation" and to rescue "the Arab Eritreans from the reactionary Ethiopian terror, which colludes with imperialism and cooperates with Zionism."[11]

Sabbe increased the connection to the PLO by moving to Amman and later to Beirut and by cultivating personal ties with Yasser Arafat and many other PLO leaders. Not only was he effective in persuading them that the Eritrean revolution was an Arab one, but he was also ready to cooperate with the PLO in its new methods of air piracy and international terrorism. After 1967, according to Sabbe's aide, Sabbe established a small unit that engaged in such activities.[12] He stated time and again that he wanted to make the Eritrean Arab struggle "a main pillar of the Palestinian revolution."[13]

By 1969, relations between Sabbe's men in the field and the PLO had become closer. Eritreans were training in PLO camps in Jordan, while Palestinian experts, notably Hasan Salameh (later head of the Black September organization and architect of the 1972 massacre of Israeli athletes at the Munich Olympic Games) were training Eritreans in the Danakil desert in eastern Eritrea. Early in 1970 it was estimated that some 250 Eritreans were being trained in PLO camps. Some of them were said to participate in fighting on the side of the Palestinians when King Hussein of Jordan drove the PLO from Amman in "Black September" of 1970. By early 1971, according to Sabbe's aide, the volume of the PLO's aid to the Eritrean revolution was greater than that of all Arab countries combined. "If not for the distance," he wrote, "we would have been practically united into one organization."[14]

Sabbe's connection to the PLO expanded to include Muammar Qaddafi who seized power in Libya in 1969. Sabbe was introduced to the Libyan through Arafat, and the acquaintance yielded financial aid as well as a connection to South Yemen—the People's Democratic Republic of Yemen (PDRY)—where more Eritreans underwent training.

Sabbe's PLO connection had far-reaching consequences. It introduced the Eritreans to a new sphere of guerrilla warfare and terrorism at a time (post-1967) that they appeared to be losing their momentum. More significantly, it enabled eastern Eritreans to maintain their independence from the western Bani 'Amir fighters who controlled the ELF institutions.

Tension between these two wings and between their respective *wilayya*s aggravated as young Christian Tigreans began joining the movement. The majority of them, following the logic of geography and history, opted to join the eastern *wilayya*s, which were now supported by Sabbe, by his Foreign Mission and by the PLO-Qaddafi connection. After a complicated series of political in-fighting Sabbe and some of his associates founded an organization that rivaled the ELF, called the Popular Liberation Forces (PLF) in a PLO camp in Amman, in November 1969.[15] From these beginnings, the Eritrean Popular Liberation Forces (EPLF) was born in

1972, comprising field commanders such as Ramadan Muhammad Nur, the Christian Issayas Afeworqi, and the Foreign Mission under Sabbe. Twenty years later, the EPLF would emerge victorious and establish an independent, yet non-Arab, Eritrea.

In the early 1970s, the more the PLO was drawn into internal Lebanese conflicts, the less it contributed to the Eritrean cause. In Beirut, the PLO contributed to the production of the ELF Arab literature, to which we shall soon turn. However, in military and political terms it was now the turn of the Iraqis to carry the torch of Eritrea's Arabism. Their role, viewed from the perspective of later years, was to create unity among the "Eritrean Arabs" in order to save them from forces that, later in the decade, would cause the group's demise.

In the early 1960s Sabbe was attempting to build an Iraqi-Eritrean connection and managed to be introduced to the president, 'Abd al-Karim Qasim, and later to President 'Abd al-Rahman 'Arif. Both offered some lip service to Arab solidarity but provided no real help.[16] In July 1968 the Ba'th Party came to power in Baghdad, aided by the Ba'thist Syrian exiles (headed by 'Aflaq), and adopted Eritrea's Arabism. As one Baghdad publication reported: "The Arab masses all over the Arab countries and all the fighters in the name of Ba'th Arab socialism live and breathe the Eritrean revolution with all their souls and consciousness . . . [for] in principle the Eritrean revolution is an inseparable part of the Arab revolution."[17]

Despite their intense rivalry with the Syrians, the Iraqis opted to join with the ELF General Command. They rejected 'Uthman Sabbe, perhaps because he was too dependent on the PLO and Qaddafi. As the Syrians lost interest, many young ELF fighters from western Eritrea left to undergo training in Iraq.

The main role of the Iraqis, however, was as mediators between the rival Eritrean wings. The split in the movement was formalized when the ELF created its Revolutionary Council (RC) in November 1971, and the EPLF was formed in February 1972. Following the Haile Selassie–Numayri agreements in 1972 the Sudanese border was nearly sealed. With the continued closing of the Suez Canal the Eritrean movement deteriorated. For their part, the Iraqis attempted to unify the movement and send mediators to the field. As it was described by one of their mumber, As'ad al-Ghuthani, the main difficulty in mending fences between the two fronts of "Arab Eritrea" were the growing number of young Christians joining the movement. They resented the Arabization of their cause and sought the establishment of working-class parties in their respective fronts. In the ELF-RC an Eritrean Labor Party was formed by Heruy Tedla Bairu, the son of a prominent leader in Eritrean Christian politics of the federation period, Tedla Bairu. Within the EPLF, an Eritrean Peoples' Revolutionary Party was formed (in fact even prior to unification with Sabbe's PLF), headed by Ramadan Nur and Issayas Afeworqi.

According to al-Ghuthani the leaders of both parties met in Aden in 1972 but they failed to unite. Nonetheless, they agreed on fighting the rhetoric and ideology of Arabism in the Eritrean movement.[18]

In addition, the young EPLF members, Christian and Muslim alike of the Revolutionary Party, were now adopting Marxist terms of class struggle, giving the concept of Eritrea's revolution an entirely different meaning from the Arabic *thawra* (revolution). The latter, an early twentieth-century Arab and Egyptian nationalist term, revived by the Ba'th Party and by Nasserites, was used extensively by the Arabized ELF (and became the standard term for revolution in Eritrean Tigrinya). It was an idealistic, nationalist concept, denoting fighting against an alien, a non-Arab oppressor, and containing a nonmaterialistic social message. This difference in seeing the social and nationalistic aspects of the Eritrean revolution would later have far-reaching consequences for the victory of the EPLF over the ELF. The nationalist Eritrean (-Arab) concept of the ELF failed to attract a new generation of mainly young Christian Tigreans, while the Marxist terminology of the EPLF bridged religious backgrounds and served to stimulate the construction, beginning in the late 1970s, of a stronger and authentically Eritrean revolutionary organization.

In the early 1970s, however, the influence of Christian Eritreans, and of these parties, began to grow after the removal of Asrate Kassa as the Ethiopian governor of Eritrea in 1972 (to which we shall return), and as the brutality of the Ethiopian army drove more young Christians to the cause of Eritreanism.

The Iraqi effort to unite the wings of an Arab movement met with little success. The Iraqis were more successful in helping their trained youth to gain positions of power within the ELF-RC. In May 1975 the Iraqi-trained Ahmad Nasser took over the leadership of the organization after toppling the Syrian-trained old guard. The new leaders emphasized that they were an integral part of the Arab world. Several months later, in September 1975, the Iraqi mediators, amid a much-publicized conference in Khartoum, finally managed to unite the ELF-RC with Sabbe's Foreign Mission of the EPLF. By that time, however, the Tigrean Christian element in the Eritrean movement had grown to the extent that this unity was only marginal in importance. Other developments to which we shall turn in our conclusion were already at work pushing the Arabism of Eritrea into the sidelines.

THE TERMINOLOGY AND
LITERATURE OF ERITREA'S ARABISM

Except in Egypt, where countries of the Nile always remained a subject of great interest, very little was published on Ethiopia during this period in other Arab countries. The Arabic press demonstrated little curiosity, and even the drama of 1974 and the fall of Haile Selassie in September yielded only brief mention. Eritrea, although regarded as part of the Arab world by the Ba'thists, the PLO, and many others, fared little better. In fact, the Arab press virtually ignored the internal developments in Eritrea. Eritrea was discussed more in the context of the region's Red Sea strategy than as the center of a struggling Arab liberation movement.

The Muslim Eritrean pioneers of the ELF, who had gone into exile and who had undergone training in the Arab countries, produced most of the literature on Eritrea's Arabism. They were seeking Arab support and they therefore worked to spread the concept of Eritrea's history as both unique and Arab. They also sought to spread the idea of Ethiopia's inherent aggressiveness, and of its alliance with "Zionist imperialism." The premise of that literature was that an Eritrean victory would make a substantial contribution to pan-Arabism.

The ELF adopted Arabic and Tigrinya as its two official languages, but until the emergence of the Christian-Tigrean wing in the mid-1970s nearly all of the official publications were in Arabic. Arabic, we reiterate, was always a vehicle of Islamic politicization in the Horn of Africa, and a language promoted by all those who had worked for the unification of local Islam as an antithesis to Ethiopia's Christian identity and statehood. Of the fifteen titles listed in an ELF Arabic-language book in 1970, *Eritrea's Struggle,* only one was published in both Arabic and Tigrinya. The rest were written during the 1960s for the consumption of Middle Eastern Arabs. Three of these were: *Eritrea, A New Algeria; Eritrea, Algeria of the Red Sea;* and *Algeria of the African Coast.* They emphasized the similarities between the ELF and the FLN and spread the notion of their common Arab anti-imperialist ideology. Other titles included *Eritrea Under the Devilish Ethiopian Imperialism* and *Facts on the Genocide in Eritrea.* Three other titles concerned Eritrea's history.[19]

The Eritrean Struggle (no place of publication mentioned) carried a clear message conveyed even by the cover drawing: it depicts a map of the Red Sea area, with Eritrea a part of the Arab world, and an angry Eritrean, backed by an angry Arab, stabbing Ethiopia with a dagger. The name of Ethiopia comes with three question marks symbolizing its being—like Israel—"a self-styled state," an artificial temporary entity. The book consists mainly of a chronology of the ELF battles until October 1969. A major section is dedicated to those who had died in the struggle as well as to a discussion of the enemy. Of the latter, *Ras* Asrate Kassa, Eritrea's governor, is mentioned as the suppressor of the use of Arabic in Eritrea and as a friend of the Israelis who supported the atrocities committed by the Ethiopian special services. The Amharization policy of Asrate, according to the book, would fail, for the young Eritreans who had gone to the Arab countries had returned to the field and were teaching Arabic in the ELF-liberated areas.[20]

Of significance is the book's terminology. It is clearly derived from similar PLO literature, with the same methods and techniques. Terms such as martyrdom (*istishad*) and strugglers (*munadilun*), with their heavy Islamic-Arab symbolism, are used throughout, and there is a similar use of words like "refugees" and "genocide." The term *thawra*, a "revolution" in the Arab nationalist liberation sense rather than the traditional political one, is prominent in this book as well as in most ELF publications.

The man who was the moving spirit behind much of the Eritrean Arab literature was 'Uthman Salih Sabbe. He was not only the most active promoter of the Syrian connection, the PLO, Qaddafi, and the PDRY, but also a prolific and talented writer, well versed in Arabic. His appearing prominently in our chapters should not, however, be misleading. The Eritrean-Ethiopian history of this period developed in the fields of Eritrea itself, where Sabbe had had negligible influence from the start.

Sabbe published dozens of articles and gave innumerable interviews, but it was in two books that he elaborated his concept of Eritrea. One was published in Beirut in 1974, under the title *Eritrea's History*.[21] In the intro duction Sabbe admitted to being an amateur historian but his work has a professional quality. He made two main points: the first is that Eritrea was always unique and Middle Eastern. This argument is supported by a wealth of information and is based on the assumption that Eritrea is, and was, a diversified albeit cohesive entity shaped by many influences: Ottoman, Egyptian, Italian, Sudanese, among others. In his argument, Sabbe took great pains to play down or ignore any influence from Ethiopia (for example, he failed to mention *Ras* Alula's government in Asmara) and exaggerated the influence of Arabs and of Arabic, which he admitted is only one of Eritrea's languages, but implied it is *the* language of Eritrean unity.[22]

The other point he made throughout his book is the illegitimacy of Ethiopia's claim to Eritrea, indeed, the illegitimacy of Ethiopia as a Red Sea entity. A main thrust of Sabbe's argument was his contention that the Aksumite kingdom had nothing to do with the future Ethiopia. Aksum was a part of the Oriental East, which disappeared five hundred years before the appearance in the thirteenth century of the Solomonides and the birth of "Amharic" Ethiopia. Aksum, according to Sabbe, was not Abyssinian. When he ran into difficulty in narrating the story of Muhammad and the *najashi,* he disposed of it quickly, failing to mention that in the Arabic and Islamic terminology of the period, Aksum was *al-Habasha* and that the Prophet was said to have left a *hadith* with a message of gratitude to the Ethiopians (p. 70). (Sabbe was too well read not to be aware of that saying. In any case, in a book by one of his followers, it was reported that Sabbe had met in the early 1960s the *imam* of Yemen, whom Sabbe asked to support the Eritrean separatists, and who then reminded Sabbe of the *utruku al-habasha* legacy.)[23]

Ever since they founded their landlocked kingdom, the Amhara had strived to reach the sea at the expense of Eritrea, according to Sabbe. For that purpose they joined forces with the powers of Western imperialism—Europeans, Americans, and Zionists. The Middle Easterners, he wrote, have always helped the Eritreans against these enemies.

This argument was presented even more forcefully in Sabbe's *The Struggle over the Red Sea,* published in about 1972. Although I have been unable to find the book itself, it is extensively summarized in a 1974 book by Sabbe's chief aide, the Sudanese Muhammad Abu al-Qasim Hamad, during their period in Damascus.[24]

Entitled *The International Dimensions of the Eritrean War,* Hamad's book is mainly dedicated to Sabbe's work in the Arab world. Its premise is that Eritrea was always the Middle Eastern bridgehead in the struggle against an Ethiopian-Western imperialist alliance that sought to deprive the Red Sea region of Islam and the Arabs. Thus, the Persians separated Ethiopia and Byzantium, the Ottomans disrupted an Ethiopian alliance with the Portuguese, and now it is up to the Arabs to prevent an Ethiopian-Zionist-American imperialistic plot to accomplish the same goal. The Red Sea, the author quotes Sabbe as saying, was always the key to the Middle East and the Mediterranean. It is even more important in modern times than ever before because of the importance of oil. And the key to the Red Sea is what Sabbe depicted as *The Crucial Triangle,* the Assab-Massawa-Asmara area. There, argue Sabbe and his aide, the future of the Red Sea will be determined. The Eritrean revolution can give Arabism this precious gift if the Arabs come forward with the necessary aid.

The book makes two arguments. First, that the eastern Red Sea part of the Eritrean battlefield, that of the EPLF, is far more important than the western Eritrean wing of the ELF. Sabbe had made this point elsewhere, such as in his introduction to the Arabic translation of G.K.N Trevaskis's *Eritrea: A Colony in Transition.*[25] (Sabbe argues that the British administrator, Trevaskis, overstated the importance of the 1940–1950s Muslim League of Western Eritrea, a group that can be seen as the original ELF. Sabbe added that Trevaskis, the embodiment of imperialism, ended overseeing the British 1967 flight from Aden, then returned to Britain, wounded by an Arab grenade.)

Hamad laments the lack of Eritrean unity (and the ELF failure to recognize the supremacy of eastern Eritrea). He also laments the Arab failure to respond to the call to liberate *The Crucial Triangle.*[26] The Ba'thist Syrians and Iraqis helped the ELF while the Egyptians, the Algerians, the Saudis, and others did little more than pay lip service to their cause. After the Suez Canal was closed as a result of the Six Day War, it was difficult to convince these busy governments of the importance of the triangle, and the book is filled with details on the frustrating negotiations in the Arab capitals.

In Sabbe's view, the main ray of hope was the PLO. Sabbe missed no opportunity to praise the Palestinian organization as the most authentic supporter of Eritrea's Arabism. In *Filastin al-thawra* of 19 September 1973, to quote one example, he stated that "the Palestinian people is the true friend of the Eritrean people and its chief ally. The Eritrean revolution for its part should work to move the Arabs to unite in standing by the Palestinian struggle." The PLO press and radio station spoke in the same language, and Abu al-Qasim Hamad illustrates it by quoting a long poem written by the Palestinian poet Samih al-Qasim:

> I heard of a girl immersing herself in her blood
> to purify the dust and the tears from her doors
> and expel the ghosts from her skies.
> It is said that her face is ripe with fertility
> and the sun, and Arabism.
> And who is she—Eritrea. (pp. 148–149)

The PLO helped and subsidized Sabbe in his effort to publicize the issue of Eritrea's Arabism. Of the relevant literature thus produced in Beirut in the mid-1970s I shall mention only Khalaf al-Munshidi's *Eritrea from Conquest to Revolution* (1973), Sa'id Ahmad al-Janahi's *Eritrea on the Threshold of Victory* (1975), and Muhammad 'Abd al-Mawla's *The Eritrean Revolution and the International Struggle in the Red Sea* (1976).[27] In their basic premises they share much with Sabbe; they reflect a tendency to ignore Ethiopia. There is no real discussion, not even a mention of Ethiopian affairs as meriting some interest. Ethiopia, like some of the Palestinian writings on the conflict with Israel, is depicted as an artificially created nation that deserves to be ignored.

In fact, the literature of Eritrea's Arabism mentioned Ethiopian affairs mainly in the context of the country's unholy alliance with Israel. One case in point is the booklet "Israeli Penetration into Eritrea" (no author mentioned) issued by the PLF in 1970.[28] The booklet contains much information on Israeli involvement in Ethiopia, in such fields as agriculture, education, health, transportation, and security. By 1970, the relations between the two countries had reached the stage of a near alliance, with dozens of Israeli experts busy in the capital, the rural areas, and in Eritrea. The booklet gives some details of this activity in an effort to prove that Ethiopia is the enemy of the Arabs, which fell into the hands of the "Zionist-American octopus." The Zionists, according to the booklet, promote the Ethiopian Jewish "Falasha" community so that it will serve to further undermine the Ethiopian people as Jews had been long doing in Europe and America (p. 37). Essentially, the booklet asserts, Ethiopia in itself is as inherently imperialistic as Israel, and Menelik's circular letter of 1891 to the European governments is quoted as proof.

A list of Israeli economic enterprises in Eritrea, primarily the Incode meat factory at Asmara and a fishery in Massawa, is presented as evidence that Eritrea is the main target of this imperialism. Israeli penetration into Eritrea was increased after the appointment of *Ras* Asrate Kassa as Eritrea's governor in 1964. The *ras* and the Israelis, the booklet recounts, worked to build up the Ethiopian forces that were quelling the Eritrean revolution. A base near the town of Decamere served as the Israeli-run training camp for the Ethiopian Eritrean commandoes (mostly local Eritrean Christians). The author writes that Eritrea was a prime Israeli-Ethiopian colonial target. It was both the base to insure that the Red Sea would not be an Arab lake and the gateway to Israeli and U.S. imperialist expansion into the continent of Africa. The PLF publication concludes:

> It is a fact that world Zionism as exemplified by its racist and imperialistic base [Israel], shares certain dreams and common interests with the autocratic Ethiopian regime, . . . for both, where international affairs are concerned, find themselves linked to the USA. Both pursue a political line which is an exact replica of American aggressive policies. Each of them is involved in the persecution of a whole people in an attempt to impose a racist and settler colonialism. Thus, a puppet state which was politically created by world Zionism, led in turn by the US, in direct contradiction to the historical dialectic, has succeeded in subjecting a whole people to the attacks of a hateful settlers' invasion supported by the US on Palestinian soil. . . . And this same Zionism occupies our land by force and imposes a coercive union on us in an attempt to enlarge the borders of the Ethiopian empire, and to place the Red Sea coasts in his hands. The Red Sea coast would thus remain the legal gateway open to world Zionism from which entry into Africa would be gained. . . . This . . . [is] to insure the success of America's strategic plans.
>
> It is not surprising that we should find this close cooperation between Israel and Ethiopia, since the two of them are two sides of the same bad coin . . . two sides which are not different at all in the political implications of their racism and chauvinism. . . . Supported by Arab revolutionary forces the PLF's role is to liquidate the foundation of Ethiopian-Zionist imperialism in Eritrea. (pp. 46–47)

The literature of Eritrea's Arabism was produced mainly in the 1960s and 1970s by Eritrean Muslims and their PLO supporters. In the final analysis, it promoted not only the idea that Eritrea was Arab and was not Ethiopian but also the concept that Ethiopia's legitimacy was questionable.

The idea of Eritrea's Arabism was widely accepted by Middle Eastern Arabs at this time. In Egypt, however, it was widely accepted that Eritrea was historically unique. (Sayyid Harraz of Cairo University, whose book *Modern Eritrea, 1557–1941* was published in 1974, makes no mention of Arabism.)[29] In the press of the Ba'thist countries of Syria and Iraq Eritrea's Arabism was simply assumed. The Lebanese (Christian Maronite and leftist) historian, Yusuf Ibrahim Yazbak, to cite but one more example, wrote the introduction to Sabbe's *History of Eritrea,* in which he confessed little knowledge of Eritrea's background and history, yet we read that Eritrea "is a part of the Arab entity. . . . Her future is inseparable from that of the Arab homeland . . . and . . . it is the duty of the Arabs . . . to stand by that sister in her effort to realize her just demands."[30]

But what of Ethiopia itself? As noted, the amount of literature produced in Arab countries on Ethiopia proper (as distinct from the Arabs' interest in the Eritrean conflict) was astonishingly small. Of the available literature a comparison of two books published in Iraq illustrates the general Arab attitude in the 1970s toward Ethiopia.

The only book on Ethiopia proper discovered in the course of research for this study was published in Baghdad in 1975 under the title, *The Abyssinians Between the Marib and Aksum.*[31] The author, Mumtaz al-'Arif, came to Ethiopia by chance as an agricultural expert for the United Nations' Food and Agriculture Organization and spent eight years in various African countries before returning home to Baghdad in 1969. Although he visited nearly the entire continent of Africa, he was impressed only by Ethiopia. The rest of the continent, he writes, is composed of artificial countries with no real cultures, only poor creations of the colonialists. Ethiopia, by contrast, is authentic and valid, a nation that was able to maintain its sovereignty for thousands of years. He decided to write about that country to reacquaint the Arabic reader with Ethiopia (pp. 3–7). It is only African in a geographic sense. Other than that Ethiopia is Oriental, with an Oriental sense of continuity of religions and other aspects of life. The Arab Peninsula's origins of Ethiopian culture are clear, says Mumtaz al-'Arif, to the point that when he was in Ethiopia he often thought he was visiting 'Asir, Jizan, and Yemen.

The premise of the book is that Ethiopia is not an African Christian entity but rather an Oriental one, Islamic, Christian, and Jewish (he puts the number of *Falasha*s at no fewer than 60,000). He recounts the country's long history, emphasizing the role of the Muslims (there is a long chapter, pp. 230–241, on *Lij* Iyasu), and makes a point in another chapter (10) that the majority of the Ethiopians are, in fact, Muslims. The chapter on the Eritrean conflict does not mention Arabism, and there is also no mention of depriving Muslims of Arabic and Arabism. To the contrary, the Amharic language is even praised as the all-Ethiopian language and a symbol of national unity. The general attitude toward Ethiopia is one of respect. In a short passage he concludes that the Arabs were right in denouncing Haile Selassie for his alliance with Israel, but since the emperor's days were numbered (the book was written in 1974) it is up to his successors, the young officers, to open Ethiopia to Arab friendship (pp. 6–7).

As'ad al-Ghuthani's book, *The Events in the Horn of Africa and the Truth about the Ethio-Eritrean Struggle,* was published in Baghdad in 1980. The author had been one of the Ba'thists we have already seen trying to mediate between the Eritreans. He makes no mention of Mumtaz al-'Arif's book, but his own volume reads like an official response to the latter's call to accept Ethiopia. His reply is negative. The book considers only the Eritrean Arab side and is derogatory whenever it briefly refers to Ethiopia. Haile Selassie, the author asserts, hated the Arabs and suppressed the Arabic language in Eritrea. He spread anti-Arab propaganda. His policy stemmed from his concept of a Christian nation under Islamic-Arab siege, and his country was therefore hateful and aggressive. He and his successor, Mengistu Haile Mariam, shared this view of Arabs, and they allied themselves with Israel. The Arabs, the book predicts, will recognize Ethiopia only after the Arab self-determination of the Eritreans and the Somalis has been accomplished.[32]

ISRAEL AND THE FALL OF HAILE SELASSIE

MUTUAL CONCEPTS

The main practical significance of the literature of Eritrea's Arabism was its impact on the Ethiopian political establishment. The literature conveyed a threat to Ethiopia's existence, and that message was magnified by Arab diplomatic pressure on Ethiopia to sever its relations with Israel. This pressure mounted to become a factor in Ethiopia's internal power game. It intensified particularly after 1972 when Haile Selassie reached the age of eighty and the issue of imperial succession polarized the network of rivalries. Finally, in October 1973 (during the Yom Kippur War and four months before the collapse of Haile Selassie's regime)[1] the wing in the political establishment that had stood for appeasing the Arabs managed to undermine its rivals and persuaded the emperor to break with Israel.

Seven years earlier, in the aftermath of the Six Day War, Haile Selassie's government appeared to have reached a plateau of stability. Nasscrism had been shattered, and the closing of the Suez Canal, although it created economic difficulties, also reduced the importance of the Red Sea. Israel, which was now considered the strongest power in the region, became a main supporter of Ethiopia, involved in nearly all aspects of Ethiopian domestic politics.

The Israeli presence in Ethiopia in the late 1960s and early 1970s was almost unique in the Israeli diplomatic effort; the Israeli diplomatic community in Ethiopia was Israel's second largest, next only to New York. Some seventy Israeli families were in Addis Ababa, about ten in Asmara, and the quality of the Israelis was exceptional. Many of them had come from or would later enter the top echelons of Israeli life. In Ethiopia they were trusted advisers in the fields of economic planning, agriculture, education, transportation, health, industry, and banking.

The Ethiopian attitude toward Israel was a mixture of trust and fear. The trust stemmed from the traditional sense of biblical Zionist brotherhood, which was an organic dimension of Ethiopian Christianity and culture. Indeed, the Ethiopian religious self-awareness of being *dakika Esrael,* "the children of Israel," has been from the very beginning a pillar of

Ethiopia's historical identity, due to strong Hebraic and Judaic influences in various formative stages. A fuller analysis of Ethiopia's traditional attachment to the concept of Israel would entail a detailed discussion of Ethiopia's basic culture, which is outside this book's scope.[2] These traditions, however, were strengthened by, and in turn contributed to, the modern trust, verging on admiration, for the Israeli modern abilities at various vital fields. The fear aroused by the Ethio-Israeli connection was part of the "*Gragn* syndrome," namely, the idea that a strategic alliance with Israel might well result in a renewed Islamic Arab onslaught. The Israelis, for their part, brought into the picture a somewhat different approach, more practical, less culturally and historically oriented.

Ethiopia entered the history of modern Zionism during the Abyssinian Crisis. But unlike the multifaceted argument over the historical significance of Ethiopia, which was so central in 1935 to the politics of Middle Eastern Arabs, Ethiopia in itself was hardly on the agenda of the Jewish *yishuv* (community) in Palestine. Immersed in anxieties over its very existence Jewish public opinion was focused on European and Middle Eastern developments. An extensive reading of the Hebrew Zionist press of that year would reveal a consensual support for British policy combined with an effort not to overly alienate Mussolini. The Italian dictator was still on record as an admirer of the Zionist enterprise, and it seemed wise not to provoke him into an alliance with either Hitler or the Arab nationalism of the Shakib Arslan type.[3] Of the two leading Hebrew papers in Palestine, the "general Zionist" *Ha'arets* conveniently refrained throughout 1935 from discussing Ethiopia, let alone elaborating on the moral aspects of its contemporary fate. Only the socialist *Davar* was openly anti-Italian,[4] and it published occasionally some informative material on Ethiopian history.

The articles in *Davar* were written mostly by A. Z. Aescoly, a journalist and historian who had published articles and books on the Ethiopian community in Jerusalem and on the *Falasha*. In the summer of 1935 he started assembling these pieces into a book which appeared later in the same year. Entitled *Abyssinia: The People, the Country, the Culture, the History, the Government, the Politics,* it was the first modern Hebrew book on Ethiopia.[5] It opened with a question: "A political storm which casts a shadow over the whole world has put on our agenda the name of a near yet a distant country, an entity that was floating between the legendary and the real, between the concrete and the imagined. Is it really 'a state': a country of black inhabitants ruled by a black emperor, which is connected by its religion to the civilized world?"[6]

In trying to answer this question Aescoly summarized the basic literature on Ethiopia. He emphasized legendary elements of the country's image, devoting substantial parts to the Western concept of Prester John, and to the Ethiopian Solomonian ethos.[7] He also discussed Mussolini's policy, which, behind the new Fascist terminology was for the author merely the continuation of nineteenth-century Italian imperialism. The book reflected a measure of indifference. Nowhere in the book is there an out-right condemnation of the Fascists' brutal strategy nor is there any clear moral identification with Ethiopia and Haile Selassie. Ethiopia is depicted throughout as a curiosity. It deserves sympathy, but there is no hint that the issue of its survival bears relevance to the fate of Jews and Zionism. A sim-ilar general attitude, a blend of curiosity and detachment, was reflected in other Hebrew publications of the same year, including Ben-Zion Furman's *Habash.*

Soon, however, the impact of Mussolini's victory on the Arab Middle East rendered Ethiopia very relevant. When the defeated Haile Selassie entered Jerusalem in May 1936, a couple of weeks after the beginning of the Palestinian Arab Revolt, *Ha'arets* wrote:

> The coming of the *negus* to Jerusalem is a matter of great interest for us not only because the king of Ethiopia, who considers himself a descen-dent of the Hebrew royal dynasty, returns to the land of his ancestors in an hour of plight. . . . It is of importance because the events in Ethiopia had, and will continue to have in the future, an enormous influence on the situ-ation in this country. It is a fact that the beginning of the war in Abyssinia was the first push towards instability in Palestine. It was first felt in the economic field, then in politics. Who can really deny the role of these developments in creating the crisis which today storms Palestine?
>   . . . And in this complex of global escalation there plays a central yet so tragic a role a state with which we are most vitally connected, Ethiopia.[8]

The seed of Ethiopian-Israeli relations was indeed planted that year. As the Palestinian Arab Revolt intensified a British guerrilla expert, Orde Wingate, was assigned to modernize the *Hagana* Jewish militia. His 1938-initiated "Night Squads" were to become the conceptual and organizational nucleus of the future Israeli Defense Forces (IDF). Motivated by biblical, Christian attachment to the people of Israel, Wingate's contribution to the development of the Israeli strategic thinking was seminal. He won the nick-name "The Friend" and a very special place in the Israeli security ethos. In 1940 Wingate was assigned to oversee the return of Haile Selassie from Khartoum to Addis Ababa. He brought with him from Palestine one of his Jewish disciples, Avraham 'Aqavia, and appointed him his secretary and personal aide. 'Aqavia accompanied Wingate all the way from the begin-ning in Khartoum to the entrance of the emperor and the "Gideon Force" to Addis Ababa. (A Palestinian unit, Commando 51, mostly Jewish with a few Arabs, fought under British flag in Eritrea and Tigre.) In Ethiopia, Wingate implemented the guerrilla principles he had taught in Palestine and through the services of 'Aqavia he left some of the lesson to the future first com-mander of the IDF, Ya'aqov Dori. More important, however, was 'Aqavia's own account. Back in Palestine he published in 1944 (the year Wingate was killed in Burma) his book *With Wingate in Abyssinia*. It was the first Hebrew book on the war, and against the tragic news infiltrating from Europe it was a story of victory and resourcefulness. It soon became a best-seller, selling 4,000 copies, an enormous number for a community only one hundred times more.

With Wingate in Abyssinia was not only a tribute to a founder of Israel's strategic concepts but also a very favorable and a lively description of Ethiopia. It followed the spirit of Wingate himself, who molded his own biblical attachment to both the Zionist enterprise and to Ethiopia. He told 'Aqavia: "The war to liberate Ethiopia is a war for all the oppressed peoples, it is a war for the liberation of the Jews. Anyone who is a friend of Ethiopia is automatically a friend of the Jews. . . . In your work here and in Ethiopia you can help me, and if I succeed there I can better help Zionism. So it is for Zionism that you fight in Ethiopia."[9]

With Wingate in Abyssinia made fascinating reading and was instrumental in shaping the initial Israeli concept of that country. Its legacy combined reliance on a daring military approach with an awakening of the biblical attachment between Ethiopia and Israel.[10] Turning into a near classic, it introduced Ethiopia to a new generation of Israelis.

The Israeli concept of Ethiopia, however, was never romantic. The Solomonian ethos and Haile Selassie being the "Lion of Judah" made little impression in 1935, as we saw, when Ethiopia was struggling for survival. It was only when Ethiopia became a part of the Israeli security ethos that it won a special place in the Israeli consciousness. When in 1959 David Ben-Gurion started pursuing his "periphery strategy," the idea of Ethiopia's relevance to Israel's struggle for survival in the Middle East had been long entrenched. The fact that the Ethiopians were "Zionist" in their own eyes only added some flavor.

RELATIONS UP TO THE FALL OF HAILE SELASSIE

During the 1940–1941 campaign 'Aqavia befriended young *Lij* Asrate Kassa, already Haile Selassie's most trusted aide. Asrate, later a *ras,* would become the Ethiopian chief promoter of an Ethiopian-Israeli alliance. The relations, however, as we have seen above, developed tentatively and slowly. In the 1940s and later, the emperor entrusted his legal affairs to the Palestinian Jew Nathan Marein, a lawyer from Jerusalem, who had helped in 1936 to counter the Italian Fascists' claim to Ethiopian property in Jerusalem. Marein was later instrumental in preparing the 1955 constitution.[11] In the 1950s and early 1960s Israeli experts had been dispatched all over the country, but it was only after the Six Day War victory that Ethiopia's trust in Israel increased. Beginning in 1967, Israelis were invited to advise Ethiopia on all positions of sensitivity, the security branches, the secret services, the police forces, the territorial army, to train the elite units (mainly the paratroopers), to teach in the army's staff college, and to advise in the various military units, mainly in Divisions III and IV, in some cases, including even the battalion levels. In about 1970, the Israeli embassy in Addis Ababa appeared to be one of the country's major nerve centers, with Israeli Ambassador Uri Lubrani joking that he made it a rule to update the emperor about what was going on in Ethiopia at least once a week.

In the spring of 1968, the two countries agreed in principle to work secretly for the establishment of a military alliance. Following a meeting between Israeli officials and the emperor, an Ethiopian mission spent a week in Israel in mid-April. A program under the code name "Coffee Project" was designed. It involved a close Ethio-Israeli military cooperation in the Red Sea, the turning of Assab Port into a joint naval base, with Israel obtaining ground facilities for the use of its air force on Ethiopian soil. In return, Israel was to build a new mechanized brigade and supply Ethiopia with a sophisticated radar system. Moreover, a joint committee was appointed to plan close cooperation in military intelligence. Israel was also to extend its involvement into further modernization of the Ethiopian armed forces. The whole project was to lead to a tripartite alliance with the Iranians.[12]

On the Israeli side the project was taken most seriously. The IDF chief of staff, Lt. General Tsur, wrote:

> Our interest is to prevent turning the Red Sea into an Arab-Soviet lake. We have been courting Ethiopia for years now, but lately they have become more responsive, for they are worried because of Eritrea. They lead us now to believe that we have a chance to sign a military and political alliance. Since we are very interested in deepening our presence in Ethiopia and turning it into our close military and political ally, we have to respond to Ethiopian demands.[13]

One such demand to which Israel was ready to respond concerned the issue of Deir al-Sultan. As noted, the Ethiopians had lost their rights to the monastery in 1838 when their fellow Copts, the Egyptian monks, took possession of the keys to its gates. Ever since, Ethiopian emperors had made repeated efforts to regain the rights over what was considered Ethiopia's share in the holiness of Jerusalem. In the preceding pages we followed these efforts by Tewodros II, Yohannes IV, Menelik II, the Ottomans' plan to offer the keys to *Lij* Iyasu, and Haile Selassie's attempts to get them from the British. We also noted that the last rulers in East Jerusalem, the Jordanians, decided in December 1960, after a long legal procedure (with the Ethiopians receiving legal advice from the Israelis) to return the keys to the Ethiopians. But forty days later they took them back, under pressure from the Egyptians. When Jerusalem was united during the Six Day War, the Ethiopians laid the matter at Israel's doorstep again.

As the Coffee Project was under way, the Israelis finally responded. On 26 May 1969, a ministerial committee authorized Israeli Foreign Minister Abba Eban to announce to Haile Selassie during his June 1969 visit to Ethiopia:

> I have the honor and pleasure to inform Your Highness that the Government of Israel has decided to recognize the historical rights of the Ethiopian Church to Deir al-Sultan, without prejudice and detriment to the historical status and rights of other Christian denominations.
>
> The Government of Israel will therefore and as a token of friendship to the Emperor's Government and people of Ethiopia assist the Ethiopian Church in the restoration of their rights, including the possession of the key to the South Gate and the key of the Church of the Angel Michael.
>
> Taking into consideration the manyfold complexities of this problem, it is proposed that the modalities for this charge will be worked out between the Ethiopian Church authorities and the Israel Government authorities concerned.[14]

The Israelis even helped the Ethiopian monks to change the locks at midnight 25 April 1970. As a result, the Egyptian Copts filed a legal complaint, and on 16 March 1971 the Israeli Supreme Court ruled that the keys should be returned to the Egyptians. But at the same time it also ruled that the Israeli government could itself become a party to the action and make suitable temporary arrangements before reaching a final judgment.[15] Under these temporary arrangements, the keys are still with the Ethiopians.

On another sensitive international issue, Israel refrained from troubling Haile Selassie about the matter of Ethiopia's Jews, the Beta Israel or the *Falasha*. The Israeli Foreign Ministry simply shelved the matter. Coincidentally, Israel's Chief Rabbinate denied the *Falasha* recognition as Jews, which would have meant they were eligible for Israeli citizenship under the Law of Return. (Recognition was finally given by the Sepharadi and Ashkenazi rabbis in 1973 and 1974, respectively, but by then the entire political climate had changed.)

In Ethiopia, the issue of the alliance with Israel became an important subject of domestic debate.

Internal Ethiopian politics, usually a competition among government elites over proximity to the emperor, entered an intensively competitive stage in the mid-1960s. The members of the imperial establishment were maneuvering and planning for the post–Haile Selassie period. The prominent political figures were taking sides with various potential heirs. Heading the two main rival groups were Aklilu Habte-Wold, the prime minister, and *Ras* Asrate Kassa. The latter, as noted earlier, had his power base in Eritrea, of which he had been governor since 1964. With the help of the Israelis he had built special counterinsurgency units in Eritrea to quell the separatists. His policy in Eritrea sought to attract the support of the local Christians (without sacrificing the emperor's prescribed

Amharization), but he was mainly concerned with preparing for the upcoming struggle over succession in Addis Ababa. Close to the emperor by virtue of old family relations and his long-proven loyalty, Asrate was also the guiding spirit behind the Israeli connection. In this, he was joined in the aftermath of the Six Day War by Foreign Minister Ketema Yifru.[16]

Aklilu had been the chief opponent of the Israeli alliance. As prime minister, he controlled the regular Ethiopian army and favored its units, rather than Asrate's special Eritrean Police, in dealing with the Eritrean rebels. At the same time, as noted earlier, Aklilu, a born diplomat, was in favor of appeasing the Arabs. On 1 March 1968 he attended the meeting between the Israeli Foreign Ministry officials and the emperor in which the Coffee Project was conceived. He said:

> Ethiopia is interested in a strong Israel the same as Israel is interested in a strong Ethiopia. However, the two countries have their problems and limitations, and whenever we try to work out some cooperation the differences in basic approaches are revealed. . . .
> Ethiopia is a Christian island in a Muslim sea, and the Muslims make no distinction between religious and political goals. Their aim is to destroy Ethiopia, and they criticize her for every step she takes together with Israel. Recently the Egyptian delegate to the OAU told us they knew about every detail in the Ethio-Israeli context. . . . If they find out about the suggested project, about a joint base in Assab and the like, they will do everything to destroy Ethiopia. . . . Ethiopia's enemies might assault her in order to pre-empt any such strengthening. The Arabs may also leave the OAU if they hear we have a treaty with Israel.[17]

Until the end of 1970 the emperor allowed the two rivals to compete on an equal footing. Aklilu allowed the Israelis to train the Ethiopian army but insisted on their not appearing at official occasions wearing Israeli uniforms. Under Akilu's supervision, negotiations on the Coffee Project dragged on at a pace that was irritatingly slow to the Israelis. The same foot-dragging occurred on the issue of an Ethiopian embassy in Israel. Consul Yiftah Demitrios, fluent in Hebrew, was the toast of Jerusalem's diplomatic community, but he was never promoted to ambassador. The Israelis insisted on an Ethiopian embassy in Jerusalem. The Ethiopians continued to procrastinate, claiming to have decided in favor of it, then suggesting the possibility of moving to Tel Aviv to avoid angering the Arabs. Eventually they allowed the issue of the embassy to die unresolved.

Meanwhile, Aklilu scored a major victory over Asrate. In 1970, the situation in Eritrea deteriorated (due in great measure to new guerrilla and terrorist attacks introduced by PLO and PDRY operatives in central and eastern Eritrea).

The assassination of an Ethiopian general and other acts of political sabotage helped Aklilu to convince Haile Selassie that Asrate was losing his grip on the province. In December 1970 the emperor removed Asrate from Eritrea and appointed him to head the Crown Council in the capital. Ethiopia's central army was given a free hand to solve the Eritrea problem its own way.

In 1971, only one Coffee Project meeting on intelligence cooperation was convened. It was the last of the project. A visit by the IDF chief of staff Lt. Gen. Haim Bar-Lev brought no progress, and Arab press attacks on Ethiopia led to the dispatching of the country's minister of defense to Cairo. Aklilu launched a diplomatic campaign in the Arab capitals that resulted in a 1972 agreement with Numayri at Addis Ababa and an agreement with the PDRY against the Eritreans.

The emperor then adopted Aklilu's policy, and a new foreign minister, Minasse Haile, was appointed to help implement it. The emperor was particularly concerned with the integrity of the OAU and his position as its figurehead. To ensure that the Arabs would not secede from the organization or undermine the emperor's position, beginning in mid-1971 Ethiopia took the lead in condemning Israel for occupying the "African territories" (meaning the Sinai Desert), captured in the Six Day War. Israeli officials, alarmed at the harshness of the Ethiopian position, were reassured by Aklilu and Minasse that all was well. The general director of the Israeli Foreign Ministry rushed to Ethiopia twice in the first half of 1972. Aklilu assured him that that Ethiopia had to pretend to be siding with the Arabs, but in fact it favored a strong Israel in the Middle East and an Israeli presence in Ethiopia. But, he said, it had to be done without publicity, "because otherwise all the Arab hatred would be focused on Ethiopia, which is weak economically and socially, poor, and torn by the civil war in the north." This pretense, Aklilu said, "is good for Israel, because what Israel needed is a strong Ethiopia." Asrate's advice was quite different: "You have to do your utmost to deepen the economic presence and aid. . . . Our future depends on our economic development. If we will not succeed in bettering the economic situation most substantially in the very immediate future, we will be facing a tremendous crisis."[18]

In late 1972, after he had failed to persuade Haile Selassie to begin transferring power to his designated heir, Asrate gave up and moved to London. Meanwhile, Aklilu and Minasse had intensified their campaign in the Arab countries. Their overtures to Syria, Iraq, and Yemen were, however, futile. Although they had failed in early 1972 to convince Qaddafi to stop helping the Eritreans, they kept trying.[19] In April 1972 Qaddafi paid Idi Amin to expel the Israeli mission from Uganda. In May 1973 when Qaddafi dared to attack Haile Selassie at an OAU meeting in Addis Ababa, they tried to convince the emperor to sever relations with Israel. They were also seeking Saudi goodwill: when King Faysal met with Haile Selassie in September 1973 at the nonaligned conference in Algiers, he promised the emperor Arab financial aid on condition that the Israelis would be expelled.[20] In March 1973 an Egyptian researcher and journalist, 'Abd al-

Tawwab 'Abd al-Hayy, was invited to Ethiopia to meet with the emperor. He was also allowed to see the Ethiopian schemes for the Blue Nile and was flown to Bahr Dar to see the actual sites. These activities paved the way for a meeting between Haile Selassie and Sadat at the May 1973 OAU meeting. At that meeting, the Ethiopian emperor promised the Egyptian president that his country would not interfere with the flow of the Nile without an agreement among the riparian countries.[21] These were welcome words for Sadat, but not quite enough. In October 1973, after Egypt had launched war on Israel, Sadat sent messages to Haile Selassie pressuring him to sever his relations with Israel. "It is time to act," he cabled on October 19th, "no more talking between us. Do what you have to do, but do not just talk."[22]

At this time Aklilu formed a committee to examine Ethiopia's relations with Israel. The foreign minister prepared a survey on Israeli aid since the relations were established, and those who took part in the consultations were told the purpose of the survey was merely to lower Israel's profile. The army's chief of staff, invited to testify, resisted strongly, arguing that the army should not be deprived of its advisers, and especially not at a time when the Somalis were renewing their threats to invade the Ogaden. He warned of a crisis in the army and said it was high time to strengthen it, not to subject it to a sudden shock. A few days earlier the United States had finally turned down Ethiopia's request for new arms. After reviewing Sadat's cable, the emperor invited the committee to his resort outside Addis Ababa for the weekend, and it was then that the decision to sever the relations with Israel was made. Announcing the decision to Israeli ambassador Hanan 'Aynor, on 23 October 1973, Foreign Minister Minasse Haile said:

> Ethiopia has nothing against Israel for not supplying us with advanced arms. We know you are fighting now for your lives and you cannot spare us anything significant. Every Ethiopian knows your situation and every Ethiopian hopes for your victory, for we know you are right in your war with the Arabs. But we have to take care of our interests, and this calls upon us today to break the relations with you. It is not a popular move and we have no doubt that it will help us in the short run only. We hope that the moderate Arabs, the Egyptians, the Moroccans, Tunisia, and Jordan will restrain the radical ones, Somalia, Syria, Libya, who target at us, and that they, the moderates, will not allow them to attack us. . . . It is with great sorrow that we do it, and we hope that the breaking of relations will not last long.[23]

The same day, the emperor announced the severing of relations on Radio Addis Ababa.[24]

During the Yom Kippur War sixteen African countries broke relations with Israel. It was a dramatic culmination of a process that had started two years earlier. Among the reasons were the influence of the Arabs and the Soviets as well as the loss of Israeli contributions of the 1960s. But

Ethiopia was a different case from the other fifteen African states, both in terms of the historical background and the consequences. Of the background, Ambassador 'Aynor wrote:

> The Ethiopian public was taken by surprise and reacted with amazement upon hearing this unexpected news. The roots of historical, religious, and emotional ties between Christian Ethiopia and Israel are so deep and rich that they occasionally verge on the irrational. The cutting of relations while Israel is struggling for survival had a stunning effect on many, for on top of all that it had the smack of betrayal and a stab in the back. . . . Among the members of the establishment as well as by the masses there was first disbelief, then followed grief. . . . Soon the issue was added to the growing resentment by the masses against the regime. Ethiopian political humor resorts to double meaning rhymes and the following line was heard all over: "I, Haile Selassie the first, Ethiopia's Emperor, the Lion of Judah, betrayer of Israel."
> . . . It may be the case that some, not all, of the Muslims are happy about it, but there is no doubt that the overwhelming majority of Christian Ethiopians, from the royal family, the nobility, down to the peasants in the remotest provinces conceive the breaking of relations a matter of great shame and little benefit. The basic Ethiopian historic concept is fundamentally anti-Islamic. What was done is seen as an act of surrender to Arab blackmail, an act for which Ethiopia is soon to pay dearly. In the eyes of the Ethiopians Israel has a special status with Providence. Any hurting of Israel cannot but yield the worst of evils.[25]

In February 1974 Haile Selassie's regime collapsed. A popular protest movement spearheaded by the students and by the army's intermediate- and low-ranking officers was fueled by the fast-deteriorating economic situation. Some of the factors leading up to the 1974 revolution in Ethiopia were Middle Eastern. These included the long-term effects on Ethiopia's economy of the 1967 closing of the Suez Canal; the immediate effects of the 1973 oil crisis; and the dramatic rise of oil prices following the October 1973 war. King Faysal's promise to reward Ethiopia with Arab aid if it broke off relations with Israel was not fulfilled. Soon after the severing of relations with Israel, he sent a cable to Haile Selassie congratulating him for getting rid of Zionism, "which aims at controlling the world." He promised again that the action would be rewarded with friendlier Arab-Ethiopian relations.[26] But beyond words, he did nothing. In January 1974 Haile Selassie was warmly received in Riyad. King Faysal pledged a token 35 million dollars and urged the emperor to initiate the construction of a new grand mosque in Addis Ababa. Ethiopia was no longer "taking the offensive"; thus he left Ethiopia.

By the end of February 1974 the officers who had revolted arrested the upper echelons of the armed forces and some members of the political establishment. They formed committees, which took over the army's various battalions. In the following months a complicated power struggle ensued. The country's elite was in confusion and had no control of most of the armed forces, as the rival wings continued their internal struggle. They did so riding, even fueling, a growing spontaneous revolt, in the armed forces, the rural areas, and the urban centers, which they did not understand. The young officers slowly organized, astonished to find themselves acting against a helpless establishment.

On 5 April 1974 *Ras* Asrate landed in Paris. He contacted the Israeli embassy and arranged for an immediate meeting with a high official. Asrate told him that the Ethiopian security services had totally failed to understand the situation. For that and for other reasons everyone in Ethiopia was saying that if the Israelis were not expelled, chaos would not have ensued. The paratroopers who were trained in Israel were the only reliable force left. *Ras* Asrate then added that he had convinced the emperor to create a new intelligence service, and that on behalf of the emperor he had been asked to transmit to Colonel Avraham Orli, the Israeli military attaché until 1971, and to the minister of defense, Moshe Dayan, that Ethiopia urgently requested an Israeli expert to be secretly sent to Addis Ababa to assess the situation and reopen the office of the Mosad there. Asrate told them:

> In spite of the problems I am confident that the Emperor will prevail. The masses and the bulk of the army are still loyal to him. He is active and knows what he is doing, and so far he compromised with the rebels for tactical considerations only. If you give him a hand now, in spite of what he did to you in the last months, and although the situation looks confused, it would be a very wise step on your behalf. It will be greatly appreciated in due course by the Emperor and by those who will be party to your effort.[27]

It was in late September, only after General Aman Andom had been proclaimed Ethiopia's new head of state, that his old friend General Orli flew to Nairobi and reestablished contact. By then all the important members of Haile Selassie's elite were in prison. The most prominent among them, together with General Aman, were executed or killed on 23 November 1974 by the officers of the *Derg* (the Committee). Major Mengistu Haile Mariam was on his way to power.

To what extent was the expulsion of the Israelis a factor in the demise of Haile Selassie's regime? Clearly, many causes produced that result. However, at least two points must be emphasized. First, the Israeli advisers were so deeply involved in the army's various battalions that in many cases, up to the moment they were expelled, they served as the daily link between the generals and the intermediate officers. Their removal accelerated the already deepening crisis within the army. It also created a certain vacuum in the units that enabled the organization and activation of the various intermediate officers battalions' committees without the upper echelon of the army even noticing.[28]

The second point is that many observers were impressed that the expulsion of the Israelis significantly added to the state of disorientation and confusion among the country's elite. Haile Selassie himself, a prominent member of the royal family later said, behaved as someone vulnerably exposed, uprooted from his own history after he announced the expulsion. He was not the same person afterward.[29]

Ethiopians are very reluctant writers of memoirs, and when they do write them, very rarely do they reveal their emotions. The following is a page from the draft memoirs of Ahadu Sabure, a part of which I shall quote at length for it reflects some of the important concepts and allows a glimpse into the inner thoughts of Haile Selassie's elite. Ahadu Sabure, in his long career, had served as a provincial governor, an editor of various official journals, a journalist, Ethiopia's ambassador to Somalia (1961–1966), and as a governmental minister (Information) in 1974. While in the *Derg*'s prison he wrote his Amharic diary, *Years of Darkness and Trial:*[30]

> Today [1 December 1976] while Ketema Yifru [Foreign Minister in the late 1960s] and I were sunning ourselves, I asked him to tell me why it had been decided to break relations with Israel in 1973, and who had pressured the government to do this. After mentioning that those who pushed hard for this were Prime Minister Aklilu Habte-Wald and [the then] Foreign Minister Minasse Haile, he said the matter was submitted to the Council of Ministers, and when all the other ministers approved . . . only he took a different stand and voiced his objections. He explained to me in details the reasons he objected.
>
> He told me that the briefing he gave the Council of Ministers was in brief the following: "It seems to me the reason we are planning to break our diplomatic relations with Israel is to please the Arabs and win their friendship. However, I doubt that we will be able to win the friendship of the Arabs no matter what we do. The Arabs will not place any value on this thing we are going to do and will not change the hatred they have for us nor their policy. They will not halt aid they are giving the Eritrean secessionists. It is best that we not be deceived in this respect. It does not seem good policy to me to break the relations which we have with a reliable friend of ours for something we know we will not derive any benefit from. I fear that if we do this, the Arabs will become more arrogant and that it will encourage them to dictate to us in other matters."
>
> Again I asked him what was the reason Aklilu Habte-wald and Minasse Haile urged relations to be broken. He explained to me that basically the ex–prime minister was one who from the start was frightened every time the Arabs' name was mentioned, and that he believed they could hurt us in various ways, i.e., by stirring up the Muslims of Ethiopia against us, by helping the Eritrean secessionists with arms and money, and also by supporting our neighbor and antagonist Somalia, and that when it was planned to establish official diplomatic relations with Israel in 1962 he opposed this proposal, and that Minasse Haile's views were not much different [than Aklilu's].
>
> . . . (My [Sabure's] views and comment). The Saudi King Faisal's telling His Majesty in Algiers that Ethiopia's having relations with Israel,

which was the Arabs' enemy, had been grieving them for some time was basically nothing new. It was the Arabs' plaint, which they had been uttering for some years and which was getting terribly boring. The fact that they were singling out Ethiopia from among 80 or 90 countries with which Israel had official relations and indicting and accusing her, clearly indicates the extent of the hatred they have for our country. Previously, during the years from 1941 to 1960, one used to hear repeatedly the song that went, "Many kinds of wrong are being perpetrated on the Muslims living in Ethiopia. All rights are denied them. They are oppressed". . . . While they were repeating this song until the record got old and everyone got tired of it, the establishment of diplomatic relations with Israel unexpectedly fell into their hands and they rejoiced. They were jubilant. After that, who could withstand them? On account of that matter they threw upon us all the putrid cud they had been ruminating on for ten years. They sprayed us with their poison. . . . There is no bad name or insulting appellation they did not apply to us. The Arabs are a people who are very sophisticated in insults and insolence and have no peers. . . . If insulting words could kill and bury one's enemies, they would have reduced Israel and America to dust in one minute.

King Faysal said in Algiers that if Ethiopia broke diplomatic relations with Israel, he would try hard for Ethiopia to get much aid from the Arabs and for the Eritrea problem . . . to be peacefully resolved. However, he did not keep his promise. To please him and the Arabs Ethiopia canceled in one day the diplomatic relations she had with Israel. In exchange she got nothing. . . . On the contrary it was confirmed that the amount of aid in arms and money given to the Eritrean bandits after the Algiers Conference was even much greater than before. During the time he ruled in Ethiopia for more than fifty years Haile Selassie used to think that there was no leader who was more sophisticated than he in the arts of politics, trickery, and cunning. However, it is only to be regretted that he died still hoodwinked without understanding that the Arabs were our enemies who for a long time had never let up in wounding and bleeding us by looking for opportunities to attack us and injure us, that leaders like Gamal 'Abd al-Nasser and King Faysal were the uttermost faithless knaves who made their principal work gulling Ethiopia and other black African states with sweet words and promises, whose breaths stank, whose pledges were completely untrustworthy, who used prevarication as a major political method and instrument and who, while they turned their face five times a day toward Mecca and prostrated themselves in worship to Allah, were only plotting this swindling action of theirs.

The former Emperor's cunning and trickery never went beyond the stage of causing clashes and divisions among his ministers. . . . We ought not to judge him if he was unable to cope with foxes like Faysal and his ilk. Even if the pickpockets of downtown Addis Ababa were a thousand times more skillful, there is no one who would wager that they could be considered the equals of the hamstringers of Cairo, Baghdad, Damascus, or Riyad. If God in His subtle wisdom had not confronted the Arabs with a deadly enemy, namely Israel, who would trample them under his feet whenever they got arrogant, the Arabs would be devils who would be good for no one and would be upsetting all creation without letup.

Ahadu's views can only be understood as a reflection of traditional

Ethiopian concepts that began with the Ahmad *Gragn* trauma. The fear of Middle Eastern Islam (or Arabism) joining hands with local repoliticized Islam to destroy Ethiopia was a product of a long history. In itself, as we have seen, this history was far from simple, but facts are always more complicated than beliefs.

Also rooted in the past was Ethiopia's inherent trust in Israel. It was because of a religious attachment combined with the Ethiopians' ancient yearning for a reliable anti-Islamic ally. Haile Selassie's expulsion of the Israelis, giving in to Arab pressure, went against the grain of Ethiopia's culture. There was no precedent in Ethiopian history for such an act of political capitulation. It had a significant impact on the course of events in the crucial year of 1974. It contributed to the disorientation and paralysis of the imperial establishment and to the unexpected effectiveness of a protest movement led by young army officers.

The officers who led the 1974 revolt, much to the sorrow of Ethiopia, were far from being their country's best and brightest. They were not what Ethiopia deserved. Ethiopia was surely ripe for change, and thousands of highly educated young people were ready to revolutionize Ethiopian politics and society. In 1974 it was inevitable that Ethiopia's patriarchal system would be toppled by the energy of a younger generation. The young generation was waiting—liberals, Marxists, bureaucrats, professionals, a rapidly growing intelligentsia—both in Ethiopia and in exile. Some of these people of quality were in uniform, especially the graduates of the Harar military academy and the officers of the air force. With less confusion, disorientation, and cultural crisis, and with a modicum of intelligence, things could have turned out differently. The year 1974, and the years that immediately followed, might have been more in keeping with the traditions of Ethiopia's historical continuity, but this was not to be. That out of all the great and proud history of Aksum and Ethiopia would emerge the ruffians of the *Derg* and the brutal dictatorship of Mengistu Haile Mariam was perhaps only to be expected in that most unexpected of years.

14

CONCLUSION: THE STRUGGLE FOR DIVERSITY

—

We have followed the history of Ethiopia within the context of the Middle East to the year 1974, a good point to end for two major reasons:

First, we have, in 1994, sufficient perspective to see that an era ended in 1974, in both Ethiopia and the Middle East. A revolution in Ethiopia shattered the imperial regime and led to the emergence of the Mengistu Haile Mariam dictatorship. In the Middle East, from the Ethiopian perspective, the era of political pan-Arabism was coming to an end. By 1977, both the regime in Addis Ababa and the gist of the Middle Eastern strategy had changed irrevocably.

The second reason for concluding this history in 1974 is that we *lack* the perspective to go beyond that cataclysmic year, even though we have a wealth of information, and the importance of the Middle East to Ethiopia and of Ethiopia and Eritrea to the Middle East have only increased since 1974.

ETHIOPIA AND ERITREA: FROM SHIFTA TO FRONTS

In Ethiopia the period beginning in 1974 seems to be defined by the nature of the revolution that took place there. What Mengistu labeled a "revolution" was really an attempt on his part to overcentralize Ethiopia's entire system of government. Domestically, he betrayed Ethiopia's tradition of flexibility in political, social, and cultural spheres. In foreign policy, he sought a Soviet connection. Seeking to imitate the structures and terminology of the Communist countries and to link Ethiopia to the Communist bloc, Mengistu did his best to sever his country not only from its own past but also from the Middle East. Mengistu saw the Arabs as Ethiopia's reactionary enemies, who were supporting the rebellion in Eritrea. He maintained contact with pro-Soviet Arab countries, but alienated the most important of these: Sadat's Egypt, Numayri's Sudan, the Saudis. At the beginning, he flirted briefly with Israel. In 1975 he invited the Israelis to rebuild part of the now politicized and disbanded army. The Israelis formed a new division and new special units, unaware that they were, in fact, equipping Major Mengistu with the wherewithal to eliminate his political rivals. As soon as Mengistu was sure of his Soviet connection, when the Soviets and the Cubans rescued him from the July 1977 Somali invasion to the Ogaden, he unceremoniously expelled the Israelis at the war's end in February 1978.

The Ogaden War, which was conducted between two Marxist states, was nonetheless a twentieth-century chapter in Ethiopia's *Gragn* story. Like his two great *jihadi* predecessors, *Gragn* and the *mawla,* Siyyad sought to cement the fragmented Somali society through an external war. His failure, again, resulted with disastrous dismemberment. Siyyad's siege in the second part of 1977 on the strategic town of Harar was conceived in both countries as a battle on Ahmad *Gragn*'s medieval capital, the historic and symbolic center of political Islam. This notion—for a while—helped Mengistu to mobilize Ethiopian society around old national collective memories. The Cubans and Soviets who helped expel the Somalis from the walls of Harar resorted to the terminology of Communist brotherhood. For many in Ethiopia they nevertheless played the Christian role of the Portuguese in 1540–1543.

But it was in Eritrea that the real battle over the future of Ethiopia was waged. Eritrea, as has been reflected throughout Ethiopia's long history, had two historical roles. One was as a Middle Eastern bridgehead into Ethiopia—the 'Umayyads in Dahlak, the Ottomans' Habesh *Eyaleti,* the Egyptians in Massawa, Mussolini's Red Sea–Mediterranean dream, the "Arabism of Eritrea." The other was as an autonomous part of a decentralized Ethiopia—the Bahr Midir of *Bahr Negash* Yishaq, *Ras* Alula's Asmara, the autonomy and federation of 1952–1962. It was, as we have seen, Haile Selassie's destruction of the Eritrean-Ethiopian autonomy that led to the province becoming a potential bridgehead of pan-Arabism (rather than being a parliamentarian autonomy that might well have influenced the beginning of political openness in Ethiopia).

Mengistu's crude attempts at solving the Eritrea problem brutally with military force drove the Christian Tigreans of the province into the EPLF. The more Ethiopia became identified with Mengistu's brutality, the more the younger generation of Eritrea abandoned the hope for Ethiopian pluralism and resorted to separatism. Believing in Eritrea's nationalist uniqueness, the core of the Eritrean Tigrean youth achieved victory over Mengistu in 1991. In April 1993 Eritrea finally achieved full statehood.

However, the struggle over Eritrea never ceased being a battle over Ethiopia as a political system. Indeed, the struggle itself made possible the emergence of a potential change.

Mengistu changed Ethiopia's political vocabulary and introduced new political structures, but his absolute dictatorship prevented a real political revolution. In spite of his new Workers' Party of Ethiopia (established in 1984) and the other seemingly modern institutions, the political transformation was only skin deep. Politics remained, even was fostered, as a highly personified hierarchy of power, a game of endless individual intrigues, different essentially from the imperial "no-party system" only by its borrowed symbols and gross brutality. A real revolution, the introduction of authentically institutionalized politics, was beginning on the political periphery, in the oppositional "liberation fronts."

The *shifta* (the bandit), we recall, was, in fact, the institution of the opposition in traditional Ethiopian politics. Being a culturally legitimate institution it reflected Ethiopia's political permissiveness. But the *shifta,* an ambitious natural leader who sought to advance his personal position, was part of the Ethiopian system rather than a promoter of change. Successful *shifta*s were accepted and appointed, some making it all the way to the imperial throne. *Shiftnnet,* as a flexible tradition encouraging and accommodating individual political initiative, was thus useful in preventing the emergence of political modernizations: It kept fresh energy in Ethiopian politics. Also, Ethiopian society never experienced a long anticolonial struggle that created such popular uprisings and the ensuing political modernization in other Afro-Asian countries. A proper discussion of Ethiopia's political *shiftnnet* would lead us from medieval Ethiopian internal politics and foreign relations, from the days of *Bahr Negash* Yishaq to the 1950s. During the 1936–1941 Fascist occupation, guerrilla resistance was led by individual *arbannyoch* (patriots, guerrilla fighters), but they failed to form a modern movement. The 1943 *Woyane* rebellion in Tigre came close to being a combination of traditional *shiftnnet* and a popular protest movement, but it, too, failed to form a valid synthesis. In post–World War II Eritrea, Ethiopian *shiftnnet* was successfully orchestrated and subsidized by the emperor to terrorize and destroy the political modernization of Eritrean autonomy, its parties, and its constitutional parliamentarianism. It was only the creation of the fronts in the 1970s, in rural Ethiopia, that started the introduction of modern structured politics. The roots of this change in Ethiopia's political culture extend to the EPLF, the ELF, and to its birth in the Arab Middle East.

Indeed, the anti-Mengistu struggle was for Ethiopia what their anti-colonialist periods were for other countries. Out of the opposition there emerged parties, movements, and fronts, but those at the center were crushed by the regime. Those who emerged victorious had come from the political periphery, and mainly from the northern, Tigrean People's Liberation Front (TPLF) and Eritrea's EPLF. They were effective partly because they had easy access to offices, and could develop connections in Middle Eastern capitals, but mainly because they were able to integrate into the front the political energy of the Christian Ethiopian *shifta* tradition. This amalgamation of the imported structure (which would itself undergo substantial modification) and the highly energetic Ethiopian permissive politics represented a major change. It proved efficient in forming a force that was successful at waging modern guerrilla warfare and toppling a dictatorship undermined by its own betrayal of the country's political culture. But the question we must answer is whether these fronts—and the other fronts of the same era, which joined to form new governments in Addis Ababa and in Asmara in 1991—are capable of further development that will lead to the formation of political parties representing the diversity of Ethiopian culture. Or will they fall back upon traditional Ethiopian instinct of individualistic power games, and erode whatever they have thus far achieved in terms of pluralism? The answer to this question is still unclear, but it may well determine the very existence of the country: whether it will be reunited through a modern cultural and political dialogue or whether it will be again immersed in bloodshed and chaos.

THE MIDDLE EAST AND ETHIOPIA: ISLAM, ARABISM, AND DIVERSITY

For its part, the Middle East, during much of the period beginning in 1974, conveyed to Ethiopia a message that was distinct from the pan-Arabist threat of the 1960s.

It did not appear so different at the beginning. In the period from 1975 to 1977, just after the reopening of the Suez Canal, the slogan of "Arabism of the Red Sea" was raised again and interpreted in Addis Ababa as the Arab menace of yore. It activated the *Gragn* syndrome and led Mengistu to see a renewed pan-Arab plot behind the Eritreans, a concept which he conveniently adapted to his ends.

But the 1975–1977 Arab politics in the Red Sea region was not what Mengistu believed. It was, rather, an attempt to stem Soviet penetration into Somalia, into the PDRY, and into Ethiopia. Indeed, the three countries behind the "Arabism of the Red Sea" campaign of the mid-1970s, Sadat's Egypt, Numayri's Sudan, and the Saudis, were far from advocating the revolutionary all-Arab Ba'thist ideology, or an all-regional, subversive machinery, such as that of Nasser in the 1950s and 1960s. Seen from the Eritrean perspective, there appeared to be little coordination in 1975–1977 between this Arab Red Sea effort, and the Arab ELF-RC, led by Iraqi-trained and other Arab revolution-oriented cadres. The latter were about to lose the leadership of the Eritrean movement to the EPLF, which, as we have seen, resented the Arabization of the Eritrean cause. In the 1980s, the EPLF's dialogue with most Arab countries was at best problematic and yielded no significant support. The collapse of the ELF-RC earlier in the decade and the diverting of the strategic attention of the Middle East from the Red Sea to the Persian Gulf (with the break of the Iran-Iraq War) combined to render the whole concept of "Eritrea's Arabism" no longer an issue.

With the demise of pan-Arabism, Middle Eastern attitudes toward Ethiopia and Eritrea became a state-by-state matter. Syria, Iraq, and the PLO lost interest, while in Beirut, production of literature on Eritrea for the general Arab public has virtually ceased to exist as of this writing. Other Arab countries remained involved, notably Qaddafi's Libya, the PDRY, Saudi Arabia, the Sudan, and Somalia. The history of the Horn, with the war in Eritrea, the escalating war in Tigre, the rise of the Afars and the Oromos, the Ethio-Somali and the Ethio-Sudanese complications, the drought and starvation, and the involvement of the Great Powers, was central to the strategies of the Red Sea and the Nile Basin, and of particular interest for these Middle Eastern countries. But pan-Arabism was no longer the motivating force.

As in the past, it was again Cairo and Jerusalem that mattered most, and their message underlined the fact that a post–pan-Arab Middle East was ready to invite Ethiopia into its fold.

In 1977, Sadat went to Jerusalem, culminating his historic withdrawal from active pan-Arabism and from his alliance with the Soviets, and his reorienting of his country back to Egyptianism. At the same time Mengistu was moving in the opposite direction, as he betrayed Ethiopianism. He fell into the hands of the Soviets, and allied himself, as well, with Qaddafi and the PDRY. When Mengistu began discussing anew the old idea of interfering with the flow of the Nile, Sadat labeled him one of the region's greatest dangers. Yet in 1977 Sadat authorized Boutros Boutros-Ghali to initiate a diplomatic movement toward Ethiopia, characterized by restraint and appeasement. It came to be known as the Boutros-Ghali Thesis, and it has continued into the early 1990s to guide Egyptian policy toward Ethiopia.

Boutros-Ghali brought with him the terminology of *Al-Siyasa al-Duwaliyya* (the quarterly we discussed above, International Politics), with the emphasis on the historical attachment between Ethiopia and Egypt. His purpose was to strengthen diplomatic relations with the Nile countries to ensure the regular flow of the river to Lake Nasser beyond the Aswan Dam. The importance of Ethiopia as the provider of more than four-fifths of the flood waters (and some two-thirds of the annual quantity) made Boutros-Ghali's diplomatic efforts to bridge the gap between Cairo and Addis Ababa a matter of the highest priority for Egypt.

Its magnitude was dramatically illustrated in the summer of 1988. After several years of drought in Ethiopia the water level in Lake Nasser fell from 175 meters above sea level to below 150 meters. Production of electricity was interrupted, and the irrigation of some crops was stopped. The leaders of Egypt could hardly conceal their anxiety. One more dry year in Ethiopia, the experts told them, and it would not be only electricity and irrigation, but the very existence of the Egyptian economy that would be threatened. At a level of 123 meters, not a far-fetched eventuality (perhaps a matter of two more similar years) the Nile in Egypt would be virtually dry. The potential consequences had no precedent in the history of natural disasters along the Nile.

The rains of 1988 in Ethiopia brought some relief. Egypt's concern focused on Ethiopia's plans to use the waters of the Blue Nile and of the other tributaries for its own needs. Boutros-Ghali's effort to establish a diplomatic dialogue with Mengistu were helped when Mubarak took Sadat's place after his 1981 assassination, bringing a more relaxed style and better chemistry with the Ethiopian dictator. Mengistu, for his part, enjoyed the Egyptians' anxiety. He refused to join a forum of Nile countries, which Boutros-Ghali initiated in 1983. When the latter warned in early 1985 that the next war in the Middle East would probably be over water, Mengistu took note. He nonetheless authorized various spokesmen to emphasize Ethiopia's right to exploit the Nile waters and to stress that the 1902 agreement that Menelik had signed with the British, under which the emperor undertook not to act unilaterally, had long since expired. When, in 1987, Boutros-Ghali established Endugu, the organization of the Nile riparian countries, Ethiopia was the only one to join solely as an observer.

In the same year, change began to take place. The Soviets grew impatient with Mengistu's centralization of economy and society and with his penchant for costly wars. Returning from Moscow in April, Mengistu landed in Cairo and opened a dialogue with Mubarak. The two leaders drew closer in later years, but the Egyptian political establishment and public remained worried. Subjects of intense interest in the Egyptian press in the early 1990s were: the Nile; Eritrea and its break with Ethiopia; the fall in May 1991 of Mengistu; the nature of the new regime in Addis Ababa; implications on the Red Sea; and Israeli renewed involvement. Academic conferences were held and a new political literature came into being to examine these issues. In general, the government position was in line with the Boutros-Ghali Thesis.

Israeli interest in Ethiopia also increased during this period. When Menachem Begin became prime minister in 1977, it signaled a change in the Israeli foreign policy. Begin continued to attach importance to Ethiopia's role in the strategy of the Red Sea and the Nile, but the expulsion of the Israelis from Ethiopia by both Haile Selassie and Mengistu, and the fall of the *shah* in Iran in 1979 ended the so-called "periphery strategy" that had been established by David Ben-Gurion. Begin made peace with Egypt in 1979, and the strategic importance of Ethiopia to Israel was thus greatly reduced.

A new focus of interest was the Ethiopian Jews, the Beta Israel, the so-called *Falasha*. The old guard of the Israeli political establishment, in power until May 1977, had ignored the issue that these Jews posed. At the time, Israel preferred not to irritate Haile Selassie; in addition, the Israeli chief rabbis were not yet ready to recognize the Beta Israel as full Jews.

But by the time Begin came to power such recognition, implying entitlement under the "Law of Return," had been granted (1973, 1974), and Jewish organizations in the West were much involved in increasing international awareness of the problem as well as in organizing the *Falasha* in the field. Begin brought to the picture his own concepts of Israel's biblical roots, his hatred of the Soviets and of their client Mengistu, and his own attachment to the Oriental Jewish diaspora. He saw the redemption of Beta Israel as a Zionist obligation of the highest priority. Moreover, the 1975 United Nations Resolution equating Zionism with racism (for which Ethiopia had voted) strengthened Begin's resolve to bring "the black Jews of Ethiopia" to Israel.

"Operation Moses" (1984–1985) and "Operation Solomon" (1991) by which Israel (and Jewish American organizations) organized the *Falasha* and brought them to live in Israel are too complex to be dealt with in this volume. However, they placed Ethiopia on the Israeli agenda more intensively than ever. Moreover, they resulted in the establishment in Israel of an Ethiopian community of some 40,000 new citizens, a substantial size by Israeli standards. The process of their integration into Israeli society, the relatives they left behind (many of whom had long converted to Christianity and lost their rights under the "Law of Return") and the energy of the community's young leadership, suggest that Ethiopian-Israeli relations will continue to be of much mutual interest.

In spite of its peace with Egypt and the rupture of its relations with Ethiopia, Israel refused to succumb to the constant pressure brought by Egypt to return the keys of Deir al-Sultan to the Egyptian Copts. (For his part, Mengistu, in order to counter the Egyptians, had sent to Jerusalem a permanent representative of the Ethiopian Ministry of Culture.) In 1987, when Mengistu sensed he lost his *carte blanche* with the Soviets, he was ready to revive the old connection to Israel. Diplomatic relations were resumed between the two countries in 1989. However, Mengistu allowed himself to believe that this resumption of relations would be similar to the 1960s, with Israel courting Ethiopia and seeking to take the Soviets' place as suppliers and advisers to the Ethiopian army. Few Israeli strategists imagined that they would do any such thing, and many in the establishment remembered Ethiopia's questionable record of reliability. Those who did toy with the idea of assisting Mengistu's Ethiopia met with stiff U.S. resistance to any arming of the tyrant. As Mengistu exerted pressure on Israel to receive planes, sophisticated bombs, and military advisers he became a figure of mockery in defense circles. Some token shipments of arms were sent to avoid having the *Falasha* treated as hostages.

Soon the Israeli-*Falasha*-Mengistu connection would have an impact on Ethiopia's history: In May 1991, as the forces of the TPLF (allied with others to form the Ethiopian People's Revolutionary and Democratic Forces [EPRDF]) besieged Addis Ababa, Mengistu seemed on the brink of turning the capital into his own Stalingrad. Because of the simultaneous Israeli "Operation Solomon," the Americans joined the action with a full diplomatic effort. Four days after Mengistu was persuaded to flee Addis Ababa, thirty-five Israeli Air Force and ten El-Al planes landed at Addis Ababa Airport to take the *Falasha* to Israel. Under an agreement with the Americans the EPRDF forces kept their distance. They entered the town two days later, and the dreaded battle of Addis Ababa was thus avoided.

Israeli and Egyptian interest in Ethiopia is, at this writing, far from being a matter of amicability and shared interests. The Egyptians are especially anxious about what they consider Israeli presence near the sources of the Nile. The Israelis are unhappy with the Egyptian record of working to undermine Ethio-Israeli relations. The Deir al-Sultan issue adds another element of uncertainty. There are countless grievances between Addis Ababa and Jerusalem and between Cairo and Addis Ababa. But given the lessons of history, the very existence of such a new triangular axis of regional diplomacy is a development of great significance for Ethiopia. Egypt and Israel are still the most powerful states of the Middle East. Their orientation to the West and their mutual recognition is the key to the Middle East having a chance to survive in the face of the current assault of Islamic radicalism (or an eventual resurgence of pan-Arabism). The struggle over the future of the Middle East is not yet over, but the receptive attitudes toward Ethiopia in both Cairo and Jerusalem may well carry a promise of good things to come.

Tolerance for diversity is necessary for both the survival of Ethiopia and its acceptance within the Middle East. After more than fourteen and a half centuries of exclusion one can only hope that the great potential may one day be realized in the economic, cultural, and political spheres for Ethiopia to be a bridge between the worlds of the Middle East and Africa. But the threat from the Middle East is no less than its promise. It comes from the very force that threatens the region's diversity: radical Islam.

In the beginning of this study we noted the theoretical concept of Ethiopia as seen by today's Islamic radicals. In Chapter 1, we saw a sample of the vehemently anti-Ethiopian literature produced by those circles in Cairo during the 1980s. Their theological and historical premise is that the Aksumite Ethiopians rather than saving the *sahaba* attacked the pioneers of Islam, and that ever since that episode the historical role of Ethiopia has been to join hands with the infidels of Europe to destroy Islam. Their legacy is clear: Ethiopia is an illegitimate entity that should be dismembered and integrated into the state of Islam. Indeed, an extensive reading of such contemporary material leads to the conclusion that today's radical Muslims' denial of Ethiopia is expressed in terms far harsher than those used by pre-modern *jihadi* anti-Ethiopian movements. Much of the new terminology is in fact a recycling of the writings of Shakib Arslan, Yusuf Ahmad, and the other Fascist-inspired propagators of the anti-Ethiopian campaign during the Abyssinian Crisis of 1935. Publications filled with such anti-Ethiopian rhetoric in the name of Islam are even produced outside the Middle East. The message that Ethiopia is illegitimate and is destined to be dissolved into Islam is being conveyed by a variety of other means. Qaddafi's 1991 declaration that the Ethiopians are actually Arabs is but one case in point. The establishment in the Sudan of a radically Islamic government, allied since 1992 with the Islamic government of Iran, and committed (like the Mahdist state in its time) to the spread of Islamic revolution to the entire Middle East, may well turn anti-Ethiopian literature into anti-Ethiopian action.

Throughout history, we have seen, Ethiopia faced the three political identities and forces of the Middle East. The Islamic core empires, for a variety of reasons, refrained from seriously attempting a conquest of the Ethiopian citadel. Their orthodox Islam, from the very beginning, proved tolerant of Ethiopia's existence but denied it acceptance within the region and condemned it to isolation. Part of the Islamic force—what is known today as radical Islam—denies Ethiopia's legitimacy.

The modern Arab political force of the Middle East derived much of its ideas about Ethiopia from radical Islam. Pan-Arabism became a central idea amid the Abyssinian Crisis, and in the 1950s and the 1960s worked to undermine Ethiopia by adopting the concept of Eritrea's Arabism. Now that an independent Eritrea, non-Arab and non-Islamic, finally exists, has the impact on Ethiopia of the pan-Arabists or the radical Muslims been spent? We do not yet know.

The third force of the Middle East, that of its being a land of Oriental diversity, was always receptive to Ethiopia. From the Aksumite kingdom to the Easternism of Muhammad Lutfi Jum'a, the Egyptian aid during the Abyssinian Crisis, to the Israeli periphery strategy, and the Boutros-Ghali Thesis, this receptivity can be seen. Can Ethiopia and the new Eritrea benefit from the current supremacy in the Middle East of the spirit of diversity? The answer largely depends on their own ability to accept pluralism as the key to their own survival. Thus, the struggle for diversity has yet to be won.

HISTORY AND HISTORIANS

As mentioned in the preface, my initial idea was to survey the modern relations of Ethiopia with the Middle East. But in trying to understand the basic cultural concepts behind the relevant politics I had to turn to their medieval roots. Moreover, as both Ethiopian and Middle Eastern civilizations are strongly history oriented, all modern issues involved fundamental discussions of earlier formative chapters. The legacies of the past—and the arguments over their interpretations—were so central to the making of the unfolding contemporary, that I could not escape dealing with historical junctures spreading over fifteen centuries.

To some of the numerous issues along such a long sequence I hope I made informative and analytic contribution. However, they all deserve far more intensive research and study, for which there is no lack of source material. In fact, in most cases I felt that I was just scratching the surface under which a wealth of evidence, documents of varied natures, waits to be used. None of these issues—all going to the very heart of Ethiopia's history and some of importance to the history of the Middle East—is the subject of a definitive study.

Although I hope to be challenged by new studies and expect to be corrected on various issues, I feel quite sure about the validity of my overall thesis: that in spite of the pivotal centrality of the Middle East to Ethiopian history, the eye contact between the two worlds is very problematic. John Markakis's description of the mosque in Negash, Tigre, housing the presumed grave of the *najashi* and invisible from the nearby church of the very same village,[1] is reflective of the entire story. The Ethiopians, still captive of the Ahmad *Gragn* trauma, and the Middle Easterners, still inclined to "leave alone" their Ethiopian peculiar neighbor, should both reexamine their mutual concepts. Such reexamination is needed for the demystification of history as well as to prepare for a better future.

Ethiopian politicians of the last two generations have hardly served to build such understanding. Haile Selassie, we saw, initiated in 1958 his Africanization of Ethiopia's foreign policy, culminating with the establishment in 1963 of the Organization of African Unity's headquarters in Addis Ababa. Though in itself very compatible with Ethiopia's historical identity the move was no less aimed at artificially disconnecting from the then Nasserite Middle East. Mengistu missed the opportunity to rebuild relations with a post–pan-Arab Middle East. Pursuing a pro-Soviet line, a brutal policy of centralization, and a military solution in Eritrea, he only aggravated Ethiopia's sense of siege. Both Mengistu and Haile Selassie, like Tewodros and Yohannes in their times, conceived the Middle East through the Ahmad *Gragn* syndrome. One can only hope that a new reality in the Middle East will justify restoring a modern version of Menelik's relaxed and confident diplomacy.

In any event the transmission of history's messages is the responsibility of historians. But, unfortunately, in our case the generation of Ethiopianists emerging since the 1960s have done little to maintain the proper scholarly balance between Ethiopia's African and Oriental souls. Educated in the new, excellent university of Addis Ababa, the African History Department of the School of Oriental and African Studies of London University, or in other leading European and U.S. universities, the overwhelming majority of the new scholars defined Ethiopian history as a part of the then rising African studies. This in itself, as I mentioned in the preface, was needed in order to better understand Ethiopia's ethnic and cultural diversity and in order to better integrate approaches stemming from social and political sciences into the historiographical texture. In this respect my generation of Ethiopianists, and the emerging new one, have scored major achievements, balancing the contributions of the previous guard, led mostly by Orientalists. But, with only a few exceptions, it was all done at the expense of the Middle Eastern dimension. The impact of the Middle East on various internal developments, the study of Islam in Ethiopia and its contacts with the Middle East, even the role of the Middle East in Ethiopia's sphere of foreign relations, were all grossly marginalized.

Even the old guard of Ethiopianist Orientalists (Conti Rossini, Cerulli, Guidi, Trimingham, Ullendorff, and others) paid little attention to the actual history of Middle Eastern–Ethiopian relations. The majority were not historians of the Middle East, and they worked during a period in which the Arab Middle East was still under Western occupation. But since the 1950s the central importance of the Middle East to the making of Ethiopia's history, both domestic and external, was renewed and became apparent in nearly every avenue. It had been central to Ethiopia from its birth.

In an extensive article surveying the recent historiography of Ethiopia a call was made to break "the old line between the study of Ethiopia and the rest of Africa . . . [and] draw Ethiopia into the mainstream of African historiography."[2] If the idea is to further relate Ethiopian history to the experiences of societies in Kenya, Nigeria, and Zimbabwe at the expense of researching the historical connections with Egypt, Yemen, Somalia, Israel, Sudan, Saudi Arabia, and the rest of the Middle East, then I beg to differ. To overemphasize the Africanism of Ethiopia at the expense of advancing scholarly awareness of the multidimensional contributions of the Oriental East, and to further academically marginalize the ever-active legacies of the Ethio–Middle Eastern common rich past is misleading. Historians should work for the restoration of direct contact between civilizations. They should not allow politicians, who may occasionally be interested in blurring such contact, to reshape history and its meaning. After two thousand years of history Ethiopia struggles today with its own identity. In searching for a better tomorrow Ethiopians should look back to their diversified past, both African and Oriental.

NOTES

CHAPTER 1

1. For the latest discussion of Aksumite culture and its relations to Arabia, see also the 1991 issue of *Henock, Journal of Historical and Philosophical Thought,* Vol. 2, articles by Wosene Yefru, A. K. Irvine, Getachew Haile, A. G Loundin, and J. Michels. Recent Eritrean and also Arab historians have argued that Aksum was not the cradle of Ethiopia, but an Eritrean entity. I am not going to enter into such debate, and the following passages on ancient and medieval history are based on the mainstream literature.

2. For the history of Aksumite Ethiopia, consult Sergew Hable Sellassie, *Ancient and Medieval Ethiopian History to 1270* (Addis Ababa, 1972); and A.H.M. Jones and Elizabeth Monroe, *A History of Ethiopia* (Oxford, 1935) and later reprints. For Hebraic and Hellenic cultural influences as well as for a general introduction on related dimensions and aspects see E. Ullendorff, *The Ethiopians* (Oxford, 1960). For the most updated analysis of Hebraic and biblical influences on Aksumite Ethiopia, see S. Kaplan, *The Beta Israel (Falasha) in Ethiopia* (New York, 1992), Chapters 1–2, especially pp. 13–43.

3. For the relations between the churches of Ethiopia and of Egypt, see Otto Meinardus, *Christian Egypt: Faith and Life* (Cairo, 1970), mainly Appendix 4: "The Coptic Church and the Church of Ethiopia," pp. 369–398.

4. For a fresh and a detailed analysis of the Aksumite involvement in the affairs of Arabia in the fifth and sixth centuries, see Z. Rubin, "Byzantium and Southern Arabia—The Policy of Anastasius," in D. H. French and C. S. Lightfoot (eds.), *The Eastern Frontier of the Roman Empire* in *British Archeological Reports International Series,* 553 (2), 1989, pp. 383–419. The article, based on hitherto insufficiently noticed Persian sources, argues that the main purpose of the Roman policy in Arabia in that time was to maintain and consolidate a commercial route to the Far East, a route that would circumvent the Persian Sasanian monarchy and enable Roman trade, especially the silk trade, to avoid the exorbitant customs duties imposed by the Sasanians. In this policy the eastern Roman Empire shared a common interest with the Ethiopian kings of Aksum. This, Rubin argued, was the background to the conversion of the Aksumite Empire to Christianity and to the persecution of Christians in the realm of Himyar in Yemen by its Jewish king Dhu Nuwas. The attempts of this king to establish an independent block between the great powers caused concern in both Constantinople and the Sasanian kingdom. The Aksumites, already long involved in the affairs of Himyar, invaded in the year 524 the kingdom of Himyar in accordance with Roman policy. (This was the second or even third invasion of Himyar by the Aksumites.)

5. See Bernard Lewis, *Race and Slavery in the Middle East: An Historical Enquiry,* (New York, 1990), Chapter 3.

6. Ibid., p. 24. See also Yusuf Ahmad, *Al-Islam fi al-habasha* (Cairo, 1935), p. 7.

7. Lewis, *Race and Slavery,* pp. 90–91.

8. See Sadiq Basha al-Mu'ayyad al-'Azm, *Rihlat al-habasha* (Cairo, 1908), p. 319.

9. See Husein Ahmed, "The Historiography of Islam in Ethiopia," *Journal of Islamic Studies,* 3(1), 1992, pp. 15–46; Shehim Kesim, "The Influence of Islam on the Afar," Ph.D. thesis, University of Washington, 1982, p. 45.

10. See details and analysis in Muhammad 'Abd al-Fatah 'Aliyyan, *Al-Hijra ila al-habasha wa-munaqashat qadiyyat Islam al-najashi* (Cairo, 1987); also Yusuf Ahmad, *Al-Islam fi al-habasha* (Cairo, 1935), pp. 11–20.

11. The following passage on the *sahaba* in Aksum is based on A. Guillaume, *The Life of Muhammad, Translation of Ibn Ishaq's Sirat Rasul Allah* (Oxford, 1955); al-'Azm, *Rihlat al-habasha;* J. S. Trimingham, *Islam in Ethiopia* (second impression, London, 1965); Hable Sellassie, *Ethiopian History;* and E. Van Donzel's article "Al-Nadjashi" in his edited *Encyclopedia of Islam* (Leiden, 1993), pp. 862–863. For more details and compilation of medievel Islamic writings on the episode see also: Ahmad al-Hifni al-Qina'i al-Azhari, *Kitab al-Jawahir al-hisan fi ta'rikh al-hubshan,* Cairo 1905.

12. For the full list see al-'Azm, *Rihlat al-habasha,* pp. 193–194.

13. The story summarized here is according to the Islamic medieval sources. Various modern scholars dispute substantial parts of it. For a critical version see Montgomery Watt, *Muhammad: Prophet and Statesman* (Oxford, 1961), pp. 65–70. Watt, and many others, accepts the story of persecutions against the *sahaba* but contends that Muhammad had presumably other plans and ideas in sending them to Aksum, one being mobilizing the Aksumite might against Mecca.

14. See A. Guillaume, *A Translation of Ibn Ishaq's Sirat Rasul Allah* (Oxford, 1955), p. 657.

15. On his names see more in 'Aliyyan, *Al-Hijra,* p.74.

16. Most Western modern historians dispute the story about two hegiras to Aksum. See Watt, *Muhammad,* pp. 65–70.

17. There is no consistency as to their number; the figure quoted is from al-'Azm, *Rihlat al-habasha.* In 'Aliyyan, *Al-Hijra,* for example, the number is 101. See a list of their names on pp. 15–16. According to Ibn Ishaq's *Sirat Rasul Allah,* the number of men ("apart from the little children") was 83. See also Guillaume, *Ibn Ishaq's Sirat,* p 148.

18. See Guillaume, *Ibn Ishaq's Sirat,* pp. 148–149; also Hable Sellassie, *Ethiopian History,* pp. 182–183.

19. See E. Cerulli, "Ethiopia's Relations with the Muslim World," in *Cambridge History of Africa: Africa from the Seventh to the Eleventh Century,* p. 575.

20. See details in al-'Azm, *Rihlat al-habasha,* pp. 312–313.

21. Ibid., p. 196.

22. 'Aliyyan, *Al-Hijra,* pp. 77–81; the last quotation from Ibn Kathir, *Al-Bidaya wal-nihaya* (Cairo, ND). But see Watt, *Muhammad,* pp. 194–195, arguing that such versions of Muhammad's letters must have been fabricated later in order to justify universal *jihad.* Muhammad, in his time, Watt contended, was not pursuing such policy, and his letter to the Ethiopian king must have been on matters such as his marriage to 'Umm Habiba and the call for the other members of the *sahaba* to return to his camp.

23. See also E. Van Donzel, *A Yemenite Embassy to Ethiopia, 1647–1649* (Stuttgart, 1986), p. 242, Note 7.

24. See also Ibn Ishaq's version of the correspondence between Muhammad and the *najashi* in Guillaume, *Ibn Ishaq's Sirat,* p. 657.

25. Of the Western historians it seems that only Wallis Budge, the British historian, accepted that the *najashi* did convert to Islam. The *najashi* did so, Budge argued, to avoid provoking the power of Islam and to thus enable Christianity to flourish in Ethiopia. See E. A. Wallis Budge, *A History of Ethiopia* (London, 1928, rep. New York, 1970), pp. 270–273. For refuting the Muslims' contention that the *"nadjashi"* adopted Islam see Van Donzel, "Al-Nadjashi," pp. 862–863; and also J. Cuoq, *L'Islam en Ethiopie: Des origines au XVI siecle* (Paris, 1981), pp. 32–35.

26. According to Ibn Ishaq; "Ja'far b. Muhammad told me on the authority of his father that the Abyssinians assembled and said to the *negus,* 'you have forsaken our religion,' and they revolted against him. So he sent to Ja'far and his companions and prepared ships for them, saying, 'Embark in these and be ready. If I am defeated, go where you please; if I am victorious, then stay where you are.' Then he took paper and wrote, 'He testifies that there is no God but Allah and that Muhammad is His slave and apostle; and he testifies that Jesus, son of Mary, is His slave, His apostle, His spirit and His word, which He cast into Mary.' Then he put it in his gown near the right shoulder and went out to the Abyssinians, who were drawn out in array to meet him. He said, 'O people, have I not the best claim among you?' 'Certainly,' they said. 'And what do you think of my life among you?' 'Excellent.' 'Then what is your trouble?' 'You have forsaken our religion and assert that Jesus is a slave.' 'Then what do you say about Jesus?' 'We say that he is the Son of God.' The *negus* put his hand upon his breast over his gown, (signifying), 'He testifies that Jesus, the Son of Mary, was no more than *this.*' By *this* he meant what he had written, but they were content and went away. News of this reached the Prophet, and when the *negus* died he prayed over him and begged that his sins might be forgiven." See A. Gillaume, *Ibn Ishaq's Sirat,* pp. 154–155.

27. Cerulli, "Ethiopia's Relations."

28. See al-'Azm's *Rihlat,* p. 320.

29. For a short summary of Islamic presence on Dahlak Islands at that period see Cerulli, "Ethiopia's Relations."

30. For a discussion on the painting "The Family of Kings" found in the ruins of Qusayr 'Amra (50 miles east of Amman), which was produced between 712 and 750 A.D., see R. Ettinghausen, *Arab Painting* (Geneva 1977), pp. 30–31, 190; Oleg Grabar, "The Painting of the Six Kings at Qusayr 'Amrah" in *Ars,* no. 1 (1954), pp. 185–187; K. A. Creswell, *Early Muhammedan Architecture* (London 1932), vol. 1, pp. 263–264; and Hana Taragan, *The Umayyad Sculpture,* Ph.D. thesis, Tel Aviv University, 1991, p. 191. While the early scholars like Creswell interpreted the painting as implying submission to the 'Umayyads, the more recent scholarship found the painting to be of a conciliatory character, reflecting respect to these rulers as members of "the family of kings," from which the 'Umayyads themselves wanted to derive legitimacy. I am indebted to Dr. Taragan of Tel Aviv University for her help.

31. The *hadith* is first found in Abu Dawud, *Sunan Abi Dawud.* See Van Donzel, "Al-Nadjashi," in *Encyclopedia of Islam,* 1993. Suliman Abu Dawud died in 888.

32. See Hussein Ahmed, "The Historiography of Islam in Ethiopia," *Journal of Islamic Studies,* 3(1), 1992, pp. 15–46; see also I. Guidi's article "Abyssinia," in *First Encyclopedia of Islam* (Leiden, 1987); and Jones and Monroe, *A History of Ethiopia,* p. 44.

33. "Red" in Arab tradition meant people of swarthy skin color; in Ethiopian tradition "red" [*qay*] meant light-skinned Ethiopians.

34. Lewis, *Race and Slavery,* p. 34.

35. Ibid., p. 33.

36. Ibid., p. 35.

37. See more in M. Abir, *Ethiopia and the Red Sea* (London, 1980), pp. 7–9.

38. Lewis, *Race and Slavery,* Chapters 5 and 7.

39. See D. Levine, *Greater Ethiopia* (Chicago, 1974), pp. 43–44, 151–152.

40. See Majid Khadduri, *War and Peace in the Law of Islam* (Baltimore, 1955), Chapter 12, "Neutrality."

41. Van Donzel, "Al-Nadjashi," pp. 862–863.

42. Khadduri, *War and Peace,* p. 267.

43. See M. Abir, "Trade and Christian-Muslim Relations in Post-Medieval Ethiopia," in R. L. Hess (ed.), *Proceedings of the Fifth International Conference on Ethiopian Studies* (Session B) (Chicago, 1978), pp. 411–414.

44. An interview with *Shaikh* Nimr al-Darwish, Kafr Qasim, March, 1994. At the time of the interview the *shaikh* was in the middle of preparing for publication a pamphlet on the legacy of the *sahaba-najashi* story. The Ethiopian precedence legitimizing recognition of a non-Islamic yet benevolent government is the subject of numerous articles by *Shaikh* Nimr in the movement's publications, *Sawt al-haqq* and *al-Sirat.*

45. Muhammad 'Abd al-Fattah 'Aliyyan, *Al-Hijra ila al-Habasha wa-munaqashat qadiyyat islam al-najashi* (Dar al-turath, Cairo, 1987).

46. See a bibliographical survey of the literature relevant to the question of the *najashi* conversion, in Hussein Ahmad, "The Historiography of Islam in Ethiopia," *Journal of Islamic Studies,* 3(1), 1992, pp. 15–46.

47. 'Aliyyah, Al-Hizra, pp. 77–81, 85, 93, 97.

48. Ibid., pp. 8–9, 97, 106, 111.

49. See the quotation from Ibn Ishaq's *Sirat Rasul Allah* in Note 26.

50. 'Aliyyah, Al-Hizra, see pp. 103, 106, 108.

51. 'Abd al-Halim Muhammad Rajab, *Al-'Alaqat al-siyasiyya bayna muslimi al-Zayla' wa-nusara al-habasha fi al-'usur al-wusta* (The Institute of African Research and Studies, Cairo University, 1985).

52. Ibid., pp. 3, 7, 254.

53. See Ahmad al-Hifni al-Qina'i al-Azhari, *Kitab al-jawahir al-hisan fi ta'rikh al-hubshan* (Cairo, 1904), p. 4, and introductory note by Isma'il Rafit ("A history teacher at al-Azhar").

CHAPTER 2

1. Hable Sellassie, *Ethiopian History,* Chapters 9 and 10; also Taddesse Tamrat, *Church and State in Ethiopia, 1270–1527* (Oxford, 1972), pp. 31–34.

2. For a discussion of Ethiopia's diversity and its internal cultural-political dynamism in historical perspective see Donald Levine, *Greater Ethiopia* (Chicago, 1974).

3. See Sadiq Al-'Azm, *Rihlat al-habasha,* p. 172; 'Abdallah Husayn, *Al-mas'ala al-habashiyya* (Cairo, 1935), p. 20; I. Guidi, *Il Fetha Nagast o Legislazione dei Re* (Rome, 1899).

4. See analysis in Levine, *Greater Ethiopia,* pp. 92–108.

5. See the most recent analysis in Marilin E. Heldman, "Architectural Symbolism, Sacred Geography and the Ethiopian Church," *Journal of Religion in Africa,* Vol. 3 (1992), pp. 222–241.

6. See more details in Otto Meinardus, *Christian Egypt; Faith and Life* (Cairo, 1970), pp. 369–399.

7. The relevant modern data are as follows: Some 84 billion cubic meters of water reach the Aswan area annually, some 10 billion having evaporated en route. Of these 94 billion the Blue Nile supplies 54, the Atbara 11, and the White Nile 29 billion. The data for the four months of Egypt's summer floods are: Of a total 76 billion cubic meters 50 stem from the Blue Nile, 11 from the Atbara, and 15 from the White Nile. See Arnon Sofer and Nurith Kleaot, *Water Plans in the Middle East*, a Study Presented to the Israeli Foreign Ministry, Haifa University, 1988 (in Hebrew), quoting M. Shain, *Hydrology of the Nile Basin* (Amsterdam, 1985).

8. On the relations between the Zagwe kings and Egypt see more in Hable Sellassie, *Ethiopian History,* pp. 268–270.

9. The most authoritative study of the period in Ethiopia, containing also a wealth of analyzed information on external relations, is Tamrat, *Church and State.*

10. See details and analysis in M. Abir, *Ethiopia and the Red Sea* (London, 1980), p. 6.

11. See J. Plante, "The Ethiopian Embassy to Cairo of 1443," *Journal of Ethiopian Studies,* Vol. 13(2), pp. 133–140.

12. See a summary of Islamic literature on the Mamluks and the Ethiopians in 'Abd al-Halim Rajab, *Al-'Alaqat,* pp. 38–42. See also Elizabeth-Dorothea Hect, "Ethiopia Threatens to Block the Nile," *Azania,* 23, 1988, pp. 1–11.

13. See also Zahir Riyad, *Misr wa-Ifriqya* (Cairo, 1976), pp. 81–104, "The Mamluk Period as the Climax of the Ethiopian-Egyptian Connection." Also, Zahir Riyad, *Al-Islam fi Ityubya,* pp. 95–152.

14. Yusuf Ahmad, *Al-Islam fi al-Habasha,* p. 32; Abir, *Ethiopia and the Red Sea,* p. 29.

15. See 'Abd al-Halim Rajab, *Al-'Alaqat,* p. 36, quoting Ibn al-Athir.

16. For a detailed analysis of the commercial aspect behind the history of the conflict between the Islamic sultanates of southern Ethiopia and the Christian kingdom of Ethiopia see Abir, *Ethiopia and the Red Sea,* especially Chapter 1. Also, R. Pankhurst, *A Social History of Ethiopia, from Early Medieval Times to the Rise of Emperor Tewodros II* (Addis Ababa, 1990).

17. See Yusuf Ahmad, *Al-Islam fi al-habasha* (Cairo, 1935), p. 68. For more on Massawa and Zeila see R. Pankhurst, *History of Ethiopian Towns, from the Middle Ages to the Early Nineteenth Century* (Wiesbaden, 1982), pp. 54–64, 80–94.

18. The paragraphs above and below are based on Enrico Cerulli, *l'Islam di Ieri e di Oggi* (Rome, 1971). This volume combines much of Cerulli's writing on the subject, ten articles, assembled in the section "L'Islam in Ethiopia," pp. 99–394. For a condensed summary of his main theses see Cerulli, "Ethiopia's Relations with the Muslim World" in *Cambridge History of Africa, Africa from the Seventh to the Eleventh Century,* pp. 575–585. Also Trimingham, *Islam in Ethiopia,* pp. 58–76, 138–143; I. Guidi, "Abyssinia," in *First Encyclopedia of Islam* (Leiden, 1987); Tamrat, *Church and State* and "Ethiopia, the Red Sea and the Horn" in the *Cambridge History of Africa,* Vol. 3, edited by R. Oliver, pp. 99–182 ; Zahir Riyad, *Al-Islam fi Ityubya* (Cairo 1964), pp. 49–94; J. Cuoq, *L'Islam en Ethiopie* (Paris, 1981), pp. 119–192. Also Ulrich Braukamper, "Islamic Principalities in Southeast Ethiopia Between the Thirteenth and Sixteenth Centuries," *Ethiopianist Notes,* Vol. 1(1), 1977, pp. 17–55, and Vol. 1(2), pp. 1–42. Also the detailed description in Rajab, *Al-'Alaqat.*

19. See Abir, *Ethiopia and the Red Sea,* especially pp. 19–23.

20. For a succinct analysis of such "northern policy" and the *bahr negash* see F. A. Dombrowski, *Ethiopia's Access to the Red Sea* (Leiden, 1985), pp. 11–15.

21. See Abraham Demoz, "Moslems and Islam in Ethiopic Literature," *Journal of Ethiopian Studies,* 1972, 10(1), pp. 1–12; G.W.B Huntingford (ed.), *The Glorious Victories of Amda Seyon, King of Ethiopia* (Oxford, 1965), pp. 57–58.

22. See E. Cerulli, "Il Sultanato dello Scioa nel Seolo XIII Secondo un Nuovo Ducumento Storico" in his *L'Islam di Ieri e di Oggi,* pp. 207–243; Yusuf Ahmad, *Al-Islam fi al-habasha* (Cairo, 1935), pp. 23–28.

23. See E. Cerulli, "L'Islam Etiopico" in his *L'Islam di Ieri e di Oggi,* pp. 113–133.

24. 'Abd al-Halim Rajab in his interpretation of medieval history in the Horn called the Muslims "Zayla'iyyun," after the town of Zayla', and in distinction from the *habasha* who were the Christians.

25. See, for example, an article under that title by the greatest Islamic opponent of Ethiopia in the twentieth century—Shakib Arslan—in his edited translation into Arabic of L. Stoddard's work, *Hadir al-'alam al-islami* (Cairo, 1933), Vol. 3, pp. 78–119.

CHAPTER 3

1. B. G. Martin, "Arab Migrations to East Africa," *International Journal of African Historical Studies,* Vol. 7(3), 1974, pp. 367–390. Also his "Mahdism, Muslim Clerics, and Holy Wars in Ethiopia, 1300–1600" in H. Marcus (ed.), *Proceedings of the First United States Conference on Ethiopian Studies,* 1973 (East Lansing, 1975), pp. 91–100.

2. Rajab, *Al-'alaqat,* pp. 4, 67–76, 221–226.

3. See Chihab ed-Din Ahmed Ben Abd el-Qader (Arab Faqih), *Futuh al-habasha—Histoire de la Conquête de L'Abyssinie* (Trans. and ed. R. Basset), Paris, 1897.

4. See R. Basset's edition of 'Arab Faqih's *Futuh al-Habasha,* pp. 29–30; also 'Arab Faqih (Shihab al-Din Ahmad ibn 'Abd al-Qadir al-Jayzani), *Tuhfat al-zaman aw Futuh al-habasha,* edited by Fahim Muhammad Shalut (Cairo, 1974), especially Chapter 4, "Miracles that Happened to the Imam." Also J. Couq, *L'Islam en Ethiopie* (Paris, 1981), pp. 221–222.

5. In his *Islam in Ethiopia* the Egyptian scholar Zahir Riyad analysed the whole chapter of *Gragn*'s conquest of Ethiopia under the title of *thawra,* a revolution in modern Arabic. See Riyad, *Al-Islam fi Ityubya,* Chapter 5.

6. See a summary of the controversy in Hussein Ahmed, "The Historiography of Islam in Ethiopia," *Journal of Islamic Studies,* 3(1), 1992, pp. 15–46.

7. For Abir's interpretation of the demographic-economic aspect see his *Ethiopia and the Red Sea,* pp. 87–92.

8. For an Ethiopian interpretation of the conflict with Ahmad *Gragn* see Takla-Tsadiq Makuriya, *Ya'ityopia tarik, ka'atse Lebna Dengel eska atse Tewodros* (Addis Ababa, 1953 E.C., A.D. 1961), pp. 71–196. The volume covers more than three hundred years of history in 455 pages, and the *Gragn* story consumes nearly a third of it. See also his later, expanded version, *YaGran Ahmad Warara* (Addis Ababa, 1966 E.C., A.D. 1974).

9. See also J. Couq, *L'Islam en Ethiopie,* pp. 242–244.

10. Sylvia Pankhurst, *Ethiopia, A Cultural History* (London, 1955), p. 329.

11. See Abraham Demoz, *Moslems and Islam.*

12. B. G. Martin, *Arab Migrations.*

13. Cengiz Orhonlu, *Habesh Eyaleti* (Istanbul, 1974), pp. 26–30.

14. J. R. Blackburn, "The Ottoman Penetration of Yemen," *Archivum Ottomanicum,* Vol. 6, 1980, pp. 55–100.

15. See analysis in Dombrowski, *Ethiopia's Access,* pp. 16–20.

16. The extensive summary of *Futuh al-habasha* was included in the chapter "Muslimu al-habasha" (The Muslims of Ethiopia), by Shakib Arslan, in the Arabic edition of Lothrop Studdard's book *Hadir al-'alam al-Islami* (Cairo, A.H. 1352, A.D. 1933), pp. 78–119. The above quotation on the vision in which the Prophet said it was God's will that *Gragn* would "bring peace [and Islam] to Ethiopia" is on p. 88.

17. Al-'Azm, *Rihlat al-habasha,* p. 186.

18. Orhonlu, *Habesh Eyaleti,* pp. 26–30.

19. See Rajab, *Al-'alaqat,* pp. 197, 207, 226–239, 256.

20. The most detailed study on the subject of the Ottomans and their Ethiopian Province enterprise is the work of Orhonlu, *Habesh Eyaleti.* Many of the details below are from that book. I am grateful to my student Elda Yerushalmi for helping me with the Turkish text. The definition of *habesh* is on p. 21 of that book.

21. On Debaroa see R. Pankhurst, *History of Ethiopian Towns,* pp. 65–72.

22. Orhonlu, *Habesh Eyaleti,* pp. 30–50.

23. Ibid., pp. 48–58.

24. The following reconstruction of the relations between the Ottomans and the Bahr Negash is based on Orhonlu, *Habesh Eyaleti;* Carlo Conti Rossini, "La Guerra Turco-Abbisina del 1578," *Oriente Moderno,* Vol. 1, 1922, pp. 634–636, 684–691, and Vol. 2, pp. 48–57; Also E. Van Donzel, "Les Ottomans et L'Ethiopie au XVIIe siecle," a paper presented at an Ottomanists' conference, Paris, April 1992, and his article "Massawa" in his edited *Encyclopedia of Islam.* I am most grateful to him for his help.

25. This is how Conti Rossini titled his above-mentioned detailed article.

26. More on the subject is given in Abir, *Ethiopia and the Red Sea,* pp. 124–130, 142–150; Dombrowski, *Ethiopia's Access,* pp. 19–24.

27. Abir, *Ethiopia and the Red Sea,* p. 127.

28. Van Donzel, "Les Ottomans."

29. See Orhonlu, *Habesh Eyaleti,* pp. 58–61.

30. See B. Lewis, *Race and Slavery in the Middle East* (Oxford, 1990), Illustrations 17 and 18.

31. Van Donzel, "Massawa"; Trimingham, *Islam in Ethiopia,* pp. 99–102; Dombrowski, *Ethiopia's Access,* pp. 29–30.

32. See R. Pankhurst, "Some Notes on the Historical and Economic Geography of the Mesewa Area (1520–1885)," *Journal of Ethiopian Studies,* Vol. 13(1), 1975, pp. 89–116. The famous Ottoman traveller, Evliya Celebi, visited Massawa in 1672. But unlike the detailed and insightful descriptions he dedicated to other regions of the Ottoman empire the passages on Massawa and the province of Habesh are quite dull. See Evliya Celebi, *Siyahatname* (Istanbul, 1938), vol. 10, pp. 942–946.

33. See E. Van Donzel, *Foreign Relations of Ethiopia, 1642–1700* (Leiden, 1979), pp. 1–38; also his "Correspondence Between Fasiladas and the Imams of Yemen," in G. Goldenberg (ed.), *Proceedings of the Sixth International Conference of Ethiopian Studies* (Rotterdam, 1986), pp. 91–100. Also E. Van Donzel, *A Yemeni Embassy to Ethiopia 1647–1649* (Stuttgart, 1986).

34. See also Dombrowski, *Ethiopia and the Red Sea,* pp. 30–31.

35. Van Donzel, *A Yemeni Embassy,* pp. 235–240.

36. This is a main thesis of his *Ethiopia: The Era of the Princes* (London, 1968).

37. See Abir's *Ethiopia and the Red Sea,* pp. xix, xx.

38. See Takla Tsadiq Makuriya, *YaGran Ahmad Warara* (Addis Ababa, 1966 E.C.), p. 11.

CHAPTER 4

1. J. S. Trimingham, *Islam in Ethiopia* (London, 1965), p. 101.

2. See Braukamper, *Islamic Principalities,* p. 28.

3. On Islam in Ethiopia during the period under discussion see *inter alia:* Trimingham, *Islam in Ethiopia,* pp. 98–114; Cerulli, "L'Islam Etiopico," and "L'Islam in Africa Orientale" in his *L'Islam di Ieri e di Oggi* (Rome, 1971); Hussein Ahmed, "The Historiography of Islam in Ethiopia," *Journal of Islamic Studies,* 1992, pp. 15–46; M. Abir, "Ethiopia and the Horn of Africa," in R. Gray (ed.), *The Cambridge History of Africa,* Vol. 4 (Cambridge, 1975), pp. 537–577; Abir, *Ethiopia and the Red Sea;* Abir, *The Era of the Princes;* A. Demoz, "Muslims and Islam in Ethiopian Literature," *Journal of Ethiopian Studies,* 1972, pp. 1–12; Abussamad H. Ahmad, "The Gondar Muslim Minority in Ethiopia: The Story Up to 1935," in *Journal of the Institute of Muslim Minority Affairs,* Vol. 9(1), 1988, pp. 76–85.

4. See E. Van Donzel, *A Yemeni Embassy to Ethiopia, 1647–1649* (Stuttgart, 1986), which is an English-annotated translation of al-Haymi al-Hasan bin Ahmad, *Sirat al-habasha.* An Arabic edition was prepared by Murad Kamil (Cairo, 1958). See also E. Van Donzel, "Correspondence between Fasiladas and the Imams of Yemen," in Gideon Goldenberg (ed.), *Proceedings of the Sixth International Conference of Ethiopian Studies* (Rotterdam, 1986), pp. 91–100.

5. The above is based on John Markakis, *Ethiopia: Anatomy of a Traditional Polity* (Oxford, 1974), pp 62–67; C. H. Walker, *The Abyssinian* (London, 1928), pp. 18, 71; E. Ullendorff, *The Ethiopians* (Oxford, 1960), p. 114; and M. Volpe, "Unity Through Enmity; Ethiopian Christian Attitudes Towards Muslims," a draft article. I am grateful to Dr. Volpe for letting me see this draft.

6. See Zahir Riyad, *Al-Islam fi Ityubya* (Cairo, 1964); the main thesis of the book is that relations between Muslims and Christians in pre-modern Ethiopia were good and relaxed; and were spoiled only due to external influences.

7. See Markakis, *Ethiopia,* p. 62n.

8. See also Mohammed Hassen, *The Oromo of Ethiopia: A History, 1570–1860* (New York, 1990). This is the most recent research on the Oromo, though controversial in claiming that the Oromos always lived in the territories of southern Ethiopia.

9. The Ethiopian monk Bahrey wrote in 1593 *A History of the Galla.* He explained his purpose: "To make known the number of their tribes, their readiness to kill people, and the brutality of their manners. If anyone should say . . . 'why has he written a history of bad people?' . . . I would answer by saying, 'search in the books and you will find that the history of Mohammed and the Moslem kings has been written and they are our enemies in religion.'" See "Ye-Galla Tarik," translated by C. F. Beckingham and G.W.B. Huntingford, in *Some Records of Ethiopia, 1593–1646* (Cambridge, 1954). See more in P. Henze, *The Horn of Africa: From War to Peace* (London, 1991), pp. 23–24.

10. See Trimingham, *Islam in Ethiopia,* pp. 112–113, 234–235, 242–243. See also B. G. Martin, *Muslim Brotherhoods in Nineteenth-Century Africa* (Cambridge, 1976), Chapter 7.

11. See "Eritrean Colony, Historical Notes, on Muslim Religion and Division of Islam in Eritrea" by Adorizzi Dante (Asmara, 1916), translated and edited by F.

Lijian, in *Asmara University, IAS Research work* (Asmara, 1986); Trimingham, *Islam in Ethiopia,* pp. 244–245.

12. Trimingham, *Islam in Ethiopia,* p. 252.

13. See a summary in S. Rubenson, "Ethiopia and the Horn" in J. F. Flint (ed.), *The Cambridge History of Africa,* Vol. 5 (Cambridge, 1976), pp 51–98.

14. See B. Lewis, *Race and Slavery in the Middle East,* Chapter 11. For more on Islam and slaves in Ethiopia see R. Pankhurst, *Economic History of Ethiopia* (Addis Ababa, 1968), Chapter 3; R. Austen, "The Islamic Red Sea Slave Trade: An Effort at Quantification," in R. Hess (ed.), *Proceedings of the Fifth International Conference of Ethiopian Studies* (Chicago, 1978), pp. 433–468.

15. See also R. Caulk, "Harar Town and Its Neighbors in the Nineteenth Century," *Journal of African History,* Vol. 18(3), 1979, pp. 369–386.

16. See U. Braukamper, "The Islamization of the Arsi-Oromo" in Taddese Beyene (ed.), *Proceedings of the Eighth International Conference of Ethiopian Studies* (Addis Ababa and Frankfurt, 1988), pp. 767–777.

17. Personal communication from Professor Getachaw Haile, 1993.

18. Concerning *Shaikh 'Ali Musa'* mosque in Gondar see S. Rubenson (ed.), *Correspondence and Treaties, 1800–1854* in *Acta Aethiopica,* Vol. I (Lund, 1987), p. 93.

19. Analysis and details in Abir, *Era of Princes.*

20. In the following chapters, which include references to Egyptian and other Middle Eastern modern developments relevant to our discussion, I shall avoid mentioning the sources on internal Middle Eastern issues. They are too numerous and mostly have little to do with Ethiopian history. Much of that material is derived from my two Hebrew-language series: *Introduction to Modern History of the Middle East* (five volumes) (Tel Aviv, 1987–1990), and *The Middle East Between the World Wars* (six volumes, the first three, titled *The Middle East During the 1920s,* already published) (Tel Aviv, 1991–1993). (The three volumes on the 1930s up to 1945 are in preparation.)

21. See R. Pankhurst, *History of Ethiopian Towns,* p. 243.

22. See M. Abir, "The Origins of the Ethiopian-Egyptian Border Problem in the Nineteenth Century," *Journal of African History,* Vol. 8(3), 1967, pp. 443–461; Abir, *Era of Princes,* p. 102; F. Dombrowski, *Ethiopia's Access,* pp. 44–48. Also Muhammad Rajab Harraz, *Iritriya al-haditha, 1557–1941* (Cairo, 1974), pp. 35–53.

23. See Ras 'Ali's letters to Muhammad 'Ali, in Rubenson, *Correspondence and Treaties 1800–1854,* especially his letter of 7 June 1844, pp. 94–95. Also Ras 'Ali to Ahmad Mankili, same day, pp. 96–97. See also Aleme Eshete, "Une Ambassade du Ras Ali en Egypte; 1852," *Journal of Ethiopian Studies,* Vol. 9(1), 1971, pp. 1–8.

24. See Abir, "Border Problem."

25. S. Rubenson, *The Survival of Ethiopian Independence* (London, 1976), p. 99.

26. Abir, "Border Problem." Also O. Meinardus, *Christian Egypt: Faith and Life* (Cairo, 1970), pp. 389–390.

27. For the latest historiographical survey and discussion of Tewodros see Shiferaw Bekele, "Kasa and Kasa: The State of Their Historiography" in Taddese Beyene, R. Pankhurst, and Shiferaw Bekele (eds.), *Kasa and Kasa: Papers on the Lives, Times and Images of Tewodros II and Yohannes IV (1855–1889)* (Addis Ababa, 1990), pp. 289–347. For a condensed yet thorough analysis of Tewodros and Ethiopian history from his period to the fall of Haile Selassie see Bahru Zewde, *History of Modern Ethiopia, 1855–1974* (London, 1991).

28. S. Rubenson, "Shaikh Kassa Hailu" in S. Rubenson (ed.), *Proceedings of*

the Seventh International Conference of Ethiopian Studies (Addis Ababa, Uppsala, and Michigan, 1984), pp. 279–285.

29. Rubenson, Ibid.: "In all probability Arabic was used in seals as well as in letters simply because it was convenient to do so. The chance that the message would be read and understood outside Ethiopia was greater when Arabic, rather than Gi'z or Amharic, was used."

30. Trimingham, *Islam in Ethiopia,* pp. 117–118.

31. D. Crummey, "Tewodros as a Reformer and a Modernizer," *Journal of African History,* Vol. 10(2), 1969, pp. 457–469.

32. See Trimingham, *Islam in Ethiopia,* p. 119. For a slightly different version from the P.R.O., see S. Rubenson, "Ethiopia and the Horn" in J. E. Flint, *The Cambridge History of Africa,* Vol. 5 (Cambridge, 1976), pp. 51–98.

33. See Harraz, *Iritriya al-haditha,* pp. 53–59.

34. Ibid., pp. 57–59.

35. See Rubenson, *The Survival,* p. 237; Chapter 4 (pp. 172–287) provides the most authoritative analysis of Tewodros's relations with the Ottomans and Egypt.

36. P. M. Holt, *Egypt and the Fertile Crescent* (Ithaca, 1966), p. 192.

CHAPTER 5

1. For details consult, among others, G. Douin, *Histoire du Regne du Khedive Ismail,* especially Vol. 3 (Cairo, 1933–1941); Sven Rubenson, *The Survival of Ethiopian Independence* (London, 1976), pp. 288–406; W. M. Dye, *Muslim Egypt and Christian Abyssinia* (New York, 1880); Muhammad Rif'at Bek, *Jabr al-Kasr fi al-khilas min al-asr* (Cairo, 1896); H. Erlich, *Ethiopia and the Challenge of Independence* (Boulder, 1986), Chapter 2; Hesseltine and Wolf, *The Blue and the Gray on the Nile* (Chicago, 1961).

2. On Yohannes' history see two different versions by Ethiopian scholars: Zewde Gabre-Selassie, *Yohannes IV of Ethiopia* (Oxford, 1975), and Takla-Tsadiq Makuriya, *Atse Yohannes ena Yaltyopia Andnat* (Emperor Yohannes and Ethiopia's unity), (Addis Ababa, 1989). On Yohannes's way to power see Bairu Tafla, *A Chronicle of Emperor Yohannes IV (1872–1889)* (Stuttgart, 1977). See more on Yohannes and the period in H. Erlich, *Ethiopia and Eritrea During the Scramble for Africa, A Political Biography of Ras Alula, 1875–1897* (East Lansing and Tel Aviv, 1982).

3. On the Ethio-Egyptian border relations in the period under discussion see Erlich, *Ethiopia and Eritrea,* Chapters 1–6.

4. Perhaps the most critical assessment of Yohannes as a diplomat was produced by a British visitor to his court: G. Portal, who wrote *My Mission to Abyssinia* (London, 1892). Working in the Library of Congress, Washington, D.C., I found in the catalogue that an Arabic translation of that book was published in Cairo in 1984 (titled: "Al-Ba'tha al-Injliziyya ila malik al-habasha, Yuhanna, sanat 1887"). Why was such a book reproduced for the Egyptian public in 1984? I wanted to discuss it later in the proper context, but unfortunately the book itself (with, most probably, an introduction by the translator) was lost.

5. See Rubenson, *Survival;* H. Marcus, *The Life and Times of Menelik II* (Oxford, 1975).

6. This is the title of the relevant chapter in P. J. Vatikiotis, *The History of Egypt: From Muhammad 'Ali to Sadat* (Second Edition, London, 1980).

7. For a discussion of Isma'il as continuing the Egyptian tradition of expansion rather than as heralding Western imperialism see G. Talhami, *Suakin and Massawa under Egyptian Rule, 1865–1885* (St. Louis, 1979). See also her article

"Massawa under Khedive Isma'il," in R. Hess (ed.), *Proceedings of the Fifth International Conference of Ethiopian Studies* (Chicago, 1978), pp. 481–494.

8. See H. Erlich, *Student and University in Twentieth-Century Egyptian Politics* (London, 1989), Introduction and Chapter 1. More details on Egyptian Copts serving in Menelik's educational effort are given in Zahir Riyyad, *Misr wa-Ifriqya* (Cairo, 1976), p. 168.

9. The comparison below between Alula and Ahmad 'Urabi is based mainly on my book on *Ras* Alula (*Ethiopia and Eritrea*) and the following on 'Urabi: W. S. Blunt, *Secret History of the English Occupation of Egypt* (reprint, Cairo, 1980); N. Keddie, *Sayyid Jamal ad-Din al-Afghani* (Los Angeles, 1972); 'Isa Salih, *Al-Thawra al-'Urabiyya* (Beirut, 1972); 'Abd al-Rahman al-Rafi'i, *Al-Thawra al-'Urabiyya wal-ihtilal al-Injilizi* (Cairo, 1949); 'Urabi Ahmad, *Mudhakirat Ahmad 'Urabi Basha* (Cairo, 1975).

10. Al-Sayyid Ahmad 'Urabi al-Husayni al-Misri, *Kashf al-sitar 'an sirr al-asrar* (Cairo, 1929), pp. 30–50.

11. See Muhammad Rajab Harraz, *Iritriya al-haditha*, Introduction and p. 146.

12. Muhammad Rif'at, *Jabr al-kasr fi al-khilas min al-Asr* (Cairo, 1896).

13. See Ahmad al-Hifni al-Qin'i al-Azhari, *Kitab al-jawahir al-hisan fi ta'rikh al-hubshan* (Cairo, 1905). In the history and geography chapter there is no significant mention of Ahmad *Gragn*'s conquest of Ethiopia (pp. 16–17); Tewodros is discussed with little reference to his conflict with Islam (pp. 19–20); and Yohannes's policy against Islam is mentioned but not elaborated (pp. 21–23). Altogether the book, written from an Islamic religious point of view, refrains from passing judgment on the issue of Ethiopia's legitimacy.

14. Yusuf Ahmad, *Al-Islam fi al-habasha* (Cairo, 1935), pp. 43–44. More information on the Egyptian government in Harar is given in two works by the same Egyptian historian: Shawqi 'Atallah al-Jamal, *Siyasat Misr fi al-bahr al-ahmar fi al-nisf al-thani min al-qarn al-tasi' 'ashar* [Egyptian policy in the Red Sea during the second half of the nineteenth century] (Cairo, 1974); and his earlier *Al-Watha'iq al-ta'rikhiyya lisiyasat Misr fi al-bahr al-ahmar, 1863–1879* [The historical documents on Egyptian policy in the Red Sea, 1863–1879] (Cairo, 1959).

15. For an Ethiopian description of the period reflecting also attitudes toward Islam, the Egyptians, and the Mahdiyya see Erlich, "A Contemporary Biography of *Ras* Alula: A *Ge'ez* Manuscript from Manawe, Tamben," Chapter 5 in my *Ethiopia and the Challenge of Independence* (Boulder, 1986). It was first published in the *Bulletin of the School of Oriental and African Studies*, Vol. 39, 1976, pp. 1–46, 287–327. (The manuscript was translated by Roger Cowley.)

16. R. A. Caulk, "Religion and State in Nineteenth-Century Ethiopia," *Journal of Ethiopian Studies*, Vol. 10(1), 1972, pp. 23–41. This is the best analysis of Yohannes's Islamic policy; the paragraphs above and below the quotation are based on it.

17. Abdussamad Ahmad, "The Gondar Muslim Minority in Ethiopia; The Story up to 1935," *Journal of the Institute of Muslim Minority Affairs*, Vol. 9(1), 1988, pp. 76–84.

18. Caulk, "State and Religion."

19. Trimingham, *Islam in Ethiopia*, p. 123.

20. Erlich, *Ras Alula*, Chapter 8.

CHAPTER 6

1. The best detailed analysis of the Mahdist state is P. M. Holt, *The Mahdist State of the Sudan, 1881–1898* (Oxford, 1970). See it also for a summary of existing

bibliography, pp. 267–277. I shall refer below only to new sources published later.

2. For more on the political and international aspects see R. Caulk, "Yohannes IV, the Mahdists, and the Partition of North-East Africa," *Transafrican Journal of History,* Vol. 1(2) 1971, pp. 23–42. Also Zewde Gabre-Sellassie, *Yohannes IV of Ethiopia.*

3. For Kufit and later confrontations between Ethiopia and the Mahdiyya see details in my *Ras Alula.* Chapter 7, devoted to the confrontation at Kufit, is titled: "The Year in Which the Dervishes Were Cut Down," a quotation from a popular Ethiopian contemporary poem.

4. See al-Athir.

5. See Na'um Shuqayr, *Ta'rikh al-Sudan,* a new edition prepared and annotated by Muhammad Ibrahim Abu Salim (Beirut, 1981), pp. 728–729. The original composition: Naum Shoucair, *Ta'rikh al-Sudan al-qadim wal-hadith wa-jughrafiyatuhu* (Cairo, 1903) is one of the wealthiest sources on the Mahdiyya and its relations with Ethiopia.

6. See my *Ras Alula,* p. 65.

7. Muhammad Sa'id al-Qaddal, *Al-Mahdiyya wal-Habasha, dirasa fi al-siyasa al-dahiliyya wal-harijiyya lidawlat al-mahdiyya, 1881–1898* (Beirut, 1992), pp. 121–123 (quoting Shoucair's *Ta'rikh,* 1903 edition, pp. 1073–1074). Al-Qaddal's study is based also on new documentary sources and is richer than Holt in describing the Ethio-Mahdist conflict.

8. See "A Contemporary Biography of Ras Alula" in my *Ethiopia and the Challenge of Independence,* p. 96.

9. Al-Qaddal, *Al-Madiyya,* pp. 39–40.

10. Isma'il Ibn 'Abd al-Qadir al-Kurdufani, *Al-Tiraz al-manqush bibushra qatl Yuhanna malik al-hubush.* The manuscript was edited and published in Khartoum in 1971 by Muhammad Ibrahim Abu Salim. It was recently republished under the title: *Al-Harb al-habashiyya al-sudaniyya, 1885–1888,* by Muhammad Abu Salim and Muhammad Sa'id Qaddal (Beirut, 1991).

11. In countries under Islamic sovereignty, until the mid-nineteenth century, Christians were not allowed to have bells in their churches.

12. See Abu Salim and al-Qaddal, *Al-Harb al-habashiyya al-sudaniyya,* pp. 59–60.

13. Holt, *The Mahdist State,* p. 150.

14. Ibid., pp. 151–152.

15. See Zewde Gebre-Sellassie, *Yohannes IV,* p. 526, and a similar version in D. Levine, *Wax and Gold* (Chicago, 1965), p. 28. Another, similar version is in Bairu Tafla, *A Chronicle of Emperor Yohannes IV* (Wiesbaden, 1977), p. 155.

16. See details in Erlich, *Ras Alula,* pp. 110–140.

17. Al-Qaddal, *Al-Mahdiyya,* pp. 122–123.

18. See both quotations, from a Ge'ez contemporary biographies of *Ras* Alula, and of *Ras* Gubana, in Erlich, *Ras Alula,* p. 128.

19. Bairu Tafla, *A Chronicle of Emperor Yohannes* (Wiesbaden, 1977), p. 157.

20. For Yohannes's policy leading to fighting the Mahdiyya at Mettema and to the ensuing loss of Eritrea to the Italians, see my *Ras Alula,* Chapters 12, 13.

21. For a detailed and comprehensive analysis of Menelik II and his period see H. Marcus, *The Life and Times of Menelik II: Ethiopia 1844–1913* (Oxford, 1975). See there a bibliography on the period.

22. G. N. Sanderson, "Conflict and Co-Operation Between Ethiopia and the Mahdist State, 1884–1898," *Sudan Notes and Records,* Vol. 2, 1969; and his "The Foreign Policy of Negus Menelik II: 1896–1898," in *Journal of African History,* Vol. 5, 1964, pp. 87–97.

23. After the Egyptians were forced by the British to evacuate Harar, *Amir*

'Abdallah restored the power of the local dynasty. During the two years he ruled prior to being conquered by Menelik, 'Abdallah further intensified the spreading of Islam among the Oromos and other neighboring groups. *Amir* 'Abdallah's relevant activities were discussed in an Arabic manuscript on Menelik's conquest of Harar discovered in 1978 by Richard Caulk, then of Addis Ababa University. In 1982–1983 I helped Professor Caulk prepare the text for annotated publication. His sudden death was a great loss to the community of Ethiopianists and to Ethiopian historiography. (He was about to complete a fifteen-year effort to produce a comprehensive study of Menelik's period.) For *Amir* 'Abdallah's spreading of Islam see also Carlo Conti Rossini, "Testi in Lingua Harari," in *Rivista degli Studi Orientali,* Vol. 8, 1919, pp. 413–415.

24. The occupation of the south has been described and analyzed by many. See Marcus, *Menelik II.* See also a map in Trimingham, *Islam in Ethiopia,* p. 97.

25. See more in Kofi Darkwa, *Shewa, Menilek and the Ethiopian Empire* (London, 1975), pp. 136–137.

26. Menelik's basic concepts of political Islam were perhaps revealed in his famous circular letter of April 1891 to the heads of state of Britain, France, Germany, Italy, and Russia, in which he stated: "Ethiopia has been for fourteen centuries a Christian land in a sea of pagans. . . ." See text in R. Greenfield, *Ethiopia: A New Political History* (New York, 1965), p. 464. In practice, however, he refrained from following the religiously motivated policies of Yohannes and Tewodros.

27. For a detailed history see E. Cerulli, *Etiopi in Palestina, I and II* (Rome, 1943 and 1947).

28. The following passages on the nineteenth-century history of the Ethiopian community in Jerusalem and the related activities of Ethiopian modern emperors is based on Kirsten Pedersen, *The History of the Ethiopian Community in the Holy Land from the Time of Emperor Tewodros II until 1974* (Jerusalem, 1983). (See there also a bibliographical list.) Also her articles (in Hebrew): "Bney malkat Shva beZion" in *Haetiopim hanotsrim beYerushalaim* (Tel Aviv, 1992), pp. 3–40, and her "Dir al-Sultan" in E. Shiler (ed.), *Sefer Ze'ev Vilnai* (Jerusalem, 1984), pp. 155–163; also Yehushua Ben-Arie, "Habatim haEtiopim mihuts lahomot" in his *Yerushlaim hahdasha bereshita* (Jerusalem, 1979), pp. 423–430; H. Scholler, "The Ethiopian Community in Jerusalem from 1850 to the Conference of Dar-el-Sultan 1902: The Political Struggle for Independence" in G. Goldenberg, *Proceedings of the Sixth International Conference of Ethiopian Studies,* pp. 487–500.

29. For Yohannes's correspondence regarding the monastery see appendices in Bairu Tafla, *A Chronicle of Emperor Yohannes IV;* for Tewodros's diplomatic effort consult Rubenson's *Survival,* Chapter 4; and for the period just before Tewodros see *Letters from Ethiopian Rulers (Early and Mid-Nineteenth Century),* translated by D. Appleyard and A. K. Irvine, annotated by R. Pankhurst (Oxford, 1985), pp. 91–134.

30. G. Orhonlu, *Habesh Eyaleti,* p. 164.

31. See details in Chris Prouty, *Empress Taytu and Menilek II: Ethiopia, 1883–1910* (London, 1986), Chapter 14, "Jerusalem and Ethiopia," pp. 247–256.

32. Sadiq al-Mu'ayyad al-'Azm, *Rihlat al-habasha* (Arabic translation by Rafiq al-'Azm and Haqqi al-'Azm) (Cairo, 1908).

33. Information given to me by his grandson, Professor Sadiq al-'Azm of Damascus University, in Washington, D.C., 1993.

CHAPTER 7

1. Sadiq al-'Azm al-Mu'ayyad, *Habesh Siyahetnamehsi,* Istanbul 1322 H (1904). The Ottoman-Turkish Original book (484 pp) is available in Tel Aviv University's Library.

2. The passages above and below are based on G. Orhonlu, *Habesh Eyaleti,* pp. 165–167.

3. See H. Marcus, *Life and Times of Menelik II, Ethiopia 1844–1913* (Oxford 1975), Chapter IX, and his *Haile Sellassie I, The Formative Years, 1892–1936* (Berkeley, 1987), Chapter One.

4. Getachaw Haile, "Religion in Ethiopian Politics" (Paper presented at the Michigan State University International Conference of Ethiopian Studies, East Lansing, April 1992).

5. For a comprehensive analysis of Iyasu see the last chapter in H. Marcus, *Life and Times of Menelik II,* and the first chapter in his *Haile Sellassie: The Formative Years, 1892–1936* (Berkeley, 1987). See the latter for a bibliography.

6. Of the vast literature on the *mawla* perhaps the best analysis of his Islamic dimension is B. G. Martin, "Sayyid Muhammad 'Abdallah Hassan of Somalia," Chapter 7 in his *Muslim Brotherhoods in Nineteenth-Century Africa* (Cambridge, 1976).

7. *Turkey; Sublime Porte, Ministere des Affaires Etrangeres, UH (General War), Dossier 120.* (Hereafter Turkey, UH 120.) The correspondence between Mazhar and Istanbul in this dossier was studied by the late C. Orhonlu for his book *Habesh Eyaleti,* where Mazhar's policy and his relations with Iyasu are discussed on pp. 167–175. Sven Rubenson persuaded the Turkish scholar to translate this correspondence into English. I am grateful to Professor Rubenson for letting me photocopy these translations. (A set of copies is available also at the Institute of Ethiopian Studies, Addis Ababa University.)

8. Turkey, UH 120, Mazhar to Istanbul, 14 December 1914.

9. Turkey, UH 120, Mazhar to Istanbul, 17 March 1915.

10. Turkey, UH 120, Mazhar to Istanbul, 13 February 1915.

11. See Alame Eshete, "A Page in the History of the Ogaden—Contact and Correspondence Between Emperor Minilik of Ethiopia and the Somali Mahdi, Muhammad Abdullah Hassan (1907–1908)" in S. Rubenson (ed.), *Proceedings of the Seventh International Conference of Ethiopian Studies,* pp. 301–314.

12. Turkey, UH 120, Istanbul to Embassy in Berlin, 23 August 1916. See also B. G. Martin, *Muslim Brotherhoods in Nineteenth-Century Africa* (Cambridge, 1976), Chapter 7, "Sayyid Muhammad Abdallah Hasan."

13. Turkey, UH 120, Istanbul to Mazhar Bey, 22 May 1916.

14. Turkey, UH 120, Mazhar to Istanbul, 4 September 1916.

15. In his *Ethiopia and Germany, Cultural, Political and Economic Relations, 1871–1936* (Wiesbaden, 1981), Bairu Tafla asserts that a decision to restore the monastery of Deir al-Sultan in order to lure Ethiopia to enter the war on their side was made by the governments of Germany and the Ottomans in early 1915. However, as he narrates on pp. 133–134, the Germans were unable to pass the information to Ethiopia prior to October 1915. It is not clear from Bairu's text if by the information he had from the German documents the matter was subsequently discussed with Iyasu or *Ras* Mika'el. It is probable that Mazhar, whose strategy was to build up an Islamic momentum through Iyasu and the *mawla,* convinced the Germans to shelve the matter.

16. 'Ali Mahmud 'Ali Ma'yuf, *Ta'rikh harakat al-jihad al-islami al-sumali didd al-isti'mar (1899–1920)* (Cairo, 1992). This book on the *mawla* and his holy war against imperialism is based also on research in the British archives. The passage is from pp. 230–231, in which there is a summary and a reference to Public Record Office (PRO) Colonial Office (CO), 535\43 "Translation of Proclamation Exhibited in Harar, August, 1916."

17. See the genealogy and other details on Iyasu's Islam, in E. A. Wallis Budge, *A History of Ethiopia* (London, 1928), pp. 542–547.

18. Al-Ma'yuf, *Ta'rikh harakat,* pp. 232–233, quoting CO, 535\43 "Précis of Abyssinian Intelligence received in Somaliland during weeks ending 23, 30 September 1916."

19. Turkey, UH 120, Mazhar to Istanbul, 4 September 1916.

CHAPTER 8

1. See in the volumes of *Berhanena Selam* the following pieces (summary of the titles): 18 March 1926, p. 87: Pilgrims in Jerusalem; 26 August 1926, p. 271: The *London Times* on water from Ethiopia to the Sudan; 2 September 1926, p. 279: Sudan, Ethiopia, Egypt, water affairs; 23 September 1926, p. 303: Egypt wants to join the League of Nations; 10 March 1927, p. 73: An Egyptian newspaper on Ethio-Egyptians relations; 14 April 1927, p. 113: On Deir al-Sultan; 7 February 1929, p. 43: Ethio-Egyptian relations; 21 February 1929, p. 60: Correspondence between the Egyptian king and the Coptic Patriarch; 29 February 1929, p. 60: An Egyptian consul appointed to Addis Ababa; 13 June 1929, p. 197: Appointment of bishops from Egypt; 4 July 1929, p. 215: Ethiopian religious functionaries return from Egypt; 5 September 1929, p. 294: On conflict between Jews and Arabs in Palestine; 25 January 1930, p. 25: The Voyage of the patriarch from Egypt to Ethiopia; 21 May 1931, p. 163: On the religious connections between Ethiopians and Egyptians in Jerusalem; 22 February 1935, p. 64: On appointment of Ethiopian consul to Jerusalem; 19 March 1935, p. 86: Water floods in Palestine; 30 May 1935, p. 178: On Arabic press. I am grateful to my ex-student and friend El'azar Rahamim for helping me with *Berhanena Selam.* For church affairs as the main interest in the Middle East at the period under review see also Haile Selassie's descriptions of his 1924 visits to Egypt and to Jerusalem, in E. Ullendorff, *The Autobiography of Emperor Haile Selassie, "My Life and Ethiopia's Progress, 1892–1937,"* Chapters 21 and 48.

2. The only exceptions are Egyptian Copts, who are naturally interested in Ethiopia. I shall mention below the works on Ethiopia by some prominent Copt scholars, notably Murad Kamil, Zahir Riyyad, Boutros Boutros-Ghali, and others.

3. See C. A. MacDonald, "Radio Bari, Italian Wireless Propaganda in the Middle East and British Countermeasures, 1934–1938," *Middle Eastern Studies,* Vol. 13, 1977, pp. 195–207.

4. I have analyzed the internal situation in Egypt and the impact of the Abyssinian Crisis on Egyptian youth during the stormy and detrimental 1935 in my *Students and University in Twentieth-Century Egyptian Politics* (London, 1989), Chapter 3. See also H. A. Ibrahim, "The Italian Conquest of Ethiopia as a Factor for the Conclusion of the 1936 Anglo-Egyptian Treaty," in Taddese Beyene (ed.), *Proceedings of the Eighth International Conference of Ethiopian Studies,* Vol. 2 (Addis Ababa, 1989), pp. 225–231.

5. Erlich, *Students and University,* p. 115.

6. Italian reports on Arab Middle Eastern countries during the Abyssinian Crisis, their policies and public opinion, are to be found in Rome in the series *Ministero degli Affari Esteri, Archivio Storicho, Etiopia Fondo la Guerra, Affari Politici Etiopia* (hereafter *ASMAE*), Buste (folders) 6–137. The reports from Egypt are in Buste 37, 38, 61, 62, 68, 97, 102, 117, 125. The report on the mission to contact the Sanussis is from 28 July 1935.

7. *Al-Ahram* (newspaper), 1 August 1935; *ASMAE,* Report from Alexandria, 4 August 1935.

8. See details on the al-Azhar mission in Yusuf Ahmad, *Al-Islam fi al-*

habasha (Cairo, 1935), pp. 69–74; 'Abdallah Husayn, *Al-Mas'ala al-habashiyya* (Cairo, 1935), pp. 29–32.

9. *Al-Ahram,* 10 April 1935; 15 April 1935.

10. *Al-Ittihad,* 28 August 1935; Abdallah Husayn, *Al-Mas'ala al-habashiyya,* p. 86.

11. *Al-Ahram,* 10 October 1935; 18 October 1935.

12. 'Abdallah al-Husayn, *Al-mas'ala al-habashiyya, min al-ta'rikh al-qadim ila 'am 1935* (Cairo, 1935).

13. Ibid., p. 16. 'Abdallah al-Husayn was also an editor of a law journal and the author of a book entitled *The New Woman and How Shall We Treat Her,* a highly sensitive subject that had been tackled already by the early pioneers of Egyptian liberalism.

14. *Al-mas' ala al-habashiyya,* pp. 18–19.

15. Muhammad Lutfi Jum'a, *Bayna al-asad al-Ifriqi wal-nimr al-Itali, Bahth tahlili ta'rikhi wanafsani wa'ijtima'i fi al-mushkilla al-habashiyya al-Italiyya* (Cairo, 1935).

16. See Ahamd Lutfi Jum'a, *Hayat al-sharq* (Cairo, 1932), as the best elaboration of the idea of a pluralist modern East.

17. Jum'a, *Bayna al-asad wal-nimr,* p. 9.

18. Yusuf Ahmad, *Al-Islam fi al-habasha, watha'iq sahiha qayyima 'an ahwal al-muslimin fi mamlakat Ithyubya min shuruq shams al-Islam ila hadhihi ayyam* (Cairo, 1935). A graduate of law studies in Cairo, Yusuf Ahmad's main field was Arab architecture and Arabic language. He served as inspector of Arab antiquities and then as a teacher of Arabic calligraphy. The book is decorated with quranic verses in *Kufi* script in an attempt to lend the book an air of Islamic piety.

19. See Muhammad Husayn Haykal, *Hayat Muhammad* (Cairo, 1935), pp. 168–172, 178–179. Also: A. Wessels, *A Modern Arabic Biography of Muhammad* (Leiden, 1972), pp. 59–60, and I. Gershoni, "The Reception of Muhammad Husayn Haykal's Biography of Muhammad, 1936–1939" in *Poetics Today,* Vol. 15(2), Spring 1994 (forthcoming). I am indebted to my friend Israel Gershoni of Tel Aviv University for this information as well as for many other points of information and interpretation.

20. Yusuf Ahmad, *Al-Islam fi al-habasha,* pp. 11–12.

21. See Al-'Azm's description of the uncleanliness of the Ethiopian Christians in Chapter 6.

22. Bulus Mas'ad, *Al-Habasha, aw Ithyubya fi munqalab min ta'rikhiha* (Cairo, 1935). Bulus Mas'ad collaborated with Yusuf Ahmad, exchanging material and views. The two finished their books at the same time (they were published on the 18th and 20th of November 1935), and each thanked the other for his help. They both were subsidized by the Fascists, as will be pointed out below.

23. The reader can make no mistake about the connection between the Italians and Bulus Mas'ad. Just as he opens the book he finds a set of pictures hastily glued to the bindings, which were supplied by the Fascist perpetrators of "the civilizing mission." It is the well-known Italian-made visualization of backwardness and cruelty: Ethiopians carry horrible diseases, babies from the Eritrean frontier castrated by Ethiopians, thieves flogged in Addis Ababa, mutilated or hung on a tree. And, ranking first: Ethiopia the slave house: crippled slaves in Harar, a slave market in Addis Ababa. All this was old early-twentieth century stuff recycled by the Italian propaganda machine. Finally, a picture just arrived from the war field, "Italian officers liberate a slave" in the newly Italian-captured Makkale.

24. See a file on Bulus Mas'ads book in *ASMAE,* 1936, Busta 125.

25. See a file on Yusuf Ahmad and his book in *ASMAE,* 1936, Busta 125.

26. *Al-Balagh,* 29 December 1935; 17 January 1936; 27 January 1936.

27. *Al-Jazira,* 9 January 1936.

28. See the volume of *Al-Hilal,* 1936, pp. 355, 476–477.

29. Yusuf Ahmad, pp. 100–102.

30. The book by 'Abd al-Halim Muhammad Rajab *(Al-'Alaqat al-siyasiyya)* that I quoted in my opening chapter as an example for contemporary radical Islamic attitudes toward Ethiopia, draws substantially from Yusuf Ahmad's book. See above p. 18. I shall return briefly to this point in my conclusion.

CHAPTER 9

1. The Italians collected carefully nearly every newspaper piece that had to do with their Ethiopian enterprise. The material is kept in Rome in the series *Ministero degli Affari Esteri, Archivio Storicho, Etiopia fondo la Guerra, Affari Politici, Etiopia,* 1935, 1936 (hereafter *ASMAE*), Buste 6–167. Material on Islam in Ethiopia is in B. 6, press reports from Egypt are in B. 37, 38, 61, 62, 97, 102, 117, 125, 151, 165, 166; press reports from Palestine in B. 49, 121, 130, 152, 166; from Syria and Lebanon B. 49, 50, 97, 131, 166; from Iraq B. 49, 65, 121, 128, 154, 167. There are also pieces from Morocco, Iran, Turkey, Yemen, and Saudi Arabia. These files contain unsystematically the pieces themselves, translations, summaries, general reports, and so on. Nearly all the articles I quote below are from that enormous collection. I also worked separately on the volumes of the Egyptian newspapers: *al-Ahram, al-Hilal,* and *al-Musawwar,* 1935–1936.

2. A particularly vicious series of articles titled "Slavery in Ethiopia" was published in *Al-Waqit* of Aleppo starting 4 December 1935.

3. See, for example, *Al-Ahram,* 22 July 1935.

4. *Filastin,* 25 September 1935, 2 October 1935.

5. *Al-Qabas,* 1 December 1935.

6. *Al-Tariq,* 10 October 1935.

7. "The Ethiopian Virgin" *(Azra' Ithyubya),* as reproduced in Anwar Shawul's autobiography, *Qisat hayyati fi wadi al-Rafidin* (My life in Mesopotamia) (Jerusalem, 1980), pp. 216–219. I am grateful to Dr. Reuven Snir and Professor Sasson Somekh of Tel Aviv University for this information.

8. See Shakib Arslan's biography of Rida and his analysis of their relations: *Al-Sayyid Rashid Rida, aw ikha' arba'in sanah* ("The Master Rashid Rida, or forty years of brotherhood") (Beirut, 1937), quoting two letters of Rida to him, from 24 January 1935 on p. 766, and from 10 May 1936 on p. 783.

9. For his general role in Islamic-Arab history see William L. Cleveland, *Islam Against the West: Shakib Arslan and the Campaign for Islamic Nationalism* (Austin, Texas, 1985).

10. Arslan, *Rashid Rida,* p. 791.

11. Shakib Arslan, "Muslimu al-Habasha" in his edited and extensively annotated and expanded Arabic translation (by 'Ajaj Nuyahid) of Lothrop Stoddard's work, *Hadir al-'alam al-Islami* (Cairo, 1933), Vol. 3, pp. 78–119.

12. See Arslan's article in *Al-Ayyam* of Damascus, 10 November 1935. Arslan wrote an article on 'Abd al-Karim al-Khattabi in *Hadir al-'alam al-Islami.*

13. Arslan, *Rashid Rida,* p. 794.

14. The text and a photograph of that letter were published on 18 March 1935 in the Jaffa-based *Al-Jami'a al-Islamiyya,* a journal rival to the *mufti.* The pro-*Mufti* press responded with counter-allegations and contended that the letter was a forgery coordinated with the British and aimed at discrediting *Hajj* Amin. The issue of the letter's authenticity produced a long scandal. (See a long article in the Hebrew jour-

nal *Ha'arets,* 22 April 1935; also articles on 19 March, 21 April, and 10 May 1935.) *Hajj* Amin himself refrained from denying the letter nor was he tempted—as yet— to provoke the British by personally expressing an opinion on the Ethio-Italian cri- sis. But his press started hosting Arslan's anti-Ethiopian campaign, and his alliance with Arslan was further cemented in the following years.

15. *Al-Ayyam,* 10 November 1935.

16. Reports on the conference in *Al-Jazira* and *Alif Ba* of Damascus, 16 September 1935, 21 September 1935. Two Fascist Orientalists, V. Vilieri and A. Barbiglieni (who had converted to Islam), participated.

17. *Al-Jihad,* Aleppo, 18 April 1935.

18. Salim Khayyata, *Al-Habasha al-mazluma, fatihat akhar niza' lil-isti'mar fi dawr inhiyarihi* ("The oppressed Ethiopia: The beginning of the last battle of impe- rialism in a period of its demise") (Beirut, 1937), Introduction p. 3. The author, a Communist, produced a highly emotional anti-Fascist composition which, other than the reference to Arslan and general praise for Ethiopia, has little to offer to our discussion.

19. Arslan, *Rashid Rida,* p. 783.

20. *Al-Ayyam,* 24 January 1936.

21. *ASMAE,* 1935, B. 49, "Repercussions in Palestine to our action," 3 October 1935.

22. Arslan, *Rashid Rida,* p. 791.

23. *Al-Ayyam,* 15 April 1935.

24. *Al-Balagh,* 6 April 1935.

25. *Akhir Sa'a,* 7 April 1935.

26. *Al-Ahram,* 3 June, 22 July 1935.

27. *Egyptian Gazette,* 19 July 1935.

28. *Alif-Ba,* 9 November 1935.

29. See *Al-Ahwal,* 18 March 1936; *Al-Jazira,* 6 May 1936; *Al-Ayyam,* 7 July 1936.

30. *Al-Taqaddum,* 7 May 1936.

31. *Al-Jazira,* 12 May 1936.

32. *Al-Waqit,* 19 May 1936.

33. *Al-Jazira,* 5 June 1936.

34. It is worth noting that not only *Hajj* Amin al-Husayni became an admirer of Hitler, but also his opponent in 1935, and the then defender of Ethiopia, the Jaffa-based newspaper *Filastin,* adopted in 1938–1939 a pro-Nazi line.

35. The journalist Yunis al-Bahri, whom we mentioned leading in 1935 the anti-Ethiopian line in the Iraqi press, became a Middle Eastern analyst for Radio Berlin during World War II.

36. On Ethiopian missions to San'a and Jidda see reports in 1935, *ASMAE,* B. 50 and 56.

37. See also the *Autobiography of Haile Selassie* (trans. and ed. E. Ullendorff), p. 238. See mainly Tariq al-Ifriqi's book in Note 39.

38. See *Al-Ayyam,* 8 June 1936, 10 July 1936, 15 July 1936.

39. Muhammad Tariq Bey (al-Ifriqi), *Mudhakkirati fi al-harb al-habashiyya al-Italiyya, 1935–1936* (Damascus, 1937).

40. *ASMAE,* B. 131, Report from Beirut, 2 June 1936, quoting the local paper *Al-Ittihad al-Lubnani; Al-Jazira,* 4 June 1936; *Al-Ayyam,* 29 June 1936.

41. Alberto Sbacchi, *Ethiopia Under Mussolini: Fascism and the Colonial Experience* (London, 1985), pp. 161–165; the quotation is from pp. 164–165.

42. *Al-Qabas,* 14 May 1936; *Al-Jazira,* 20 May 1936.

43. *Al-Ahram,* 9 September 1936.

44. *Al-Waqit,* 12 June 1936.

45. *Al-Jazira,* 7 July 1936.

46. Muhammad Tayasir Zabiyan al-Kaylani, *Al-Habasha al-muslima, musha-hadati fi diyar al-Islam* (Damascus, 1937).

CHAPTER 10

1. In September 1960 Haile Selassie told the visiting Israeli minister of agriculture, Moshe Dayan, that after World War II he had hoped that not only Eritrea but also Somalia would be united with Ethiopia. *Israeli Foreign Ministry, Papers of Ambassador Hanan Aynor,* kept at Truman Institution, Jerusalem (hereafter *IMF-Aynor*), Bar-On to FM, 16 September 1960.

2. Muhammad Rajab Harraz, *Al-'Umam al-muttahida wa-qadiyyat Irtirya 1945–1952* (Cairo, 1974). See mainly pp. 6–12.

3. According to John Spencer, Haile Selassie's adviser, this whole Egyptian diplomatic enterprise was aimed at forcing Ethiopia to negotiate an agreement on the Nile waters. As part of that effort, in April 1947 King Faruq sent two envoys to the emperor to tell him that the Egyptians had prevented an attempt to assassinate him. Spencer advised against opening to these Egyptian overtures. Years later, facing Nasserite subversion, Spencer regretted his advice. See J. Spencer, *Ethiopia at Bay* (Michigan, 1984), p. 188.

4. Just before the fall of the royal parliamentary regime in Egypt a "League for Strengthening Friendship with Ethiopia" was established in Cairo; see *Al-Ahram,* 16 June 1952.

5. See PRO FO 371/12563 "Ethiopian Egyptian Relations," a report on U.S. assessment of Nasser's policy, FO to Addis Ababa 18 January 1957. See also Tariq Ismail, *The UAR in Africa* (Evanston, Ill., 1971), pp. 178–179. Also see below Nasser's conversation with Haile Sclassie's envoy, Meles Andom, December 1956.

6. For more details see, among others: John Markakis, *National and Class Conflict in the Horn of Africa* (Cambridge, 1987, and London, 1990), Chapter 5; and Haggai Erlich, *The Struggle Over Eritrea, 1962–1978* (Palo Alto, 1983), Chapter 2.

7. Muhammad Muhammad Fa'iq, *'Abd al-Nasir wal-thawra al-Ifriqiyya* (Beirut, 1980), pp. 85–87.

8. See Jordan Gebre-Medhin, *Peasants and Nationalism in Eritrea* (New Jersey, 1989), pp. 49–53, 64–65, 77, 151–165.

9. Three hundred was the number estimated for the early 1950s; see Markakis, *National and Class Conflict,* p. 109. Seven hundred was the number estimated in 1960, *IMF-Aynor,* Bar-On to MF, 11 October 1960. 'Aynor was the Israeli ambassador to Ethiopia from 1971 to 1973 and witnessed first hand the process leading to Haile Selassie's decision to break relations with Israel. I am most grateful to him for allowing me to study the documents and correspondence he put together.

10. See PRO/FO 371/131287, H.M. Consulate in Asmara to Addis Ababa Embassy, 5 November 1958.

11. See Muhammad Abu al-Qasim Hajj Hamad, *Al-Ab'ad al-duwaliyya li-ma'rakat Irtirya* (Beirut, 1974), p. 165; also, Markakis, *National and Class Conflict,* p. 111.

12. See Erlich, *Struggle Over Eritrea,* Chapter 2. Also Khalaf al-Munshidi, *Irtirya, min al-ihtilal ila al-thawra* (Beirut, 1973), pp. 171–178.

13. Khalaf al-Munshidi, *Irtirya,* pp. 183–184.

14. PRO FO 371/125363, Furlonge to Lloyd, 16 May 1957.

15. *IMF-Aynor,* Bar-On to FM, 11 October 1960, summarizing talks between Moshe Dayan and the top Ethiopian politicians, including the emperor.

16. PRO FO 371/125363, British Embassy, Khartoum to FO, 9 January 1957.

17. *Al-Ahram,* 26 December 1957.

18. When the emperor heard of the fall of the Iraqi royal house, reported the British ambassador, he panicked. He called immediately the ambassadors of the United States, United Kingdom, the Soviet Union, and India asking for comfort, "which was not an easy thing to do," PRO FO 371/138024, "Ethiopia: Annual Report for 1958."

19. A. H. "Mediniyut mitsrayim be'africa" (Hebrew: Egyptian policy in Africa), *Hamizrah Hehadash,* Vol. 12, 1962, pp. 19–28. Also J. Spencer, *Ethiopia at Bay* (Michigan, 1984), pp. 306–309.

20. *IFM-Aynor,* Bar-On to FM, summarizing Dayan's meeting with Haile Selassie, 16 September 1960.

21. *IFM-Aynor,* D. Levin to Foreign Ministry, 7 December 1955.

22. PRO FO 371/125363, Furlonge to Bell, 22 February 1957, discussing interview in *Daily Telegraph,* 16 February 1957.

23. *Keesing's Contemporary Archives,* Vol. 11 (1957–1958), p. 15410C, 15233B.

24. *Israeli Archives, Ginzach Hamdinah* (hereafter *IGM*), Documents in Files 2403/1, 5558/201, 2414/14, 2414/13A+B, 2454/15, FO 42/16. (I am indebted to my student Itamar Levin who helped me with that material.) Divon to FO from Paris, 10 July 53, reporting on his conversation with the historian and diplomat Takla-Tsadiq Makuriya.

25. For example, in September 1956 two Arabs who had opened a business in Addis Ababa's "mercato" were deported from Ethiopia for distributing pictures of Nasser and for allegedly being engaged in other activities in the service of the Egyptians. See PRO, FO, 371/118784, Chancery Addis Ababa to African Department, 6 September 1956.

26. See a long reference to the book by Abu Ahmad Al-Ithyubi (pseud.), *Al-Islam al-jarih fi al-habasha* (Addis Ababa, 1960), in Hussein Ahmed, "The Historiography of Islam in Ethiopia," *Journal of Islamic Studies,* 1992, pp. 15–46.

27. *IMF-Aynor,* A. Levin to FM, "A conversation with Yiftah Demitrios," 23 July 1964. Yiftah, fluent in Hebrew and Arabic, was a close adviser of the emperor on Middle Eastern affairs. He was later to serve as Ethiopia's consul general in Israel.

28. *IGM,* Israeli ambassador to Paris, Y. Tsur, reporting on a conversation with Haile Selassie, 17 November 1954.

29. *IGM,* Abba Eban to Foreign Ministry, 29 November 1952.

30. *IFM-Aynor,* Consul Pilpul to FM, 16 May 1956.

31. See PRO FO 371/125355, Annual Report, 1956.

32. PRO FO 371/131241, Annual Report for 1957, 10 January 1958.

33. See R. L. Hess, *Ethiopia, The Modernization of Autocracy* (Ithaca, 1970), Chapter 10, "The Africanization of Ethiopia," mainly pp. 234–239.

34. *IFM-Aynor,* Bar-On to FM, 13 November 1958.

35. Compare, for example, Chapters 8 and 9 above to S.K.B Asante, *Pan-African Protest: West Africa and the Italo-Ethiopian Crisis, 1934–1941* (London, 1971).

36. See my *Struggle Over Eritrea,* p. 57.

37. Rashid al-Barawi, *Al-habasha bayna al-iqta wal-'asr al-hadith* (Cairo, 1961); see mainly the preface, pp. 6–8, and Chapter 7, pp. 176–186. (The book appeared in a semiofficial series: African Studies, by Maktabat al-nahda al-mis-riyya.)

38. PRO FO 371/138092. Addis Ababa Embassy to FO, 9 June 1959.

39. Details on the visit and the texts of the speeches in 'Abd al-Rahman al-Huss, *Ithyubya fi 'ahd Hayla Silasi al-awwal* (Beirut, 1960), pp. 116–146.

40. See more details in Otto Meinhardus, *Christian Egypt; Faith and Life* (Cairo, 1970), pp. 391–399. On final disconnection, see two articles in *Al-Siyasa Al-Duwaliyya,* by Murad Kamil (1967, No. 8) and Miryit Boutros-Ghali (1966, No. 3).

41. PRO FO 371/146567, *Ethiopia: Annual Report, 1959.* Also, *IFM-Aynor,* Pilpul to FM, "The Waters of the Nile," 16 December 1957. And two pieces in *Ethiopian Herald,* 12 December 1957.

42. PRO FO 371/154836, *Ethiopia: Annual Report, 1960.*

43. *IFM-Aynor,* Bar-On to FM (the date is not clear, should be late September 1960).

44. *IMF-Aynor,* MF to Embassy in Addis, 5 December 1966. Also "A Report on Deir al-Sultan" by M. Shamgar, Government's legal adviser to the minister of justice, 16 March 1971.

45. A. H. "Egyptian Policy in Africa" (Hebrew), *Hamizrah Hehadash,* 1962, pp. 19–28.

46. See details in Spencer, *Ethiopia at Bay,* pp. 305–309.

47. Bereket Habte Selassie, *Conflict and Intervention in the Horn of Africa* (New York, 1980), p. 155.

48. See, for example, a description by 'Uthman Sabbe's Sudanese assistant, Muhammad Abu al-Qasim Hamad. In the mid-1960s he went to Egypt to meet with the head of the African Section in the Republican presidency, Hasan Farnuwani, but his request for some help for the Eritreans was turned down. The description is in his book: *Al-Ab'ad al-duwaliyya li-ma'rakat Irtirya* (Beirut, 1974), p. 175. See also a discussion in Muhammad Muhammad Fa'iq, *'Abd al-Nasir wal-thawra al-ifriqiyya* (Beirut, 1980), pp. 86–87.

49. Dr. Thomas Kane, who was during that time in Addis Ababa, heard that the students of the university were planning a mass demonstration in favor of Israel but to their surprise the war ended before they could implement their plan.

50. *IMF-Aynor,* Ambassador Ben-David to FM, "Ethiopia and the Crisis in the Middle East," 22 August 1967.

CHAPTER 11

1. Murad Kamil, *Fi bilad al-najashi* (Cairo, 1949).

2. Al-Haymi al-Hasan bin Ahmad, *Sirat al-habasha,* edited and annotated by Murad Kamil (Cairo, 1972), (2d ed.). See E. Van Donzel's criticism of Kamil's work in his *A Yemeni Embassy to Ethiopia, 1647–1649* (Stuttgart, 1986).

3. See Rashid al-Barawi, *Al-habasha bayna al-iqta' wal-'asr al-hadith,* Chapter 4, pp. 76–92.

4. See *Al-Ahram,* 30 April 1955 and 24 July 1955 on Haile Selassie, the far-seeing leader, and on good relations with Egypt. A message received at the Ethiopian embassy mentioned the students in al-Azhar as Ethiopians, not Eritreans (see 24 July 1957); on greetings from Nasser to Haile Selassie see 24 July 1958. See 17 October 1957 article on a possible Egyptian-Sudanese-Ethiopian alliance. The four short pieces of chronicle from Eritrea were on 2 August 1956, 9 August 1956, 25 October 1956, and 17 September 1956; the last one on foreign students in Cairo simply mentions Eritreans. I am thankful to my student S. Press for working on *Al-Ahram* of these years.

5. A search in the collection of Nasser's speeches and in *Al-Ahram* and *Al-Jumhuriyya* during the years 1962–1967 on attitudes toward Eritrea resulted with not even one quotation on the "Arabism" of Eritrea. I am thankful to my student Hanna Hershkovitch for assisting me in that.

6. Zahir Riyyad, "Al-Islam fi Ithyubya," *Majallat Kulliyat al-Adab, Jami'at Al-Qahira,* Vol. 18, December 1957, pp. 121–142.

7. Zahir Riyyad, "Al-Shifta fi Ithyubya mundhu al-'usur al-wusta," *Majallat Kulliyat al-Adab, Jami'at Al-Qahira,* Vol. 19, 1961, pp. 215–238.

8. See G.K.N. Trevaskis, *Eritrea: A Colony in Transition, 1941–1952* (Oxford, 1960), pp. 91–96; Angelo Del Boca, *Gli Italiani in Africa Orientale, Nostalgia delle Colonie* (Rome, 1984), pp. 137–142; also PRO, FO 1015/539, "A Study of the Present Shifta Problem" by G. Trevaskis, June 1950.

9. See Zahir Riyyad, *Al-Islam fi Ityubya fi al'usur al-wusta* (Cairo), 1964.

10. Zahir Riyyad, *Ta'rikh Ithyubya* (Cairo, 1966), p. 48.

11. Zahir Riyyad, *Misr wa-Ifriqya* (Cairo, 1976).

12. *Adwa' 'ala al-habasha,* from the series "Ikhtarna laka," No. 6. "Participated in the preparation of this book: Amin Shakir, Sa'id al-'Ariyyan, Mustafa Amin," (Cairo, ND).

13. 'Abd al-Rahman Mahmud al-Huss, *Ithyubya fi 'ahd Hayala Silasi al-awwal* (Beirut, 1960).

14. Boutros Boutros-Ghali, *Qadaya 'Arabiyya* (Cairo, 1975), p. 225.

15. See articles on church relations by Murad Kamil (1967, no. 8) and Miryit Boutros-Ghali (1966, no. 3). I am thankful to my student Makram Khuri Makhul for helping me with *Al-Siyasa al-Duwaliyya.*

16. 'Abd al-Malik 'Awda, "Nahwa hall siyasi li-qaddiyat Irtirya," *Al-Siyasa Al-Duwaliyya,* 1975, No. 40.

17. Boutros-Ghali, "Al-Nasiriyya wa-siyasat misr al-harijiyya," *Al-Siyasa Al-Duwaliyya,* 1971, No. 23.

18. Boutros-Ghali, "Siyasat misr al-harijiyya fi 'ahd ma ba'da al-Sadat," *Al-Siyasa Al-Duwaliyya,* 1982, No. 69.

CHAPTER 12

1. See Erlich, *The Struggle Over Eritrea,* pp. 65–66.

2. Ibid., Chapter 5, "The Middle East and Eritrea, 1962–1974," gives a general analysis and details.

3. Muhammad Abu al-Qasim Hamad, *Al-Ab'ad al-duwaliyya li-ma'arakat Irtirya* (Beirut, 1974), pp. 165–166.

4. Muhammad Khalil, *The Arab States and the Arab League* (Beirut, 1962), Vol. 1, p. 685.

5. See Shumet Sishagne, "Notes on the Background to the Eritrean Problem" in Bahru Zawde (ed.), *Proceedings of the Second Annual Seminar of the Department of History* (Addis Ababa University, 1984), pp. 180–213.

6. John Markakis, *National and Class Conflict in the Horn of Africa* (London, 1990), p. 109; Chapter 5, "The Eritrean Revolution," is the most detailed analysis of the Eritrean movement in the years under discussion.

7. Hamad, *Al-Ab'ad,* Chapter 4.

8. Ibid.

9. Ibid., p. 167.

10. *Al-Muharrir,* 19 April 1969.

11. Voice of the Fatah, 20 November 1969, in BBC/ME 22 November 1969.

12. Hamad, *Al-Ab'ad,* p. 140.

13. *Filastin al-thawra,* 19 September 1973.

14. Hamad, *Al-Ab'ad,* p. 165.

15. See Chapter 2.

16. Hamad, *Al-Ab'ad,* p. 167; Khalaf al-Munshidi, *Iritirya, min al-ihtilal ila al-thawra* (Beirut, 1973), pp. 169–170.

17. As'ad Ghuthani, *Ahdath al-qaran al-Ifriqi wa-haqiqat al-sira' al-Ithyubi al-Iritri* (Baghdad, 1980), p. 101.

18. Ibid., pp. 12–21. Also chapter on the ELF starting p. 23 and on the EPLF starting p. 35. More on the EPLF's party led by Ramadan Nur and Isayas in Sa'id Ahmad al-Janahi, *Iritriya 'ala abwab al-nasr* (Beirut, 1975), p. 50.

19. E.g., Jabhat al-Tahrir al-Irtiriyya, *Kifah Irtiriya,* 132 pp. (no place of publication, ND). The list of ELF publications is on the back cover.

20. Ibid., especially p. 101.

21. 'Uthman Salih Sabbe, *Ta'rikh Iritriya* (Beirut, 1974). An English translation, *History of Eritrea,* was issued in the same year in Beirut.

22. Sabbe, *History of Eritrea,* Introduction, pp. 11–15, and also pp. 118, 260.

23. Hamad, *Al-Ab'ad,* p. 167.

24. Hamad, *Al-Ab'ad,* Introduction, pp. 7–14; pp. 114–120. For more on Sabbe's book, *The Struggle in the Red Sea* see also a note, "About the Author," in his *History of Eritrea,* and a quotation from the book in *Ahbar al-'alam al-Islami,* 17 March 1975.

25. Sabbe's introduction to G.K.N Trevaskis, *Eritrea: A Colony in Transition* (Arabic translation, *Musta'mara fi marhalat al-intiqal*) (Beirut, 1977).

26. Hamad, *Al-Ab'ad,* Chapter 4, "From the crucial triangle to the closed door," p. 151.

27. Muhammad 'Abd al-Mawla, *Thawrat Iritriya wal-sira' al-duwali fi al-bahr al-ahmar* (Beirut, 1976). The other two books are mentioned above.

28. Jabhat al-Tahrir al-Iritriyya, *Al-Taghalghul al-Israili fi Irtirya,* 1970.

29. Sayyid Rajab Haraz, *Irtirya al-haditha, 1557–1941* (Cairo, 1974).

30. Sabbe, *History of Eritrea,* a foreword by Yusuf Ibrahim Yazbak.

31. Mumtaz al-'Arif, *Al-Ahbash bayna Marib wa-Aksum* (Baghdad, 1975).

32. Ghuthani, *Ahdath al-qaran al-Ifriqi,* pp. 13, 54, 61, 75, 101–109.

CHAPTER 13

1. See more in Erlich, *The Struggle Over Eritrea, 1962–1978,* pp. 55–59.

2. For the best succinct analysis of the Judaic and Hebraic dimensions of Ethiopian culture and history, see E. Ullendorff, *The Ethiopians, An Introduction to Culture and People* (Oxford, 1960), mainly Chapter 5.

3. See *Ha'arets,* 21 April 1935, the editorial.

4. Two students of mine wrote B.A. papers (in Hebrew) on these two journals and Ethiopia throughout 1935. The pieces in *Davar* were assembled in Aescoly's book (see Note 5 below). See also "Repercussions in Palestine—A Survey of the Press," 3 October 1935, in *ASMAE, Ethiopia fondo la guerra,* B. 49.

5. Aharon Ze'ev Aescoly, *Habash, Ha'am, Ha'arets, Hatarbut, Divrey Hayamim, Hashilton, Hapolitika* (Jerusalem, 1935).

6. Ibid., p. 5.

7. Ibid., pp. 28–33.

8. *Ha'arets,* 5 May 1936, the editorial.

9. Avraham 'Aqavia, *'Im Wingate Behabash* (Tel Aviv, 1944).

10. Ibid. 'Aqavia published a full biography of Wingate, *Orde Wingate—Hayyav Wupo'alo* (Tel Aviv, 1993). The new book makes the connection between the building by Wingate of the first modern commando units of the *yishuv,* and the later Ethiopian campaign. Major General Wingate was killed in action in Burma, 1944.

11. See Nathan Marein, *The Ethiopian Empire Federation and Law* (Rotterdam, 1955).

12. *IFM-Aynor,* Israeli Embassy, Addis Ababa, 4 March 1968, "Report on Bitan's meeting with the emperor"; "Coffee Project—Proposals arising out of discussions between representatives of the two countries—14 April–21 April, 1968" (Tel Aviv, 24 April 1968).

13. *IFM-Aynor,* "Political and military cooperation between Israel and Ethiopia," Lt. Gen. Tsur to Finance Minister Sapir, 31 July 1969.

14. *IFM-Aynor,* "The Key," African Department to Israeli Embassy, Addis Ababa, 18 June 1969.

15. *IFM-Aynor,* African Department to Israeli Ambassador, 14 June 1969, 18 June 1969, M. Shamgar, Israeli government legal adviser to minister of justice, 16 March 1971.

16. See Erlich, *The Struggle Over Eritrea,* Chapter 3, pp. 34–42.

17. *IFM-Aynor,* "Report on the meeting between Bitan and the emperor," 4 March 1968.

18. *IFM-Aynor,* "The visit of Mr. Shim'oni to Addis Ababa—a Political Report," Aynor to African Department, 25 May 1972.

19. *IFM-Aynor,* "Conversation with Minasse Haile," 19 March 1972.

20. The memoirs of Ahadu Sabure, see Note 30.

21. 'Abd al-Tawab 'Abd al-Hayy, *Al-Nil wal-mustaqbal* (Cairo, 1988). See pp. 120–125, 141–143.

22. *IFM-Aynor,* "Ethiopia—the Breaking," by Hanan Aynor, 26 November 1973.

23. Ibid.

24. Text published in *Ethiopia Observer,* Vol. 16, 1973, p. 130.

25. *IFM-Aynor,* "Ethiopia—the breaking," Aynor, 26 November 1973.

26. *Al-Bilad* (Saudi Arabia), 25 November 1973.

27. *IFM-Aynor,* Paris Embassy to Africa Department, 8 April 1974.

28. See my *Ethiopia and the Challenge of Independence* (Boulder, 1986), Chapter 11: "The Ethiopian Army and the 1974 Revolution."

29. Interview with *Dajazmach* Zawde Gabre-Selassie, New York, April 1978.

30. Ahadu Sabure managed to find a way to smuggle out of prison the pages upon which he wrote his diary. One by one they reached Thomas Kane, one of America's leading scholars on Ethiopian languages and literature. Dr. Kane was kind enough to let me have the relevant page from the draft translation he is preparing for Ahadu Sabure's memoirs.

CHAPTER 14

1. See above p. 43.

2. See D. Crummey, "Society, State and Nationality in the Recent Historiography of Ethiopia," *Journal of African History,* Vol. 31 (1990), pp. 103–119.

SELECTED BIBLIOGRAPHY

ARCHIVES AND ARCHIVAL MATERIAL

Ministero degli Affari Esteri, Roma, Archivio Storico (ASMAE), Etiopia Fondo la Guerra, Etiopia, Affari Politici, Buste 6–137

Public Record Office, London

Israeli Foreign Ministry, papers of Ambassador Hanan Aynor (IMF-Aynor) kept at Truman Institution, Hebrew University, Jerusalem

Israel State Archives, Ginzach Hamedinah

Turkey, Sublime Porte, Ministere des Affaires Etrangeres, UH (general war), Dossier 120. Documents collected and translated by C. Orhonlu, available at the Institute of Ethiopian Studies, Addis Ababa

NEWSPAPERS AND MAGAZINES

Al-Ahram, Cairo
Al-Ayyam, Damascus
Al-Bulagh, Cairo
Berhanena Selam, Addis Ababa
Davar
Ethiopian Herald, Addis Ababa
Filastin, Jaffa
Ha'arets
Al-Hilal, Cairo
Al-Jazira, Damascus
Al-Siyasa al-Duwaliyya, Cairo
Al-Waqit, Aleppo

BOOKS AND ARTICLES

'Abd al-Hayy, 'Abd al-Tawwab, *Al-Nil wal-mustaqbal,* Cairo, 1988.

'Abd al-Mawla, Muhammad, *Thwrat Iritriya wal-sira' al-duwali fi al-bahr al-ahmar,* Beirut, 1976.

Abir, M., "The Origins of the Ethio-Egyptian Border Problem in the Nineteenth Century," *Journal of African History,* Vol. 8(3), 1967, pp. 443–461.

———, *The Era of the Princes,* London, 1968.

———, "Ethiopia and the Horn of Africa," in R. Gray (ed.), *The Cambridge History of Africa,* Vol. 4, 1975, pp. 537–577.

————, "Trade and Christian-Muslim Relations in Post-Medieval Ethiopia," in R. L. Hess (ed.), *Proceedings of the Fifth International Conference on Ethiopian Studies (Session B)*, Chicago, 1978, pp. 414–414.

————, *Ethiopia and the Red Sea*, London, 1980.

Aescoly, Aharon, *Habash, Ha'am, Ha'arets, Hatarbut, Divrey Hayamim, Hashilton, Hapolitika*, Tel Aviv, 1935.

Ahmad, Abussamad, "The Gondar Muslim Minority in Ethiopia," *Journal of the Institute of Muslim Minority Affairs*, Vol. 9(1), 1988, pp. 76–85.

Ahmad, Yusuf, *Al-Islam fi al-habasha*, Cairo, 1935.

Ahmed, Husein, "The Historiography of Islam in Ethiopia," *Journal of Islamic Studies*, Vol. 3(1), 1992, pp. 15–46.

'Aliyyan, Muhammad 'Abd al-Fattah, *Al-Hijra ila al-habasha wa-munaqashat qadiyyat Islam al-najashi*, Cairo, 1987.

Appleyard D., Irvine, A., Pankhurst, R., *Letters from Ethiopian Rulers (Early and Mid-Nineteenth Century)*, Oxford, 1985.

'Arab Faqih (Shihab al-Din Ahmad ibn 'Abd al-Qadir al-Jayzani), *Tuhfat al-zaman aw Futuh al-habasha*, in Fahim Muhammad Shalut (ed.), Cairo, 1974. (See also Chihab ed-Din)

al-'Arif, Mumtaz, *Al-Ahbash bayna al-Marib wa-Aksum*, Baghdad, 1975.

Aqavia, Avraham, *'Im Wingate behabash*, Tel Aviv, 1944.

Arslan, Shakib, *Hadir al-'alam al-Islami*, Cairo, 1933.

————, *Al-Sayyid Rashid Rida, aw ikha' arba'in sanah*, Beirut, 1937.

Asante, S.K.B., *Pan-African Protest: West Africa and the Italo-Ethiopian Crisis, 1934–1941*, London, 1971.

Austen, R., "The Islamic Red Sea Slave Trade: An Effort at Quantification," in R. L. Hess (ed.), *Proceedings of the Fifth International Conference of Ethiopian Studies*, Chicago, 1978, pp. 433–468.

Ahmad al-Hifni al-Qina'i al-Azhari, *Kitab al-jawahir al-hisan fi ta'rikh al-hubshan*, Cairo, 1905.

al-'Azm, Sadiq al-Mu'ayyad, *Rihlat al-habasha*, Cairo, 1908.

al-Barawi, Rashid, *Al-Habasha, bayna al-iqta' wal-'asr al-hadith*, Cairo, 1961.

al-'Azm, Sadiq al-Mu'ayyad, *Habesh Siyahetnamehsi*, Istanbul, 1904.

Bekele, Shiferaw, "Kasa and Kasa: The State of Their Historiography," in Taddese Beyene, R. Pankhurst, and Shiferaw Bekele, S. (ed.), *Kasa and Kasa, Papers on the Lives and Images of Tewodros II and Yohannes IV (1855–1889)*, Addis Ababa, 1990.

Ben Arie, Y., *Yerushalayim hahadasha bereshita*, Jerusalem, 1979.

Blackburn, J. R., "The Ottoman Penetration of Yemen," *Archivum Ottomanicum*, Vol. 6, 1980, pp. 55–100.

Braukamper, U., "Islamic Principalities in Southeast Ethiopia Between the Thirteenth and Sixteenth Centuries," *Ethiopianist Notes*, Vol. 1(1), 1977, pp. 17–55, and Vol. 1(2), pp. 1–42.

———, "The Islamization of the Arsi-Oromo," in Taddese Beyene (ed.), *Proceedings of the Eighth International Conference of Ethiopian Studies*, Addis Ababa and Frankfurt, 1988, pp. 767–777.

Budge, E.A.W., *A History of Ethiopia: Nubia and Abyssinia*, London, 1928 (reprinted, New York, 1970).

Caulk, R., "Religion and State in Nineteenth Century Ethiopia," *Journal of Ethiopian Studies*, Vol. 10(1), 1972, pp. 23–41.

————, "Yohannes IV, the Mahdists, and the Partition of North-East Africa," *Transafrican Journal of History*, Vol. 1(2), 1972, pp. 23–42.

————, "Harar Town and Its Neighbors in the Nineteenth Century," *Journal of African History*, Vol. 18(3), 1979, pp. 369–386.

Celebi, Evliya, *Siyahatname,* Istanbul, 1938.

Cerulli, E., *Etiopi in a Palestina, I, II,* Rome, 1943 and 1947.

———, *L'Islam di Ieri e di Oggi,* Rome, 1971.

———, "Ethiopia's Relations with the Muslim World," in *General History of Africa, UNESCO Africa from the Seventh to the Eleventh Century,* 1981, pp. 575–585.

Chihab ed-Din Ahmed Ben Abd el-Qader ('Arab Faqih), *Futuh al-Habasha— Histoire de la conquête de l'Abyssinie,* in R. Basset (trans. and ed.), Paris, 1897. (See also 'Arab Faqih)

Clapham, C., *Haile Selassie's Government,* New York, 1969.

Cleveland, W. L., *Islam Against the West: Shakib Arslan and the Campaign for Islamic Nationalism,* Austin, 1985.

Conti Rossini, Carlo, "La Guerra Turco-Abbisina del 1578," *Oriente Moderno,* Vol. 1, 1922, pp. 634–636, 684–691; Vol. 2, pp. 48–57.

Couq J., *L'Islam en Ethiopie, des origines au XVI siecle,* Paris, 1981.

Crummey, D., "Tewodros as a Reformer and a Modernizer," *Journal of African History,* Vol. 10(2), 1969, pp. 457–469.

———, *Priests and Politicians: Protestant and Catholic Missionaries in Orthodox Ethiopia 1830–1868,* Oxford, 1972.

———, "Society, State and Nationality in the Recent Historiography of Ethiopia," *Journal of African History,* Vol. 31, 1990, pp. 103–119.

Dante, A. "Muslim Religion and Division of Islam in Eritrea," *Asmara University, IAS Research Work,* Asmara, 1986.

Darkwa, Kofi, *Shewa, Menilek, and the Ethiopian Empire,* London, 1975.

Del Boca, Angelo, *Gli Italiani in Africa Orientale, Nostalgia delle Colonie,* Rome, 1984.

Demoz, Abraham, "Moslems and Islam in Ethiopic Literature," *Journal of Ethiopian Studies,* Vol. 10 (1), 1972, pp. 1–12.

Dombrowski, F. A., *Ethiopia's Access to the Red Sea,* Leiden, 1985.

Douin, G., *Histoire du Regne du Khedive Ismail,* Vol. 3, Cairo, 1933–1941.

Dye, W.M., *Muslim Egypt and Christian Abyssinia,* New York, 1880.

Eritrean Liberation Front, *Kifah Irtirya,* N.D., N.P.

———, *Al-Taghalghul al-Isra'ili fi Irtirya,* 1970. N.P.

Erlich, H., *Ethiopia and Eritrea During the Scramble for Africa: A Political Biography of Ras Alula, 1875–1897,* East Lansing and Tel Aviv, 1982.

———, *The Struggle Over Eritrea, 1962–1978,* Stanford, 1983.

———, *Ethiopia and the Challenge of Independence,* Boulder, 1986.

———, *Mavo lehistorya shel hamizrah hatichon,* 5 vols., Tel Aviv, 1987–1991.

———, *Students and University in Egyptian Politics,* London, 1989.

Eshete, Alame, "Une Ambassade du Ras Ali en Egypte, 1852," *Journal of Ethiopian Studies,* 9(1), 1971, pp. 1–8.

———, "A Page in the History of the Ogaden—Contact and Correspondence Between Emperor Minilik of Ethiopia and the Somali Mahdi, Muhammad Abdullah Hasan (1907–1908)," in S. Rubenson (ed.), *Proceedings of the Seventh International Conference of Ethiopian Studies,* Addis Ababa, Uppsala, and Michigan, 1984, pp. 301–314.

Fa'iq, Muhammad Muhammad, *'Abd al-Nasir wal-thawra al-Ifriqiyya,* Beirut, 1980.

Furman, Ben-Zion, *Habash,* Tel Aviv, 1935.

Gabre-Selassie, Zewde, *Yohannes IV of Ethiopia,* Oxford, 1975.

Gebre-Medhin, Jordan, *Peasants and Nationalism in Eritrea,* New Jersey, 1989.

Ghuthani, As'ad, *Ahdath al-qaran al-Ifriqi wa-haqiqat al-sira al-Ithyubi al-Iritri,* Baghdad, 1980.

Greenfield, R., *Ethiopia, A New Political History,* Oxford, 1965.
Guidi, I., "Abyssinia," in *First Encyclopedia of Islam,* Leiden, 1987.
————, *Il Fetha Nagast o Legislazione dei Re,* Rome, 1889.
Hable Sellassie, Sergew, *Ancient and Medieval Ethiopian History to 1270,* Addis Ababa, 1972.
Habte Selassie, Bereket, *Conflict and Intervention in the Horn of Africa,* New York, 1980.
Hamad, Muhammad Abu al-Qasim, *Al-Ab'ad al-duwaliyya li-ma'rakat Irtirya,* Beirut, 1974.
Harraz, Rajab, *Iritriya al-haditha, 1557–1941,* Cairo, 1974.
————, *Al-'Umam al-muttahida wa-qadiyyat Irtirya, 1945–1952,* Cairo, 1974.
Hassen, Muhammad, *The Oromo of Ethiopia, A History, 1570–1860,* New York, 1990.
Haykal, Muhammad Husayn, *Hayat Muhammad,* Cairo, 1935.
al-Haymi, al-Hasan bin Ahmad, *Sirat al-habasha,* in Murad Kamil (ed. and annotator), Cairo, 1958. (See also Van Donzel's *A Yemeni Embassy*)
Hect, E., "Ethiopia Threatens to Bloc the Nile," *Azania,* Vol. 23, 1988, pp. 1–11.
Heldman, M. E., "Architectural Symbolism, Sacred Geography and the Ethiopian Church," *Journal of Religion in Africa,* Vol. 3, 1992, pp. 222–241.
Henze, P., *The Horn of Africa: From War to Peace,* London, 1991.
————, *Rebels and Separatists in Ethiopia,* Santa Monica, 1985.
Hess, R. L., *Ethiopia: The Modernization of Autocracy,* Ithaca, 1970.
Holt, P. M., *Egypt and the Fertile Crescent,* Ithaca, 1966.
————, *The Mahdist State of the Sudan, 1881–1898,* Oxford, 1970.
Huntingford, G.W.B., *Some Records of Ethiopia, 1593–1646,* Cambridge, 1954.
————, (ed.), *The Glorious Victories of Amda Seyon,* Oxford, 1965.
Husayn, 'Abdallah, *Al-Mas'ala al-habashiyya,* Cairo, 1935.
al-Huss, 'Abd al-Rahman, *Ithyubya fi 'ahd Hayla Silasi al-awwal,* Beirut, 1960.
Ibn Ishaq, Muhammad, *Sirat Rasul Allah* (English edition: A. Guillaume, *The Life of Muhammad: A Translation of Ibn Ishaq's Sirat Rasul Allah,* Oxford, 1955).
Ibrahim, H. A., "The Italian Conquest of Ethiopia as a Factor for the Conclusion of the 1936 Anglo-Egyptian Treaty," in Taddese Beyene (ed.), *Proceedings of the Eighth [1984] International Conference of Ethiopian Studies,* Vol. 2, Addis Ababa, pp. 225–231.
Ismail, Tariq, *The UAR in Africa,* Evanston, 1971.
Al-Jamal, Shawqi, *Al-Watha'iq al-ta'rikhiyya lisiyasat Misr fi al-bahr al-ahmar, 1863–1879,* Cairo, 1959.
————, *Siyasat Misr fi al-bahr al-ahmar,* Cairo, 1974.
al-Janahi, Sa'id Ahmad, *Iritriya 'ala abwab al-nasr,* Beirut, 1975.
Jones, A.H.M., and Monroe, E., *A History of Ethiopia,* Oxford, 1935.
Jum'a, Muhammad Lutfi, *Bayna al-asad al-Ifriqi wal-nimr al-Itali,* Cairo, 1935.
Kamil, Murad, *Fi bilad al-najashi,* Cairo, 1949.
Kane, T., *Ethiopian Literature in Amharic,* Wiesbaden, 1975.
Kaplan, S. *The Beta Israel (Falasha) in Ethiopia,* New York, 1992.
Khadduri, M., *War and Peace in the Law of Islam,* Baltimore, 1955.
Khayyata, Salim, *Al-Habasha al-mazluma,* Beirut, 1937.
Levine, D., *Wax and Gold,* Chicago, 1965.
————, *Greater Ethiopia,* Chicago, 1974.
Lewis, B., *Race and Slavery in the Middle East: A Historical Enquiry,* New York, 1990.
MacDonald, C. A., "Radio Bari, Italian Wireless Propaganda in the Middle East and British Countermeasures, 1934–1938," *Middle Eastern Studies,* Vol. 13, 1977, pp. 195–207.

Makuriya, Takla-Tsadiq, *Ya'ityopia tarik, ka'atse Lebna Dengel eska atse Tewodros,* Addis Ababa, 1953 E.C., A.D. 1961.
————, *YaGragn Ahmad Warara,* Addis Ababa, 1966 E.C., A.D. 1974.
————, *Atse Yohannes ena YaItyopia Andnat,* Addis Ababa, 1989.
Marcus, H., *The Life and Times of Menelik II,* Oxford, 1975.
————, *Haile Selassie, The Formative Years, 1892–1936,* Berkeley, 1987.
Markakis, J., *Ethiopia: Anatomy of a Traditional Polity,* Oxford, 1974.
————, *National and Class Conflict in the Horn of Africa,* Cambridge, 1987, London, 1990.
Marein, Nathan, *The Ethiopian Empire: Federation and Law,* Rotterdam, 1955.
Martin, B. G., "Arab Migration to East Africa," *International Journal of African Historical Studies,* Vol. 7(3), 1974, pp. 367–390.
————, "Mahdism, Muslim Clerics, and Holy Wars in Ethiopia, 1300–1600," in H. Marcus (ed.), *Proceedings of the First United States Conference on Ethiopian Studies, 1973,* East Lansing, 1975, pp. 91–100.
————, *Muslim Brotherhoods in Nineteenth-Century Africa,* Cambridge, 1976.
Mas'ad, Bulus, *Al-Habasha, aw Ithyubya fi munqalab min ta'rikhiha,* Cairo, 1935.
al-Ma'yuf, 'Ali Muhammad, *Ta'rikh harakat al-jihad al-islami al-sumali didd al-isti'mar (1899–1920),* Cairo, 1992.
Meinardus, O., *Christian Egypt; Faith and Life,* Cairo, 1970.
al-Munshidi, Khalaf, *Irtirya, min al-ihtilal ila al-thawra,* Beirut, 1973.
Orhonlu, Cengiz, *Habesh Eyaleti,* Istanbul, 1974.
Pankhurst, R., *Economic History of Ethiopia,* Addis Ababa, 1968.
————, "Some Notes on the Historical and Economic Geography of Mesewa Area (1520–1855)," *Journal of Ethiopian Studies,* Vol. 13(1), 1975, pp. 89–116.
————, *History of Ethiopian Towns, from the Middle Ages to the Early Nineteenth Century,* Wiesbaden, 1982.
————, *A Social History of Ethiopia from Early Medieval Times to the Rise of Emperor Tewodros,* Addis Ababa, 1990.
Pankhurst, S., *Ethiopia, A Cultural History,* London, 1955.
Pedersen, Kirsten, *The History of the Ethiopian Community in the Holy Land from the Time of Emperor Tewodros II until 1974,* Jerusalem, 1983.
————, "Dir al-Sultan," in E. Shiler (ed.), *Sefer Ze'ev Vilna'i,* Jerusalem, 1984.
Plante, J. "The Ethiopian Embassy to Cairo of 1443," *Journal of Ethiopian Studies,* Vol. 13(2), pp. 133–140.
Portal, G., *My Mission to Abyssinia,* London, 1982.
Prouty, Chris, *Empress Taytu and Menilek II, Ethiopia, 1883–1910,* London, 1986.
al-Qaddal, Muhammad Sa'id, *Al-Mahdiyya wal-habasha, dirasa fi al-siyasa al-dahiliyya wal-harijiyya lidawlat al-mahdiyya, 1881–1898,* Beirut, 1992.
al-Qaddal, Muhammad Sa'id, and Abu Salim, Muhammad, *Al-Harb al-habashiyya al-sudaniyya,* Beirut, 1991. (An edition of the manuscript by Isma'il b. 'Abd al-Qadir, *Al-Tiraz al-manqush bibushra qatl Yuhanna malik al-hubush*)
Rajab, 'Abd al-Halim Muhammad, *Al-'Alaqat al-siyasiyya bayna muslimi al-Zayla' wa-nusara al-habasha fi al-'usur al-wusta,* Cairo, 1985.
Rif'at, Muhammad Bek, *Jabr al-kasr fi al-khilas min al-asr,* Cairo, 1896.
Riyad, Zahir, "Al-Islam fi Ithyubya," *Majallat Kuliyyat al-Adab,* Vol. 18, 1957, pp. 121–142.
————, *Al-Islam fi Ityubya fi al-'usur al-wusta,* Cairo, 1964.
————, "Al-Shifta fi Ithyubya mundhu al-'usur al-wusta," *Majallat Kuliyyat al-Adab,* Vol. 19, 1961, pp. 215–238.
————, *Ta'rikh Ithyubya,* Cairo, 1966.
————, *Misr wa-Ifriqya,* Cairo, 1976.
Rubenson, S., *The Survival of Ethiopian Independence,* London, 1976.

————, "Ethiopia and the Horn," in J. F. Flint (ed.), *The Cambridge History of Africa*, Vol. 5, Cambridge, 1976, pp. 55–98.

————, "Shaikh Kasa Hailu" in S. Rubenson (ed.), *Proceedings of the Seventh International Conference of Ethiopian Studies*, Addis Ababa, Uppsala, and Michigan, 1984, pp. 279–285.

————, "Correspondence and Treaties, 1800–1854," *Acta Aethiopica*, Vol. 1, Lund, 1987.

Sabbe, 'Uthman Salih, *Ta'rikh Iritriya*, Beirut, 1974. (English translation by Muhammad 'Azam, *History of Eritrea*, Beirut, 1974)

Sanderson, G. N., "Conflict and Co-operation Between Ethiopia and the Mahdist State, 1884–1898," *Sudan Notes and Records*, Vol. 2, 1969.

————, "The Foreign Policy of Negus Menelik II: 1896–1898," *Journal of African History*, Vol. 5, 1964, pp. 87–97.

Sbacchi, A., *Ethiopia under Mussolini: Fascism and the Colonial Experience*, London, 1985.

Scholler, H., "The Ethiopian Community in Jerusalem, from 1850 to the Conference of Dar el-Sultan 1902: The Political Struggle for Independence," in G. Goldenberg (ed.), *Proceedings of the Sixth International Conference of Ethiopian Studies*, Rotterdam, 1986, pp. 487–500.

Shawul, Anwar, *Qisat hayyati fi wadi al-rafidin*, Jerusalem, 1980.

Shuqayr, Na'um, *Ta'rikh al-Sudan* (a new edition prepared and annotated by Muhammad Ibrahim Abu Salim), Beirut, 1981. See also Na'um Shoucair, *Ta'rikh al-Sudan al-qadim wal-hadith wa-jughrafiyatuhu*, Cairo, 1903.

Sishagne, Shumet, "Notes on the Background to the Eritrean Problem," in Bahru Zewde (ed.), *Proceedings of the Annual Seminar of the Department of History*, Addis Ababa University, 1984, pp. 180–213.

Spencer, J., *Ethiopia at Bay*, Michigan, 1984.

Tafla, Bairu, *A Chronicle of Emperor Yohannes IV (1872–1889)*, Stuttgart, 1977.

————, *Ethiopia and Germany: Cultural, Political and Economic Relations, 1871–1936*, Wiesbaden, 1981.

Talhami, Ghada, "Massawa under Khedive Ismail," in R. Hess (ed.), *Proceedings of the Fifth International Conference of Ethiopian Studies*, Chicago, 1978, pp. 481–494.

————, *Suakin and Massawa under Egyptian Rule, 1865–1885*, Washington, D.C., 1979.

Tamrat, Taddesse, *Church and State in Ethiopia, 1270–1527*, Oxford, 1972.

————, "Ethiopia, The Red Sea and the Horn," in R. Oliver (ed.), *Cambridge History of Africa*, Vol. 3, pp. 98–182.

Tariq, Muhammad al-Ifriqi, *Mudhakkirati fi al-harb al-habashiyya al-Italiyya, 1935–1936*, Damascus, 1937.

Trevaskis, G.K.N., *Eritrea: A Colony in Transition, 1941–1952*, Oxford, 1960.

Trimingham, J. S., *Islam in Ethiopia*, London, 1965 (2d impression).

Ullendorff, E., *The Ethiopians*, Oxford, 1960.

————(editor and translator), *The Autobiography of Emperor Haile Selassie, "My Life and Ethiopia's Progress, 1892–1937,"* Oxford, 1976.

'Urabi, Ahmad, *Mudhakkirat Ahmad 'Urabi Basha*, Cairo, 1975.

————, *Kashf al-sitar 'an sirr al-asrar*, Cairo, 1929.

Van Donzel, E., *Foreign Relations of Ethiopia, 1642–1700*, Leiden, 1979.

————, *A Yemeni Embassy to Ethiopia, 1647–1649*, Stuttgart, 1986.

————, "Correspondence between Fasiladas and the Imams of Yemen," in G. Goldenberg (ed.), *Proceedings of the Sixth International Conference of Ethiopian Studies*, Rotterdam, 1986, pp. 91–100.

————, "Massawa," "Nadjashi," and other articles in E. Van Donzel (ed.), *Encyclopedia of Islam,* Leiden, 1993.

Vatikiotis, P. J., *The History of Egypt, From Muhammad Ali to Sadat,* London, 1980 (2d. ed.).

Walker, C.H., *The Abyssinian,* London, 1928.

Watt, M. Muhammad, *Prophet and Statesman,* Oxford, 1961.

Zabiyan, Muhammad Tayyasir, Al-Kaylani, *Al-Habasha al-muslima, mushahadati fi diyar al-Islam,* Damascus, 1937.

Zewde, Bahru, *History of Modern Ethiopia, 1855–1974,* London, 1991.

INDEX

Abba Jifar, and Jimma's autonomy, 45, 74, 78, 106, 119
Abbas Pasha, 50, 58
Abbasid dynasty, 11, 14, 23, 28, 153
Abbay, 23. *See also* Nile.
'Abd al-Hamid II, 65, 72, 74, 75, 76, 77, 78, 79, 81, 82, 83, 88, 89
'Abdallah al-Sadiq ("ra'is al-muslimin"), 79, 83, 88, 117
'Abdallah al-Ta'ishi, the Mahdi's "Khalifa," 65, 68, 70, 73
Abir, M., 39
Abu 'Anja, Hamdan, 70, 71
Adal, sultanate, 26
Afar (people), 26, 30, 33, 74, 183, 192
Afaworqi, Issayas, 156
Africa: Horn of Africa, Africanization of Ethiopia, x, xi, 3, 5, 11, 12, 13, 14, 25, 31, 33, 37, 44, 53, 55, 56, 58, 60, 72, 85, 96, 102, 103, 115, 120, 121, 122, 128, 129, 130, 131, 133–138, 139, 143, 145, 147, 148, 151, 162, 163, 172, 173, 174, 177, 186, 188–189
Ahmad, Shihab al-Din ("'Arab fafih"), 30, 33, 115
Al-Ahram, 101, 112, 123, 143, 147,
Ahmad, Yusuf, 104, 105, 106, 107, 109, 118, 125, 135, 152, 186
Aklilu Habte-Wold, 135, 136, 137, 139, 147, 151, 170, 171, 172, 173, 176, 177
'Ali, *Ras,* 45, 46, 47, 49
'Aliyyan, 'Abd al-Fattah, 17
Alula, *Ras,* 54, 58, 59, 62, 63, 66, 68, 69, 70, 71, 80, 129, 142, 159, 180
Amharic, Amharization policy, 3, 41, 117, 123, 131, 134, 158, 159, 163, 171, 176
'Amru bin al-'As, 7, 8, 113
Andom, Meles, 134

Aqavia, Avraham, 167, 168
Arabic language, 5, 13, 22, 25, 26, 28, 37, 46, 49, 61, 66, 75, 78, 81, 82, 85, 87, 96, 99, 101, 104, 107, 111, 116, 117, 122, 123, 124, 131, 132, 133, 134, 141, 143, 144, 157, 158, 159, 160, 163, 164, 200
Arab Revolt (1916), 85, 89
Arafat, Yasser, 155
Arslan, Shakib, 33, 95, 109, 111, 114, 115, 116, 117, 118, 119, 121, 124, 125, 128, 132, 135, 152, 166, 186
Asrate, *Ras,* 139, 151, 157, 158, 162, 168, 170, 171, 172, 175
Aswan Dam, 24, 138, 183
Ataturk, Mustafa Kemal, 83, 91, 96
Aynor, Hanan, xi, 173, 174, 209
al-'Azm, Sadiq al-Mua'ayyad, 10, 33, 77–81, 83, 99, 106, 108, 147

Ba'th Party, Ba'thism, 152–158, 160, 162, 163, 182
Bahr negash, Yishaq, 18, 27, 34–36, 39, 53, 180, 181
Bani 'Amir (tribe), 44, 46, 47, 130–132, 153, 155
Begin, Menahem, 184, 185
Ben Gurion, David, 137, 168, 184
Beta Israel (Falasha), 161, 163, 166, 170, 184–186
Bible, biblical, 75, 85, 165, 167, 168, 184
Bilal bin Rabah, "Bilal al-habashi," 6, 10, 37, 81
Boutros-Ghali, Boutros, 147–148, 183–184
Britain, British citizens, 36, 47, 48, 50, 51, 53–55, 57, 60, 63, 66, 68, 72, 73, 76, 80, 83, 85–90, 97–99, 103, 108, 109, 111–118, 120, 123–125, 127, 129, 130,

131, 133–135, 137, 142, 143, 146, 160, 166, 167, 169, 184
Byzantium, 4, 8, 11, 160

Cairo, 17, 18, 23, 25–27, 45, 47, 48, 52, 55, 56, 61, 81, 82, 97, 100, 101, 107, 109, 111, 113, 115, 123, 128, 130–137, 139, 141- 146, 152, 153, 162, 172, 177, 183, 184, 186
Caliphate, 23, 25, 28, 75, 89–91, 153
Cerulli, E., x, 26, 189, 195
Christianity, Ethiopian, x, 3, 4, 8, 15, 22, 23, 25, 37, 43, 44, 61, 62, 67, 68, 74, 75, 85, 103, 105, 111, 141, 142, 191, 193
Church of Ethiopia, 4, 5, 22, 26, 27, 52, 43, 50, 51, 56, 62, 69- 71, 76, 77, 95, 105, 111, 137, 138, 142, 148, 170, 188
"Coffee Project," 169–172
"Committee for the Defense of Ethiopia" (Egyptian), 100, 114, 121
Conti Rossini, C., x, 189
Copts, Coptic Church, 3, 21–25, 50, 56, 61, 75–77, 91, 95, 99–102, 112, 128, 137, 138, 141–143, 145, 147, 169, 170, 185, 205

Dahlak Island, 11, 18, 21, 25, 27, 41, 180
Dar al-hiyad (land of neutrality), 14–16, 22, 37
Darwish, Shaikh Nimr, 16, 194
Dayan, Moshe, 134, 175
Deir al-Sultan (monastery), 75–78, 88, 95, 135, 136, 138, 169, 170, 185
Derg, 175, 176, 178
Dervishes, darbush, 68, 71, 202

Easternism, 102, 187
Education, 26, 41, 42, 45, 56, 58, 131, 141, 142, 144, 145, 147, 161, 165
Egyptian nationalism, Egyptianism, Pharaohnism, x, 59, 95, 99, 102, 128, 129, 142, 183
Era of the Princes, 39, 43, 75
Eritrea, ix, 26, 27, 44, 45, 47, 53, 54, 56, 59, 61, 62, 63, 65, 66, 68–72, 88, 96, 100, 104, 106, 107, 115, 122, 125, 127–189, 209, 211, 212
Eritrean Liberation Front (ELF), 130, 132, 133, 138, 139, 141, 152–160, 181, 182
Eritrean Popular Liberation Forces (EPLF), 155–160, 181, 182

Fa'iq, Muhammad, 130–132
Falasha. See Beta Israel.
"The Family of Kings," 11, 193
Fascists, Fascism, 74, 97–100, 102, 104, 106, 107, 109, 112, 113, 115, 118–124, 137, 166–168, 181, 206
Fasiladas, Emperor, 37–39, 42, 68, 142
Faysal, king of Saudi Arabia, 172, 174, 177
Fetha Negast, 22
France, French citizens, 36, 47, 50, 51, 54, 56, 72, 85, 87, 88, 90, 97, 97, 100, 113–116, 120, 121, 132, 146
Front de Liberation National (FLN), 132, 158

Gala. See Oromo.
Galadewos, Emperor, 32, 34, 35
da Gama, Christopher, 32
Gragn, Ahmad bin Ibrahim, "Gragn Syndrome," "Ahmad Gragn trauma," 16, 29–39, 41, 42, 44, 45, 51, 62, 63, 70, 72–75, 80, 103, 105, 111, 115, 134, 135, 144, 149, 166, 178, 180, 182, 188
Greece, Greek citizens, 3, 4, 35, 48, 79
Gura, battle of, 54, 57–60, 103, 104, 106, 108

Habasha, habsh, 12–14, 16, 17, 28, 30, 45, 47, 69, 112, 159. See also "utruku al-habasha" legacy.
Habesh eyaleti (Ottoman province of Ethiopia), 29, 33–40, 46, 50 51, 85, 127, 142, 180
Hable Sellassie, Sergew, 3, 22, 191
Haile Selassie, Emperor, 91, 96, 99, 102, 104, 106, 108, 109, 111, 113, 115, 118–123, 125, 127–140, 142, 146, 147, 148, 151, 153, 156, 158, 163–178, 180, 184, 185, 188, 209, 210
Hajj, 25, 125
Harar, 26, 29, 30, 32–34, 45, 53, 60–62, 70, 73, 74, 76, 78, 79, 83, 85, 86, 88–91, 106, 108, 111, 115, 123–125, 134, 147, 178, 180, 202, 203
al-Haymi, al-Hasan bin Ahmad, 38, 39, 41
Husayni, Haj Amin al-, 115, 116, 118, 207, 208
Hussein, king of Jordan, 134, 138, 155

Ibn Sa'ud, 'Abd al-'Aziz, 114
Ifat, Emirate of, 26, 27, 41, 122

al-Ifriqi, Gen. Muhammad Tariq, 100, 121, 122
Iran (Persia), 4, 8, 11, 29, 38, 85, 96, 135, 137, 138, 160, 169, 182, 184, 187, 191
Iraq, Baghdad, 11. 23, 28, 85, 87, 89, 91, 97, 109, 111, –113, 117, 118, 120, 131, 133, 134, 151, 154–157, 160, 162, 163, 172, 177, 182, 183, 210
"*Islam al-najashi* legacy," 16–19, 72, 91, 95, 104, 107
Isma'il bin 'Abd al-Qadir al-Kurdufani, 68, 69
Isma'il, Khedive, 53–63, 72, 80, 102–104, 108, 128–130, 148
Israel, 3, 30, 134–140, 145, 149, 151–153, 155, 158, 161–189
Israeli Defense Forces (IDF), 167–169, 172
Iyasu, Lij, 83–91, 108, 111, 115, 120, 123, 127, 163, 169

Ja'far bin Abu Talib, 7–9, 16, 27, 193
jabarti, 25, 26, 41, 43, 47, 51, 62, 68, 131, 142,
Jerusalem, 3, 16, 22–24, 49, 75–77, 88, 95, 97, 111, 112, 115, 116, 118, 120, 123, 135, 166–169, 171, 183, 203
jihad, 10, 12, 15–17, 22, 28–34, 39, 62, 63, 65–69, 72, 73, 83, 85, 86, 89, 118, 127, 180, 186, 192
Jordan, 131, 134–138, 140, 149, 155, 169, 173
Judaism, judaic, 3, 4, 165, 191
Jum'a, Muhammad Lutfi, 102–104, 106, 109, 112, 137, 187

Ka'ba, 4, 18, 90
Kaleb, negus, 3, 4
Kamil, Murad, 141–143, 145, 148
Kebra negast, 22
Khadduri, M., 15, 16
al-Khattabi, 'Abd al-Karim, 115, 132, 152

Land of Islam (*dar al-Islam*), x, 11, 15–17, 31, 69, 70, 95
"Leave the Abyssinians alone" legacy. *See* "*utruku.*"
Lewis, B., 12–14
"Liberation fronts," ix, 115, 130, 132, 181
Libya, 44, 72, 85, 99, 112, 115, 119, 121, 124, 133, 149, 155, 173, 183

Mahdi, mahdiyya, Mahdist state, 16, 54, 60, 63, 65–73, 79, 80, 106, 118, 130, 142, 153, 187
Makonnen, Ras, 76, 79, 88, 108, 147
Makonnen Endalkatchw, 135
Mamluks, 12, 14, 23–25, 27–29, 75, 148
Marcus, H., 84
Markakis, J., 43, 188
Martin, B., 31
Mas'ad, Bulus, 107–109, 112
Massawa, 4, 25, 27, 32, 34–38, 45–48, 50, 53, 54, 58, 61, 65, 70, 90, 108, 122, 127, 129, 131, 132, 142, 152, 153, 160, 162, 180
"Mawla," the Somali *mawla,* Muhammad ibn 'Abdalla Hasan, 72, 83–91, 180, 204
Mazhar *bey,* 83, 85–91
Menelik II, 54–56, 61, 62, 65, 70, 71–86, 88, 90, 91, 104, 106–108, 113, 118, 120, 121, 123, 145, 169, 184, 188, 203
Mengistu Haile Mariam, 164, 175, 178–189
Minasse Haile, 172, 173, 176, 177
Mika'el, *Ras,* 62, 85, 90, 204
Mirghaniyya, 44, 45, 47, 130–132, 153
Mubarak, Hosni, 184
Mussolini, Benito, 18, 31, 74, 95–100, 107, 108, 111, 114–118, 122, 124, 127, 135, 139, 146, 152, 166, 167, 180
Muhammad, the Prophet, x, 4–19, 25, 29, 30, 37, 39, 41, 43, 66–71, 80, 81, 87, 90, 91, 101–104, 107, 111, 115, 122, 127, 145, 146, 191, 192
al-Mutawwakil 'Ala Allah, Imam, 39

Na'ib of Arkiko, 38, 47, 51
Najashi (najashi Ashama), 5–19, 37, 39, 67, 72, 80, 81, 85, 91, 95, 101–105, 107, 116, 123, 137, 141, 145, 146, 148, 159, 188, 192, 193
Nashashibis, 112
Nasser, Gamal Abd al-, Nasserism, 96, 127–140, 141, 143–149, 151, 152, 154, 157, 165, 177, 182, 183, 188, 212
Nile River, Blue Nile (Abbay), x, 3, 21, 23–25, 33, 46, 48, 55, 58, 61, 98, 99, 104, 119, 127–129, 130, 133, 138, 148, 151, 157, 173, 183, 184, 186, 195, 209
Numayri, Ja'far, 130, 151, 156, 172, 179, 182
Nur, Muhammad Ramadan, 152, 156

Ogaden War, 173, 180
Operation Moses, Operation Solomon, 185, 186
Organization of African Unity (OAU), 136, 139, 147, 148, 171–173
Orhunlu, C., 33, 36
Oromo (people), 14, 32, 33, 38, 43–47, 49, 50, 61, 62, 68, 74, 84, 183, 198
Ottoman Empire, Ottoman citizens, x, xi, 11, 12, 14, 21, 24, 25, 28–43, 45- 48, 50–55, 57, 59, 65, 72–91, 95, 100, 108, 111, 121, 127, 142, 159, 160, 169, ¹80, 204
Ozdemir Pasha, 33–35, 39, 73, 142,

Palestine, Palestinian citizenss, 85, 91, 97, 109, 112, 113, 115–118, 120, 121, 123, 124, 131, 151, 152, 154, 155, 161, 162, 166, 167, 168
Palestine Liberation Organization (PLO), 154–156, 158–162, 171, 183
Patriarch, Patriarchate, 3, 22–24, 50, 137, 138, 142, 178
People's Democratic Republic of Yemen (PDRY), 155, 159, 171, 172, 182, 183
Popular Liberation Forces (PLF), 155, 156, 161, 162

Qaddafi, Muammar, 155, 156, 159, 172, 183, 187
Qaladiyos, Idris 'Uthman, 132, 153
Quran, 5, 8, 26, 41, 45, 74, 90

Ra'is al-muslimin, 79, 83, 88, 117
Rajab 'Abd al-Halim, 17, 18, 26, 29
Rida, Shaikh Muhammad Rashid, 72, 82, 99, 114, 117, 118, 128
Rif War, 132, 152
Riwaq al-Jabartiyya, 25, 26, 47, 131, 142
Riyad, Zahir, 143–145
Rubenson, S., 47

Sabbe, 'Uthman Salih, 132, 141, 152–157, 159–162
Sabure, Ahadu, 176
Sadat, Anwar, 148, 151, 173, 179, 182–184
Sahaba, 6–19, 27, 31, 37, 67, 68, 80, 103–105, 137, 146, 148, 186
Sa'id Pasha, 58, 102, 145
Sanusiyya, 72, 99, 115
Sbacchi, A., 122
Sertsa Dengel, Emperor, 35, 36, 59
Shahabandar, 'Abd al-Rahman, 100, 113

Shahada, 9, 87, 90
Shafi'i (legal Islamic school), 22
Shari'a, 122, 124
Shifta, shiftnnet, 49, 54, 61, 144, 179, 181
Six Day War, 140, 154, 160, 165, 169, 171, 172
Siyasa Duwaliyya, 147, 148, 183
Slavery, slaves, 5, 6, 10–16, 45–47, 107, 11, 112, 124, 125, 147, 206
Solomonic myth, dynasty, 22–24, 26, 49, 74, 75, 159, 166, 168
Somalia, Somali citizens, 26, 30, 53, 72, 73, 83–91, 102, 107, 125, 127, 129, 130, 134, 137–139, 148, 149, 164, 173, 176, 177, 180, 182, 183, 189, 209
Sudan, Sudanese citizens, 13, 16, 17, 44, 46–50, 53, 54, 56, 60–63, 65–74, 86, 101, 102, 108, 118, 121, 128–133, 138, 148, 151, 153, 154, 156, 159, 160, 179, 182, 183, 187, 189
Suez, Suez Canal, Suez War, 36, 50, 53, 55, 85, 98, 121, 130, 131, 141, 154, 156, 160, 165, 174, 182
Sufi movements, sufism, 29, 44, 45, 65
Suliman the Magnificent, Sultan, 31, 35
Susenios, Emperor, 37
Syria, Syrian citizens, 3, 27, 48, 75, 91, 97, 100, 109, 112, 113, 115, 116, 118, 119, 123, 124, 133, 134, 138–140, 142, 148, 151–154, 156, 157, 159, 160, 162, 172, 173, 183

Taddesse Tamrat, 22, 26
Taitu, Empress, 77, 84
Takla-Haimanot, negus, 66, 68, 70
Tariqa, 44
Tewodros II, 41–52, 54, 55, 57, 74, 76, 80, 102–105, 107, 111, 115, 120, 145, 169, 188
Thawra, 157, 159
Tigre, Tigrinya, 3, 27, 30, 35, 36, 38, 41, 43, 47, 49, 50, 53, 55, 58, 59, 71, 72, 85, 127, 131, 141, 155, 157, 158, 167, 180, 181, 183, 188
Tigrean People's Liberation Front (TPLF), 181, 185
Trimingham, J. S., x, 26, 143, 144, 189
Turk basha, 36, 59, 73

'Ubayd Makram, 99
'Ubaydalla bin Jahsh, 7, 8, 103, 105
Ullendorff, E., x, 189

'Umayyads, 10, 11, 23, 36, 193
'Umm Ayman, Baraka, 5, 7, 10, 81
'Umm Habiba, 7, 8, 192
"Ummar, calif, 9, 10, 25, 30
United Arab Republic (UAR), 134, 138, 151
United States, U.S. citizens, ix, x, 56, 58, 59, 96, 137, 145, 151, 161, 162, 173, 177, 185, 188
al-'Urabi Ahmad, 58–60, 73, 104
Uthman Diqna, 66, 68, 80
USSR, Soviet citizens, 169, 173, 179, 180, 182–185, 188
"*utruku al-habasha*" ("leave the Abyssinians alone" legacy), 3–19, 21–23, 25, 38, 51, 66, 68–70, 72, 91, 95, 159, 174, 188

Van Donzel, E., 15, 38

Wafd Party, 99, 100, 109, 112, 120
Wahhabiyya, 44, 46, 72
Wahib Pasha, Gen., 121
Walasma' (dynasty), 27, 29
Wingate, O., 167, 168, 214
Wolde-Ab Wolde-Mariam, 131, 141
Woyanc, 127, 181

Yemen, 4, 5, 13, 24, 27, 29, 30, 32, 33, 35, 36, 38, 39, 42, 45, 68, 85, 87, 89, 107, 121, 138, 139, 140, 142, 147, 149, 155, 163, 172, 189, 191
Yishuv, 166
Yoannes IV, 53–74, 76, 80, 85, 102, 103, 105–108, 111, 115, 116, 118, 119, 125, 129, 145, 169, 188
Yom Kippur War, 165, 173
Young Men's Muslim Association (YMMA), 99
Young Turks, 77, 81, 83, 88, 89

Zabiyan, Muhammad al-Kaylani, 118, 123–125
Zagwe (dynasty), 22, 23
Zanj, 13, 14, 33, 37
Zar'a Ya'qob, 24, 27, 36, 111, 148
Zawditu, Empress, 90
Zaydiyya, Yemen, 30, 32, 35, 38, 39, 72, 85
Zion, 22, 75. *See also* Jerusalem.
Zionism, Zionists, x, 95, 115, 135, 143, 155, 158, 160–162, 164, 166, 168, 174, 185